P9-DTD-814

Graphic Design Solutions for Great User Experiences

Des solutions de graphisme pour de belles expériences utilisateur

Diseño gráfico en pantalla

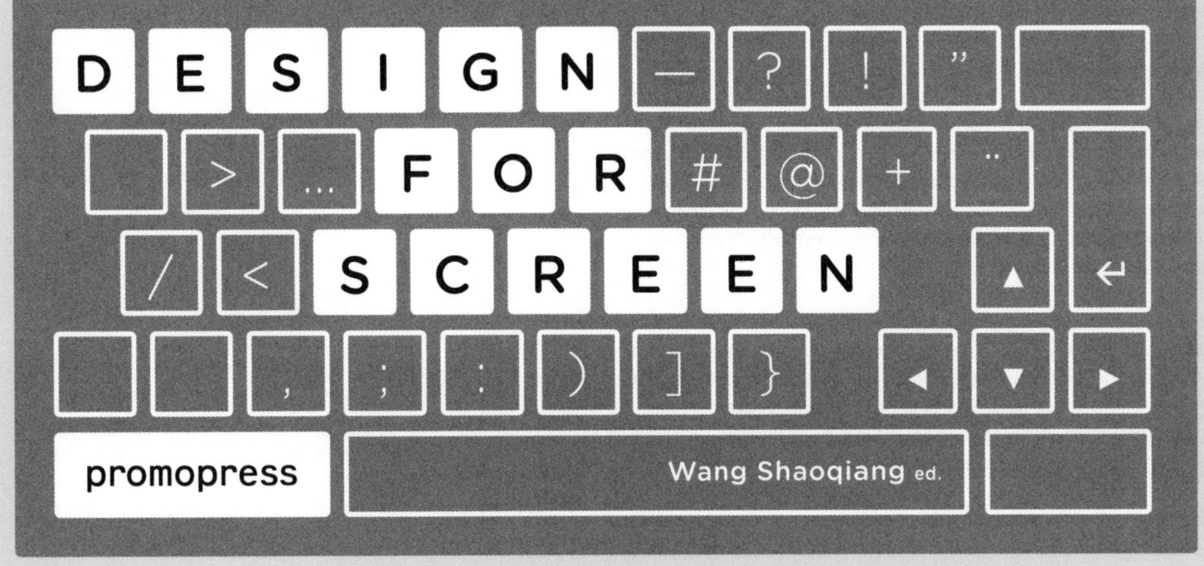

DESIGN FOR SCREEN

Graphic Design Solutions for Great User Experiences
Des solutions de graphisme pour de belles expériences utilisateur
Diseño gráfico en pantalla

Editor: Wang Shaoqiang
English preface revised by: Tom Corkett
Translators of the preface:
Leïla Bendifallah, French translation
Jesús de Cos Pinto, Spanish translation

Promopress is a brand of:
Promotora de Prensa Internacional S.A.
C/ Ausiàs March, 124
08013 Barcelona, Spain
Phone: 0034 93 245 14 64
Fax: 0034 93 265 48 83
info@promopress.es
www.promopresseditions.com
Facebook: Promopress Editions
Twitter: Promopress Editions @PromopressEd
Sponsored by Design 360°
– Concept and Design Magazine
Edited and produced by
Sandu Publishing Co., Ltd.
Book design, concepts & art direction by
Sandu Publishing Co., Ltd.
info@sandupublishing.com

Cover design:
spread: David Lorente
Cover inspired by the project of Inbal Lapidot Vidal;
Photos courtesy of Rotem Rachel Chen

ISBN 978-84-16504-56-5

Printed in China

Contents

◇◇

◊ Icon Application ◊

◊ Text & Typography ◊

Game On!

Fouad Mallouk

CEO and Founder, Phoenix the Creative Studio

The world is in constant transformation. In the last ten years, technology has evolved, but it has also changed people's way of life, as well as their relations and their expectations. There are as many people on the Web today (3.5 billion) as there were people on Earth in 1970.

Companies have experienced the impact of these technological changes on their industries. Former market leaders are threatened by emerging companies that were often born online. Mature industries are questioning themselves. Technologies are eliminating the need for intermediaries and facilitating both shopping and comparing. And the choice has never been greater for consumers, who are no longer limited to their local shops. As the *New York Times* put it recently, "No company is safe from the creative destruction brought by technological change."

Businesses know that they must adapt to this new reality in order to ensure their growth. They have never needed as much help to stay true to their vision and evolve at their customers' rhythm.

Design is everywhere. It surrounds us, and it cannot be ignored. And there is no doubt that Web design, which can account for almost 90% of a consumer's decision to choose one product or service over another, is the leader in this new reality.

But Web design is not a commodity. If a brand is a company's soul, its website is its body and voice, encapsulated through interaction and aesthetics.

When it comes to the interactive essence of one's brand, there is the good, the bad and the ugly. Bad Web design is terrible for business. And like any other form of pollution, it's bad for the soul.

It takes a dose of audacity to change one's industry. A leap of faith.

How can you create perceived value in a world where consumers are no longer satisfied with the ordinary, and how can you distinguish yourself in a way that makes your site stand out? The solution is to find innovative ways to dovetail interaction and emotion, creating experiences that resonate with each individual and make lasting impressions on them.

You should approach every project, big or small, with the desire to create something that will stand out. It's easy and tempting to follow trends, especially since everything is easily accessible nowadays. The gamble with going all-out all the time is that you don't have a template to follow. But the risk is well worth the reward.

Is there a predefined solution for creating good design? Perhaps, or perhaps not. But there are two formulas worth living by. First, content in context is king. Second, to reconstruct, we need to deconstruct.

When I founded Phoenix the Creative Studio, a human-scale agency based in Montreal, I have spent over a decade in the industry and previously run two other agencies, these were the principles that I chose to guide my new project.

Once my partner Louis Paquet and I discovered these formulas, we were reborn from our ashes in creative terms. Barely eighteen months since our rebirth, this creative audacity and technical prowess has already won Phoenix more than fifty major awards.

When we approach a new project for a client, we harness the power of reinvention. The foundation for this is the agility of our creative team, which adjusts to the needs of each project. And when it comes to the execution of the project, we reinvent old-school tools for the "always-on" culture, and we create brand experiences by revolutionizing them for the new interactive age. We're never afraid to break with the industry's standards, and we never cut corners as we seek to discover creative innovations.

Above all, we put this reinvention to use to achieve one key goal for the client: creating a connection with the customer. Because when you connect with people, they let their guards down and you get your message across.

This book has many examples of similar stories of designers and agencies that are bringing fresh ideas and philosophies to Web design.

Inspiration is everywhere. You never know when or where you'll find it. It could be while leafing through this amazing book, while browsing the Web, or simply while walking down the street to work.

Every website is an opportunity to change people's perception of your product or your brand and to trigger a chain reaction that will transform or even transmogrify your position in the market.

So put the website templates away and let innovation, artistic flair and focused creativity permeate your new digital strategy!

C'est parti ! Amusez-vous !

Fouad Mallouk

PDG et Fondateur, Phoenix the Creative Studio

Le monde change de manière constante. Au cours des dix dernières années, la technologie a évolué en changeant notre mode de vie, ainsi que nos relations et nos attentes. Le monde compte aujourd'hui autant d'utilisateurs internet (3,5 milliards) que d'individus sur Terre en 1970.

Les entreprises ont ressenti l'impact de ces évolutions technologiques sur leurs industries. D'anciens leaders de marché sont menacés par des entreprises émergentes, souvent nées sur le net. Les industries matures se remettent en question. Les technologies sont en train d'éliminer le besoin d'intermédiaires et facilitent l'achat et la comparaison. Le consommateur n'a jamais eu un si grand choix, n'étant plus limité à ses commerces de proximité. Comme le *New York Times* l'a récemment souligné, « aucune entreprise n'est à l'abri de la destruction créative apportée par l'évolution technologique ».

Les entreprises savent qu'elles doivent s'adapter à cette nouvelle réalité afin d'assurer leur croissance. Elles n'ont jamais eu autant besoin d'aide pour rester fidèles à leur vision et pour évoluer au rythme des consommateurs.

Le design est partout. Il nous entoure et il ne saurait être ignoré. Et il ne fait aucun doute que la conception de site web, qui est responsable de près de 90 % du choix d'un produit ou d'un service plutôt que d'un autre par le consommateur, est le leader dans cette nouvelle réalité.

Mais la conception de site web n'est pas un produit. Si la marque est l'âme de l'entreprise, son site est son corps et sa voix, concentrées dans des interactions et une certaine esthétique.

En ce qui concerne l'essence interactive d'une marque, il y a du bon comme du mauvais. Une mauvaise conception de site web est nuisible aux affaires. Et comme n'importe quelle forme de pollution, elle est nuisible à l'âme.

Changer son industrie requiert de l'audace. Un acte de foi.

Comment créer de la valeur perçue dans un monde où le consommateur ne se contente plus de l'ordinaire, et comment se distinguer de manière à ce que son site se démarque des autres ? La solution consiste à trouver des manières innovantes d'associer l'interaction à l'émotion, en créant des expériences qui résonnent en chacun en faisant une impression durable.

Il faut penser chaque projet, grand ou petit, avec le désir de créer quelque chose qui se démarquera. Il est facile et tentant de suivre les tendances, en particulier car, de nos jours, tout est facile d'accès. Le risque qu'il y a à toujours voir grand est qu'il n'y a pas de modèle à suivre. Mais la récompense vaut bien la peine de courir ce risque.

Existe-t-il une solution prédéfinie pour créer un bon design ? Peut-être ; peut-être pas. Mais il existe deux formules qui valent la peine d'être suivies. D'abord, le contenu dans son contexte est roi. Ensuite, il faut déconstruire pour reconstruire.

Lorsque j'ai créé Phoenix the Creative Studio, une agence à taille humaine basée à Montréal, après avoir passé plus de dix ans dans l'industrie et dirigé deux autres agences, voilà les principes que j'ai choisis pour guider mon nouveau projet.

Après avoir découvert ces formules, mon associé Louis Paquet et moi avons ressuscité de nos cendres en termes de créativité. Tout juste 18 mois après notre renaissance, cette audace créative et cette prouesse technique ont valu à Phoenix d'obtenir plus de 50 prix importants.

Lorsque nous pensons un nouveau projet pour un client, nous utilisons le pouvoir de la réinvention. La base de cette approche réside dans l'agilité de notre équipe créative, qui s'adapte aux besoins de chaque projet. Quant à l'exécution du projet, nous réinventons des outils de l'ancienne école pour la culture du « tout-connecté » et nous créons des expériences de marque en les révolutionnant pour la nouvelle ère interactive. Nous ne craignons jamais de rompre d'avec les normes de l'industrie et nous ne cherchons jamais la facilité lorsque nous sommes à la recherche d'innovations créatives.

Avant tout, nous utilisons cette réinvention pour atteindre un objectif-clé pour le client : créer un lien avec le consommateur. Car lorsque vous créez un lien avec quelqu'un, ce dernier baisse sa garde et vous pouvez faire passer votre message.

Cet ouvrage compte de nombreux exemples d'histoires similaires de créateurs et d'agences apportant des idées et philosophies nouvelles à la conception de site web.

L'inspiration est partout. On ne sait jamais quand ni où on la trouvera. Cela pourrait se produire en feuilletant ce fascinant ouvrage, en surfant sur le web ou simplement sur le chemin pour aller au travail.

Chaque site internet est une opportunité de changer la perception que le public a de votre produit ou de votre marque et de provoquer une réaction en chaîne qui transformera voire métamorphosera votre position sur le marché.

Alors éloignez-vous des modèles de sites internet et laissez l'innovation, le sens artistique et la créativité ciblée pénétrer votre nouvelle stratégie digitale !

¡Hazlo divertido!

Fouad Mallouk

CEO y fundador, Phoenix the Creative Studio

El mundo está en constante transformación. En los últimos años, la tecnología ha evolucionado y también ha cambiado la forma de vivir de las personas, así como sus relaciones y sus esperanzas. En la actualidad hay tantas personas en la web (3.500 millones) como las que formaban la población mundial en 1970.

La empresas han experimentado el impacto de estos cambios tecnológicos en los distintos sectores. Los que fueron líderes del mercado se ven amenazados por compañías emergentes a menudo nacidas en línea. Las industrias veteranas se cuestionan a sí mismas. Las tecnologías están eliminando la necesidad de intermediarios y facilitan tanto la compra como la comparación.

Y las posibilidades de elección nunca habían sido mayores para los consumidores, que ya no están limitados a las tiendas locales. Como decía recientemente el *New York Times*: «Ninguna empresa está a salvo frente a la destrucción creativa que supone el cambio tecnológico».

Las empresas saben que deben adaptarse a esta nueva realidad a fin de garantizar su crecimiento; nunca habían necesitado tanta ayuda para mantenerse fieles a sus planteamientos y evolucionar al ritmo de sus clientes.

El diseño está en todas partes, nos rodea y no podemos ignorarlo. Y no hay duda de que el diseño web–que puede influir casi en un 90% en la decisión del consumidor al elegir un producto en lugar de otro– es el líder en esta nueva realidad.

Pero el diseño web no es un lujo. Si la marca es el alma de una empresa, el sitio web es su cuerpo y su voz, envueltos en interacción y estética.

Cuando se trata de la esencia interactiva de una marca, ésta puede ser buena, mala o fea. El mal diseño web es terrible para el negocio y, como cualquier tipo de contaminación, es malo para el alma.

Cambiar la propia industria requiere una dosis de audacia. Un salto a ciegas.

¿Cómo podemos crear valor percibido en un mundo en el que los consumidores ya no se contentan con lo común? ¿Cómo podemos diferenciarnos para que nuestro sitio web destaque? La solución es encontrar maneras innovadoras de entretejer la imaginación y la emoción y crear experiencias que lleguen a todos y que dejen una impresión duradera.

Hay que abordar cada proyecto, grande o pequeño, con el deseo de crear algo destacado. Es fácil y tentador seguir las tendencias, especialmente porque hoy en día todo es accesible fácilmente. El peligro de ir siempre por delante es que no tienes una plantilla a seguir. Pero es un riesgo que vale la pena correr.

¿Hay una solución predefinida para crear un buen diseño? Tal vez, o tal vez no. Pero hay dos fórmulas que conviene tener presentes. Primero, el contenido en contexto es primordial. Segundo, para reconstruir hay que deconstruir.

Cuando fundé Phoenix the Creative Studio, una agencia a escala humana establecida en Montreal, después de pasar más de una década en el sector y de haber dirigido otras dos agencias, éstos fueron los principios que elegí para guiar mi nuevo proyecto.

Mi socio Louis Paquet y yo renacimos de nuestras cenizas en términos de creatividad cuando descubrimos esas fórmulas. Apenas dieciocho meses después de aquel renacimiento, esta audacia creativa –y la habilidad técnica– le han valido a Phoenix más de quince premios importantes.

Cuando abordamos un proyecto nuevo para un cliente, aplicamos el poder de la reinvención, un poder cimentado en la agilidad de nuestro equipo creativo, que se adapta a las necesidades de cada proyecto. Y en el momento de la ejecución reinventamos las viejas herramientas para aplicarlas a la cultura del «siempre conectados», y creamos experiencias de marca al modificarlas para la nueva era interactiva. Nunca tememos romper los estándares de la industria y nunca ahorramos esfuerzos en la búsqueda de innovaciones creativas.

Por encima de todo, ponemos en juego la reinvención con el fin de conseguir un objetivo clave para el cliente: crear una conexión con el público. Porque cuando conectas con las personas, éstas bajan la guardia y dejan que tu mensaje les llegue.

Este libro contiene muchos ejemplos de diseñadores y agencias semejantes a la nuestra que están aportando ideas y filosofías frescas al diseño web.

La inspiración está en todas partes. Nunca sabes cuándo o dónde la encontrarás. Tal vez mientras hojeas este fantástico libro, o navegando por internet, o simplemente mientras andas por la calle camino del trabajo.

Cada sitio web es una oportunidad de cambiar la percepción que tiene el público de tu producto o de tu marca e iniciar una reacción en cadena que transformará e incluso metamorfoseará tu posición en el mercado.

Así pues, deja a un lado las plantillas de páginas web y deja que la innovación, el talento artístico y la creatividad bien orientada impregnen tu nueva estrategia digital.

"The website is a source of
information so it must be able to
efficiently and effectively
deliver that information.
Being legible is a requirement."

— Vijay Mathews

Design for Screen — ❶

Color Scheme

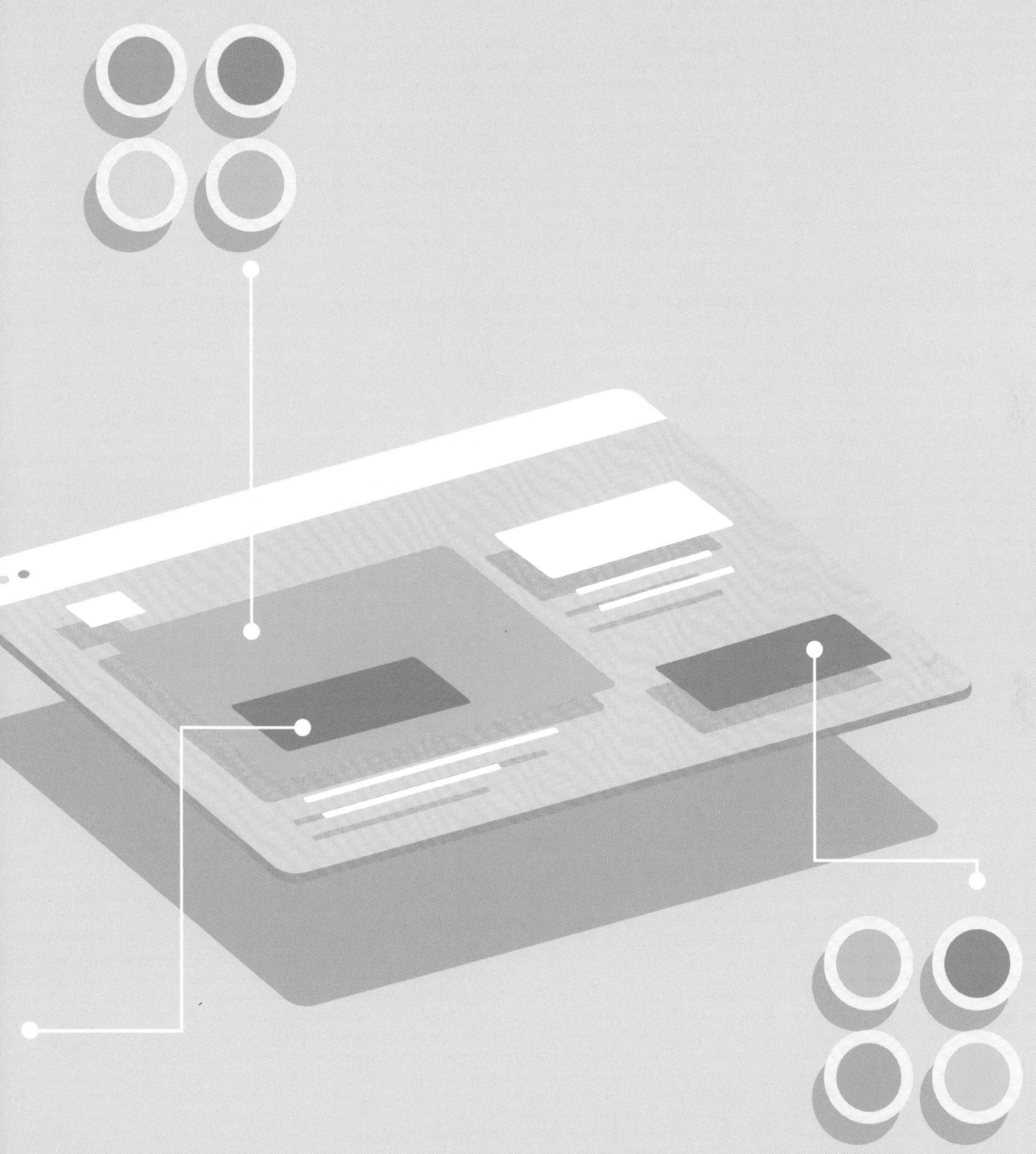

Interview with
Vijay Mathews

Graduated with a bachelor degree from Boston University in Fine Arts, Graphic Design, and Art History, Vijay Mathews is the principal of W&CO., a New York-based digital design and development studio. In addition to being a SEGD thought leader, he is also a member of the Type Directors Club, the Art Directors Club, and IxDA.

◊ Q1 ◊ Can you tell us a little bit about your background and how you came about to be doing web design?

Shortly after university, I worked as a print designer at Hatch Show Print, a letterpress print shop, then at WGBH, a television network, and at Two Twelve, a wayfinding design shop. I started experimenting with interaction design on the side. Over the course of two years, that side gig became more interesting than my full-time job, so I, along with my now co-founder Chris Auyeung, started to pursue it as a business. Designing and developing applications during those first two years allowed us to experiment with all sorts of different interactions and functions. Since we were our only client we could do anything we wanted without worrying about deliverables or expectations.

◊ Q2 ◊ Please kindly describe your design process: Is there a specific routine/technique that you adhere to?

Every project is different, but for projects that have a defined scope and deliverable we use a 4D process: Discovery, Design, Development, Deployment. During the "Discovery" phase we analyze the problem, understand the potential users and define the scope. The "Design" phase maps out those findings through an overarching sitemap, a diagrammatic wireframe as well through visual designs. The "Development" phase implements the visual designs into a working site. The "Deployment" phase is about adding all the content, testing and launching the site.

◊ Q3 ◊ A lot of web designs might look beautiful but not friendly to users. How do you take a complex chunk of information and make sense out of it?

Websites are designed for a particular purpose and for particular content. Part of the design process is developing a content strategy so that the messaging is appropriate for that medium. That process requires a thorough understanding of the information. The role of the designer is to make the complex simple.

◊ Q4 ◊ How do you determine the color scheme for a website? What makes a good color scheme?

For me color in web design shares the same importance as color in all design. There is a utility, an identification, and an emotion to it. Color is a tool that can help a user parse information.

◊ Q5 ◊ How do you think of the function of color in web design?

It can be used to establish hierarchy. Depending on the level of contrast color, it can help direct a user's attention and prioritize information. Color when used in consistency can help establish an identity through that systematic familiarity across the site.

◊ Q6 ◊ How do you think of the psychological properties of the colors using in a web?

Color can be used to establish an emotional response ranging from an electric vibrancy to something quiet and subtle. Such emotional effects are partly driven through the choices in color.

◊ Q7 ◊ The interactivity allows users to make a more direct contact with the content than print design, how does it influence the use of colors on screen?

Because websites do not allow a tactile response, color is utilized to establish a similar connection. Color in this context is needed to show various states of interactivity. For example with the usage of buttons, color is readily used to show the distinction of unselected, highlighted, selected, and active states.

◊ Q8 ◊ Given a color scheme, how to apply to a website design? Are there rules of thumb or general guidelines that help one decide which colors go where?

In my opinion there are no defining rules. What it comes down is what kind of emotional response you are trying to illicit from your users.

◊ Q9 ◊ The color scheme in your project for AIGA is very impressive. What was your initiative to use this color scheme?

The color scheme, derived from the visual identity by Mother Design, was used in a larger design program for the conference. This program included motion graphics, onsite environmental graphics, print materials and social assets.

◊ Q10 ◊ This website is designed for AIGA Design Conference, who was the target audience for this design? How did it impact your work?

The primary audience was designers. Therefore, we were able to push some of the boundaries of the website design. We could get away with certain design decisions because we knew the audience would tolerate it. In some ways, there is an almost brutal quality to the site, with overlapping elements and hard edges.

◊ Q11 ◊ How do you balance the readability and aesthetics in this project?

For us they go hand-in-hand. The website is still a source of information so it must be able to efficiently and effectively deliver that information. Being legible is a requirement.

AIGA Design Conference

Design Agency/
W&CO

Development/
W&CO

Client/
AIGA

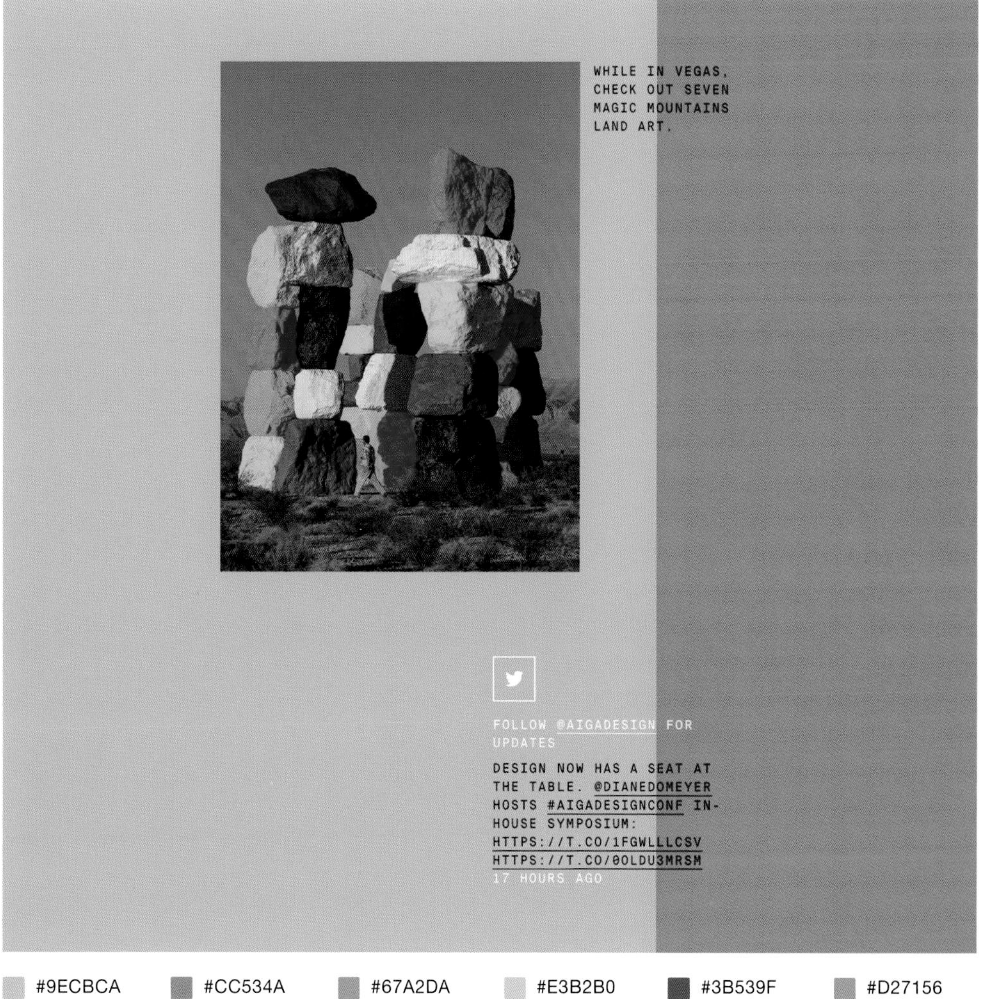

WHILE IN VEGAS, CHECK OUT SEVEN MAGIC MOUNTAINS LAND ART.
FOLLOW @AIGADESIGN FOR UPDATES
DESIGN NOW HAS A SEAT AT THE TABLE. @DIANEDOMEYER HOSTS #AIGADESIGNCONF IN-HOUSE SYMPOSIUM: HTTPS://T.CO/1FGWLLLCSV HTTPS://T.CO/0OLDU3MRSM
17 HOURS AGO

#9ECBCA #CC534A #67A2DA #E3B2B0 #3B539F #D27156

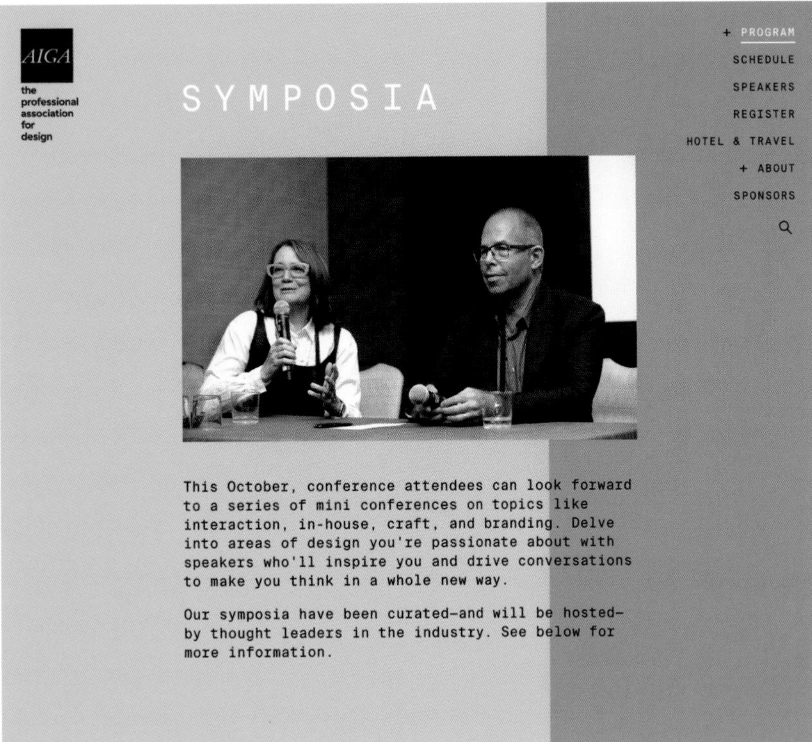

The AIGA Design Conference brings the design community together in a cross-disciplinary exchange of ideas about the changing shape of design. Built upon a strong identity by Mother Design, the website is an extension of that identity featuring dual-tone backgrounds, text transformations, and slide transitions. The website was built using customized versions of Django, React JS, and Sass.

AIGA
the professional association for design

ALL | SYMPOSIA | GENERAL SESSION | ROUNDTABLES | WORKSHOPS

+ PROGRAM
SCHEDULE
SPEAKERS
REGISTER
HOTEL & TRAVEL
+ ABOUT
SPONSORS

MONDAY 10/17 TUESDAY 10/18 WEDNESDAY 10/19

7:00 AM REGISTRATION OPENS

9:00 AM

9:00 AM - 12:00 PM
PROFESSIONAL DEVELOPMENT WORKSHOPS
Additional fee required
Pre-registration required
Fee: $75
Enhance your skills and build your practice by attending a professional development workshop with industry leaders. Pre-registration and an additional fee is required. Registration will open later this summer.

9:00 AM - 12:00 PM
EMERGING DESIGNERS SYMPOSIUM
Pre-registration required
Join Tina Essmaker from "The Great Discontent" for conversations with designers about the biggest challenges they have faced, how they have evolved, and how they define success.
The Emerging Designers Symposium is free for all registered conference attendees. Seating is limited and will be available on a first come, first served basis. Registration will open this summer.

9:00 AM - 12:00 PM
PRACTICE MANAGEMENT
Additional fee require
Pre-registration requi
This conference-within conference features ex presentations that wil valuable insights and for independent design well as design manager firms.
Errol Gerson
Ann Harakawa
Linda Joy Kattwinkel
Shel Perkins

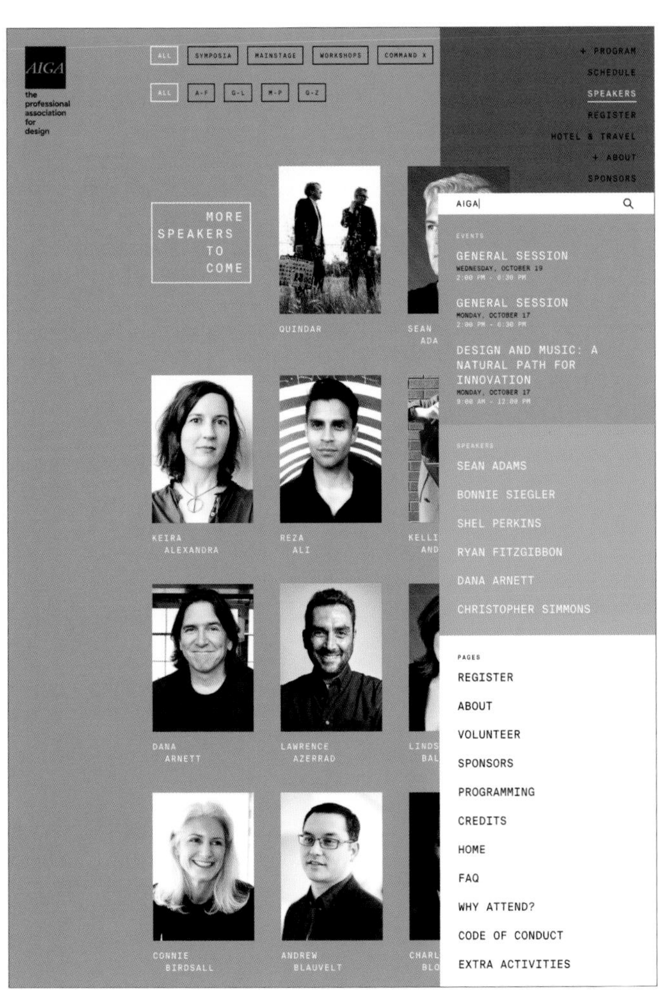
AIGA
the professional association for design
ALL
SYMPOSIA
MAINSTAGE
WORKSHOPS
COMMAND X
ALL
A-F
G-L
M-P
Q-Z
+ PROGRAM
SCHEDULE
SPEAKERS
REGISTER
HOTEL & TRAVEL
+ ABOUT
SPONSORS
MORE SPEAKERS TO COME
QUINDAR
AIGA
GENERAL SESSION
GENERAL SESSION
DESIGN AND MUSIC: A NATURAL PATH FOR INNOVATION
SEAN ADAMS
BONNIE SIEGLER
SHEL PERKINS
RYAN FITZGIBBON
DANA ARNETT
CHRISTOPHER SIMMONS
KEIRA ALEXANDRA
REZA ALI
DANA ARNETT
LAWRENCE AZERRAD
CONNIE BIRDSALL
ANDREW BLAUVELT
REGISTER
ABOUT
VOLUNTEER
SPONSORS
PROGRAMMING
CREDITS
HOME
FAQ
WHY ATTEND?
CODE OF CONDUCT
EXTRA ACTIVITIES

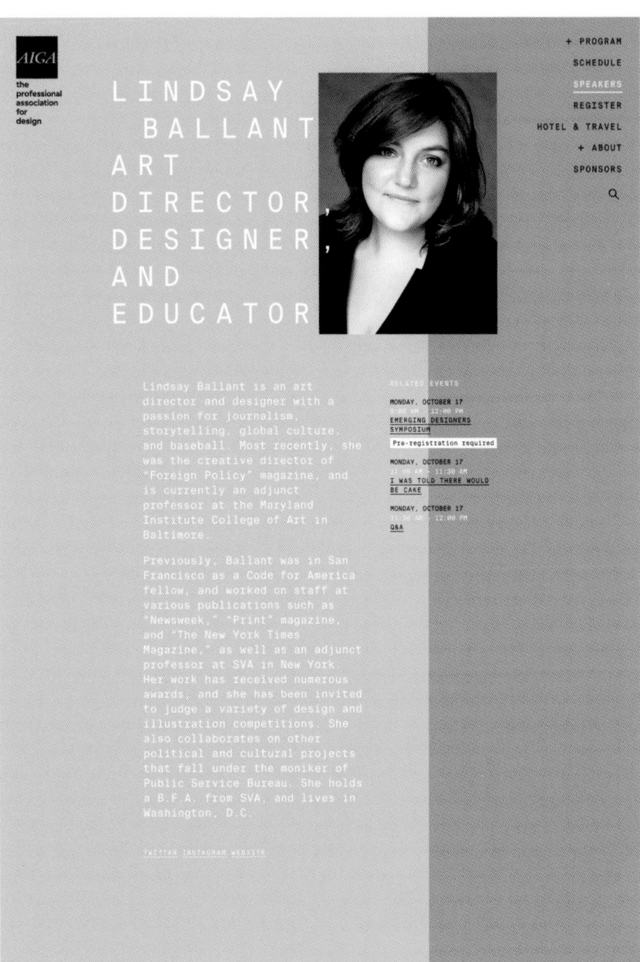
AIGA
the professional association for design
LINDSAY BALLANT ART DIRECTOR, DESIGNER, AND EDUCATOR
+ PROGRAM
SCHEDULE
SPEAKERS
REGISTER
HOTEL & TRAVEL
+ ABOUT
SPONSORS
Lindsay Ballant is an art director and designer with a passion for journalism, storytelling, global culture, and baseball. Most recently, she was the creative director of "Foreign Policy" magazine, and is currently an adjunct professor at the Maryland Institute College of Art in Baltimore.
Previously, Ballant was in San Francisco as a Code for America fellow, and worked on staff at various publications such as "Newsweek," "Print" magazine, and "The New York Times Magazine," as well as an adjunct professor at SVA in New York. Her work has received numerous awards, and she has been invited to judge a variety of design and illustration competitions. She also collaborates on other political and cultural projects that fall under the moniker of Public Service Bureau. She holds a B.F.A. from SVA, and lives in Washington, D.C.
MONDAY, OCTOBER 17
EMERGING DESIGNERS SYMPOSIUM
Pre-registration required
MONDAY, OCTOBER 17
I WAS TOLD THERE WOULD BE CAKE
MONDAY, OCTOBER 17
Q&A

MONDAY 10/17
TUESDAY 10/18
WEDNESDAY 10/19
REGISTRATION OPENS

Interview with

Jimmy Raheriarisoa

Widely-recognized by FWA, CSS Design Awards, and AWWWARDS, Jimmy Raheriarisoa is a French digital art director with 10 years experience in this field. He is the co-founder of French design studio Waaark, and he is also known as the freelance art director Nerisson.

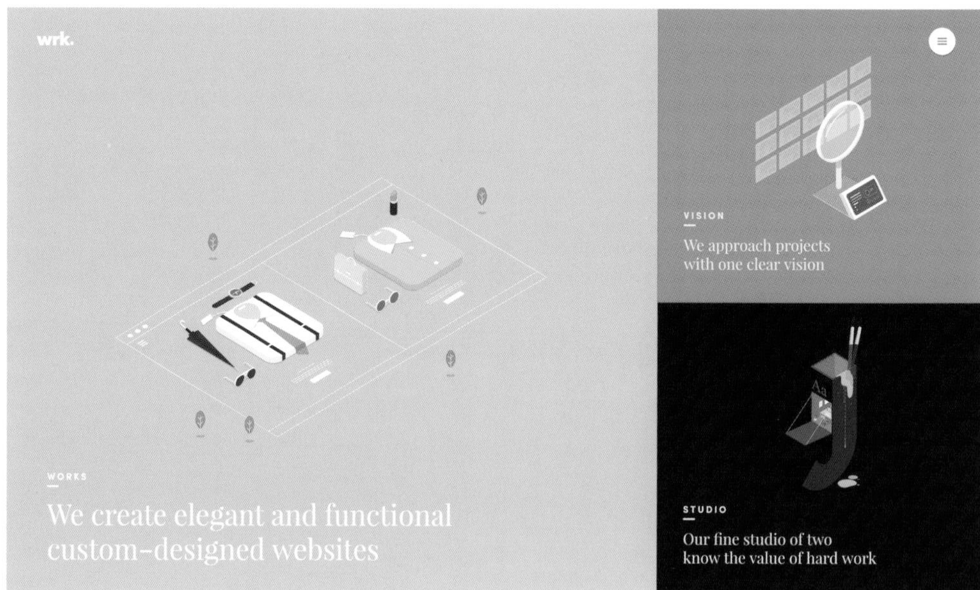

◊ Q1 ◊ Can you tell us a little bit about your background and how you came about to be doing web design?

After two-year study at the Gutenberg high school in Illkirch-Graffenstaden, France, I continued to study in web design for two years. Thereafter, I was employed into an agency to work as a web designer.

◊ Q2 ◊ Please kindly describe your design process: Is there a specific routine/technique that you adhere to?

This is my usual process:

Analyze of the project.
Creation of a web tree to organize site contents.
Creation of a wireframe for each page to define the navigation.
Creation of a moodboard to define the graphic design orientation.
Creation of the home page and the rest of the pages.
Generally this process works for every project, but sometimes it can be a bit different.

◊ Q3 ◊ A lot of web designs might look beautiful but not friendly to users. How do you take a complex chunk of information and make sense out of it?

It really depends on the client's target and values. But at Waaark, we always try to keep user experience in mind, and we don't want to make experimental projects that look more to technical demos. We try to simplify information as much as possible and keep only the essentials to make the navigation as clear as possible.

◊ Q4 ◊ How do you determine the color scheme for a website?

Generally it comes from the visual identity, and in this case we stick to it to keep the brand consistency. When the client doesn't have any identity, the color scheme comes from the moodboard, where I find inspiration in it and test several variations to find the color scheme that matches the most with the clients' needs.

◊ Q5 ◊ How do you think of the function of color in web design?

Color emphasizes information and help user to navigate with visual marker. But you always have to think about accessibility issues and make sure that color-blind person can also use the website. Colors are not the only way to spread information.

◊ Q6 ◊ How do you think of the psychological properties of the colors using in a web?

Color is important to convey an emotion and define the mood of a web site. Depending on the color scheme, you can give a strong personality to a website and enhance users' stickiness.

◊ Q7 ◊ Interactivity allows users to make a more direct contact with the content than print design, how does it influence the use of colors on screen?

I don't think that the use of colors is different between web and print design. Colors reflect the brand identity which must works the same whatever the media is.

◊ Q8 ◊ Given a color scheme, how to apply to a website design? Are there rules of thumb or general guidelines that help one decide which colors go where?

It is a really personal approach. I don't think there aren't rules that may ensure a great color combination. Great choices come from the designer sensitivity and creativity.

◊ Q9 ◊ The color scheme in your project for your official website is very impressive. What was your initiative to use this color scheme?

We first started with a moodboard to determine what our tastes and vision were. We wanted to create a delightful and colorful web site in opposition to the black or white agencies site that you usually see today. We chose a pastel color scheme to emphasize the global sweetness experience of our web site.

◊ Q10 ◊ This website, being your portfolio, showcases your aesthetic inclination and pursuit. What do you want to convey to your readers? How does your audience help decide the color scheme?

We didn't really think a lot to our potential audience when we created it. It was a personal approach and we wanted to make it our way, with the idea that it had to reflect our personality. Our main idea was to create a cool and unpretentious website, and we didn't want it to look bold or unfriendly. We tried to create things that were fun for us and that we liked, without thinking to the trends or other studio/agency website.

◊ Q11 ◊ How do you balance the readability and aesthetics in this project?

We think both of them are important and can work together. We kept the content as simple as possible, and tried to create a really clear and simple navigation. We worked with great copy writers to ensure that we could convey a clear vision with just a few words. We decided to use a scroll hijacking technique to keep each screen under control and make sure that everything is well positioned. Some people don't like it because they find it not user friendly, but we chose this solution for its aesthetics benefits.

Official Website of Waaark

Design Agency/
Waaark

URL/
http://waaark.com

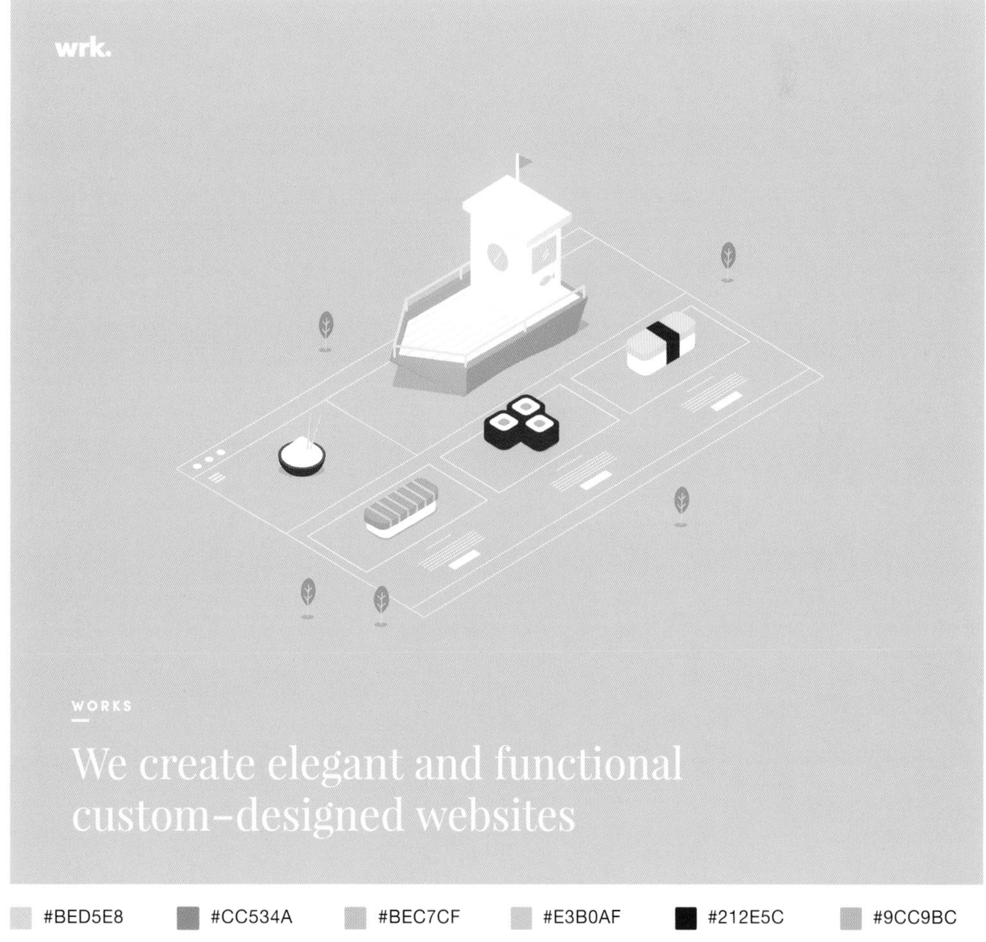

#BED5E8 #CC534A #BEC7CF #E3B0AF #212E5C #9CC9BC

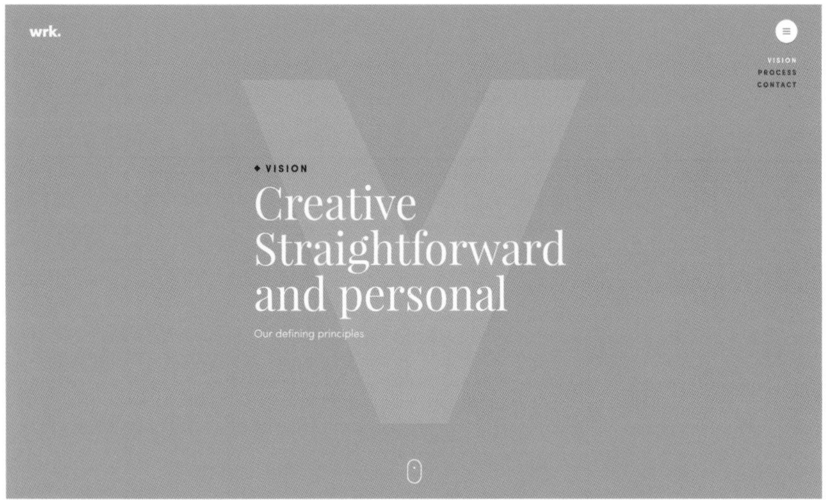

The launch of Waaark's website marked the formation and public announcement of this new studio. With a bright and fresh color scheme, playful illustrations, and smooth animations, the portfolio invites its audience into the delightful and happy half of the web industry. One of the most powerful aspects of the site is how every pixel deliberately presents the talent of its two creatives, with a constant focus on design, illustration, animation, and web development. The website is fully responsive and makes use of the most advanced techniques, such as SVG and Canvas, showing off the best example of innovation in technology.

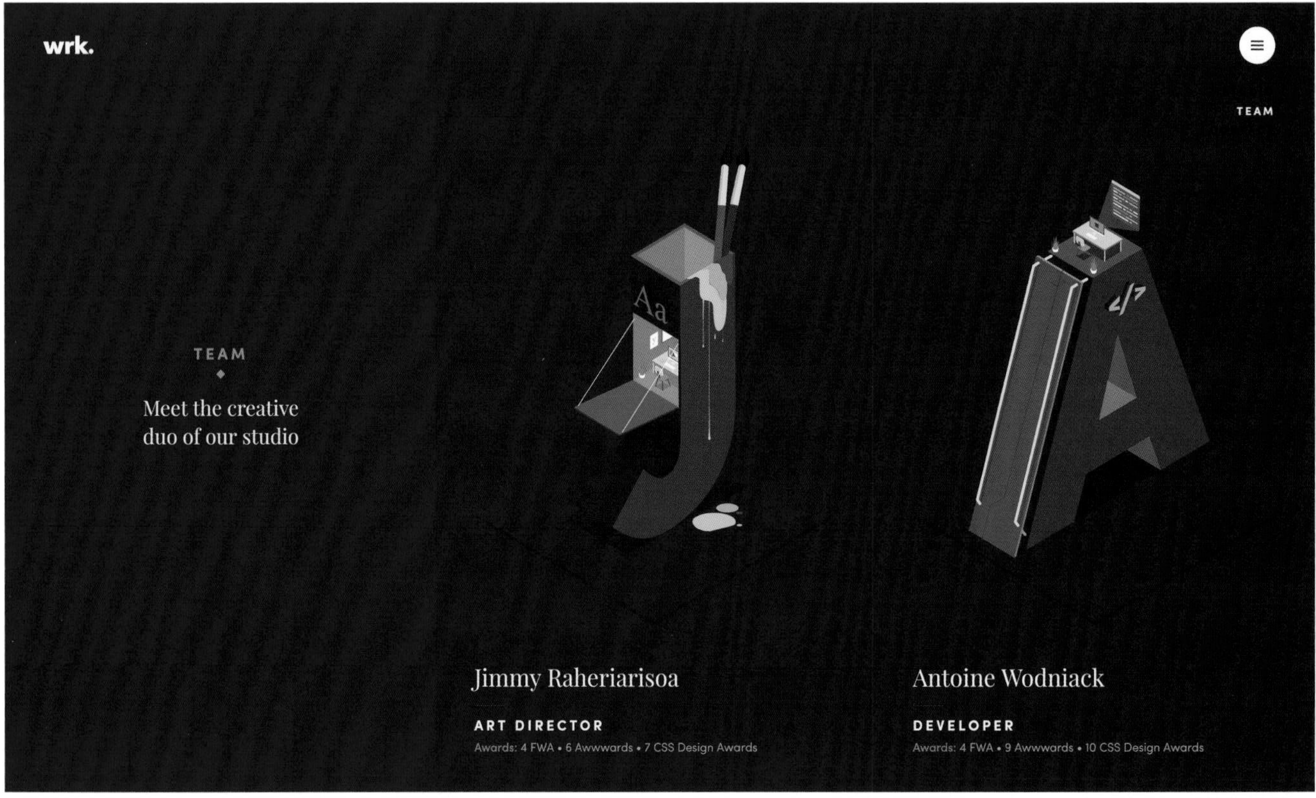

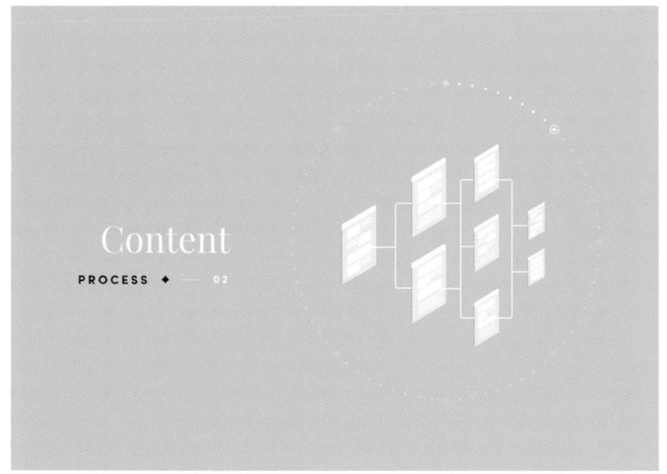
Content
PROCESS — 02

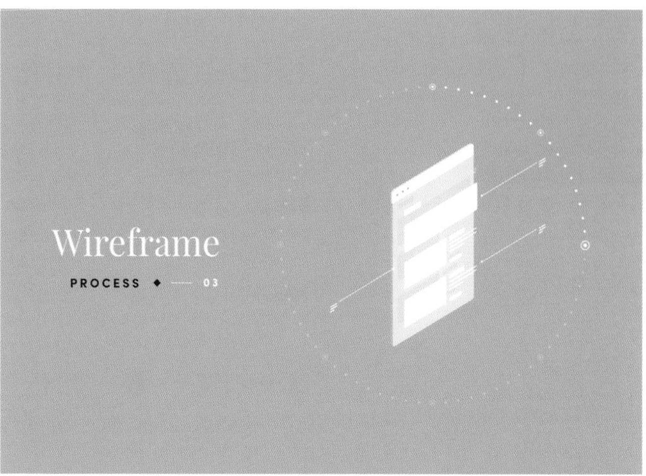
Wireframe
PROCESS — 03

Design
PROCESS — 04

Development
PROCESS — 05

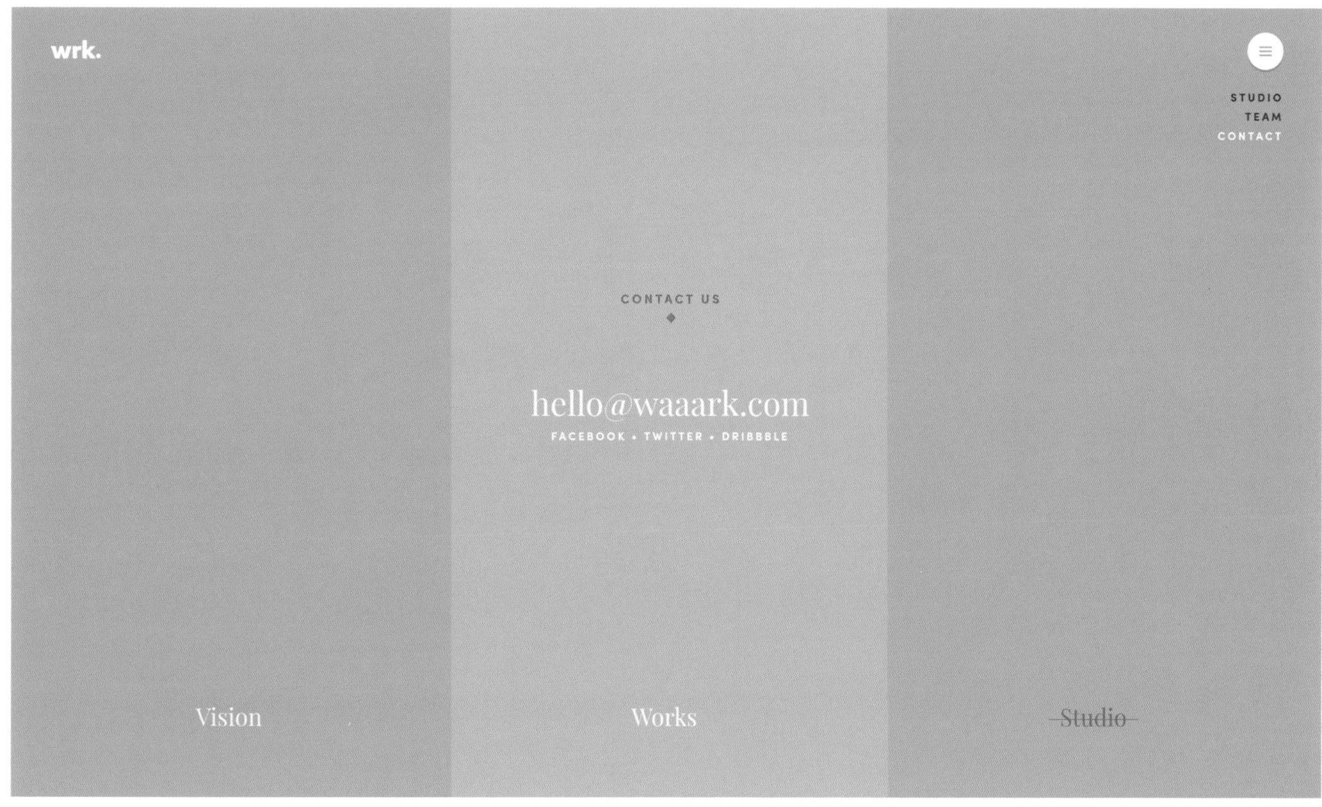
wrk.
STUDIO
TEAM
CONTACT
CONTACT US
hello@waaark.com
FACEBOOK • TWITTER • DRIBBBLE
Vision
Works
Studio

Lifeblood Agency

Design Agency/
Lifeblood Agency

Design/
Dominic Santalucia,
Travis Weihermulle

Website/
http://lifebloodagency.com

Dominic Santalucia and Travis Weihermuller, who is a design duo co-founded digital agency Lifeblood, made an eye-catching website by analyzing their DNA, and selected the unique sequences to form a pattern of lines. With a refreshing color scheme consisted of Green Cyan, Magenta Red, and Cyan Blue, the patterns are applied throughout the agency's branding. Their concept was to visualize "digital made human," and it is a result showing the power of youth.

#C52382 #2E4C9B #000000 #8AC0A6

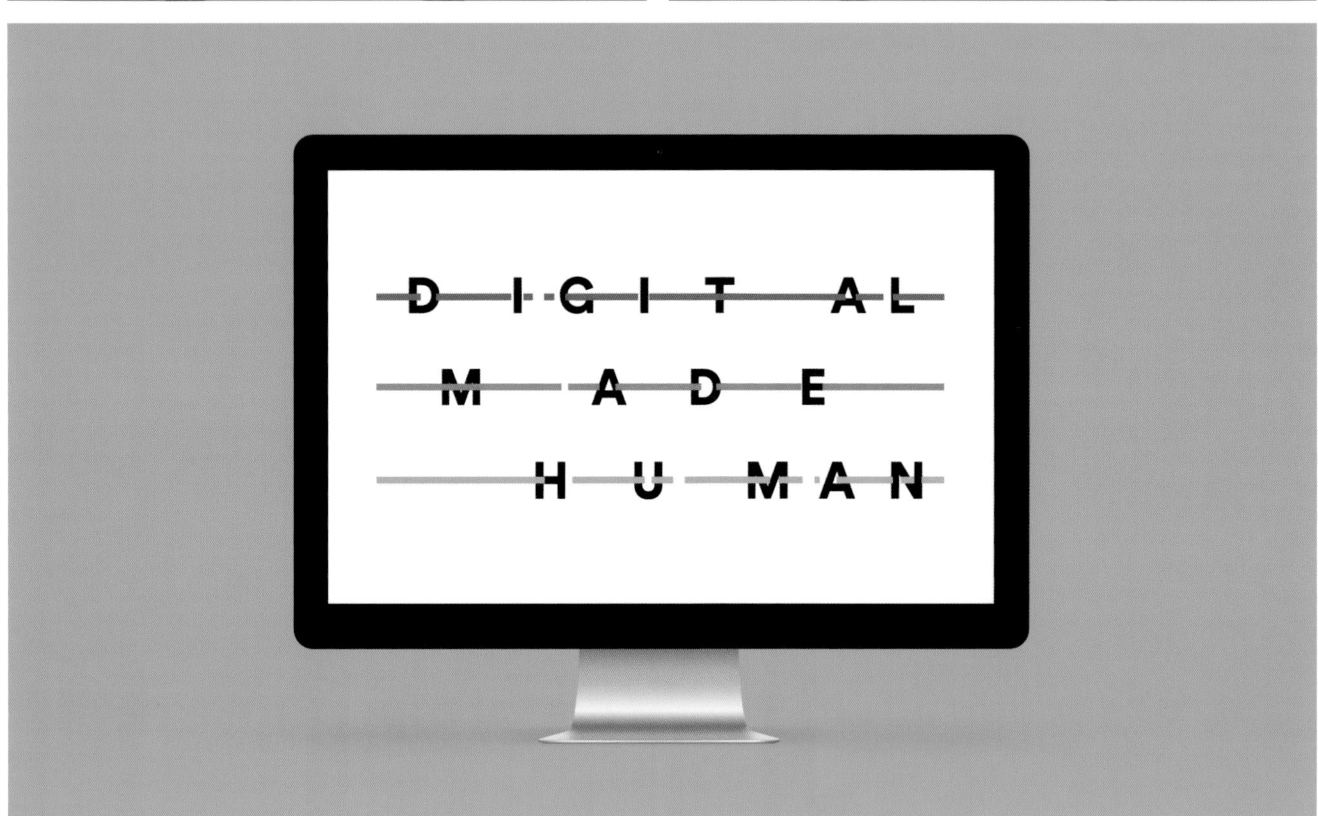

× — o www.lifebloodagency.com*

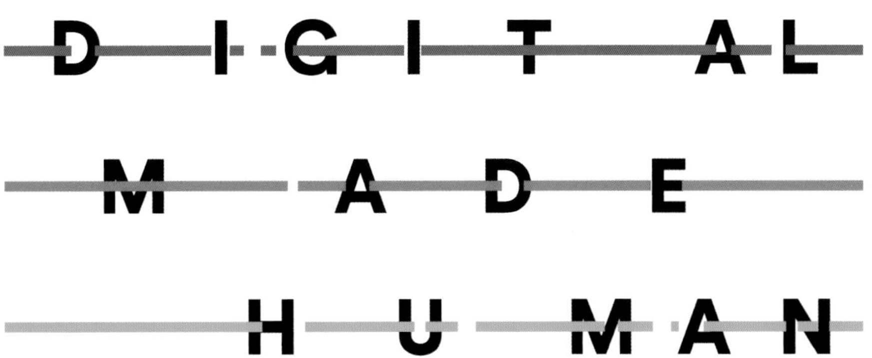

lifeblood.

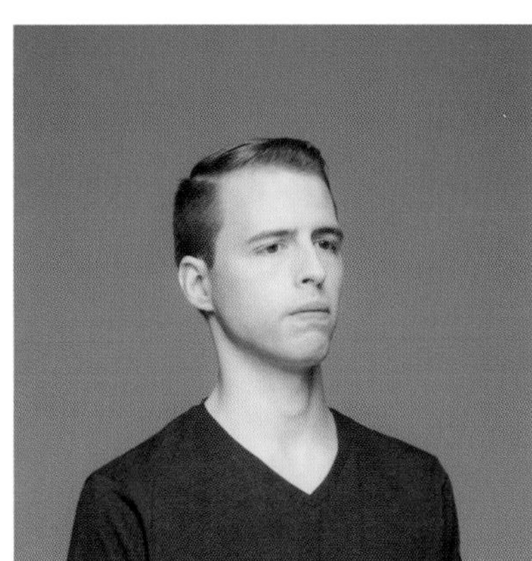

we are the collective
conciousness of creatives
who are free & fearless

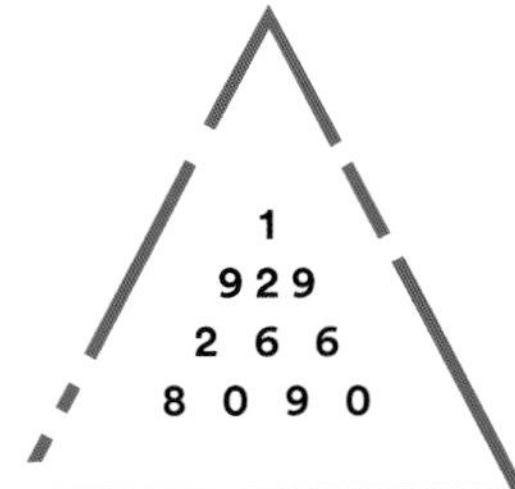

81
Prospect st.
Brooklyn
NY 11201

*For desired results view in web browser

254sound

Design Agency/
Codefrisko & Irradié

Photography/
Pierre Debusschere

Client/
254sound

URL/
http://www.254sound.com

254sound is a creative sound design studio working for Raf Simons, Terrence Fixmer, and Another mag etc.

The website is an auditory immersion with loop sampling through a simple and accessible user interface. The screen is split into two distinctive areas: the left area for vibrant images, and the right shows texts and navigation.

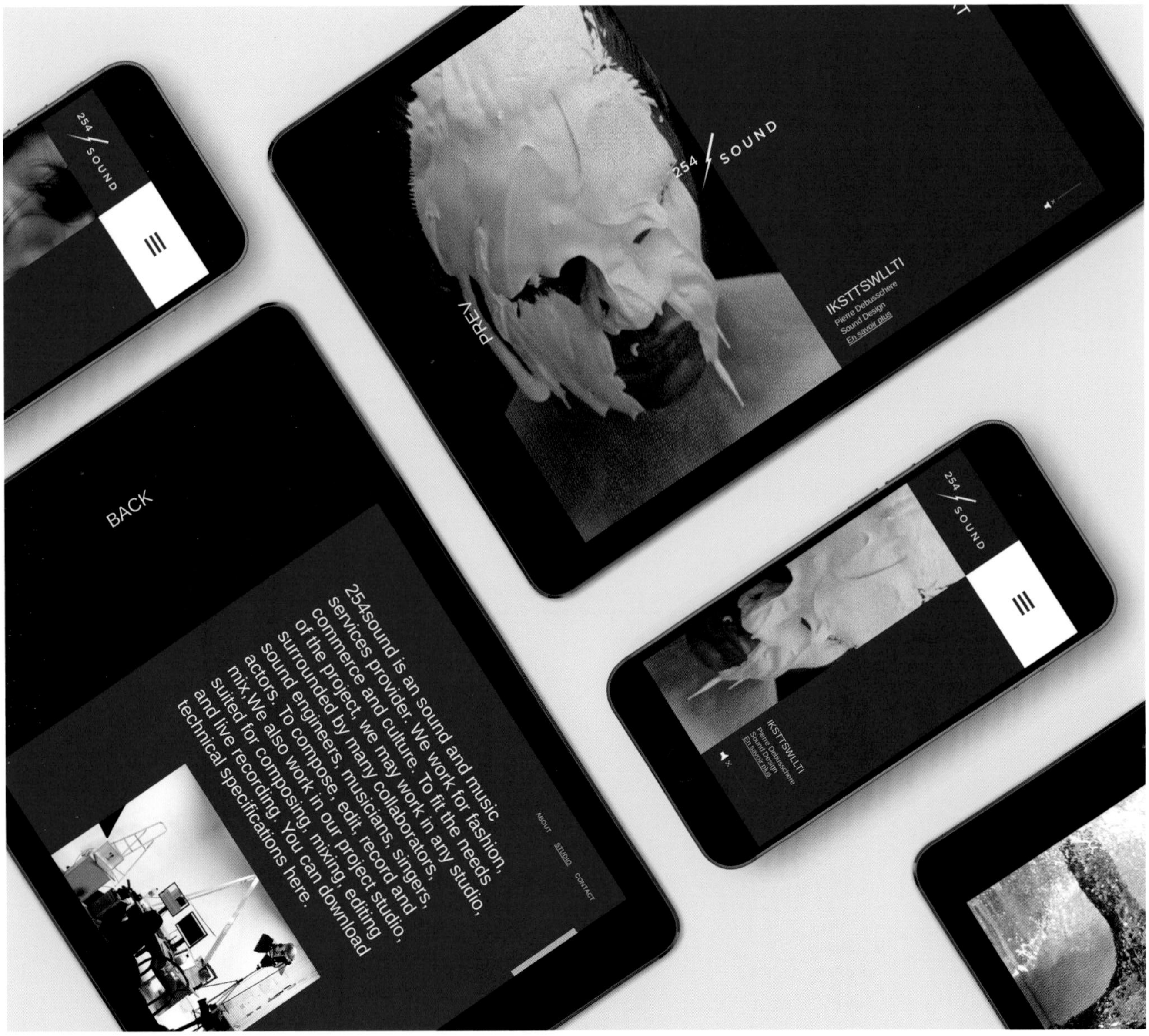

#272B82 #E3E5EF

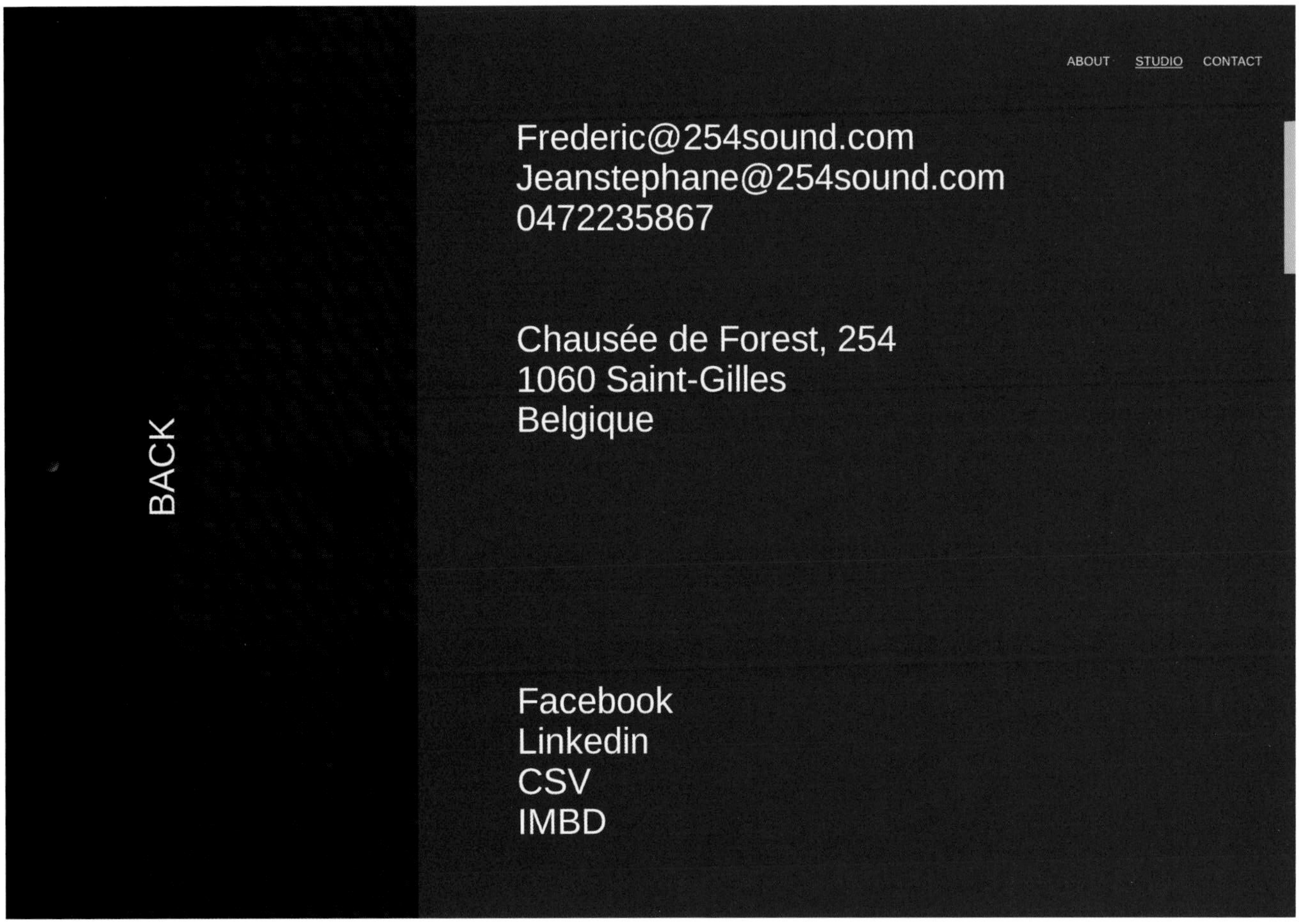

ABOUT STUDIO CONTACT

BACK

Frederic@254sound.com
Jeanstephane@254sound.com
0472235867

Chausée de Forest, 254
1060 Saint-Gilles
Belgique

Facebook
Linkedin
CSV
IMBD

254 SOUND

THE LAKE

Adriana Lima and the boys from Brazil

The Lake

The Numbers Station

CANALSAT Series

Design/
Pierre Nguyen

Client/
CANALSAT

Website/
http://www.canalsat.fr

This project was designed for CANALSAT Series, one of the major French satellite providers, to announce the new series collection available on the CANALSAT service. The wheel navigation allowed an exhaustive list of the CANALSAT offer. Each series had a page which contains cover, technical information, synopsis, video, and gallery.

The colorful layout was chosen to be coherent to the CANALSAT logotype as well as to the entertainment, broadcasting, and motion universe.

#A0377C #4786BF #FFFFFF #3C1F70

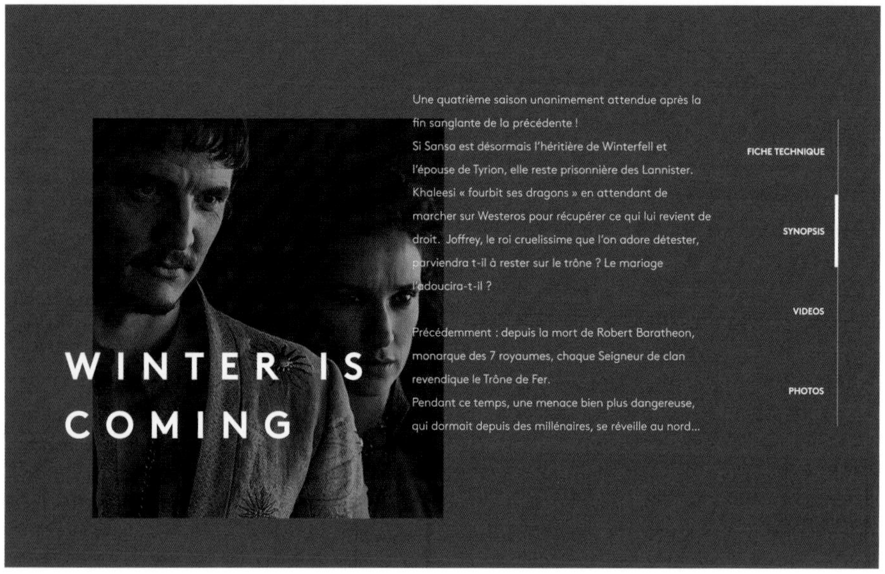

BANDE - ANNONCE
EXTRAIT
1m:16s
TEASER 1
TEASER 2
FICHE TECHNIQUE
SYNOPSIS
VIDEOS
PHOTOS

01
07

CANALSAT
AU JEU DES TRÔNES,
ON GAGNE OU ON MEURT
GAME OF
THRONES
SAISON 4
OCS
City

OFFF Italia

Design Agency/
AQuest S.r.l.

Direction/
Tomas Baruffaldi

Design/
Luca Franceschetti

Client/
Filippo Spiezia

URL/
http://www.offfitalia.com

OFFF is a community inviting all those who are eager to learn to participate and get inspired in a 3-day journey of conferences.

It's a combination of Offline/Online designers, motion designers, thinkers, sound designers, graphic designers, theorists, developers, professionals, students alike. Putting the titles aside, OFFF is made for the curious.

AQuest S.r.l. used neon colors for the site to homage the creatives and showcase their talents.

#4946FA #FFFFFF #04FCE2 #FF0202

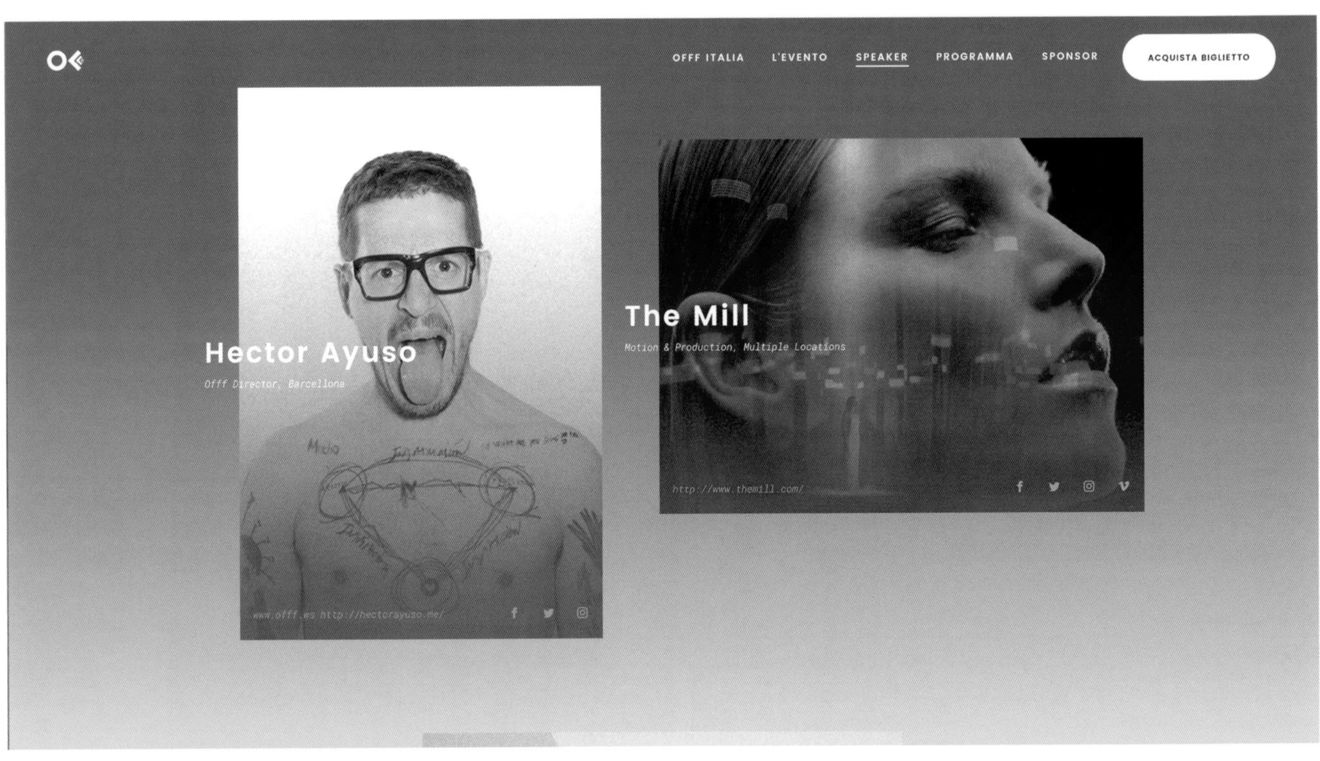

@offfitalia
SCHEDULE IS OUT! 3 magic days in which Milano becomes world capital of Digital Design. UNMISSABLE https://t.co/gMkvYIbrKT #DDD2016 #OFFF
OFFF ITALIA
Milano
28-29 Ottobre 2016
VAI ALL'EVENTO

Marta e Piotr di Ars Thanea, ...
OFFF ITALIA
Milano
28-29 Ottobre 2016
VAI ALL'EVENTO

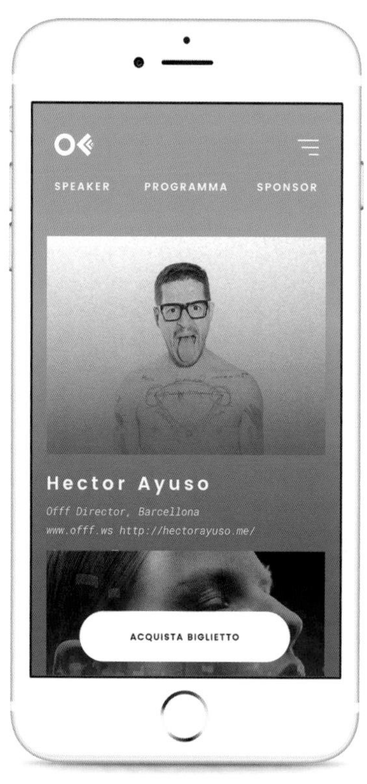
SPEAKER
PROGRAMMA
SPONSOR
Hector Ayuso
Offf Director, Barcellona
www.offf.ws http://hectorayuso.me/
ACQUISTA BIGLIETTO

Tooway Mobile Application

Direction/
Taehee Kim

Design/
Taehee Kim,
Hyemin Yoo

The TOOWAY app was created to help people to make decisions with comparisons. Users can vote anonymously about their ideas on certain topic, and, in return, receive feedbacks from the followers. To be a more casual note than ever, TOOWAY was made to share opinions on interesting occurrences and more trivial events. Specific hash tags are adopted to enhance accessibility. As in the New Post stage, users can use various templates to show their personality, and a guideline was provided for consultancy.

#4956A0 #E5E5E6 #8B8EC2 #9BC9BB

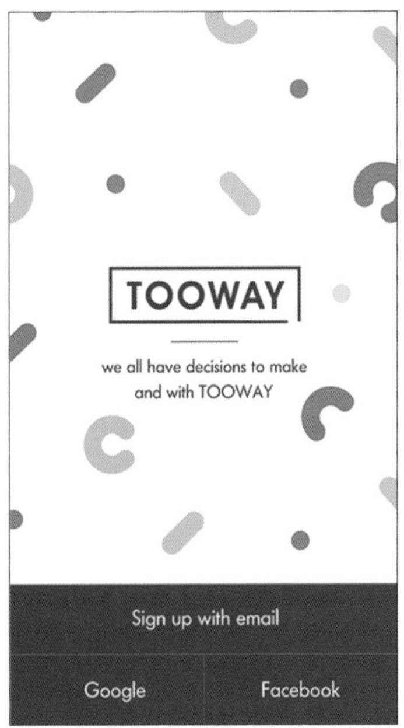

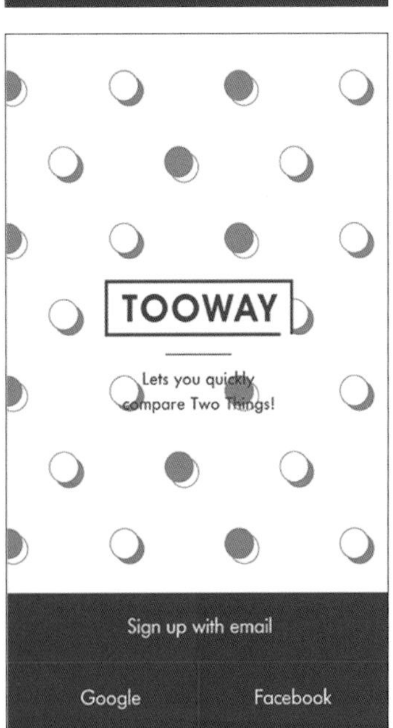

HOME PAGE

Victoria Watson
victoriaw@tooway.com
1.231 FOLLOWERS | 1.452 FOLLOWING

interests
activity
create stories
setting

sign out

NAVIGATION BAR

TOOWAY
#myhashtags
wellness fashionweek sport
new

#populartopics
WHAT ARE THE BEST WAY TO LOSE WEIGHT?
#diet #wellness
WHICH IS A BETTER CITY NEW YORK OR LONDON?
#newyork #london

#currentlynewtopics
WHAT ARE SOME OF THE BEST TRAVEL THAT —
#travel #city
EVER TRIED OF THE MILITARY DIET?
#diet #health

Arrange order of rank with text sizes.

aphicdesign sport wellness beauty
new

WHY DO PEOPLE ROMANTI-CIZE PARIS SO MUCH?
#romanticize
WHAT ARE THE HEALTH BENEFIT OF GREEN —
#greensmoothies
WHAT CAN I DO IN NEW YORK CITY IN A WEEK?
#newyork
WHAT ARE THE GOOD BUSINESS IDEAS FOR 2016?
#business #trend

ALEXSANDER JONES
1.532 FOLLOWERS
#design,#graphic
Following

ELIZABETH OLSEN
2.708 FOLLOWERS
#trend,#fashion
Follow

TOM RONINSON
434 FOLLOWERS
#journal,#news
Follow

WILLIAM HESSE
2.532 FOLLOWERS
#design,#graphic
Following

#interests
1 HOURS AGO
WHAT IS THE BEST DIET FOR LIVING A LONG PRODUCTIVE LIFE?

Information that easily become boring text add graphic

POSTING PAGE
Providing visual consistent with scroll screen
Delivering visual pleasure with changing pattern depending on hash tag.
Delivering visual pleasure while swiping motion of two choices.
IS DAIRY GOOD OR BAD FOR YOU?
#food #drink #healty #lifestyle #diet #innerbeauty
3 DAY AGO
READ MORE

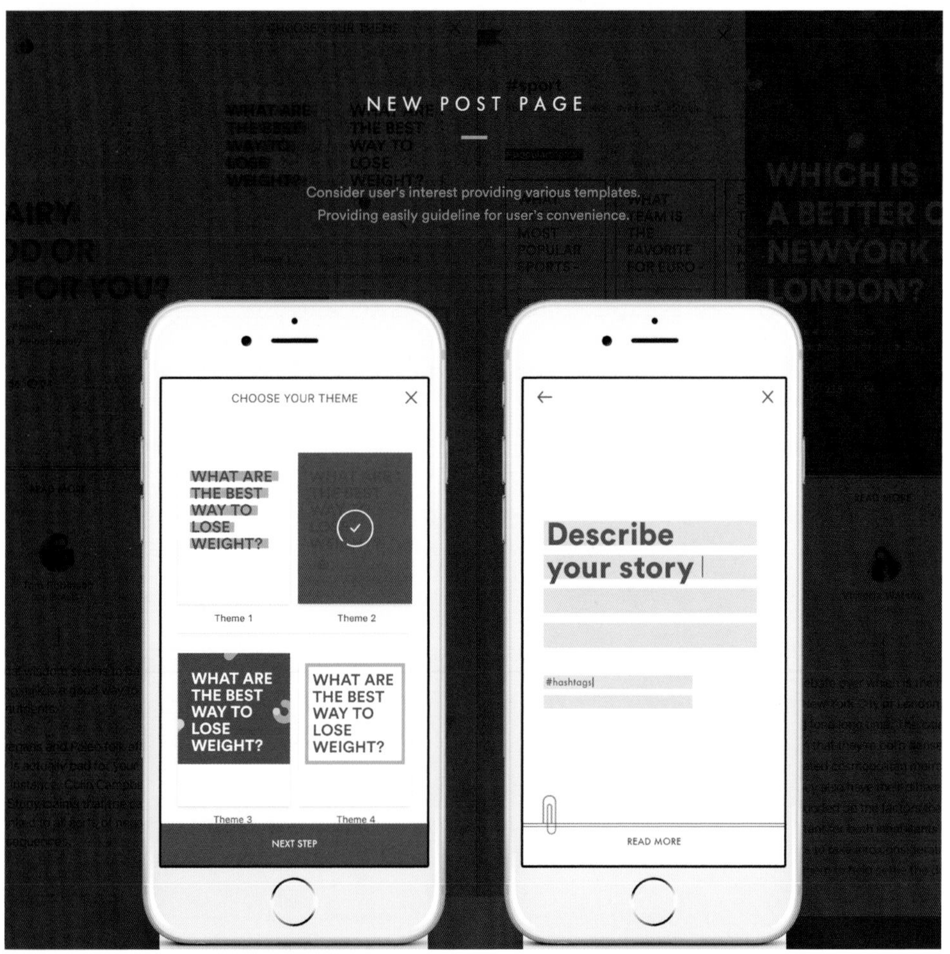
NEW POST PAGE
Consider user's interest providing various templates.
Providing easily guideline for user's convenience.
CHOOSE YOUR THEME
WHAT ARE THE BEST WAY TO LOSE WEIGHT?
Theme 1
Theme 2
Theme 3
Theme 4
NEXT STEP
Describe your story
#hashtags
READ MORE

Stadia Art Platform

Design/
Vadim Kukin

Client/
Stadia

URL/
http://www.stadia.lv

Stadia is an art community grouped by artists and served as an online gallery for the artist in the sphere of culture, arts, education, and media. It was founded for creatives to exchange ideas, forms, stories, and characters so as to realize self-development.

#3C4A99 #F4F4F4 #000000

LATVISKI

S T A D I A
art platform

ЭТО

ЛЮДИ

ПРОЕКТЫ

НЕФОРМАТ

АФИША

f

ШКОЛА

Открыт новый набор в школу
актерского мастерства

КОНТАКТЫ

Стабу 18 LV-1045

ПРОЕКТЫ

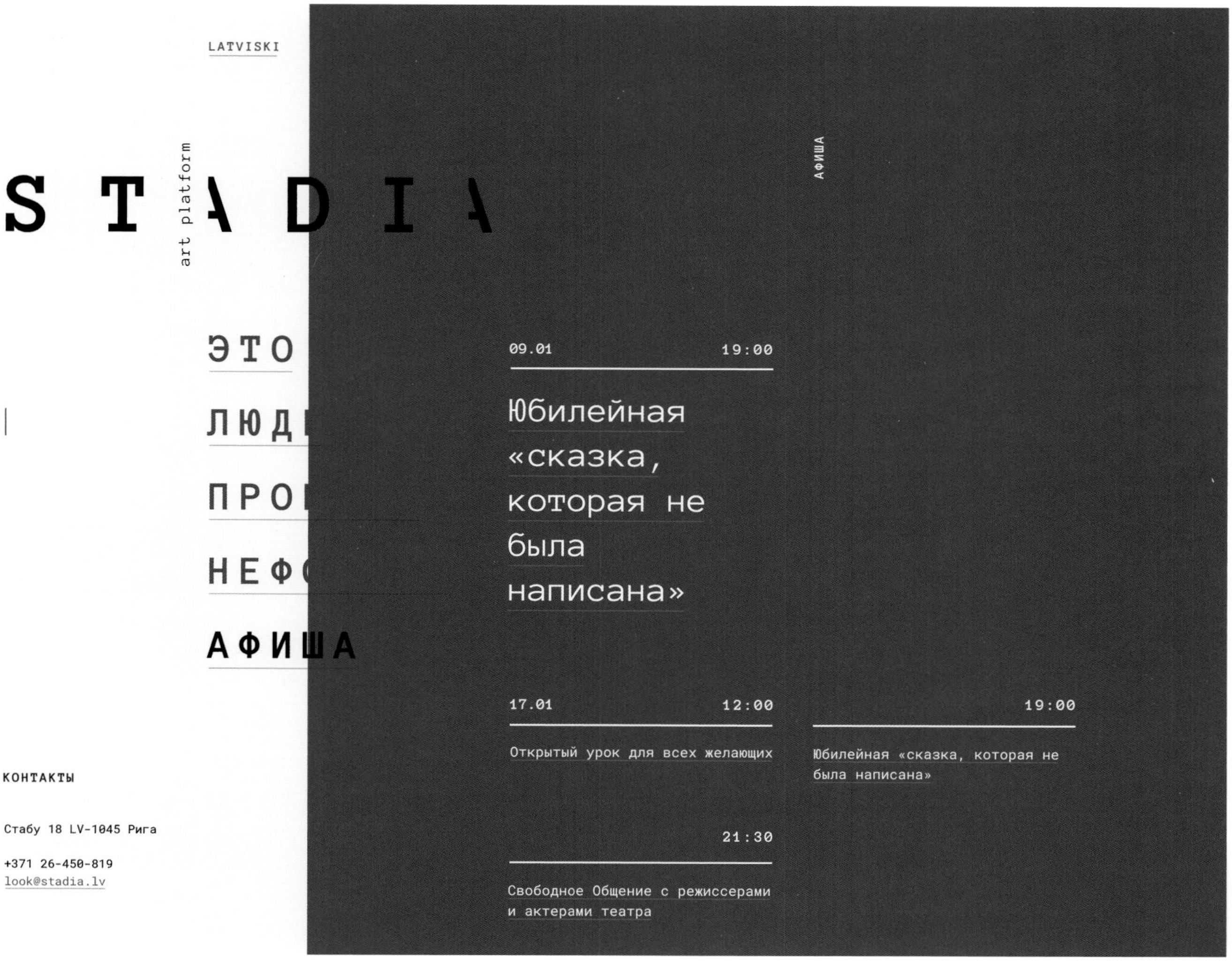

LATVISKI

S T A D I A
art platform

АФИША

ЭТО
ЛЮДИ
ПРОЕКТЫ
НЕФОРМАТ
АФИША

09.01 19:00

Юбилейная «сказка, которая не была написана»

17.01 12:00

Открытый урок для всех желающих

19:00

Юбилейная «сказка, которая не была написана»

21:30

Свободное Общение с режиссерами и актерами театра

КОНТАКТЫ

Стабу 18 LV-1045 Рига

+371 26-450-819
look@stadia.lv

Pro-té-gé

Design/
Ana Cecilia Thompson Motta

Pro-té-gé was designed as an online job-hunting site to redefine internship, which is of little regulations and may cause dissatisfaction between the two parties involved. The site connects, regulates, and assists both the employer and the intern. The log-in page is divided by white and blue equally for protégés (apprentice) and employers to represent their equal status. Unlike the typical job-hunting sites, Pro-té-gé is mainly led by images rather than texts.

#344596 #EFF6FB

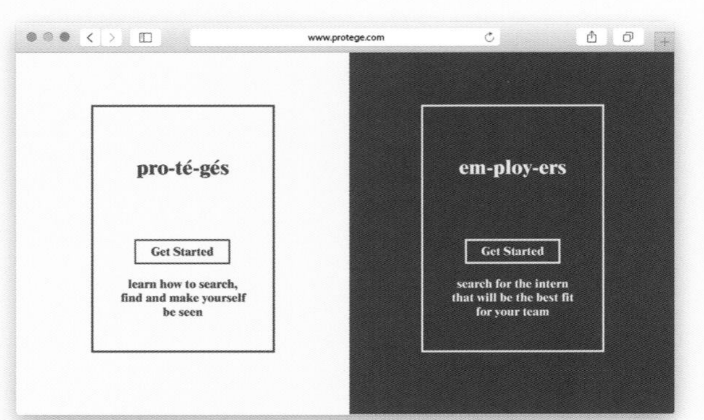

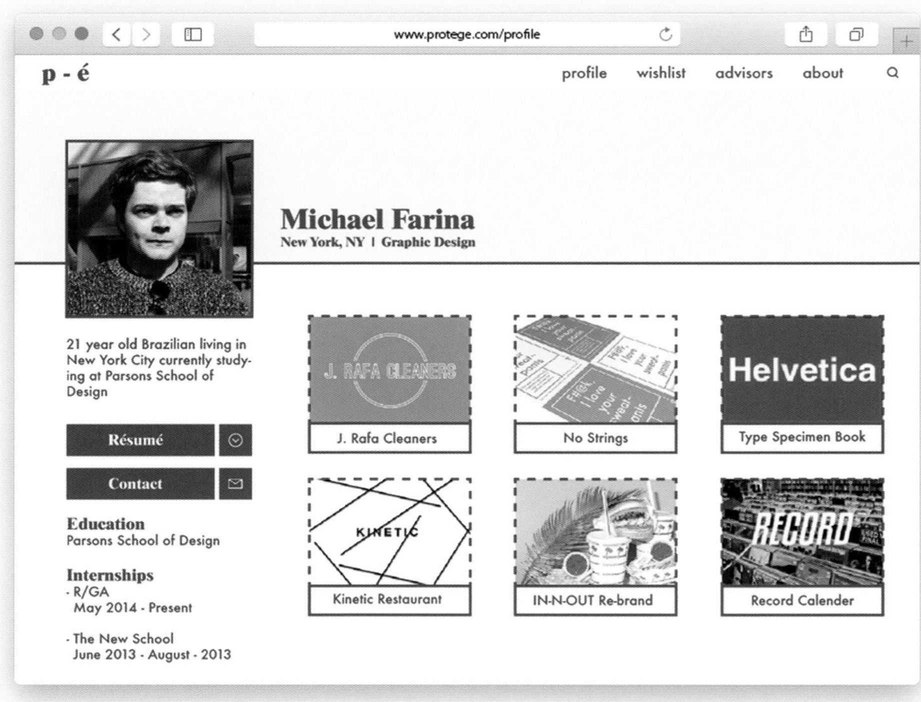

www.protege.com/educators
p - é
profile
applicants
office
about
Doubleday & Cartwright
Welcome back,
Doubleday & Cartwright
We have selected possible protéges for you
Applicants for review: 3
Most Compatible
Inye Nosegbe
Adrián Ortega
Natasha Schmidt
Isabella Caterina
Melati Diran
Popular Candidates
Inye Nosegbe
Adrián Ortega
Natasha Schmidt
Isabella Caterina
Melati Diran

www.protege.com/home
p - é
profile
wishlist
advisors
about
I want a
internship in or near
.

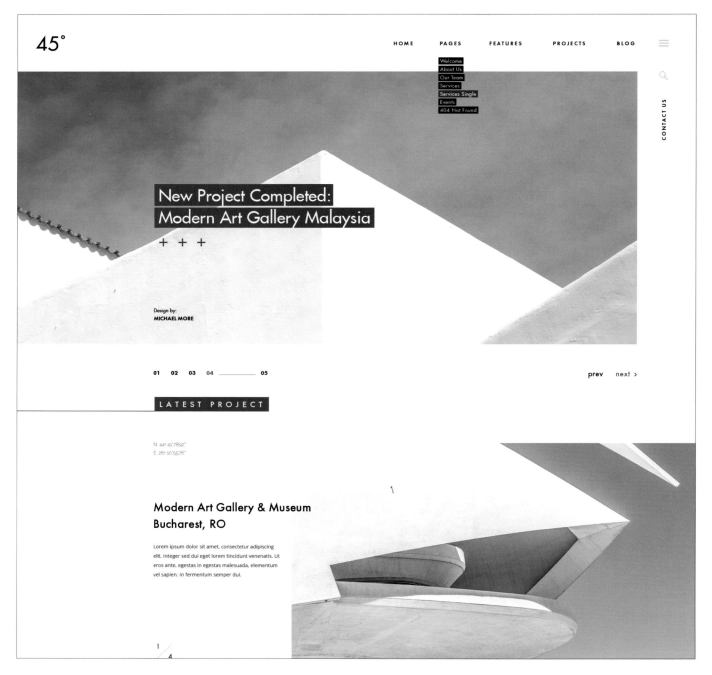

45 Degrees Architecture Studio

Design Agency/
Milo Themes

Direction/
Baldean Mihai

Design/
Loredana Papp-Dinea

Photography/
Stock Photography

45 Degrees is a site with an unconventional layout for Architecture studios, which need a modern and minimal design. The concept behind the project is simple: Milo Themes believes that design comes from nature, from simple shapes and lines and it should challenge the artistic senses. The approach is dynamic, abstract but concrete, and it builds itself around a minimalistic style.

#404D9A #000000

45°
HOME PAGES FEATURES PROJECTS BLOG
Welcome
About Us
Our Team
Services
Services Single
Events
404 Not Found
CONTACT US
New Project Completed:
Modern Art Gallery Malaysia
+ + +
Design by:
MICHAEL MORE
01 02 03 04 05
prev next >
LATEST PROJECT
N 44° 41'7892"
E 26° 10'5576"
Modern Art Gallery & Museum
Bucharest, RO
Lorem ipsum dolor sit amet, consectetur adipiscing elit. Integer sed dui eget lorem tincidunt venenatis. Ut eros ante, egestas in egestas malesuada, elementum vel sapien. In fermentum semper dui.
1/4

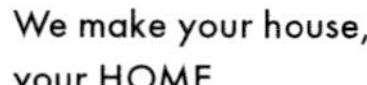

We make your house,
your HOME

Lorem ipsum dolor sit amet, consectetur adipiscing elit. Integer sed dui eget lorem tincidunt venenatis. Ut eros ante, egestas in egestas malesuada, elementum vel sapien. In fermentum semper dui. Lorem ipsum dolor sit amet, consectetur adipisc ing elit. Integer sed dui eget lorem tincidunt venenatis. Ut eros ante, egestas in eges tas malesuada, elementum vel sapien. In fermentum semper dui.

CLASSIC HOME

MODERN HOME

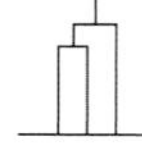

BUILDINGS

16	73	48	2
YEARS	PROJECTS	MEMBERS	AWARDS

TESTIMONIALS

Suspendisse metus turpis, blandit sed dolor quis, commodo commodo elit. Sed sagittis mollis ligula eget rhoncus. Nam blandit pellentesque odio.Sus pendisse metus turpis, blandit sed dolor quis, com modo commodo elit. Sed sagittis mollis.Sed sagittis mollis ligula eget rhoncus.

Written by:
MICHAEL MORE

‹

Concepts [3]   Interior Design [10]   Public Buildings [26]   Modern Architecture [9]

Palace Fashion Mall
PUBLIC

Palace Fashion Mall
PUBLIC

Palace Fashion Mall
PUBLIC

Crea 5 Collective

Design Agency/
Torpedov

Design/
Piotr Swierkowski

Project Management/
Agata Swierkowska

URL/
http://crea5collective.com

The site is build for a web design studio that provides business solutions for clients. It was designed to be minimalistic with cozy colors.

#AFD6E5 #FFFFFF #9EC9A7 #E5E5E2

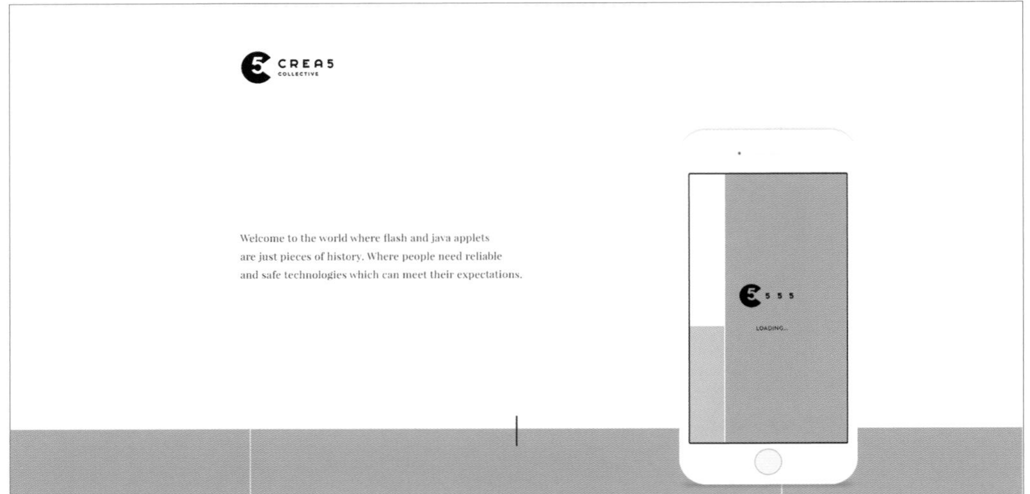

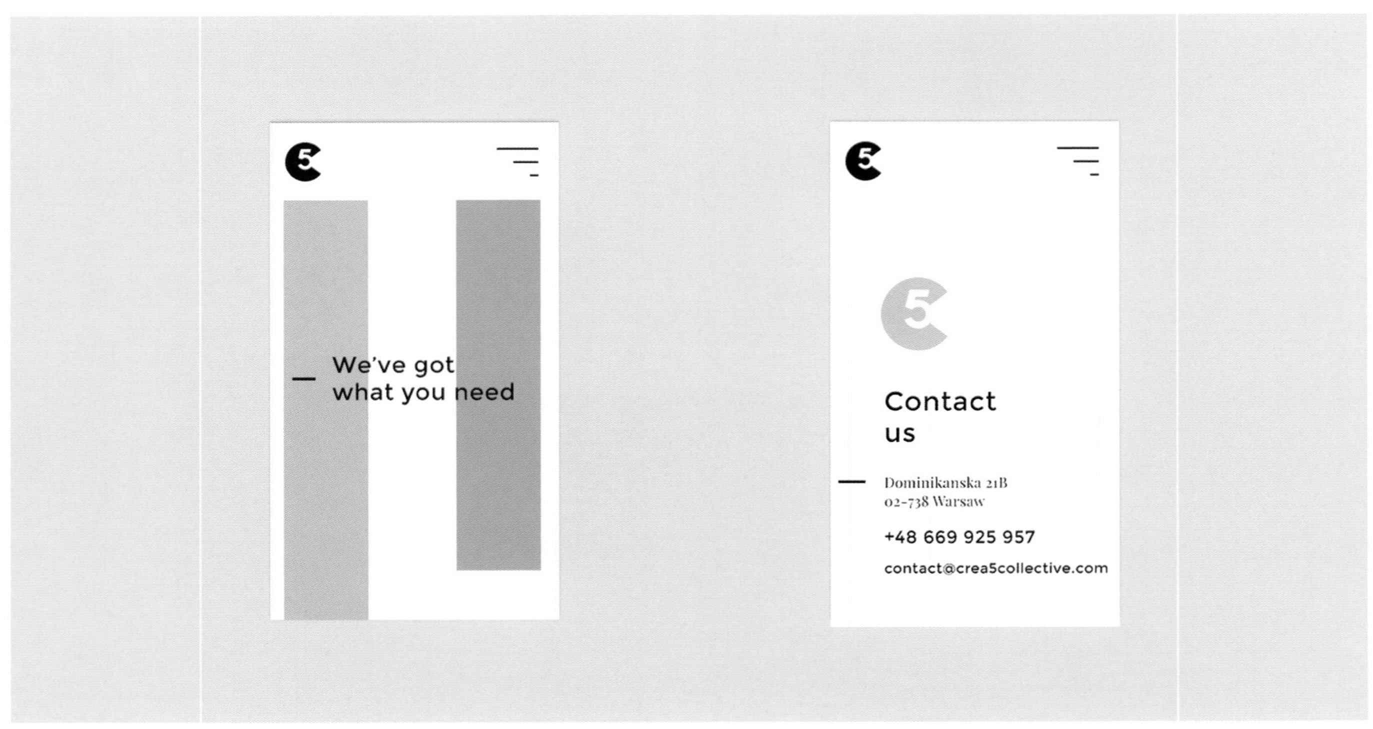

We've got what you need

Welcome to the world where flash and java applets are just pieces of history. Where people need reliable and safe technologies which can meet their expectations.

Mail us

Facebook

Twitter

scroll and discover

Our services

Advanced HTML5 creatives compatibile with leading adservers.

Advertising creatives

Creative templates

Custom solutions

Speed and performance

Advanced HTML5 creatives compatibile with leading adservers.

Mail us

Facebook

Twitter

scroll and see portfolio

Ready to start your next project with us? That's great! Give us a call or send us an email and we will get back to you as soon as possible!

Contact us

Dominikanska 21B
02-738 Warsaw

+48 669 925 957

contact@crea5collective.com

Mail us

Facebook

Twitter

back to top

Namale Creations

Design Agency/
Phoenix the Creative Studio

Design Direction/
Louis Paquet

Design/
Louis Paquet, Phoenix Team

Account Management/
Fouad Mallouk

Photography/
Jo Gorsky

URL/
http://creationsnamale.com

Namale Creations is a jewelry brand founded by a Syrian jewelry designer Feda Frangie, who was born in a jeweler's family and obsessed with the creation of jewelry. Namale is a Fijian word meaning "Unique Jewel," which perfectly represents her products that are all handmade and crafted with the finest materials available. The site is focused on showcasing the elegance and charm of her products. Phoenix used fluorescent colors ranging from Rainee to Granny Apple, and Romance to make the site looking gentle and soft.

#CEDED0 #F8F4E7 #9D9888 #FFFFFF

J
O
Y
A
U
X

N

U
N
I
Q
U
E
S

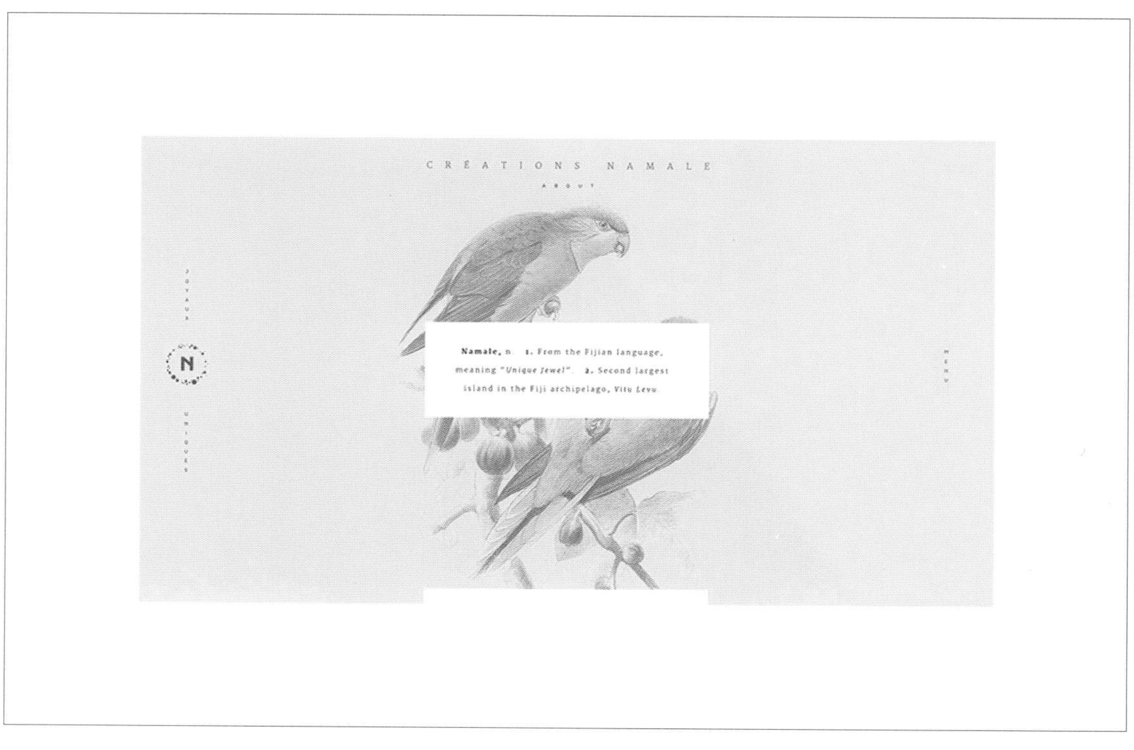

Gabriela Rubio

Design Agency/
Clase Bcn

Design Direction/
Daniel Ayuso

Design/
Héctor Sos

Client/
Gabriela Rubio

URL/
http://gabrielarubio.com

#F3DDCC #D8E8DB

The website was designed as an online portfolio for Gabriela Rubio, who is a writer and illustrator for literature about children and teenager.

The writer had specific demands: differentiating, clear, capable of showing her role between an author and illustrator. Considering that there are books written or illustrated by her, Héctor Sos created a site of minimalistic style and full of cozy illustrations. The color palate was consisted of pale greyish shade of green and baby pink, expressing a sense of innocence and quality that visitors can expect from Gabriela Rubio.

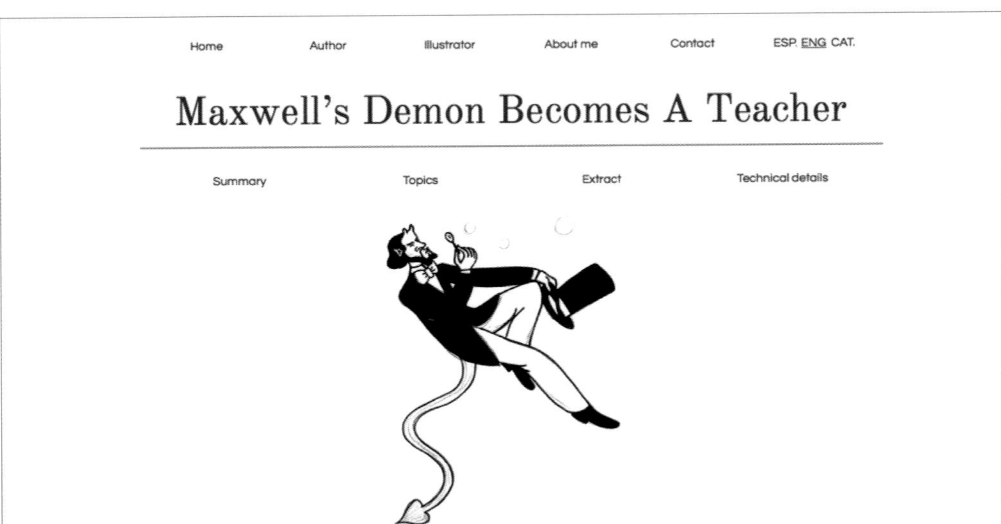

Physics. Education and good manners. Language learning. Tolerance of diversity.

27,487 words

Humour. School gangs. Fantasy tale.

Shortly after school started, our teacher had to leave due to an accident. When his substitute appeared at the classroom door, we all got a fright. Were those horns on his forehead? An elastic, flexible tail hidden under that

I tried not to be intimidated and whispered into one of my classmate's ear:

"What the teacher has written on the blackboard, is it part of our course?"

Home | Author | Illustrator | About me | Contact | ESP ENG CAT

Gabriela Rubio, illustrator

All | Press | Books for children | Text books | AWARDS

Here you can browse Gabriela's portfolios. You will find all sorts of drawings: drawings of dogs and cats, award-winning drawings, curious drawings, and much more.

Gabriela Rubio, illustrator

All | Press | Books for children | Text books | AWARDS

Here you can browse Gabriela's portfolios. You will find all sorts of drawings: drawings of dogs and cats, award-winning drawings, curious drawings, and much more.

Have you read any books by Gabriela Rubio? Tell us what you think of her books and become a literary critic. We will publish your opinion in the book's

Sushi Time

Design/
Marija Erjavec

Sushi Time is a personal project, which Marija further developed into a concept for a sushi delivery app in publishing design for Touch-screen Devices workshop at Aalto University, led by Harri Heikkilä. The Sushi Time app enables the user to order sushi directly to his or her location in a very straightforward and quick manner. It informs the user of how long will the delivery take and the cost. It also showcases all the different sushi on the menu in a playful manner.

#C9E0CE #F3E7F0 #E0A6A1 #F1D399 #CFE5ED #F6F5BC

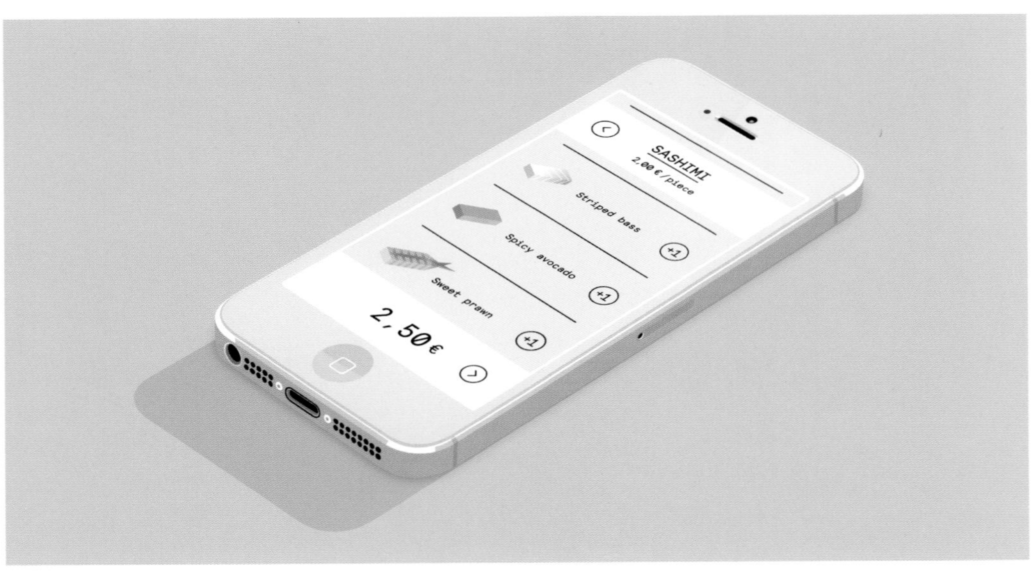

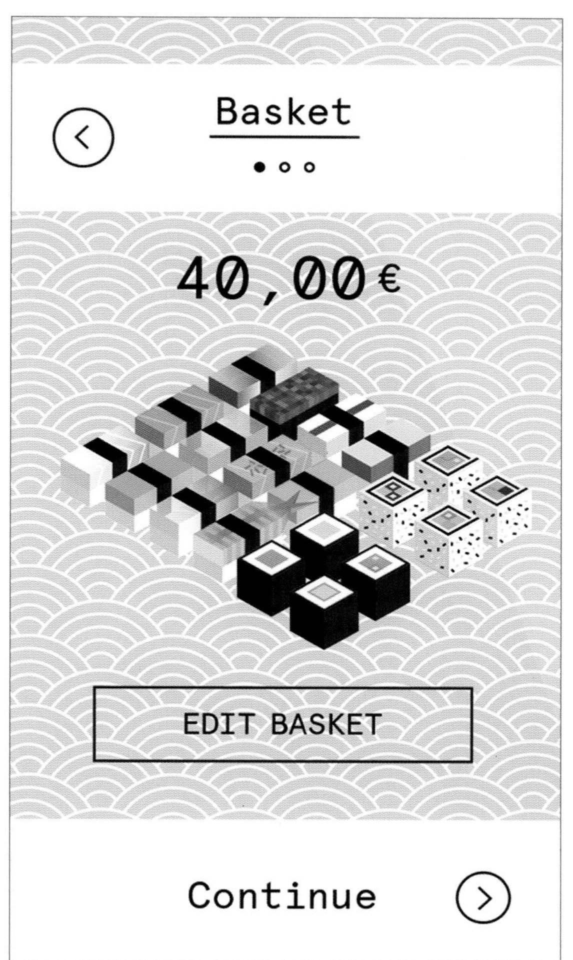
Basket
40,00€
EDIT BASKET
Continue

NIGIRI
2,50 € / piece
Salmon
+1
Grilled salmon
+1
Striped bass
+1
2,50€

Bergen International Festival

Design Agency/
Anti

URL/
http://www.fib.no

Bergen International Festival (Festspillene i Bergen) presents art in all its explorations from music to theatre, dance, opera, and visual art. Established in 1953, the festival is one of the oldest and the largest of its kind in the Nordic countries, with more than 220 events during the 15 days it lasts. Defining a strict mathematical framework for the logo allowed Anti to use the perfect square as a starting point for a rhythmic pattern. The pattern—created by applying the rule of four to the logo—provides visitors with the beat.

#CEDCDF #EAC4B8 #BEC9AD #FAEFCA

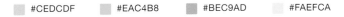

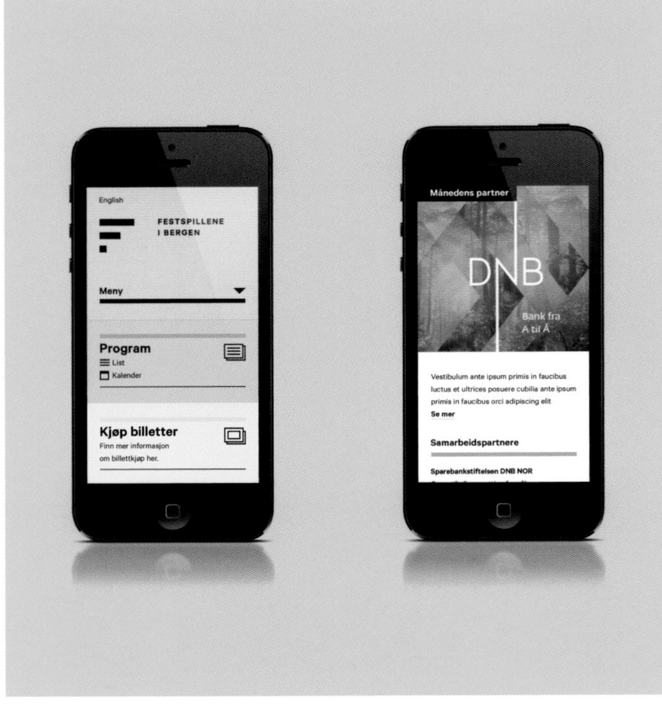

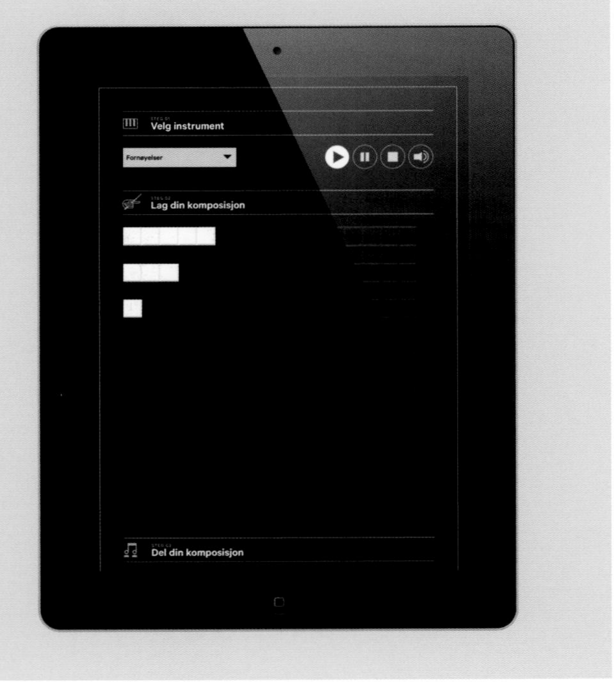

FESTSPILLENE
I BERGEN

Søk

Presse
Kontakt
English

Festspill 2013 | Om oss | Praktisk informasjon | Partnere

Program
List
Kalender

Kjøp billetter
Finn mer informasjon
om billettkjøp her

Praktisk informasjon

Samarbeidspartnere

Sparebankstiftelsen DNB NOR
Gaver til allmennyttige formål

Utvalgte forestillinger

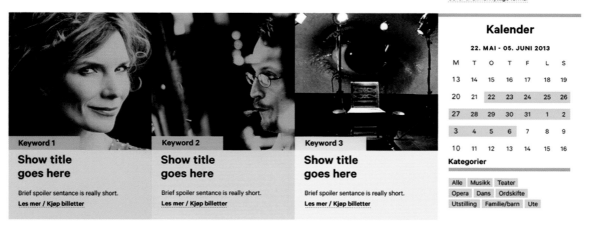

Keyword 1
Show title goes here
Brief spoiler sentance is really short.
Les mer / Kjøp billetter

Keyword 2
Show title goes here
Brief spoiler sentance is really short.
Les mer / Kjøp billetter

Keyword 3
Show title goes here
Brief spoiler sentance is really short.
Les mer / Kjøp billetter

Kalender

22. MAI - 05. JUNI 2013

M	T	O	T	F	L	S
13	14	15	16	17	18	19
20	21	22	23	24	25	26
27	28	29	30	31	1	2
3	4	5	6	7	8	9
10	11	12	13	14	15	16

Kategorier

Alle Musikk Teater
Opera Dans Ordskifte
Utstilling Familie/barn Ute

Informasjon

Månedens partner

DNB
Bank fra
A til Å

Tilbud

Billetter
www.billettservice.no

Grieghallen Tlf: +47 55 21 61 50
DNS Tlf: +47 55 60 70 80

Gruppereiser
Er dere flere som vil dra til Festspillene sammen? Grupper får selvsagt rabatt!
Les mer her

Vestibulum ante ipsum primis in faucibus luctus et ultrices posuere cubilia ante ipsum primis in faucibus orci adipiscing elit
Se mer

Nyheter

05.11 Marco Polo i multimedial drakt
15.10 Andreas Scholl til Festspillene
11.10 Vil du forske på Festspillene?
Se mer

04.09 Scenekunst.no: Kina i Bergen
04.09 BA: Slik blir festspillåpningen
06.06 Griegs Trolle denken da schon weiter
Se Mer

Matthew Galloway

Design Agency/
Sons & Co.

Creative Direction/
Timothy Kelleher

Design/
Matthew Arnold, Matthew Galloway, Paul Bright

Client/
Matthew Galloway

Website/
http://matthew-galloway.co.nz

Matthew Galloway is a writer and designer. Through collaborations, projects and publications, he has developed a practice that has a relatively broad take on traditional design outcomes.

The site is built as a portfolio site for a creative. The visual language of design always informs his approach and directly contributed to his style. The page website effectively utilizes his projects as a way to set a sense of his taste and show off his abilities with the presentation of his works. Sons & Co. used a bespoke web font and grey color palate to turn the viewpoint on the works and stress on his designs. The layout is as elegant as a magazine to engage visitors into an immersive exploration of the artistic atmosphere.

#EBEBE8 #C17CAD #FFFFFF #444A45 #EEDDDD #4C77BA

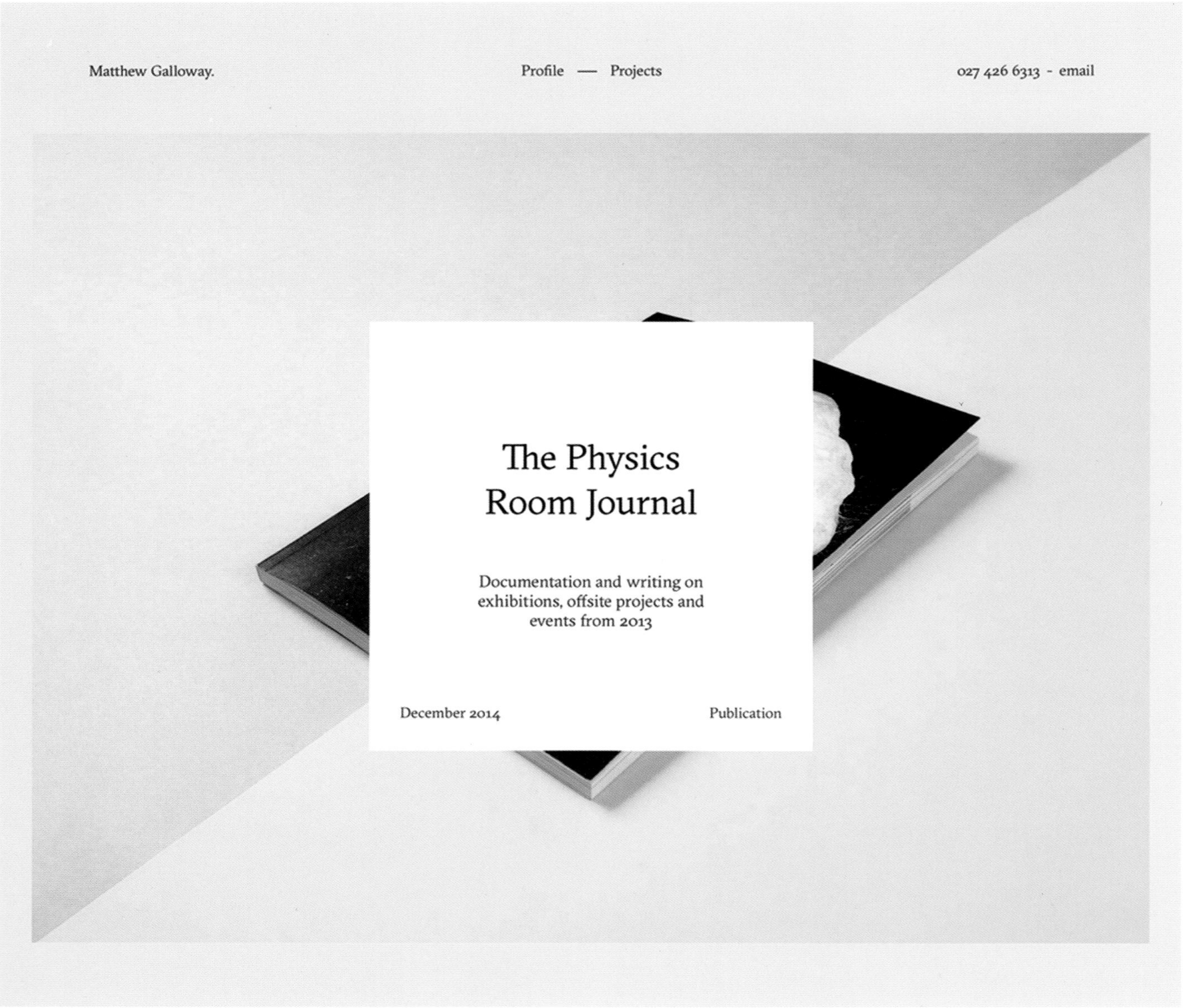

Matthew Galloway. Profile — Projects 027 426 6313 - email

The Physics Room Journal

Documentation and writing on exhibitions, offsite projects and events from 2013

December 2014 Publication

Art Over Nature Over Art

This article originally appeared in The Silver Bulletin #7.

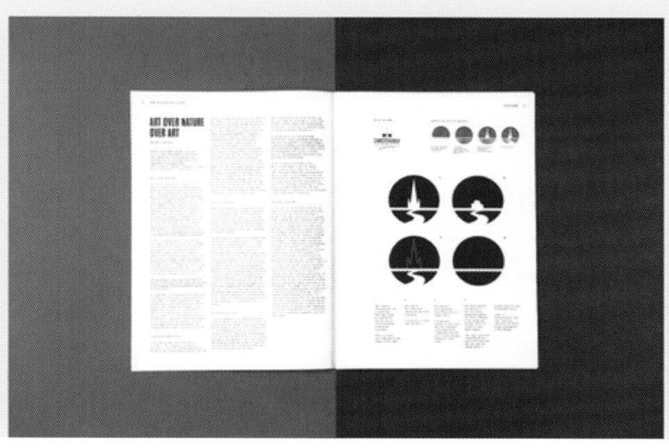

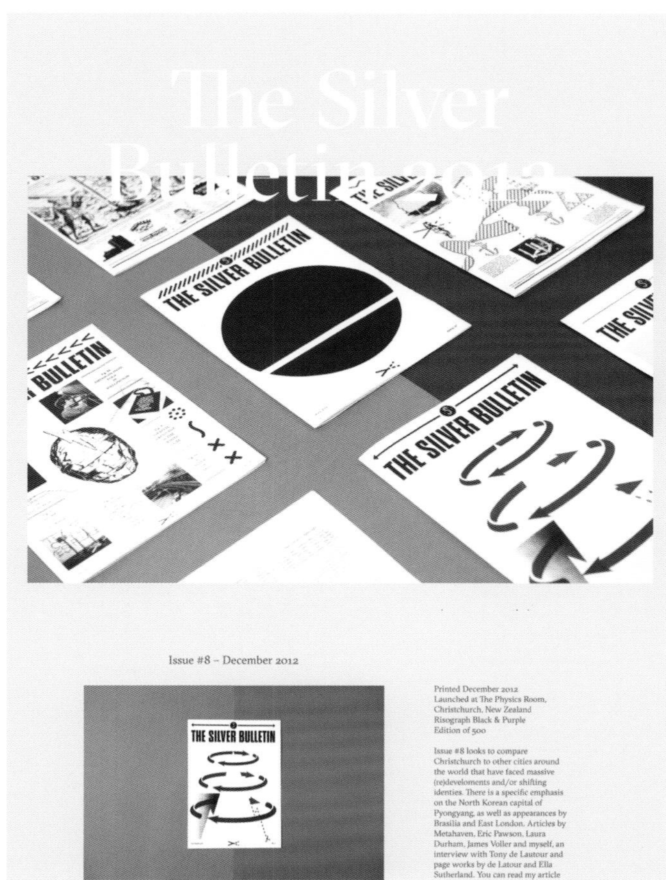

The Silver Bulletin 2012
THE SILVER BULLETIN
Issue #8 – December 2012
Printed December 2012
Launched at The Physics Room, Christchurch, New Zealand
Risograph Black & Purple
Edition of 500
Issue #8 looks to compare Christchurch to other cities around the world that have faced massive (re)develoments and/or shifting identies. There is a specific emphasis on the North Korean capital of Pyongyang, as well as appearances by Brasilia and East London. Articles by Metahaven, Eric Pawson, Laura Durham, James Voller and myself, an interview with Tony de Lautour and page works by de Latour and Ella Sutherland. You can read my article from the issue, Out of the Shadows

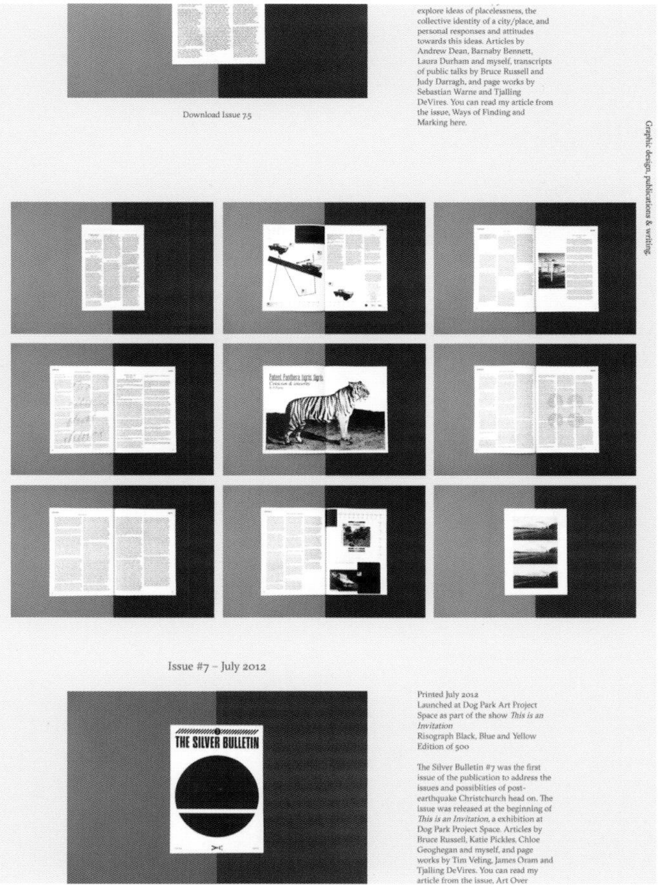

Download Issue 7.5
explore ideas of placelessness, the collective identity of a city/place, and personal responses and attitudes towards this ideas. Articles by Andrew Dean, Barnaby Bennett, Laura Durham and myself, transcripts of public talks by Bruce Russell and Judy Darragh, and page works by Sebastian Warne and Tjalling DeVires. You can read my article from the issue, Ways of Finding and Marking here.
Graphic design, publications & writing.
Issue #7 – July 2012
THE SILVER BULLETIN
Printed July 2012
Launched at Dog Park Art Project Space as part of the show This is an Invitation
Risograph Black, Blue and Yellow
Edition of 500
The Silver Bulletin #7 was the first issue of the publication to address the issues and possiblities of post-earthquake Christchurch head on. The issue was released at the beginning of This is an Invitation, a exhibition at Dog Park Project Space. Articles by Bruce Russell, Katie Pickles, Chloe Geoghegan and myself, and page works by Tim Veling, James Oram and Tjalling DeVires. You can read my article from the issue, Art Over

Programme

Design Agency/
VOLNA Studio

Design/
Ira Banana

Programme is a creative website portfolio template for designers, photographers, and agencies and studios. Photos are credited to vsco.co and unsplash.com.

Ira Banana infused a gradient color scheme, vibrant images, and minimalistic concept into an artistic, creative, and mystic world.

#FFEEF2 #FFFFFF #383838 #191919

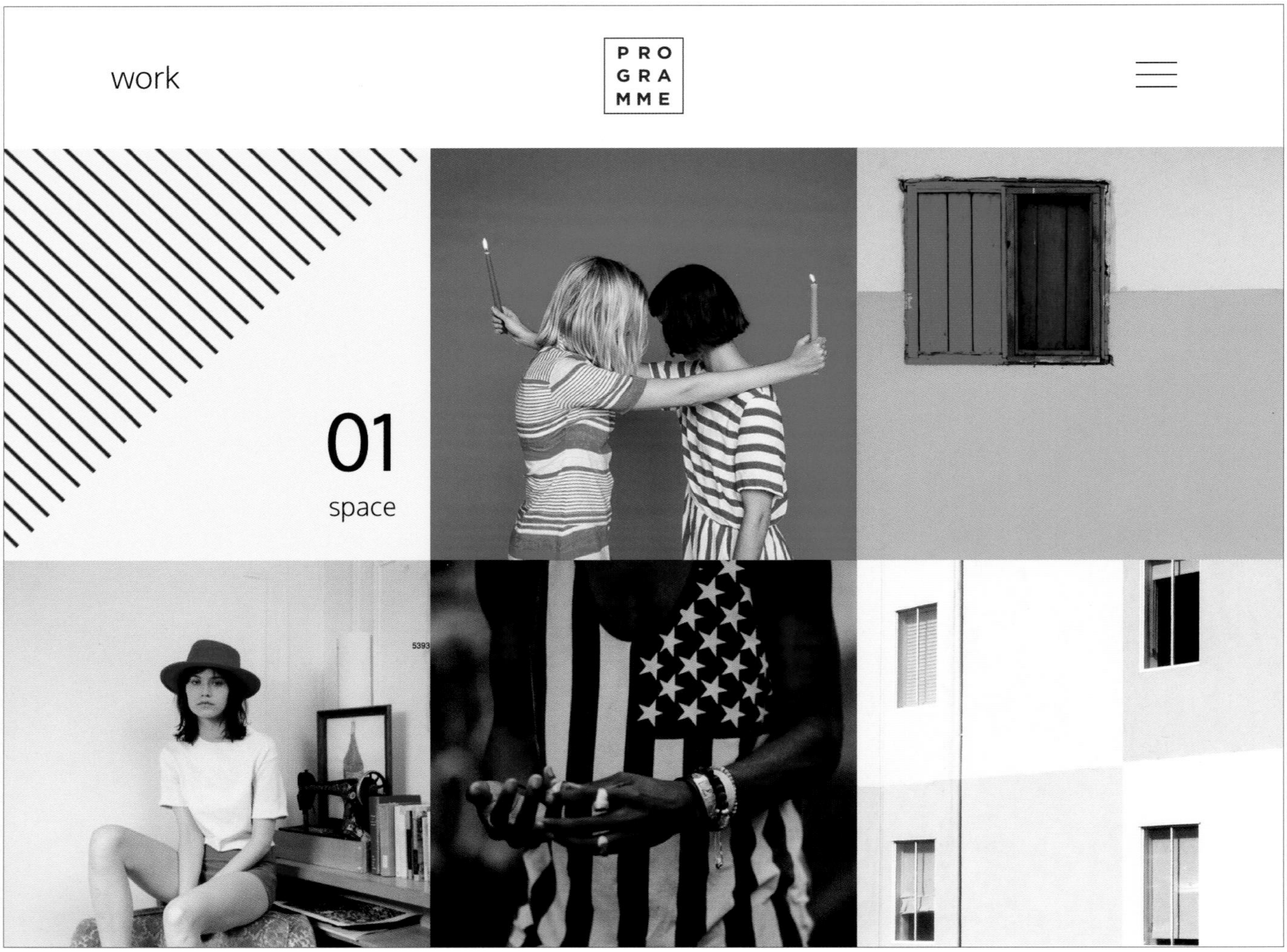

04
contrast

Lorem Impus dolor sit amet

Lorem ipsum dolor sit amet, consectetur adipiscing elit. Vivamus aliquam lorem eu enim varius volutpat. Maecenas ornare lacus mauris.

about
PRO
GRA
MME
Hi there!
Cras accumsan turpis tellus, nec luctus tellus tincidunt id. Class aptent taciti sociosqu ad litora torquent per conubia nostra, per inceptos himenaeos. Praesent lectus sapien, auctor nec metus at, laoreet consequat diam. Duis non rutrum nisl, id elementum nisl. Suspendisse dapibus ac nulla quis ornare.
P R O
G R A
M M E
© 2016 PROGRAMME. ALL RIGHTS RESERVED.

Today is Bored

Design/
Florent Gomez

Today is Bored is a web magazine born in 2014 based in Bordeaux for people who like design, images, street culture, lifestyle, photography, and beautiful things. More than that Today is Bored is a tribute to the visual culture of our time. Now the magazine is back with a completely new design and more experimental.

#C50018 #D2D4D2 #000000

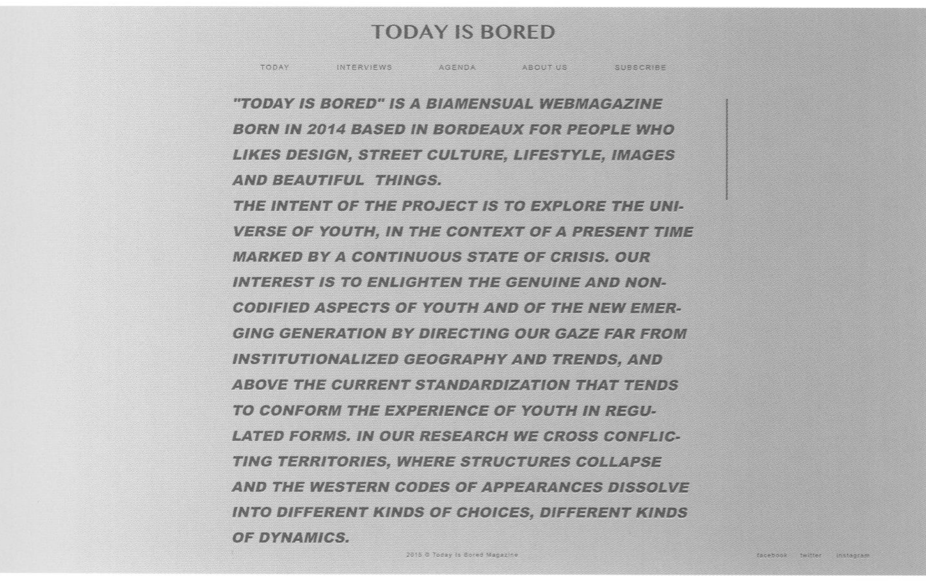

TODAY IS BORED

TODAY INTERVIEWS AGENDA ABOUT US SUBSCRIBE

Interviews

***EMILY SIMONET* - Issue #4**

Five years people will give go a week with the best graphic design, photographer, Illustrator, painters and more...

22 april 2015
Posted by TodayIsBored

1 288 743 views
203 151 likes

share

Older Interviews

NIKE x LAB - Issue #4

HORT Berlin - Issue #3

SIMPLY + STEEZY - Issue #3

The Shelby - Issue #3

Jack Lynch / Rhythm - Issue #2

KENZO - #2

facebook twitter instagram

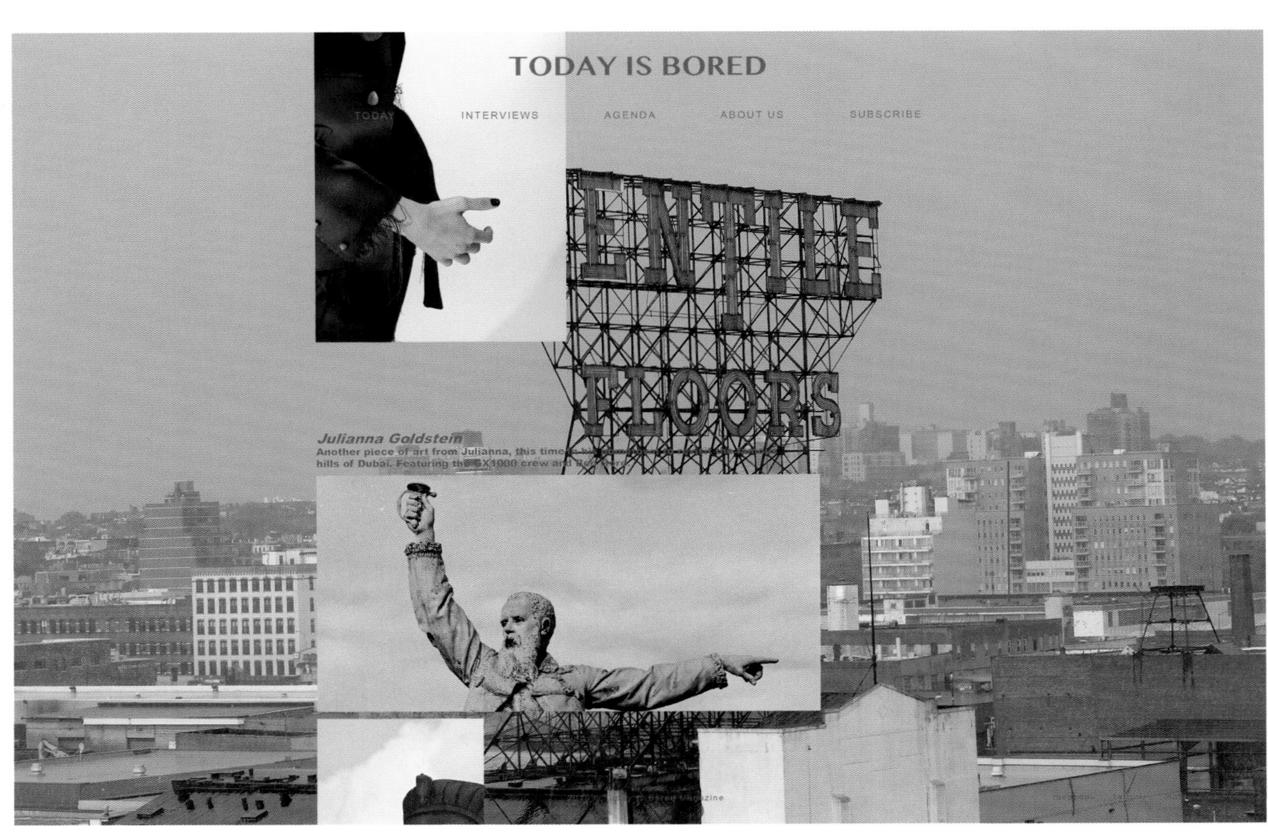

& PROJECT

Direction/
Firman Suci Ananda

Design/
Firman Suci Ananda

Photography/
Stock Image

Client/
& Project

& project is a concept for a visual design studio which is focused on commercial ads, movies, digital campaign, and advertorial design.

The idea was to deliver a modern, minimalistic, and energetic image, which was highly-valued within the studio, to its target audience. Firman Suci Ananda selected two colors: yellow contributes to refreshing impression, while grey is linked with timeless and classic.

#EFD41B #FFFFFF #C2C1BF #000000

ROLE.

Redesigning a new style of Indonesia Adidas Homepage. Exploration from the exisisting website to the next level. Played with the colors, images, elements and typography.

www.adidas.co.id

01.

02.

MOODBOARD.

After we finished our brainstorming process, we collected the great inspirations visual for the new redesign. You can see what kind of style we chose as a moodboard. Lorem ipsum dolor sit amet, consectetur adipisicing elit, sed do eiusmod tempor incididunt ut labore et dolore magna aliqua. Ut enim ad minim veniam, quis nostrud exercitation ullamco laboris nisi ut aliquip ex ea commodo consequat. Duis aute irure dolor in reprehenderit in voluptate velit esse cillum dolore eu fugiat nulla pariatur.

DESCRIPTION TITLE.

Here is the main interface, where teams spend most of their time creating the report. I worked on drag and drop interaction which seems the most evident and easy way to handle online.

STUDIO.

We're independent design studio creating online products for international clients. For our projects we collaborate with independent Talents to create outstanding content.

Our studio focused to create User Interface Design for web, Mobile Apps Design, Branding, Print Design and all digital products that cross all online channels.

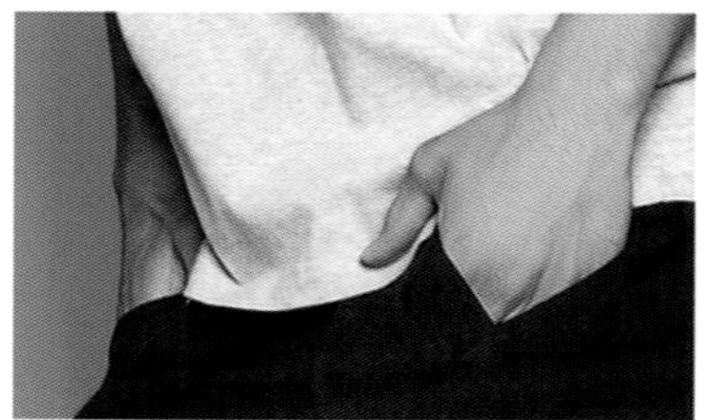

WHAT WE DO.

User Interface Design

Web & Mobile Design

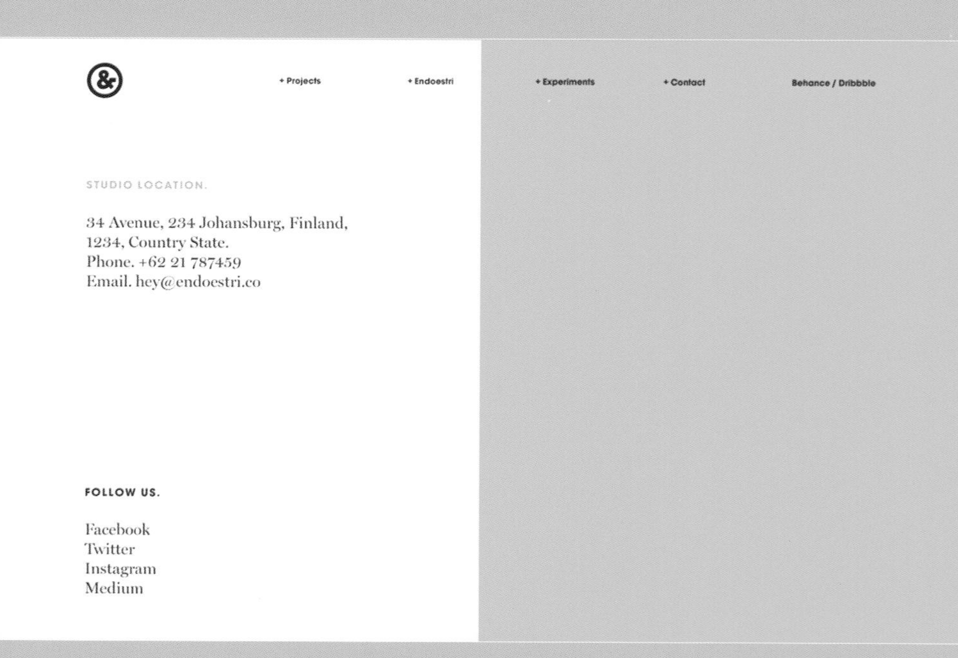

Date : **08/25/2015**

ROLE.

Redesigning a new style of Indonesia Adidas Homepage. Exploration from the exisisting website to the next level. Played with the colors, images, elements and typography.

www.adidas.co.id

MOODBOARD.

After we finished our brainstorming process, we collected the great inspirations visual for the new redesign. You can see what kind of style we chose as a moodboard. Lorem ipsum dolor sit amet, consectetur adipisicing elit, sed do eiusmod tempor incididunt ut labore et dolore magna aliqua. Ut enim ad minim veniam, quis nostrud exercitation ullamco laboris nisi ut aliquip ex ea commodo consequat. Duis aute irure dolor in reprehenderit in voluptate velit esse cillum dolore eu fugiat nulla pariatur.

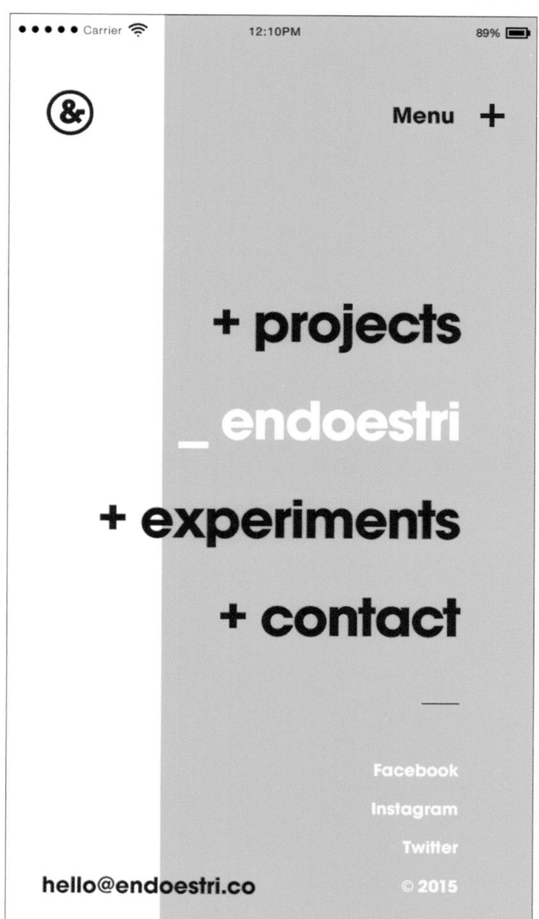

Artist portfolio website

Design/
Svetlana Tsybulevska

The idea of the project is to create a catchy portfolio site for designers. In search of a suitable structure, the website was inspired by the spiral camera shutter, which allows the animation on the site to move spirally.

The basic range of colors is a subtractive scheme of CMYK colors: cyan, magenta, and yellow. The page can be vertically scrolled to select various options, and be horizontally scrolled to look into the details in the pages for Works.

#E0A6A1 #F7EF58 #069FD5 #000000

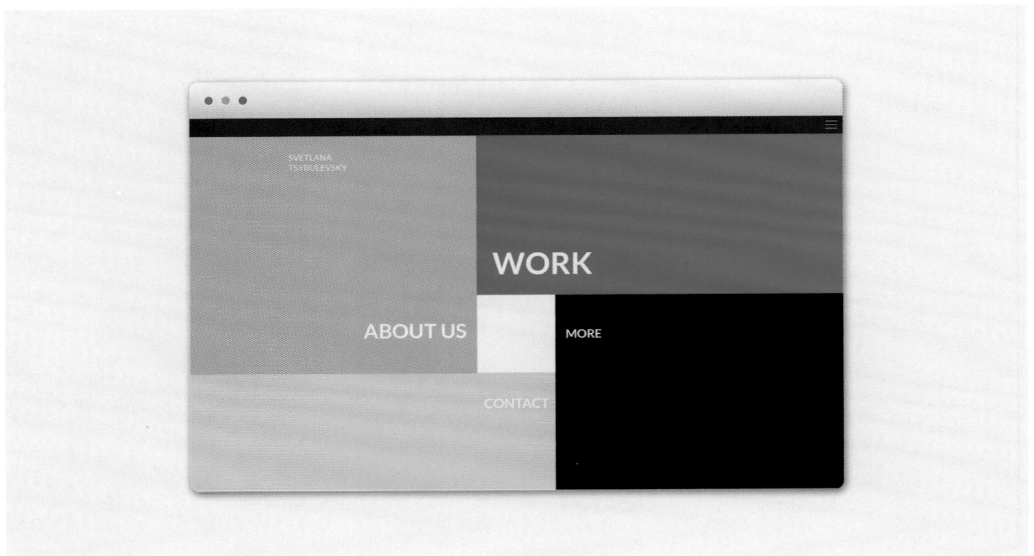

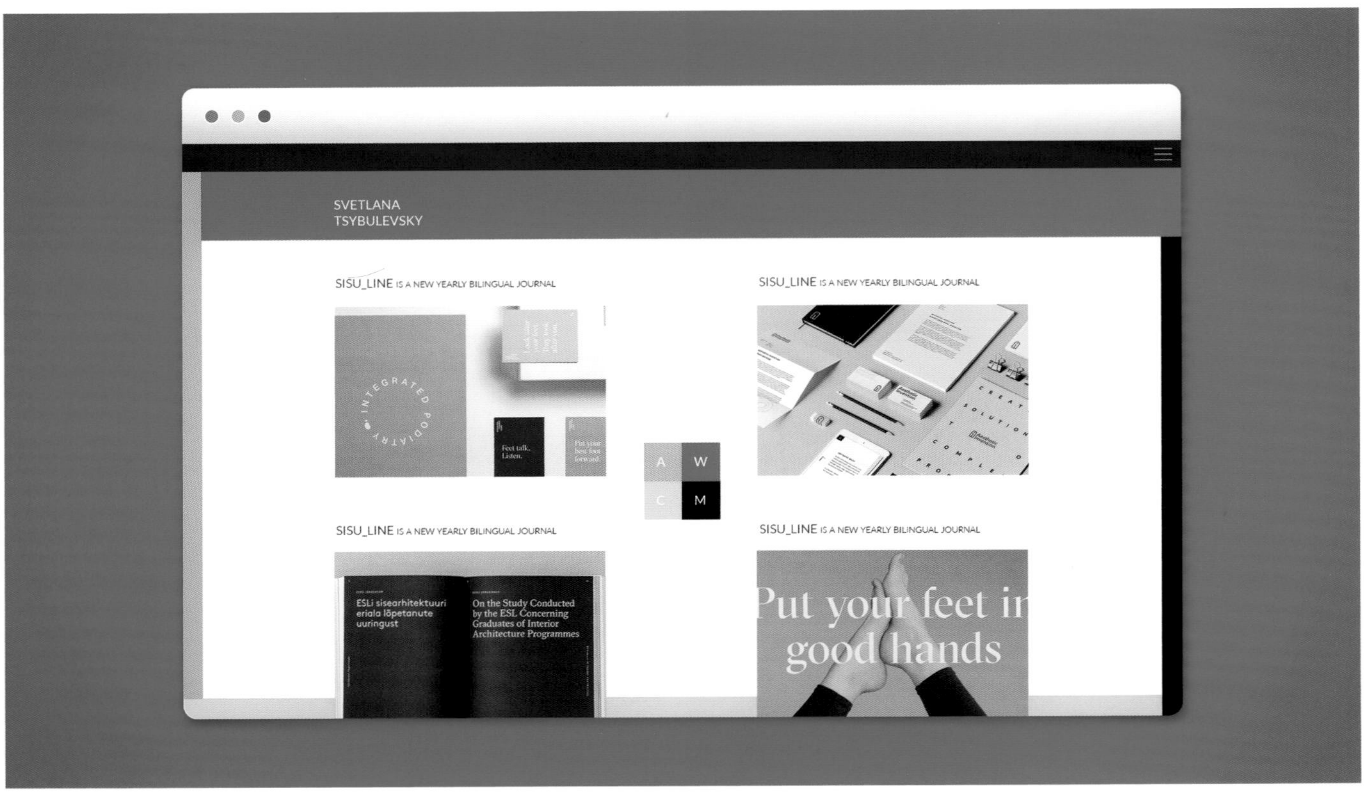

SVETLANA
TSYBULEVSKY

CLOSE

SISU_LINE

IS A NEW YEARLY BILINGUAL JOURNAL

Objekt3000

INTEGRATED PODIATRY

Feet talk. Listen.

NEXT

LINK

Garbett

Design Agency/
Sons & Co.

Creative Direction/
Timothy Kelleher

Design/
Matthew Arnold, Paul Bright, Garbett Design, Leanne Amodeo

Client/
Garbett

URL/
http://garbett.com.au

Website designed for Garbett design, one of the best design agencies in Australia.

The site offers a fairly good user experience. In the launching page, Sons & Co. plays a trick with visitors by revealing part of the images through the meshes. When the cover is removed, the projects, which are paired with large blocks of colors, are expected to engage people into a visual enjoyment. The colors chosen are matching and gentle, ensuring a comfortable user experience.

#314383 #EAE15A #EAC4B8 #6AB0A5

Follow
Contact
+612
9212-3474
Garbett
Design.
Studio.
Logos, books, posters, art & objects.
Stuart Watson
National speaker tour

SUZIE LÉO

Design/
Thibaud Sabathier

Photography/
Suzie Q, Léo Siboni

Web design for fashion photography duo based in Paris, Suzie Q and Léo Siboni. Centered on the narrative and rich colors of the photographers' works, Thibaud Sabathier kept consistency in the art direction to give it a lot of elegance and aesthetic. The homepage was designed as a long story with a flow of images, frames, and shapes. By using an interactive scroll and overlapping content, the designer referred to a magazine layout creating dynamic readability for the user experience.

#FFF002 #C40118 #000000 #394797

RECENT WORK NEWS SL ARCHIVES

Activation Nodeplus

Design/
Du Haihang

Photography/
Prussi Lin

Client/
Activation Nodeplus

URL/
http://www.activation-nodeplus.com

Activation Nodeplus is the digital subsidiary of integrated marketing agency Activation Group. It is an agency that brings brand communications to clients across Greater China and works with many premium brands. The overall design is under a modern, responsive, liquid grid layout, and subtle coding-graphic motion, presenting a striking impact that blasts through the screen of silence, as well as hyperactive yet silky smooth browsing experience to visitors.

#D4773A #C0C0BC #FFFFFF #000000

Agency
We are a forward thinking agency specialized in integrated digital solutions for brands.
Team
Meet our multi-disciplinary team and management talents. Check out opening job vacancies
Work
View our selected work and case studies under archive.
BMW BEC Beyond Geography Mobile Light App
BVLGARI Man In Black Mobile Campaign
BVLGARI Omnia Bloom with Mandala Campaign
Celebrating CNY 2015 WebGL Experience
ACNPL\WGL - Activation Nodeplus Lab featured with WebGL
Irregular Noise WebRTC / Web Audio Exp
X'Mas Greetings Light Web App

ACTIVATION NODEPLUS

Agency Team Work

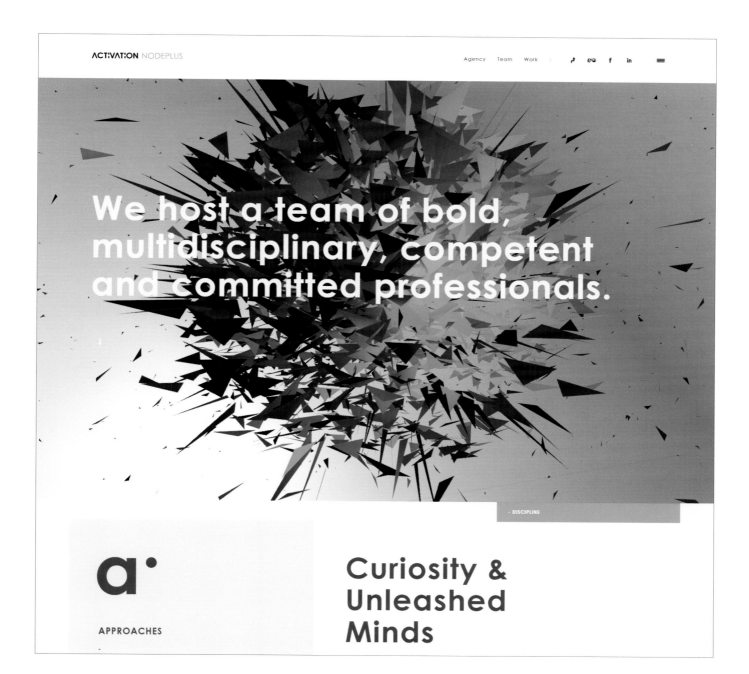

We host a team of bold, multidisciplinary, competent and committed professionals.

- DISCIPLINE

a·

APPROACHES

Curiosity & Unleashed Minds

L'Avenir, Dental Clinic

Design Agency/
Phoenix the Creative Studio

Design Direction/
Louis Paquet

Design/
Louis Paquet, Phoenix Team

Account Management/
Fouad Mallouk

URL/
https://avenirclinic.com

In order to help position L'Avenir as a leader in their field, it was imperative to review their brand as a whole and strengthen their web presence. Phoenix decided to go towards a dynamic and human image while inevitably considering the purity and perfection inherent to the dental world. The logo developed is simple yet conceal many subtle references to the dental world. The pictures used white and its purity as a metaphor for the perfection and cleanliness that every dentist tries to reach. They combine various everyday items to demonstrate what "Live brighter" might look like.

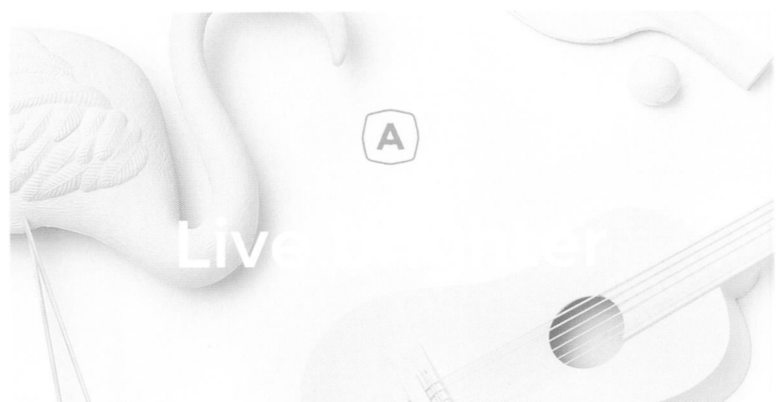

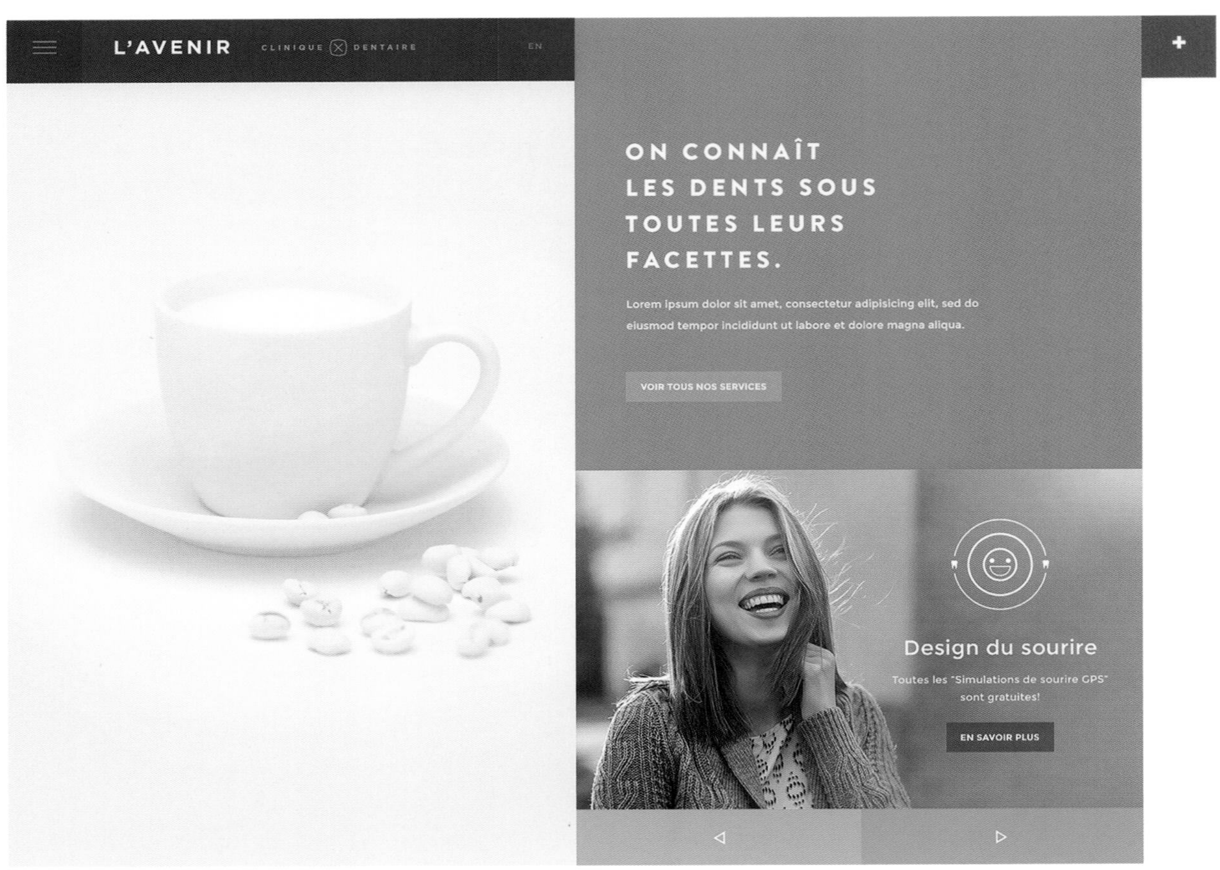

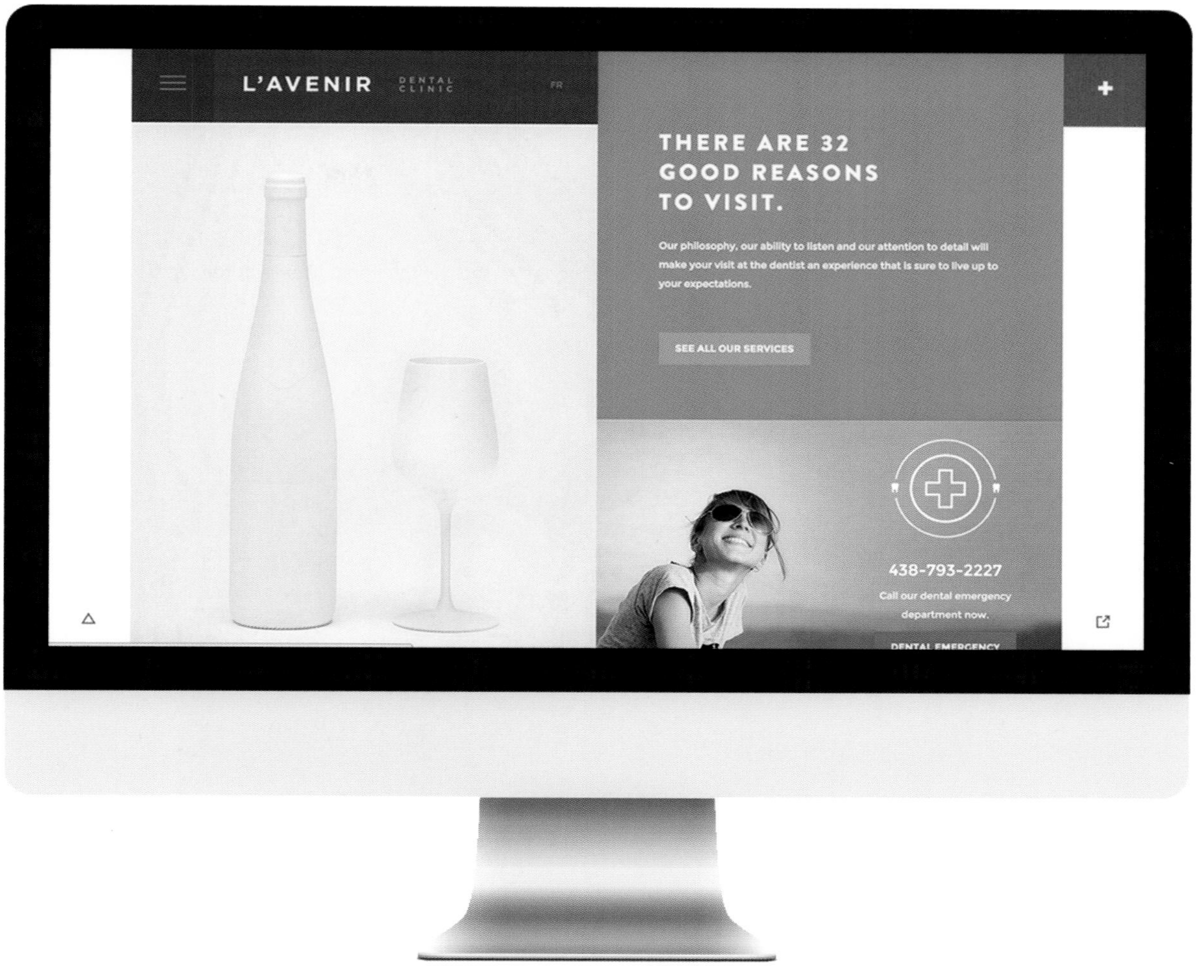

L'AVENIR
DENTAL CLINIC
FR
THERE ARE 32 GOOD REASONS TO VISIT.
Our philosophy, our ability to listen and our attention to detail will make your visit at the dentist an experience that is sure to live up to your expectations.
SEE ALL OUR SERVICES
438-793-2227
Call our dental emergency department now.
DENTAL EMERGENCY

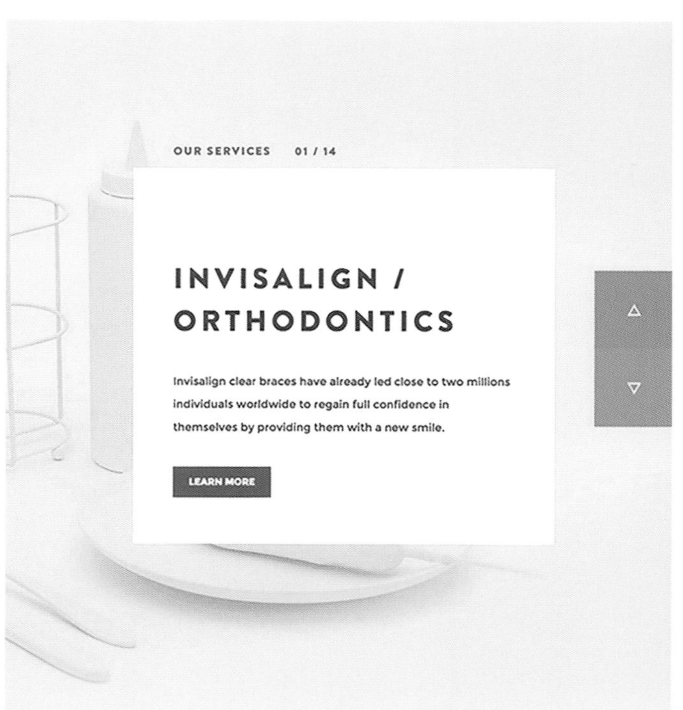
OUR SERVICES 01 / 14
INVISALIGN / ORTHODONTICS
Invisalign clear braces have already led close to two millions individuals worldwide to regain full confidence in themselves by providing them with a new smile.
LEARN MORE

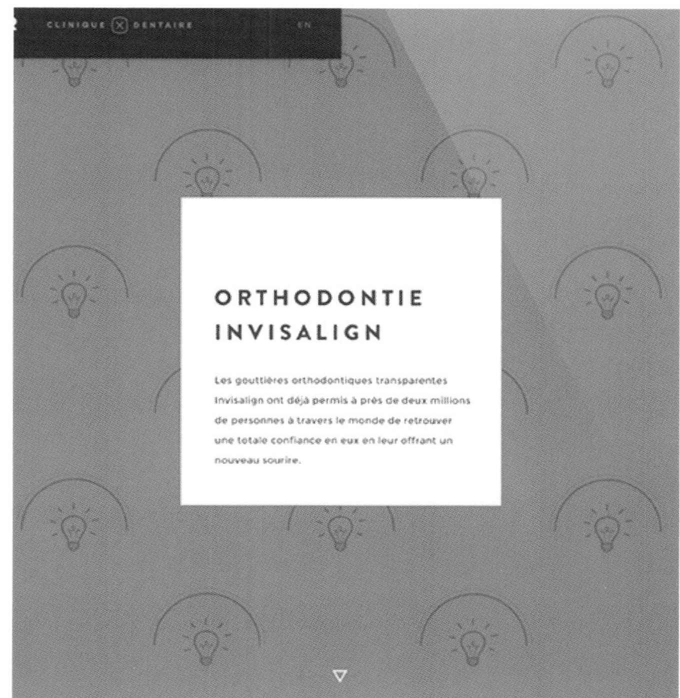
CLINIQUE DENTAIRE
EN
ORTHODONTIE INVISALIGN
Les gouttières orthodontiques transparentes Invisalign ont déjà permis à près de deux millions de personnes à travers le monde de retrouver une totale confiance en eux en leur offrant un nouveau sourire.

Fanny Agnier

Design Agency/
Studio Gambetta

Photography/
Baptiste Coulon

Client/
Fanny Agnier

URL/
http://www.fannyagnier.com

Webmaster/
Jorge Stamatio (jstamatio.com)

Web design for a jewelry brand called Fanny Agnier.

Great jewelry speak for themselves. The website confidently mixes the picture of jewelry and two equally divided colors to frame the sense of classical and timeless of the artwork with an exhibition-like clean, intuitive, and focused atmosphere. By scrolling horizontally, visitors can switch to different pages, and the details and information are hidden behind the pictures.

#D3766E #FFFFFF #706C62 #D2BC8E

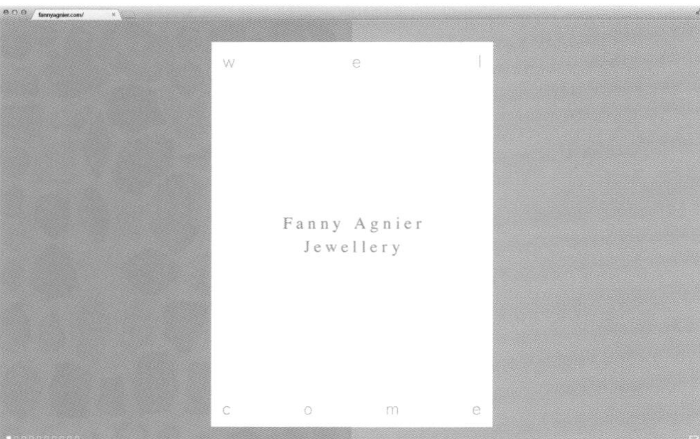

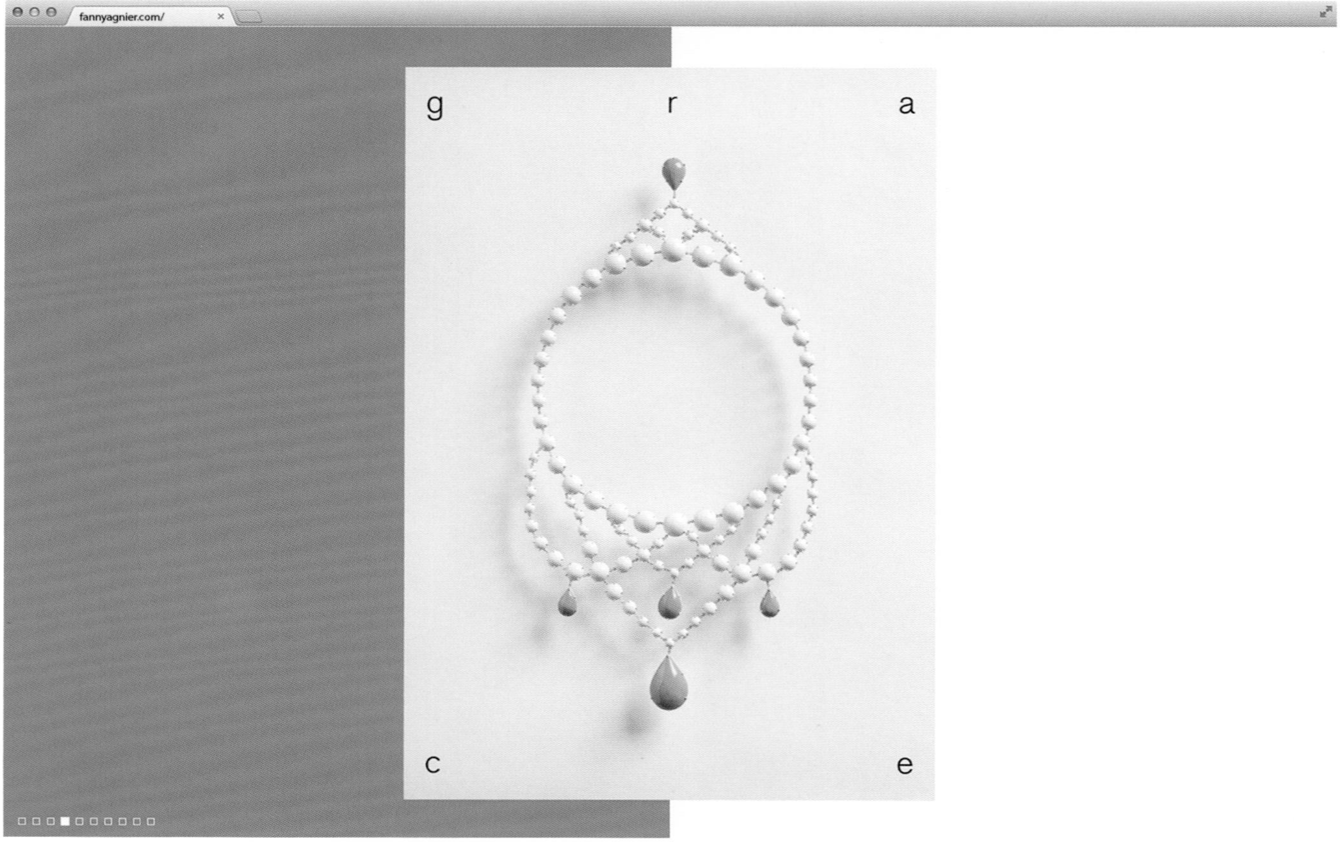

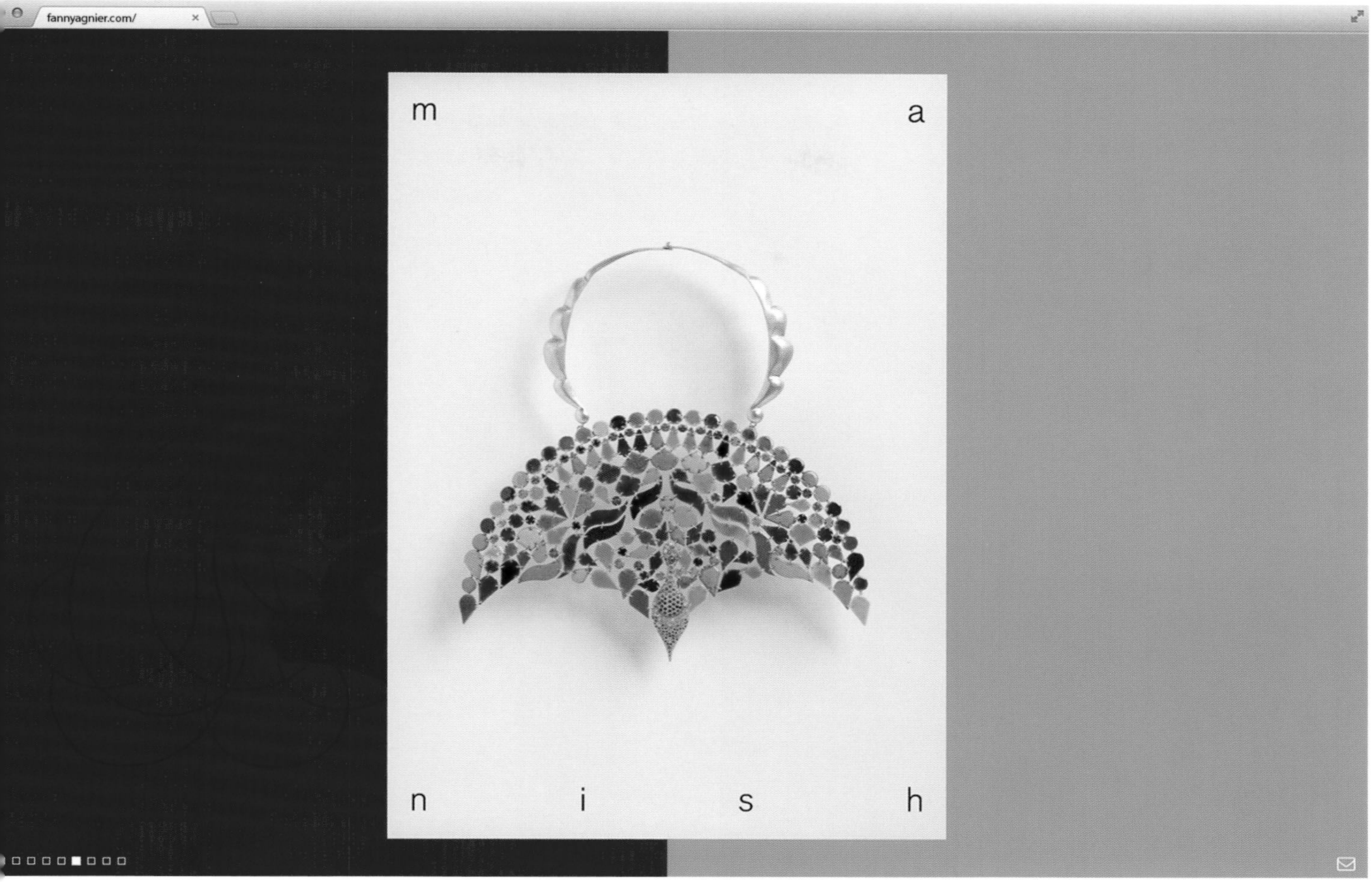

fannyagnier.com/

m a

n i s h

Enjoy Gallery

Design Agency/
Sons & Co.

Creative Direction/
Timothy Kelleher

Design/
Matthew Arnold, Greg Brown

Client/
Enjoy Public Gallery

URL/
http://enjoy.org.nz

Established in June 2000, Enjoy Gallery is a non-commercial artist-run initiative based in Wellington, New Zealand. Enjoy generates and facilitates contemporary art projects to promote the discourse of contemporary art practice in all its forms.

Ambitious to be liberated from commercial constraints, Enjoy provides both emerging and established practitioners with opportunities to develop innovative work. Likewise, the site is innovative in its form as if the pages overlap each other to achieve both a contemporary graphical expression and on-line artistic effect. Though the colors used are simple, they evoke a clear hierarchy of different contents, and cherish the communicative value and aesthetic impact.

#F5E9CE #4E6F92 #CE605F #89B668

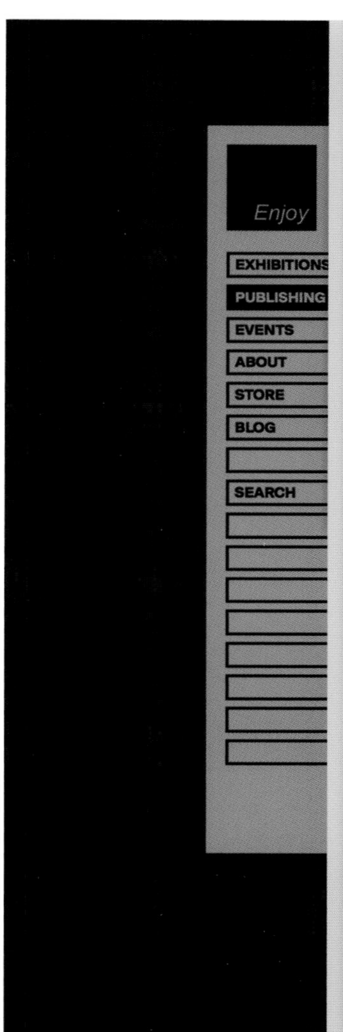
Enjoy
EXHIBITIONS
PUBLISHING
EVENTS
ABOUT
STORE
BLOG
SEARCH

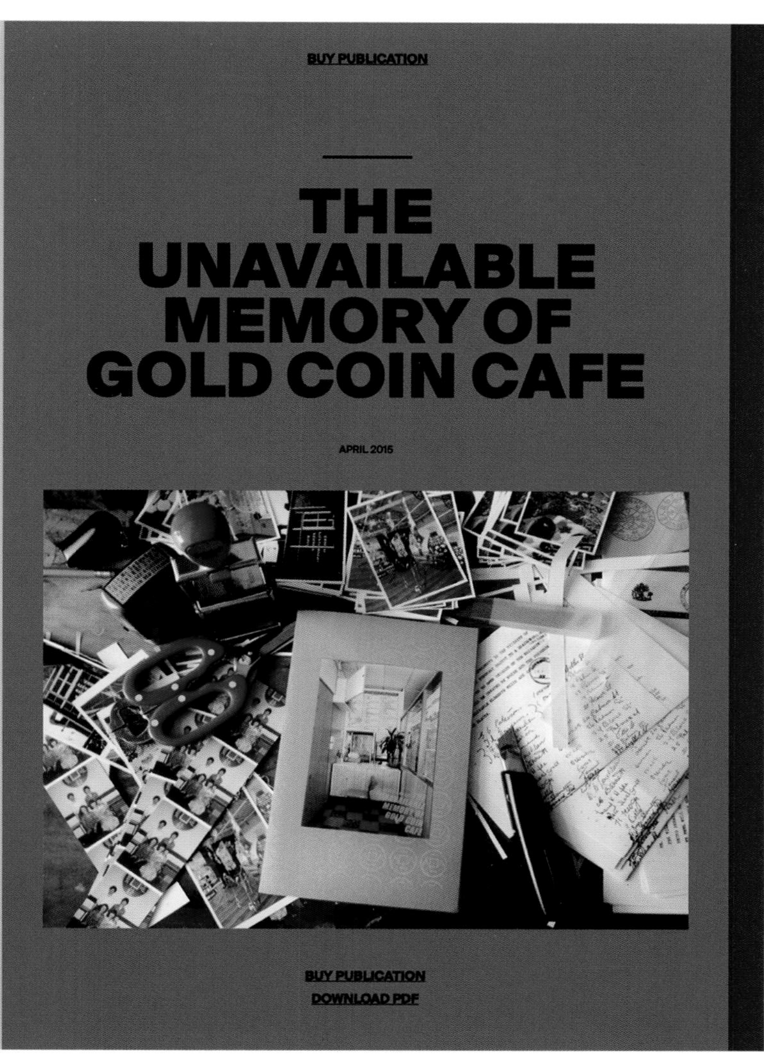
BUY PUBLICATION
THE UNAVAILABLE MEMORY OF GOLD COIN CAFE
APRIL 2015
BUY PUBLICATION
DOWNLOAD PDF

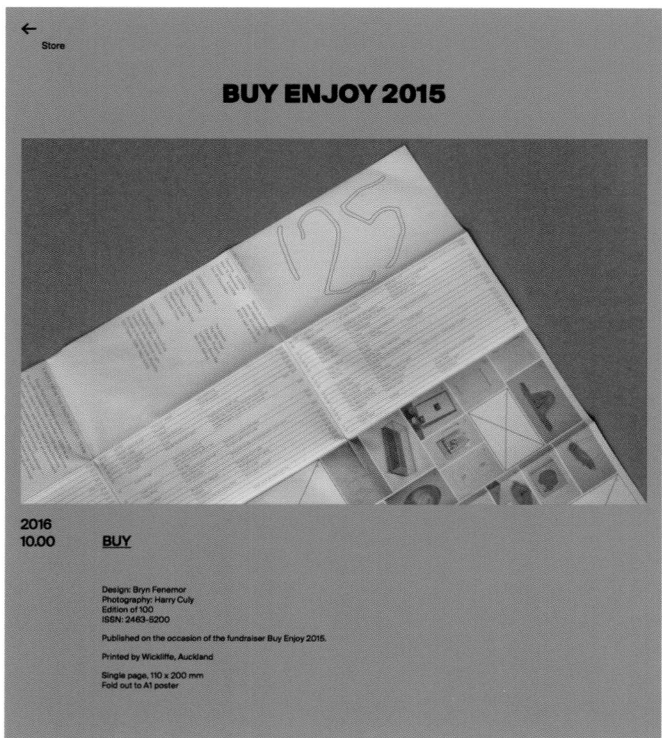
Store
BUY ENJOY 2015
2016
10.00
BUY
Design: Bryn Fenemor
Photography: Harry Culy
Edition of 100
ISSN: 2463-5200
Published on the occasion of the fundraiser Buy Enjoy 2015.
Printed by Wickliffe, Auckland
Single page, 110 x 200 mm
Fold out to A1 poster

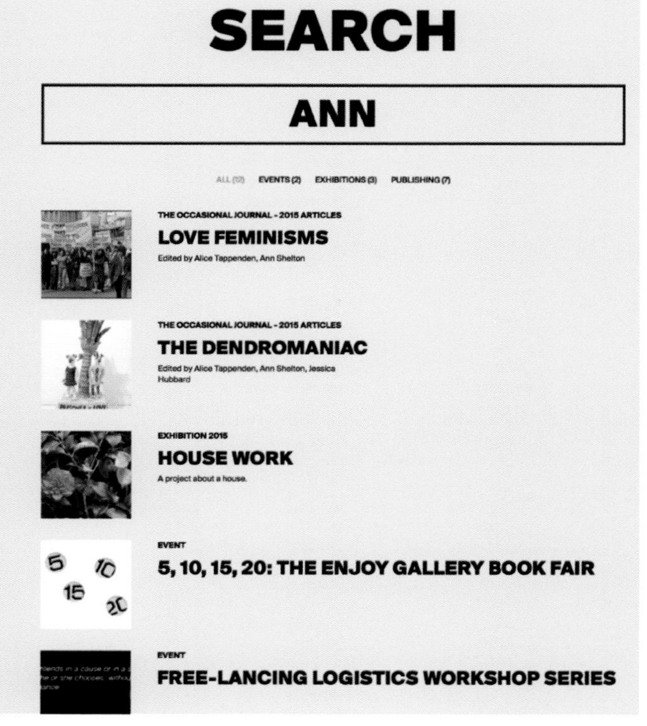
SEARCH
ANN
ALL (12)
EVENTS (2)
EXHIBITIONS (3)
PUBLISHING (7)
THE OCCASIONAL JOURNAL - 2015 ARTICLES
LOVE FEMINISMS
Edited by Alice Tappenden, Ann Shelton
THE OCCASIONAL JOURNAL - 2015 ARTICLES
THE DENDROMANIAC
Edited by Alice Tappenden, Ann Shelton, Jessica Hubbard
EXHIBITION 2015
HOUSE WORK
A project about a house.
EVENT
5, 10, 15, 20: THE ENJOY GALLERY BOOK FAIR
EVENT
FREE-LANCING LOGISTICS WORKSHOP SERIES

The Vera List Center for Art and Politics

Design Agency/
Project Projects LLC

URL/
http://www.veralistcenter.org

The Vera List Center's Art + Social Justice Working Group is an ongoing research project which examines artistic efforts to enact social change, alongside the conflicts which prompt and enrich those efforts. As a public-facing dimension of private discussions, The Working Group's website is a dynamic, continuously growing, open archive of the group's research, presenting glossary terms, case studies, and readings. Site visitors are invited to extend the group's research by adding their own thoughts and materials, extending the collaborative platform to a broader public.

#CF6A57 #81C0D9 #88BC7F #000000

ENGAGE
Events
Exhibitions
Publications
Archive

LEAD
Biennial Prize
Fellowships
Writing Awards
Art & Research Projects

LEARN
About
Focus Theme
Support
Contact & Staff

SEARCH

THE VER
FOR ART
THE NEW SC

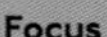

Focus

PUBLIC ART FUND TALKS AT THE NEW SCHOOL
Allora & Calzadilla
WED 13 NOV 2013 6.30PM-8.00PM

TWO-DAY FORUM, ARTIST LECTURE, AND GALLERY PRESENTATION
Theaster Gates: A Way of Working

Calendar

THE AICA-USA DISTINGUISHED CRITIC LECTURE AT THE NEW SCHOOL
Lucy Lippard
WED 30 OCT 2013 6.30PM-8.00PM

PERFORMANCE & DISCUSSION
Paulien Oltheten
WED 6 NOV 2013 6.30PM-8.00PM

PUBLIC ART FUND TALKS AT THE NEW SCHOOL
Allora & Calzadilla
WED 13 NOV 2013 6.30PM-8.00PM

Stay connected

NEWSLETTER SIGNUP

ENGAGE
Events
Exhibitions
Publications
Archive
LEAD
Biennial Prize
Fellowships
Writing Awards
Art & Research Projects
LEARN
About
Focus Theme
Support
Contact & Staff
SEARCH
THE VER
FOR ART
THE NEW SC

From "Sustaining Democracy" to the State of the Civic: 20 Years of the Vera List Center for Art and Politics

TWENTIETH ANNIVERSARY CONFERENCE
FRI 17 MAY 2013 10.00AM-5.30PM
The New School, Tishman Auditorium
66 West 12th Street
New York City
20 Years VLC => $0 Admission

On its twentieth anniversary, the Vera List Center assesses the unique role art plays at the intersection of politics and civic life. This daylong conference addresses the changing cultural and political landscape

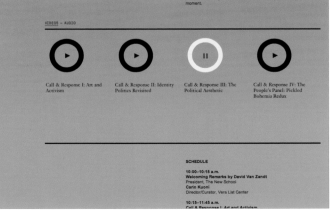

relation to their representation, their own histories, and the present moment.

VIDEOS – AUDIO

Call & Response I: Art and Activism
Call & Response II: Identity Politics Revisited
Call & Response III: The Political Aesthetic
Call & Response IV: The People's Panel: Pickled Bohemia Redux

SCHEDULE

10:00–10:15 a.m.
Welcoming Remarks by David Van Zandt
President, The New School
Carin Kuoni
Director/Curator, Vera List Center

10:15–11:45 a.m.
Call & Response I: Art and Activism

Margarita Gutman, Susan Hapgood, Sharon Hayes, Danny Hoch, Ashley Hunt, Bouchra Khalili, Lin + Lam, Kobena Mercer, Lorraine O'Grady, Olu Oguibe, Silvana Paternostro, Wendy Perron, Marjetica Potrc, Leslie Prosterman, Walid Raad, Sarah Rothenberg, Edward Rothstein, Katya Sander, Robert Sember, Joshua Simon, Elisabeth Sussman, David Thorne, and Jonathan Weinberg.

Current and past fellows

PEOPLE
Jill Magid
2013 - 2015

PEOPLE
Alexander Provan
2013 - 2015

PEOPLE
Bouchra Khalili
2011 - 2013

PEOPLE
Joshua Simon

PEOPLE
Robert Sember

PEOPLE
Lin + Lam

ENGAGE
Events
Exhibitions
Publications
Archive

LEAD
Biennial Prize
Fellowships
Writing Awards
Art & Research Projects

LEARN
About
Focus Theme
Support
Contact & Staff

SEARCH

THE VER
FOR ART
THE NEW SC

About

HISTORY
DONORS
ABOUT VERA G. LIST
ADVISORY COMMITTEE
20TH ANNIVERSARY INITIATIVES
WEBSITE

Founded in 1992 and named in honor of the late philanthropist, the Vera List Center for Art and Politics at The New School is dedicated to serving as a catalyst for the discourse on the role of the arts in society and their relationship to the sociopolitical climate in which they are created. It seeks to achieve this goal by organizing public programs that respond to the pressing social and political issues of our time as they are articulated by the academic community and by visual and performing artists. The center strives to further the university's educational mission by bringing together scholars and students, the people of New York, and national and international audiences in an exploration of new possibilities for civic engagement.

History

Twenty years ago, at the height of the culture wars, a time of rousing public debates about freedom of speech, the arts, and society's relationship to art, the Vera List Center for Art and Politics was founded at The New School with an endowment from university life trustee Vera G. List.

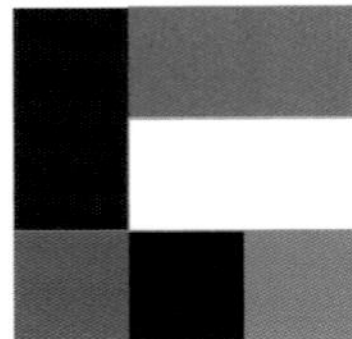

Tietgen

Design/
Morten Lybech

Client/
TietgenSkolen

Located in Odense, Denmark, TietgenSkolen is a trade educational institution consisted of 5 different departments, providing service to over 4,035 students. TietgenSkolen commissioned Morten Lybech to design a new digital platform. The hardship was to convey information of 5 departments while showing integrity. Morten adopted a sophisticated and systematically-organized color palette and layout to represent different departments so that plenty of information can be showcased in an aesthetic way.

#C74637 #3A3837 #AA9960 #17344A #FFFFFF #5C8084

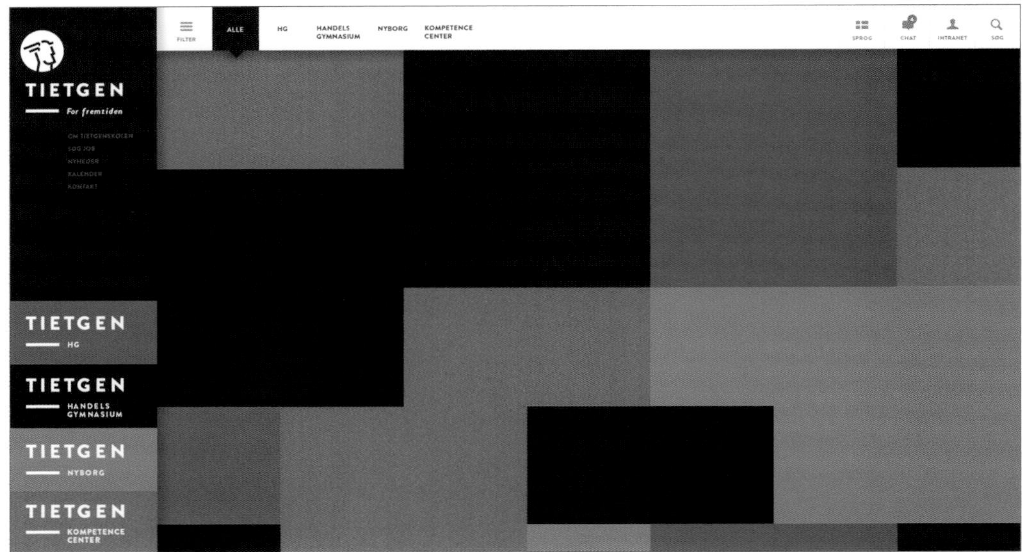

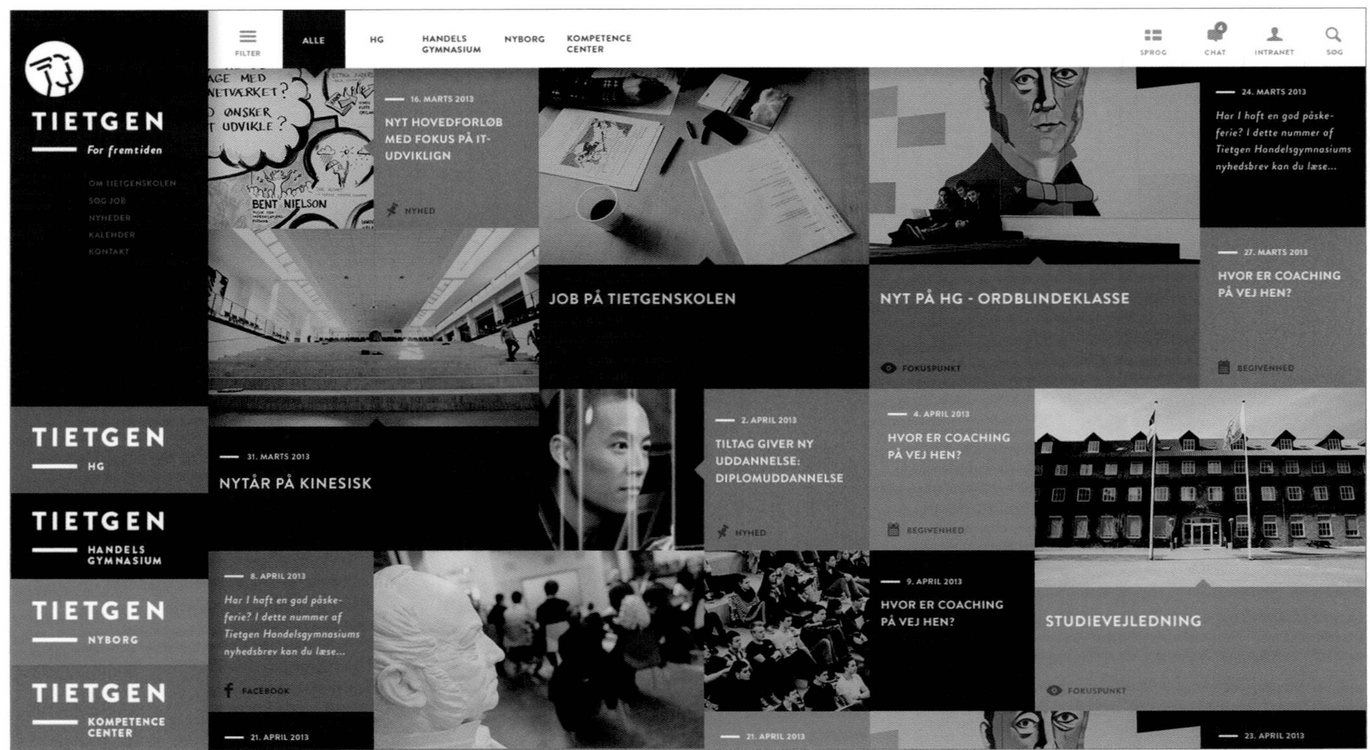

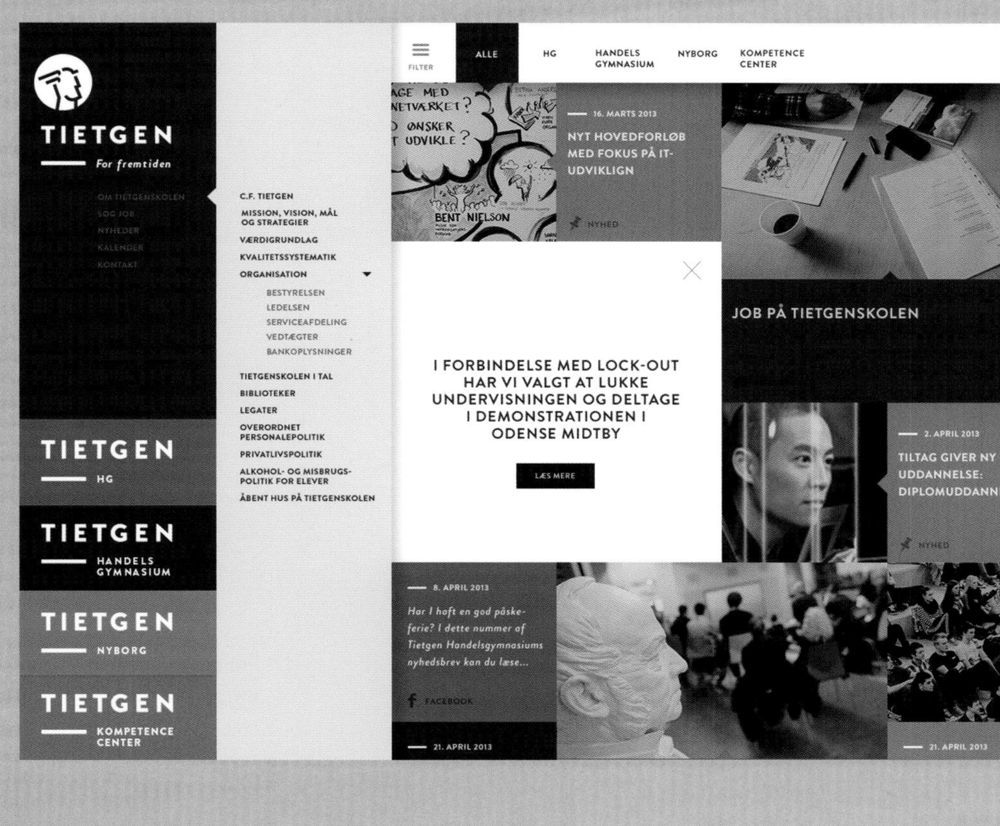

C.F. TIETGEN
MISSION, VISION, MÅL OG STRATEGIER
VÆRDIGRUNDLAG
KVALITETSSYSTEMATIK
ORGANISATION
BESTYRELSEN
LEDELSEN
SERVICEAFDELING
VEDTÆGTER
BANKOPLYSNINGER
TIETGENSKOLEN I TAL
BIBLIOTEKER
LEGATER
OVERORDNET PERSONALEPOLITIK
PRIVATLIVSPOLITIK
ALKOHOL- OG MISBRUGS-POLITIK FOR ELEVER
ÅBENT HUS PÅ TIETGENSKOLEN

TILBAGE

SPROG

CHAT

INTRANET
SØG

TIETGEN > OM TIETGEN > ORGANISATION > LEDELSEN

DEL LÆS OP PRINT

LEDELSEN

BRÆNDER DU FOR COOL BUSINESS?
Drømmer du om en karriere, hvor du er ansvarlig for økonomien i en stor virksomhed - også selvom en finanskrise kradser? Er du dygtig til at tjene penge? Kan du styre et regnskab?
Måske er økonomilinjen noget for dig?

NYT, SPÆNDENDE OG UDFORDRENDE
Økonomilinjen opleves af mange nye elever som et helt nyt fagområde. Men gør det noget? Ind imellem kan det være både sjovt og udfordrende at starte på en frisk. På økonomilinjen får du en bred viden om, hvordan en virksomhed træffer sine økonomiske beslutninger, hvordan der lægges økonomiske strategier, og hvordan der investeres.
Undervisningen veksler mellem teori og praksis - du finder hurtigt ud af, at din teoretiske viden om økonomi er noget, der også batter i virkeligheden. I løbet af uddannelsens tre år kommer du på flere studieture til økonomiske brændpunkter i Danmark og i udlandet.

KARRIEREVEJE
Økonomilinjen giver dig et optimalt afsæt til videregående uddannelser og job i erhvervslivet. Måske får du mod på at læse jura- eller økonomi på et af landets universiteter, handelshøjskoler eller erhvervsakademier? Eller måske finder du af, at du vil bruge økonomilinjen til at søge en læreplads i et pengeinstitut, et ejendomsmæglerfirma eller en revisionsvirksomhed?

EN SIKKER INVESTERING I EN SPÆNDENDE FREMTID
"Økonomilinjen handler ikke bare om en enkelt virksomheds økonomi. Det handler også om samfundets økonomi. Vi beskæftiger os på den måde med økonomi på flere planer, fordi det giver den dybeste forståelse for, hvad økonomi i grunden er for noget. Økonomi er nemlig et langt bredere fagområde, end de fleste umiddelbart tror. Det er det, der gør økonomi så interessant, synes jeg.
"Elever, der i forvejen har interesse for økonomi og samfundsforhold, klarer sig typisk rigtig godt på Tietgen Handelsgymnasium. Samtidig giver økonomilinjen den enkelte elev mulighed for en frisk start - økonomilinjen er nemlig noget nyt for alle elever. Men der kræves motivation – har man til gengæld dén, kan økonomilinjen føre til mange forskellige karrierevalg!" "Elever, der i forvejen har interesse for økonomi og samfundsforhold, klarer sig typisk rigtig godt på Tietgen Handelsgymnasium. Samtidig giver økonomilinjen den enkelte elev mulighed for en frisk start - økonomilinjen er nemlig noget nyt for alle elever. Men der kræves motivation – har man til gengæld dén, kan

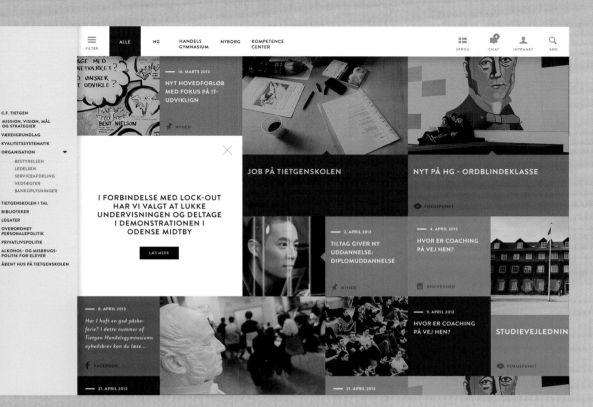

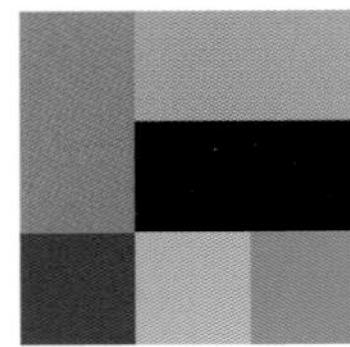

Feeling the Street — Toyota

Design Agency/
Sons & Co.

Creative Direction/
Timothy Kelleher

Design/
Matthew Arnold, Greg Brown, Matthew Wilson

Client/
Media Blanco

URL/
http://feelingthestreet.com

Feeling the Street is a global initiative from TOYOTA to celebrate the amazing, unknown artists with whom they share the world's streets. In short, it's a worldwide talent quest for street musicians. And everybody can be the judges. Over a week, the winners will experience mountains, beaches, cities and countryside on the road trip and a live performance of a lifetime!

The site has incorporated six musical icons, each pair with one modest and refreshing color, to concisely represent each theme. The design infused elements into an energetic design with colorful, yet organized layout.

#CA484E #A8A8AC #000000 #64AB8A #BFAECF #344796

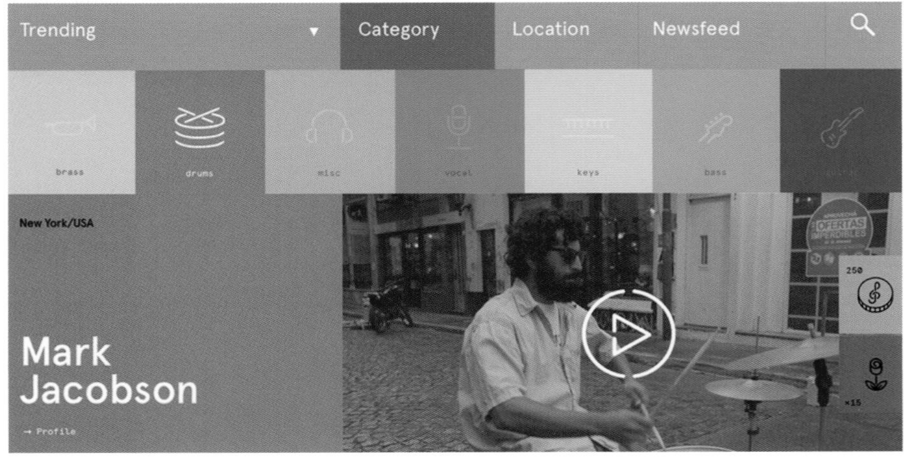

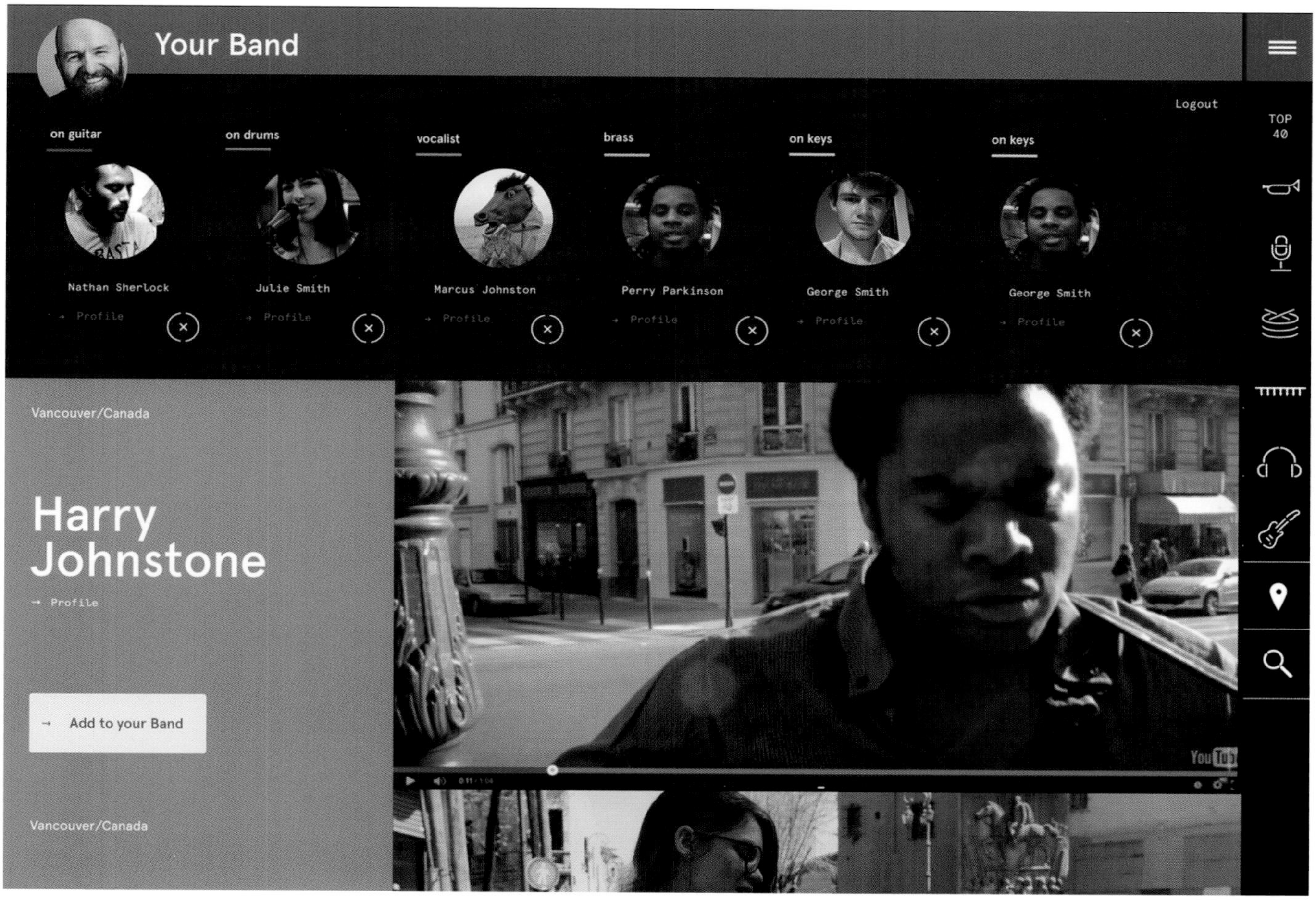

Your Band

Logout

TOP 40

on guitar — Nathan Sherlock — → Profile

on drums — Julie Smith — → Profile

vocalist — Marcus Johnston — → Profile

brass — Perry Parkinson — → Profile

on keys — George Smith — → Profile

on keys — George Smith — → Profile

Vancouver/Canada

Harry Johnstone

→ Profile

→ Add to your Band

Vancouver/Canada

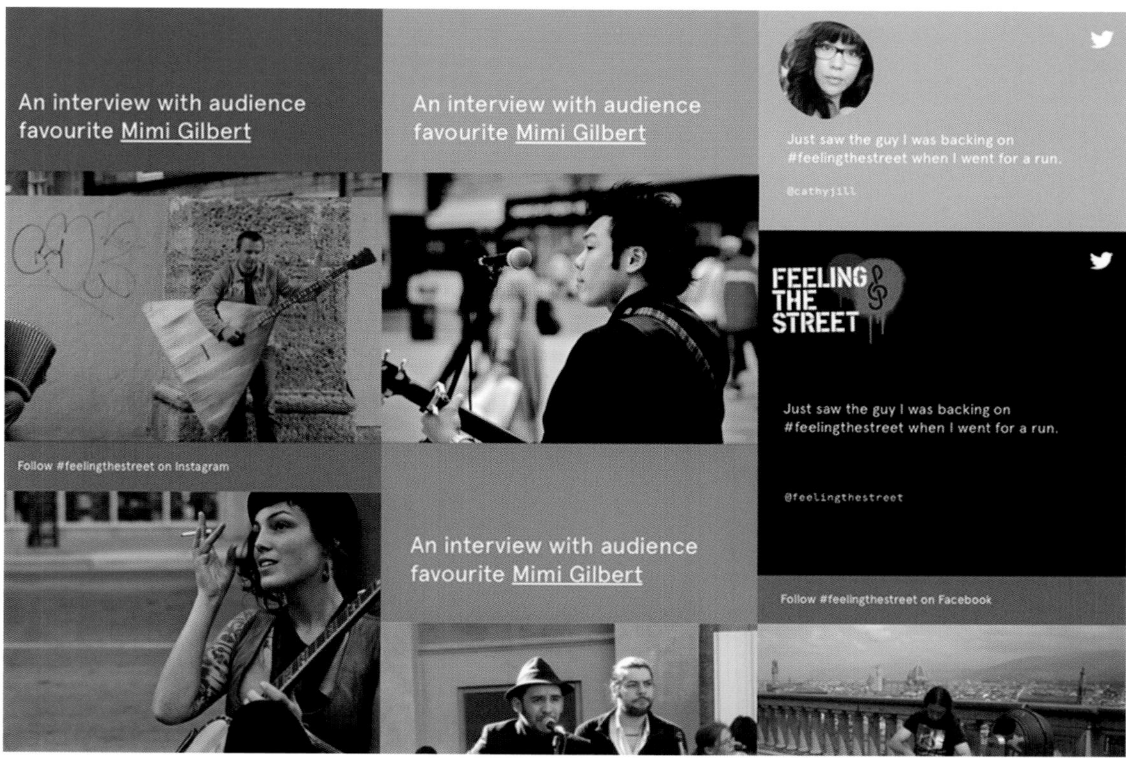

Govett-Brewster Art Gallery

Design Agency/
Sons & Co.

Creative Direction/
Timothy Kelleher

Design/
Matthew Arnold, Greg Brown

Client/
Govett Brewster

URL/
http://www.govettbrewster.com

Founded on a visionary exhibition and collection policy in 1970, the contemporary art museum Govett-Brewster Art Gallery continues to court the radical, seeks the new and provides a space for engagement and dialogue for people from all walks.

With a sophisticated layout, the site was embedded with vivid colors, clear hierarchy, and fabulous readability. When moving the mouse, the motion graphic on the headline is incredibly smooth and shows various changing forms inspired by the logo.

#102258 #E2AB7A #333331 #81B97E

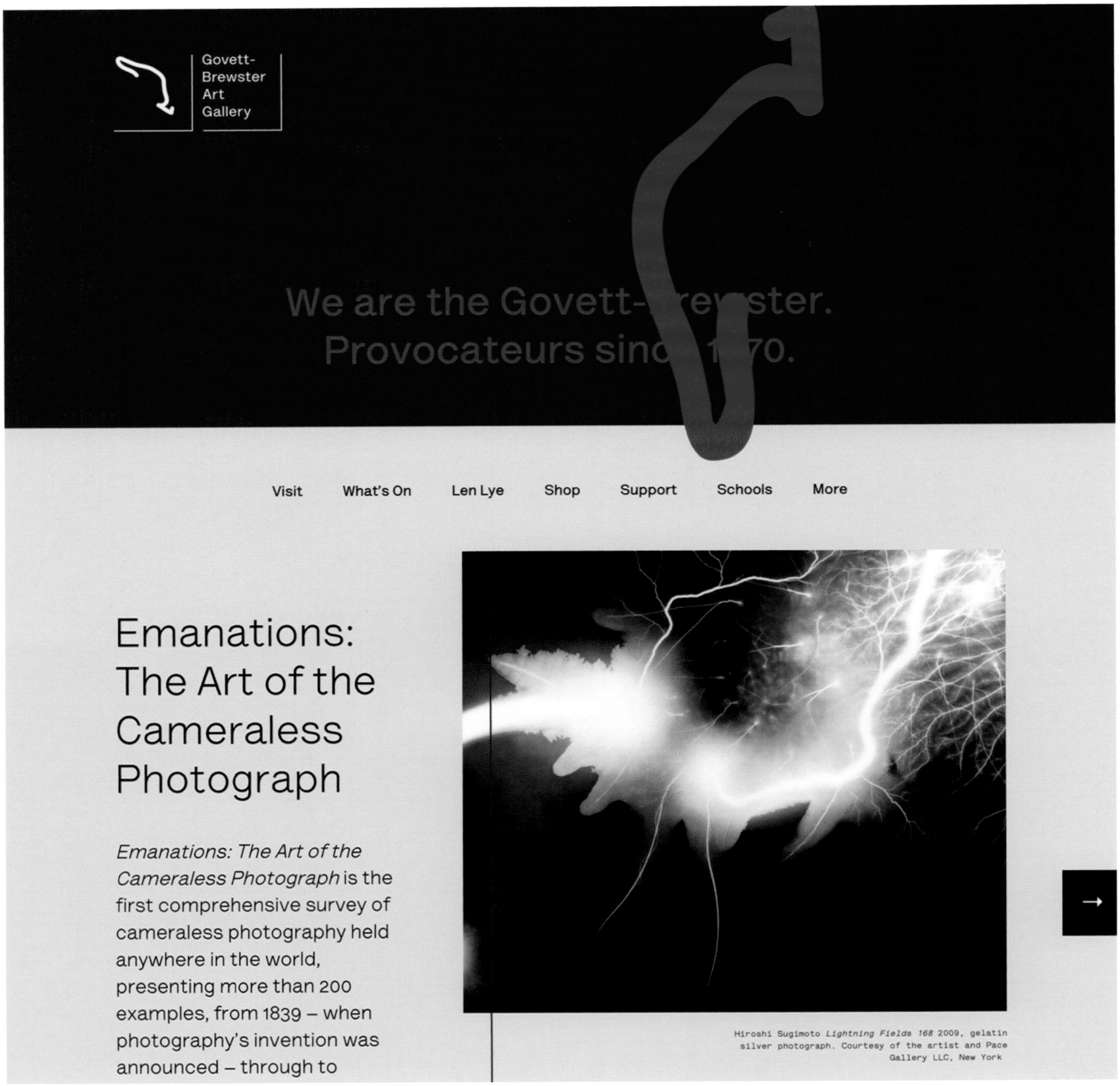

Govett-Brewster Art Gallery

We are the Govett-Brewster. Provocateurs since 1970.

Visit What's On Len Lye Shop Support Schools More

Emanations: The Art of the Cameraless Photograph

Emanations: The Art of the Cameraless Photograph is the first comprehensive survey of cameraless photography held anywhere in the world, presenting more than 200 examples, from 1839 – when photography's invention was announced – through to

Hiroshi Sugimoto *Lightning Fields 168* 2009, gelatin silver photograph. Courtesy of the artist and Pace Gallery LLC, New York

Govett-
Brewster
Art
Gallery

Len Lye
Centre

Visit What's On Len Lye Shop Support More

The Artist Len Lye Centre Len Lye's Work

The world of
Len Lye

FURNACES

Len Lye (1901–1980) is arguably one of the twentieth century's most original artists; a one-man art movement spanning several countries and multiple media over a lifetime and beyond. As a New Zealander practising in London during the pre-war years, and then a key figure in the post-war New York avant-garde art scene, Lye mapped a unique course through Modernism.

Lye spent his career pursuing an 'art of movement', a theory he initiated before he left Aotearoa New Zealand in 1924. He wanted to affect people physically and emotionally, so that art became a full body experience. Whether this was with flashing, dancing cinematography, or thunderous, oscillating metallic sculptures, his work

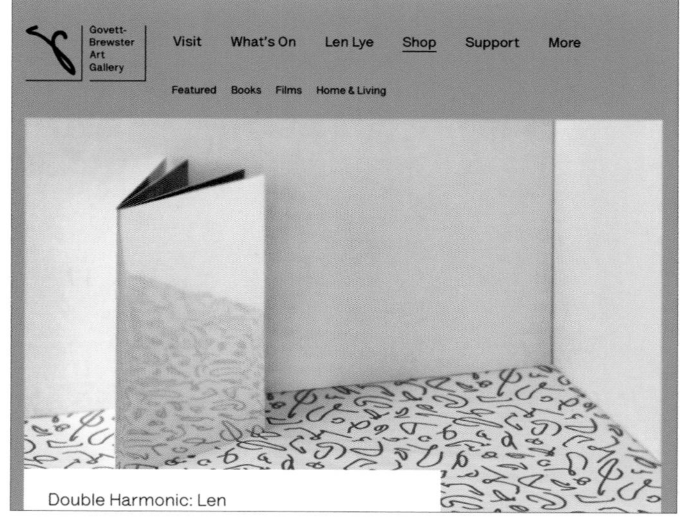

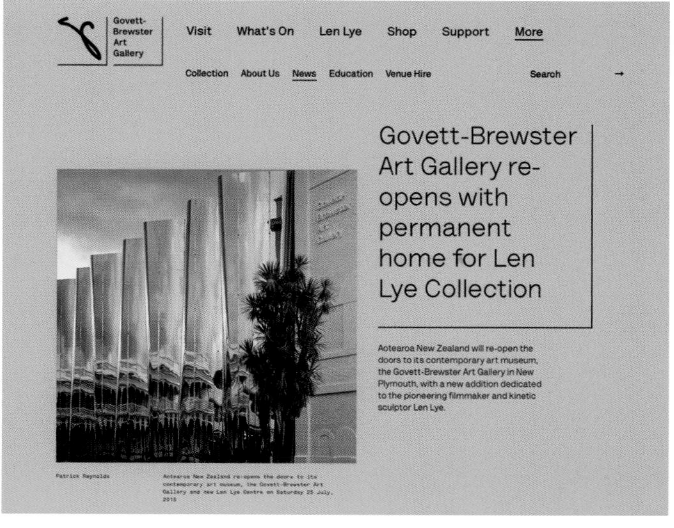

BBC Radio

Design/
Alex Yurkov

This web design is a concept website for BBC Radio. Alex Yurkov took about few months to create the youth-oriented and clean website design. Discarding all unnecessary, the site has gained a clean look with fully responsive and represents a well-thought-out modern UI and UX.

#000000 #FFFFFF #4455A0

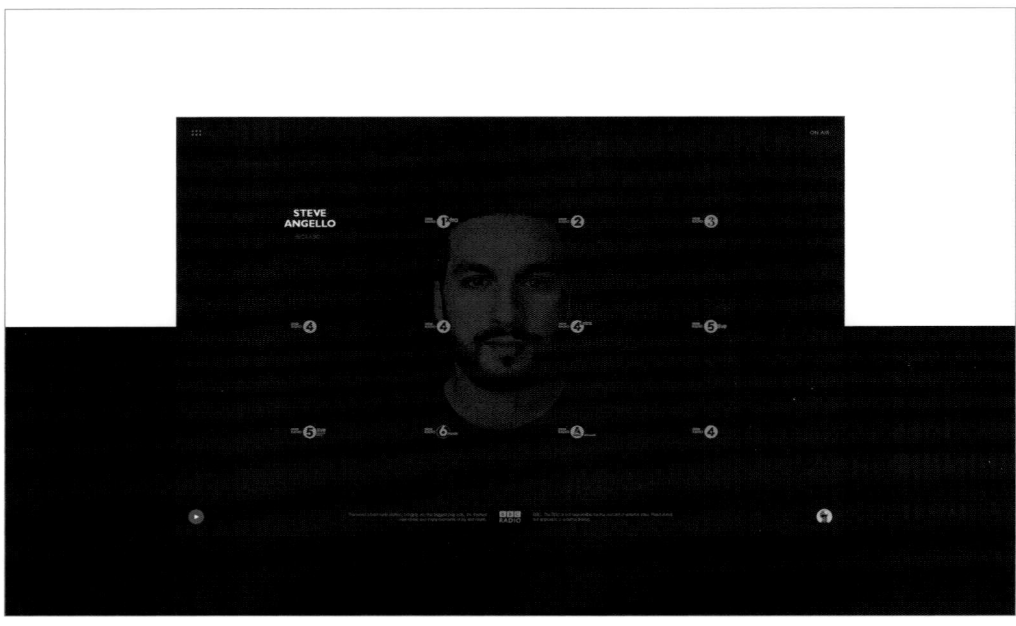

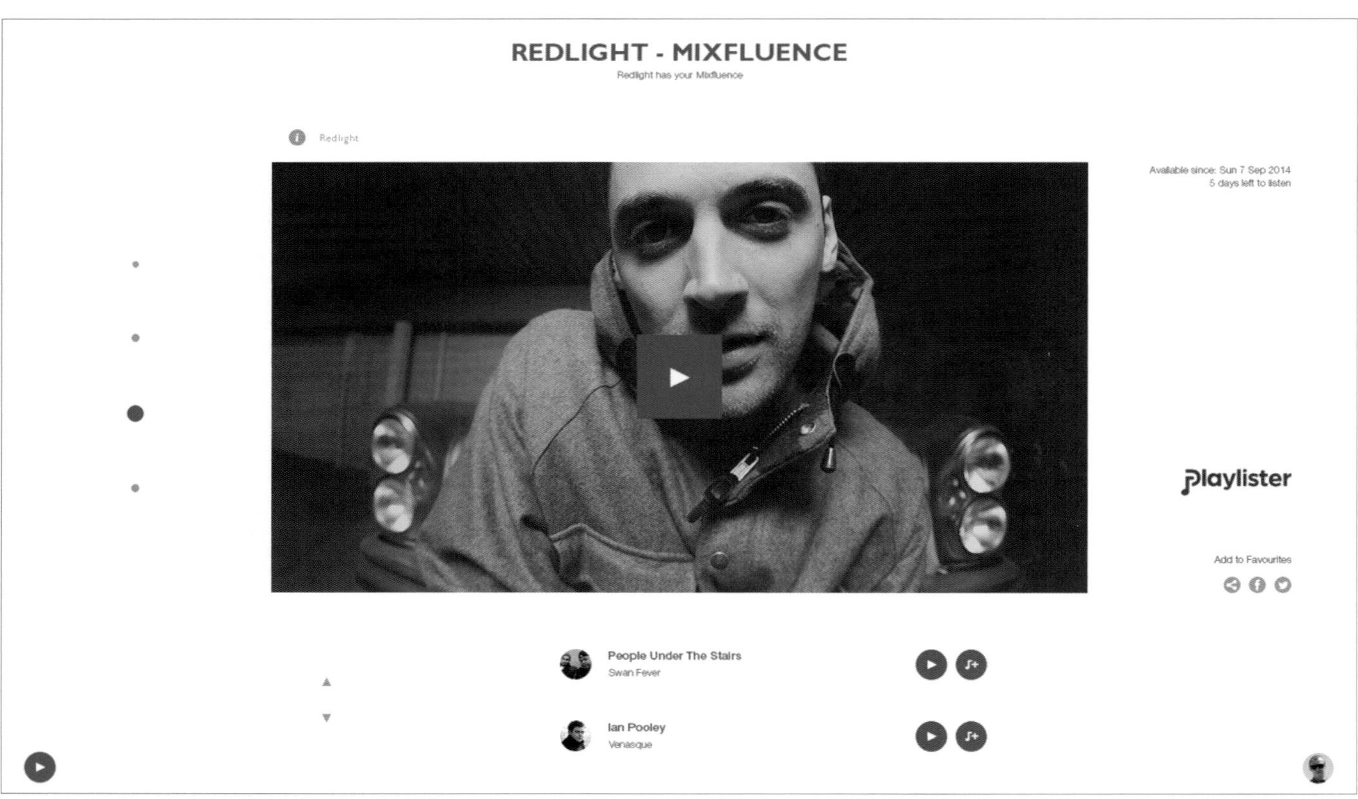

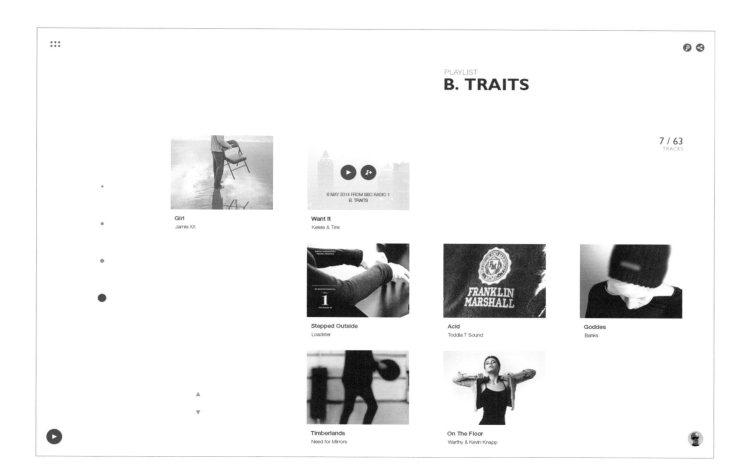

PLAYLIST
B. TRAITS

7 / 63
TRACKS

Girl
Jamie XX

6 MAY 2014 FROM BBC RADIO 1
B. TRAITS

Want It
Kelela & Tink

Stepped Outside
Loadster

Acid
Toddla T Sound

Goddes
Banks

Timberlands
Need for Mirrors

On The Floor
Warthy & Kevin Knapp

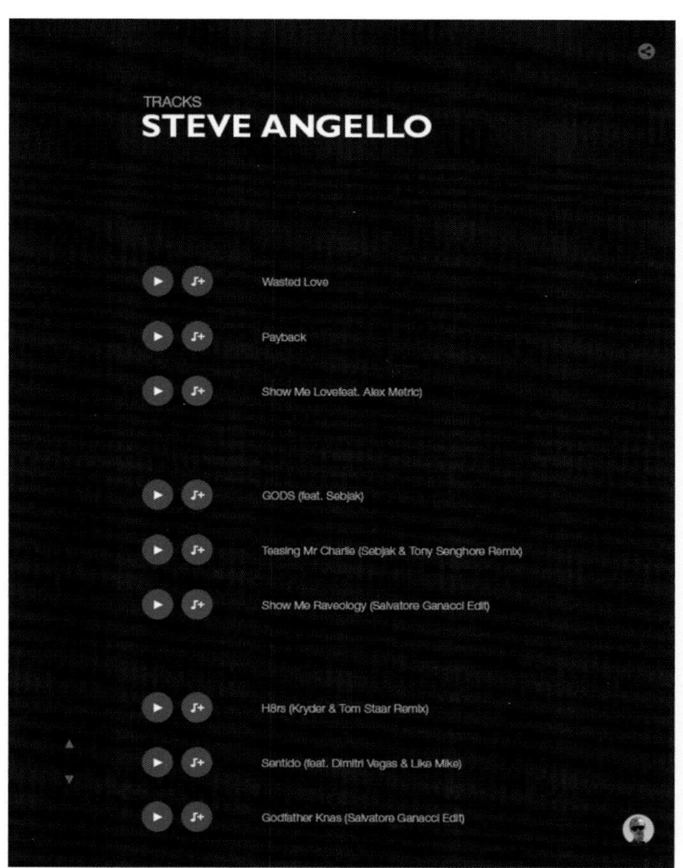

Design for Screen — 2

Grids & Layouts

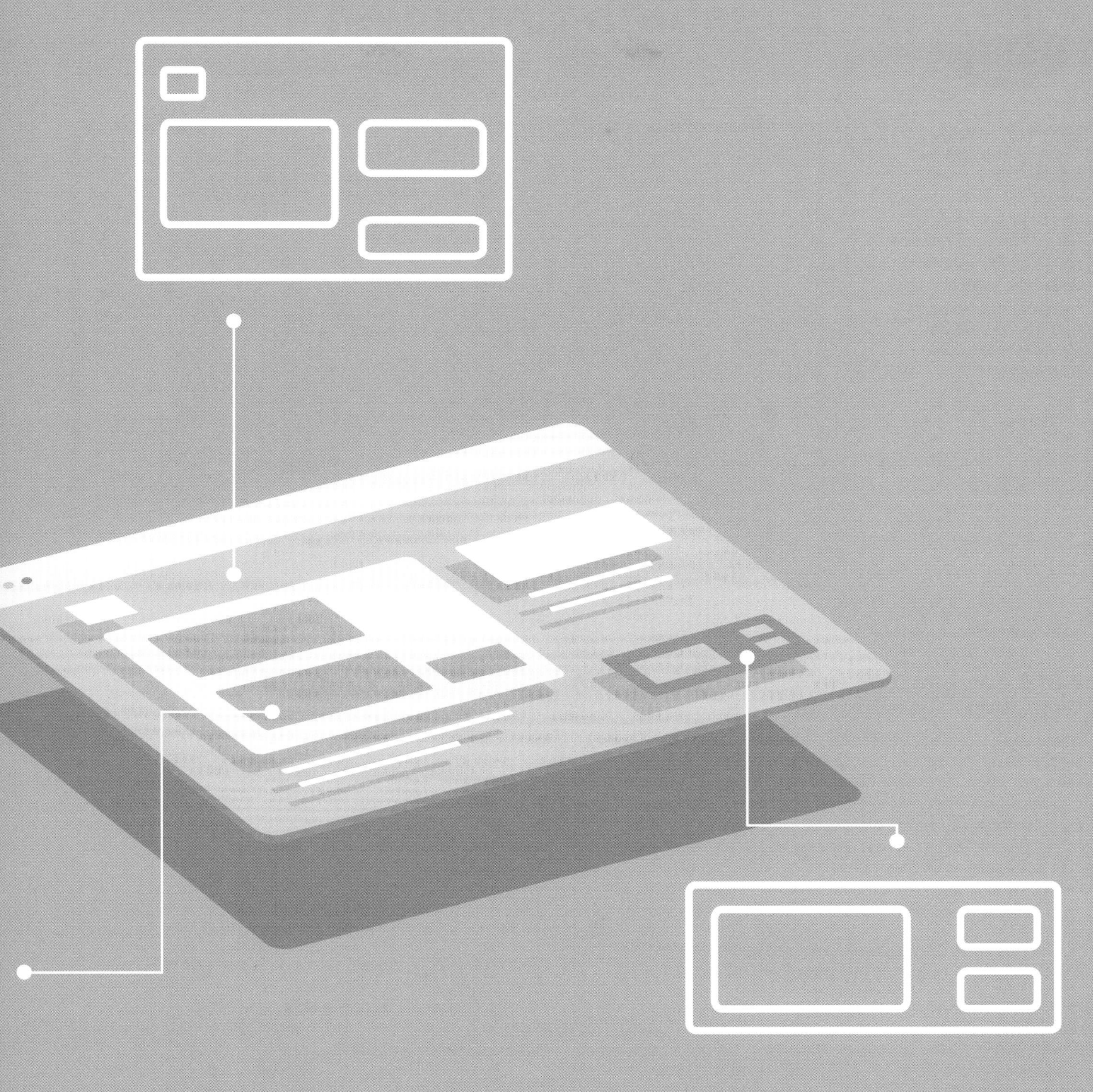

Interview with
Elisabeth Enthoven

Elisabeth Enthoven is an independent graphic designer from Amsterdam, the Netherlands. Graduated from Royal Academy of Arts in The Hague, her work is broadly involved in magazines, visual identities, web design, packaging, books, illustrations etc. in both commercial and cultural fields.

◇ Q1 ◇ Can you tell us a little bit about your background and how you came about to be doing web design?

When I was young, I was eager to be a professional violin player but after the first preparation year for conservatoire it became clear that it was not for me. When I was studying on my violin, I was a fan of drawings, painting, and letters drawings. Therefore I decided to study Graphic & Typographic Design at the Royal Academy of Arts in The Hague in The Netherlands. After working for the design studio of Scotch & Soda, a dutch fashion brand, I just returned to be a freelance graphic designer.

◇ Q2 ◇ Please kindly describe your design process: Is there a specific routine/technique that you adhere to?

What I find most important is to get to know of my client, this is a very essential part of my design process. So I start off with research on what area I am going to design for and to gain true understanding of my clients' values. My design is depended on various factors: company introduction, target audience, goals, demands, and messages to be communicated.

◇ Q3 ◇ A lot of web designs might look beautiful but not friendly to users. How do you take a complex chunk of information and make sense out of it?

The usability of a website is an essential part for a website to be a success. I always ask myself what I would like to experience on a website.

◇ Q4 ◇ How do you think of the function of grid system in web design?

Grids enable you to build a solid structure and form into your design. It is very good to use these kind of systems, in my opinion, as long as you give yourself the freedom to break all the rules that you made up for yourself. I think a grid system should be a tool and not a rule. You also have to prioritize the things that are important to the functionality of a website. The rest you can play around with.

◇ Q5 ◇ Some may argue that grid system is constrictive. Do you agree with it? How do you create a website with flexibility?

A grid system should be seen as something that will enable you to create something unique, rather than restrict you. In ways you need to think of rules and exceptions to keep your design vision clear and to make it easy to develop. A grid can only restrict you in your creativity if you are too dependent on it.

◇ Q6 ◇ It is common that nowadays designers employ 12-column and 16-column. Do you have any preference? How do you determine the grid system?

It all depends on the design. I vary a lot with my grids. The grid system is based on my first raw sketch, how I am going to use the text or images and what their purpose is on the website. It happens sometimes that when I am working with the grid, it does not serve me well. Then I will change it to my advantage. I do not really have a preference for a certain grid.

◊ Q7 ◊ **Is there any difference between the grid system for a website and a mobile device?**

A good responsive website will not lose it is qualities through different interfaces. It needs to capture the same feeling and usability on any screen. Typically I use a mobile-first approach. I design the mobile version first. It is easier to expand a design than to try and simplify a large layout for mobile screens.

◊ Q8 ◊ **How to use grid system to make readers focused on the key information? Please share with us your experience on it.**

It has been proven by research that specific areas of an interface will be viewed more by the audience of a website. That is why this section is normally used for important information. On the website of VanHarten I want to play with this impulse by placing the instruction 'SCROLL DOWN'. It will encourage the viewer to respond in a different way.

◊ Q9 ◊ **The narrative of this project is generated by the rich and consistent frameworks. Could you please introduce your concept?**

The client VanHarten designs very clean and modern fashion items and products. All of their items have a contradiction. A tablecloth could be made of a blouse and a blouse could have the characteristics of a tablecloth. I was inspired by these contradictions in their products and translated this in the design.

◊ Q10 ◊ **Who was the target audience for this design? How did it impact your work?**

At that time the target audience was mainly young urban professionals. It had impact on my design in the way that I had to find out what the visual preference was of this group of young, fast changing, and quick living group of people. It had to be super easy to navigate and find the core information. I wanted to make a striking statement on the homepage so it would trigger the interest of the viewer. As I am part of this peer group I could rely on my own preferences.

◊ Q11 ◊ **How do you balance the readability and aesthetics in this project?**

If you look at readability in print design, the viewer is challenged a lot more than they ever are on a website. So I tried to balance readability and aesthetics as I would do in print design. It is different from what we are used on websites as a lot of designs seem to be in blocks that are placed next to each other. In my design the blocks are next and on top of each other.

◊ Q12 ◊ **How many columns did you adopt in this website? What was your purpose?**

For the homepage: the frameworks are placed in the grid but the images are treated like a collage and are not in a grid. This way the text and the pictures are of equal importance.

VanHarten

Design/
Elisabeth Enthoven

Photography/
Lonneke van der Palen

Development/
Lisa Dalhuijsen

URL/
http://www.byvanharten.com

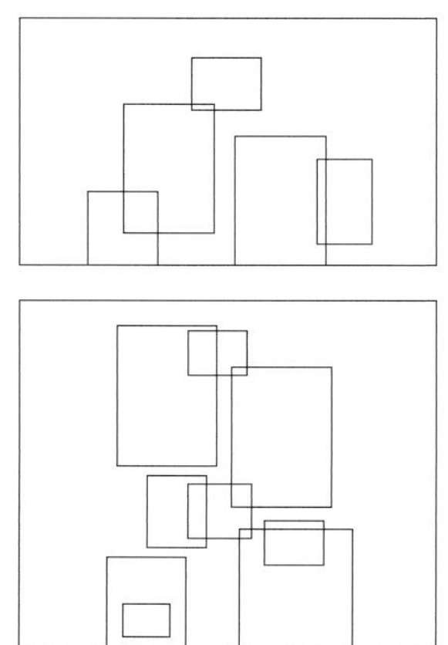

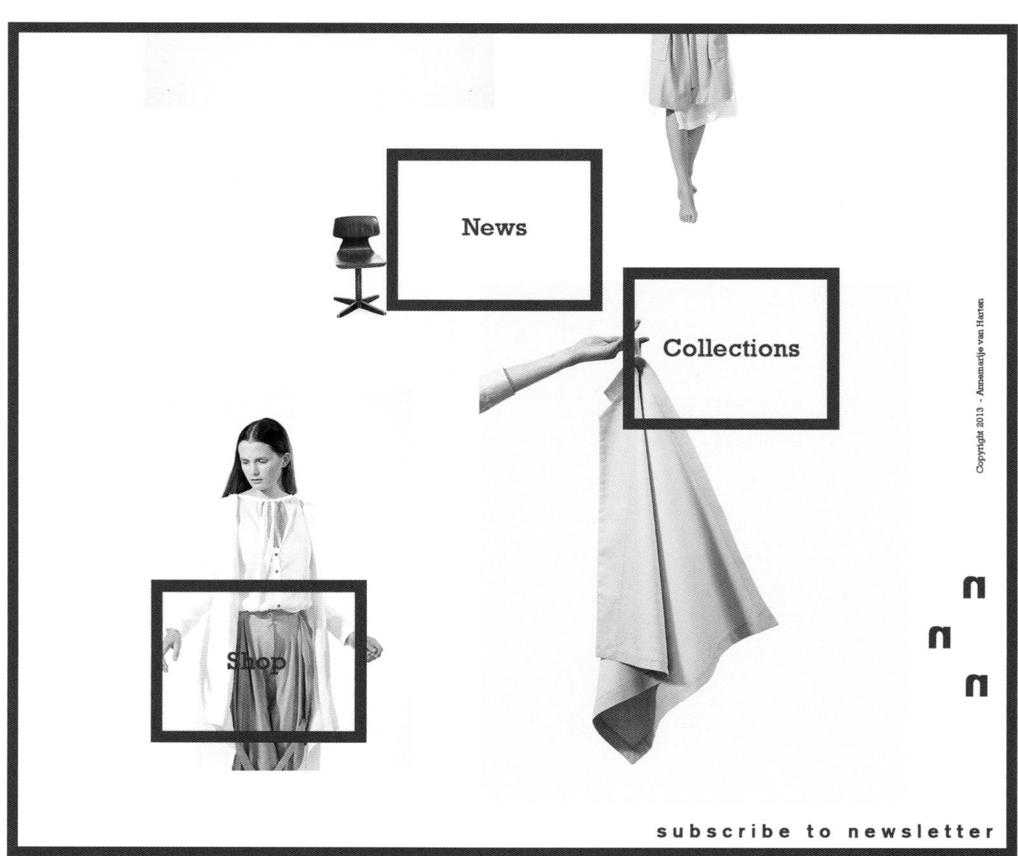

VanHarten is a Dutch fashion and product design brand reached out to Elisabeth Enthoven to re-design their logo and new website with a fresher and more modern look. One of the elements of their logo is the horizontally flipped 'n' which can be found when visitors hover over the images. The framework of the text is in several cases placed over the image, and this creates a layered feeling. The bright RGB blue color used throughout the website creates that modern and fresh look.

s c r o l l d o w n

vanharten
Fashion & Product Design

Collections
Home
News
Shop
Credits
Careers
About / Contact
v

Collection
2013
/
tablewear

Lorem ipsum dolor sit amet, consectetur adipiscing elit. Aliquam volutpat faucibus magna, eget aliquam nisl dictum eleifend. Pellentesque habitant morbi tristique senectus et netus et malesuada fames ac turpis egestas. Maecenas consequat leo sed lorem porta non placerat urna porttitor.

Collection
2013
/
Roomplays

Lorem ipsum dolor sit amet, consectetur adipiscing elit. Aliquam volutpat faucibus magna, eget aliquam nisl dictum eleifend. Pellentesque habitant morbi tristique senectus et netus et malesuada fames ac turpis egestas. Maecenas consequat leo sed lorem porta non placerat urna porttitor.

Collection
2012
/
Stoledans

Lorem ipsum dolor sit amet, consectetur adipiscing elit. Aliquam volutpat faucibus magna, eget aliquam nisl dictum eleifend. Pellentesque habitant morbi tristique senectus et netus et malesuada fames ac turpis egestas. Maecenas consequat leo sed lorem porta non placerat urna porttitor.

Contact

info@annemarijevanharten.com
+31 6 175 12 185

Address for correspondence:
Bilderdijkstraat 117B
2513 CN The Hague
The Netherlands

Visiting addres:
Willem Witsenplein 6, NO.089
2596 BK The Hague
The Netherlands

About

Vanharten is a fashion and product design studio from The Hague, The Netherlands. Annemarije is very fascinated by the curious beings called human. Their awkwardness, their doings, the way they live life and express themselves.
We are not the most important species on this planet. We are supposed to be one with nature. Sometimes we forget all about that. Annemarije reminds us with her collections we are just material and nothing more. We could be a chair, we could be a table cloth. Are we dressed or undressed?
Hier komt nog een zin maar ik weet even geen tekst.

stores
credits

shop
collections
news

Papapolitis & Papapolitis

Design Agency/
Kommigraphics Design Studio

Cient/
Papapolitis & Papapolitis

URL/
http://www.papapolitis.com

Papapoliti & Papapolitis is a leading law firm with a strong international perspective. It was established in 1898 and since then it has been engaged in pioneering legal developments that shaped part of the Greek legal landscape. Papapolitis & Papapolitis partners have chosen Kommigraphics to design their new company website, thus giving them the opportunity to present their international profile on a digital environment, where clean-cut and special aesthetics have been applied.

The company's blue corporate color has been the base of the color palette, which they combined with white and earthy tones, so that they bring out its philosophy with a modern design. The black and white photographs from well known and international cityscapes reflect the openness and long experience of the company, while all of the design are based on a strict canvas that reminds of a prestigious newspaper format. All large white surfaces as well as the few asymmetries, stand for its modern style in an otherwise heavy and special business sector.

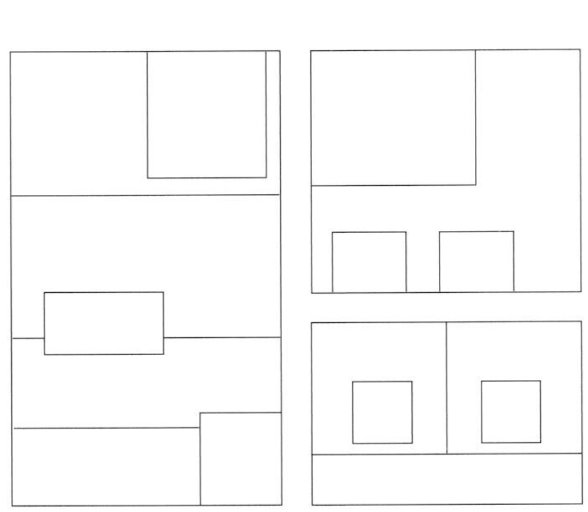

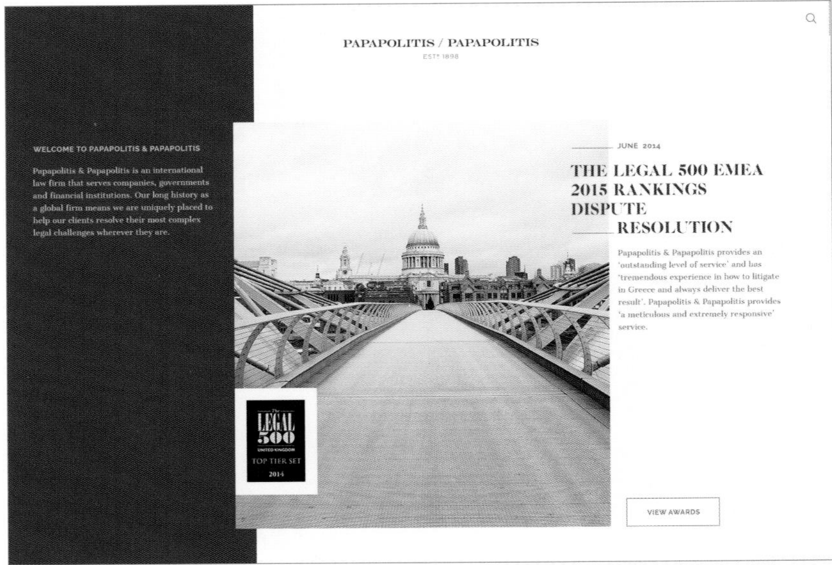

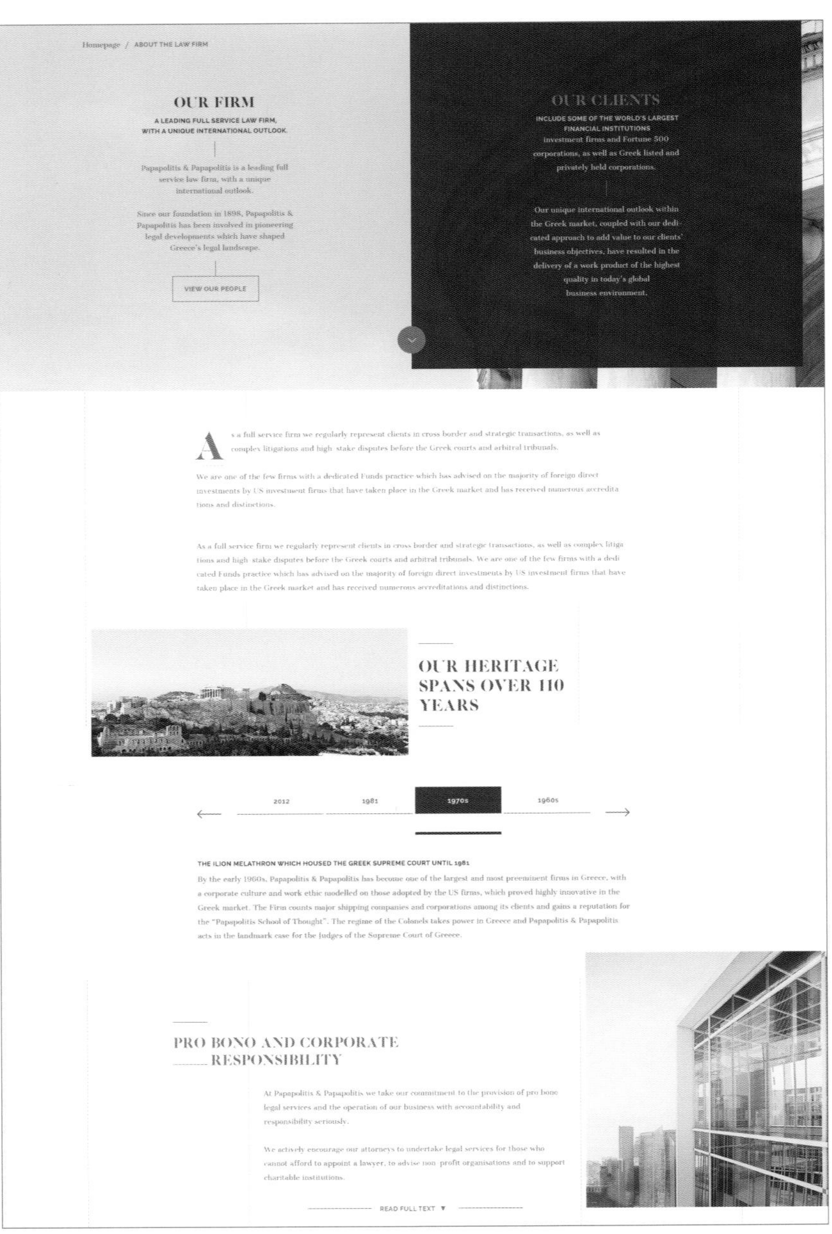

JULY 30TH, 2015
CLIENT ALERT / NEW RECOVERY AND RESOLUTION REGIME FOR CREDIT INSTITUTIONS
This Alert provides an analysis of the main provisions of the second part of the bill implementing EU Directive...
JUNE 15TH, 2015
JULY 23RD, 2015
NICHOLAS PAPAPOLITIS FEATURES IN WSJ ARTICLE
GSO/BLACKSTONE GROUP INVESTMENT IN LAMDA DEVELOPMENT SA

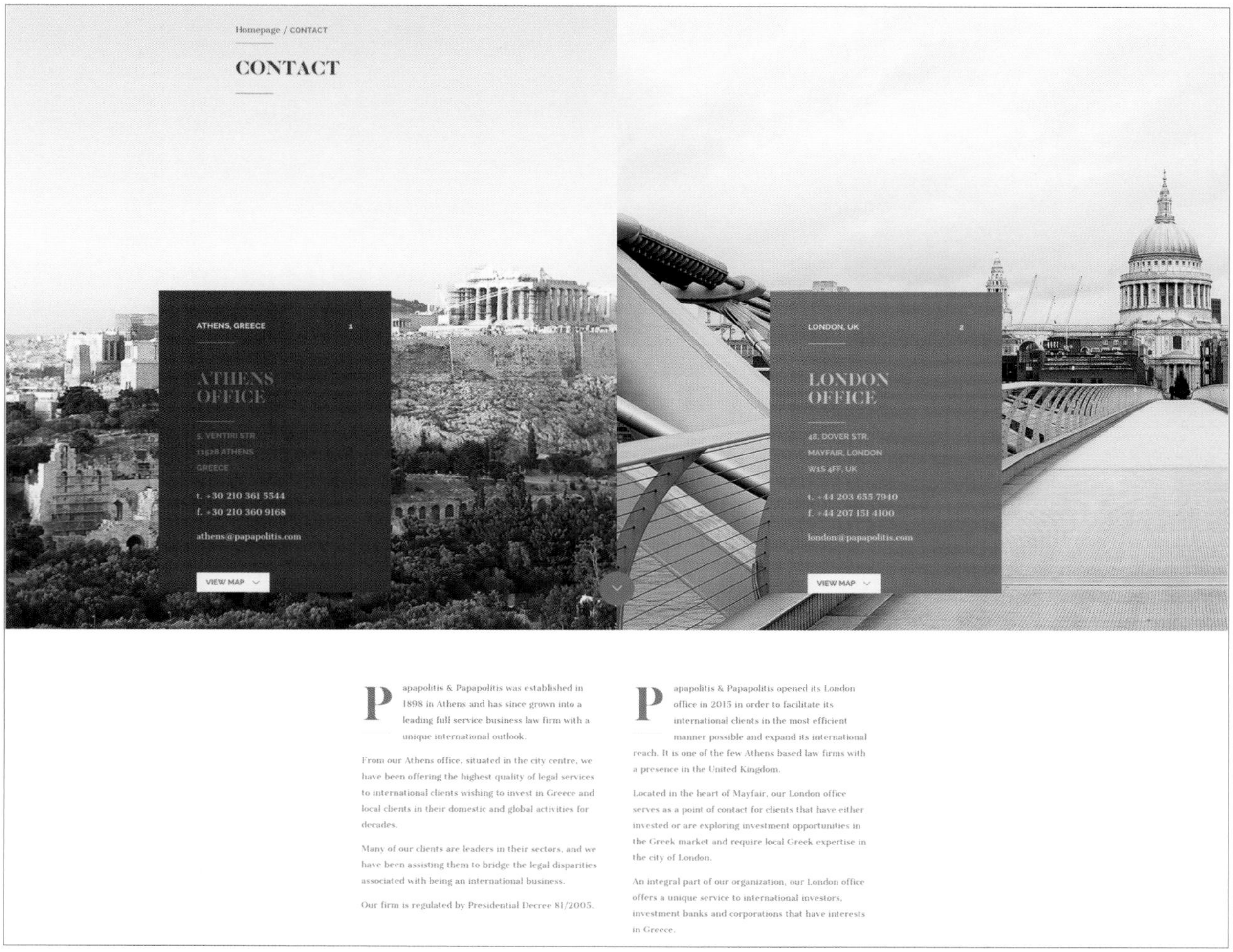

Homepage / CONTACT

CONTACT

ATHENS, GREECE 1

ATHENS OFFICE

5, VENTIRI STR
11528 ATHENS
GREECE

t. +30 210 361 5544
f. +30 210 360 9168

athens@papapolitis.com

VIEW MAP

LONDON, UK 2

LONDON OFFICE

48, DOVER STR.
MAYFAIR, LONDON
W1S 4FF, UK

t. +44 203 655 7940
f. +44 207 151 4100

london@papapolitis.com

VIEW MAP

Papapolitis & Papapolitis was established in 1898 in Athens and has since grown into a leading full service business law firm with a unique international outlook.

From our Athens office, situated in the city centre, we have been offering the highest quality of legal services to international clients wishing to invest in Greece and local clients in their domestic and global activities for decades.

Many of our clients are leaders in their sectors, and we have been assisting them to bridge the legal disparities associated with being an international business.

Our firm is regulated by Presidential Decree 81/2005.

Papapolitis & Papapolitis opened its London office in 2015 in order to facilitate its international clients in the most efficient manner possible and expand its international reach. It is one of the few Athens based law firms with a presence in the United Kingdom.

Located in the heart of Mayfair, our London office serves as a point of contact for clients that have either invested or are exploring investment opportunities in the Greek market and require local Greek expertise in the city of London.

An integral part of our organization, our London office offers a unique service to international investors, investment banks and corporations that have interests in Greece.

Jova Construction

Design Agency/
Phoenix the Creative Studio

Design Direction/
Louis Paquet

Design/
Louis Paquet, Phoenix Team

Account Management/
Fouad Mallouk

URL/
http://jovaconstruction.com

Being a one-stop shop for home improvements, Jova Construction's approach is unique: it aims to build a long-term relationship with its clientele. Maintaining house quality is essential to preserve its value and they work with clients for assistance to make their home a dreamland.

To be as professional as the brand, the information on this site are designed to be used as product tags, delivering the contents in an organized and clear way.

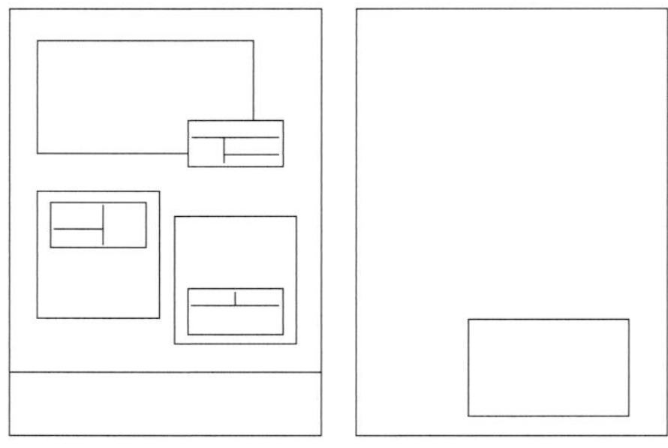

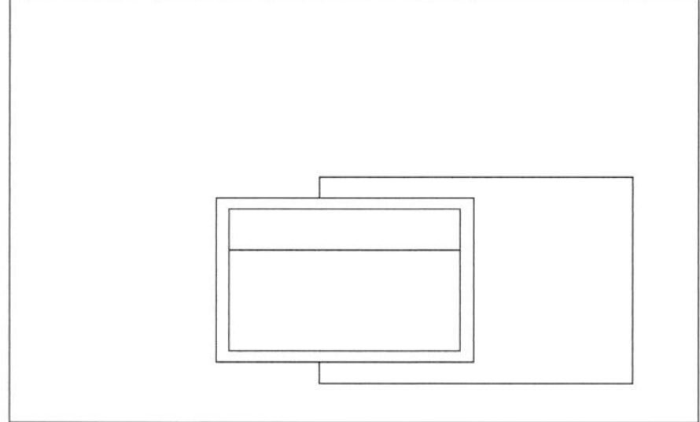

L'UNIQUE ARRÊT POUR TOUS VOS PROJETS DE RÉNOVATIONS

En savoir plus

SALON DE L'HABITAT & DU CHALET

Promotions | 5 à 10% de rabais

POUR TOUS VOS PROJETS DE RÉNOVATION

Trucs et astuces

Profil de l'entreprise | Depuis ◊ 1986

MÉTIER TRANSMIS DE PÈRE EN FILS

JOVA

514.917.JOVA (5682)

Facebook Twitter Pinterest

Québec

W H O

W E A R E

J

MENU

WHO WE ARE

Business Profile

JOVA Construction is a second (2nd) generation enterprise that offers and specializes in custom renovation. Home improvement artists (since 1986), we have also worked for more than a decade in building shops, condo towers, offices and art galleries.

Today, JOVA Construction combines these two forces to provide an exceptional service and a unique product on the market.

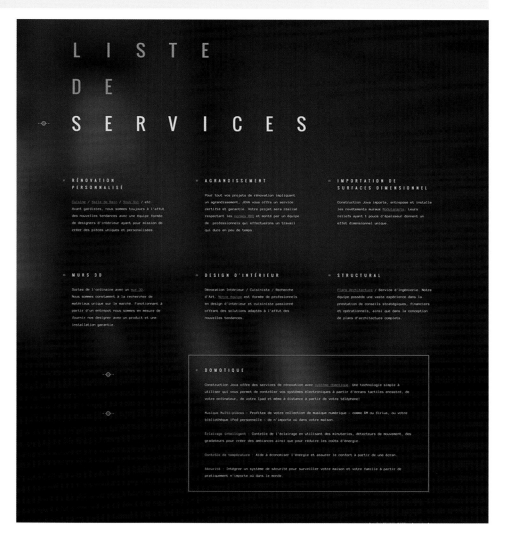

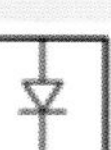

L I S T E

D E

S E R V I C E S

R É N O V A T I O N P E R S O N N A L I S É

Cuisine / Salle de Bain / Sous Sol / etc.
Avant gardistes, nous sommes toujours à l'affut des nouvelles tendances avec une équipe formée de designers d'intérieur ayant pour mission de créer des pièces uniques et personalisées.

A G R A N D I S S E M E N T

Pour tout vos projets de rénovation impliquant un agrandissement, JOVA vous offre un service certifié et garantie. Votre projet sera réalisé respectant les normes RBQ et monté par un équipe de professionnels qui effectuerons un travail qui dure en peu de temps.

I M P O R T A T I O N D E S U R F A C E S D I M E N S I O N N E L

Construction Jova importe, entrepose et installe les revêtements muraux Modularts. Leurs reliefs ayant 1 pouce d'épaisseur donnent un effet dimensionnel unique.

M U R S 3 D

Sortez de l'ordinaire avec un mur 3D.
Nous sommes constament à la rechercher de matériaux unique sur le marché. Fonctionnant à partir d'un entrepot nous sommes en mesure de fournir nos designer avec un produit et une installation garantie.

D E S I G N D ' I N T É R I E U R

Décoration Intérieur / Cuisiniste / Recherche d'Art. Notre équipe est formée de professionels en design d'intérieur et cuisiniste passionné offrant des solutions adaptés à l'affut des nouvelles tendances.

S T R U C T U R A L

Plans Architecture / Service d'Ingénierie. Notre équipe possède une vaste expérience dans la prestation de conseils stratégiques, financiers et opérationnels, ainsi que dans la conception de plans d'architecture complets.

D O M O T I Q U E

Construction Jova offre des services de rénovation avec système domotique. Une technologie simple à utiliser qui vous permet de contrôler vos systèmes électroniques à partir d'écrans tactiles encastré, de votre ordinateur, de votre Ipad et même à distance à partir de votre téléphone!

Musique Multi-pièces : Profitez de votre collection de musique numérique - comme XM ou Sirius, ou votre bibliothèque iPod personnelle - de n'importe où dans votre maison.

Éclairage intelligent : Contrôle de l'éclairage en utilisant des minuteries, détecteurs de mouvement, des gradateurs pour créer des ambiances ainsi que pour réduire les coûts d'énergie.

Contrôle de température : Aide à économiser l'énergie et assurer le confort à partir de une écran.

Sécurité : Intégrer un système de sécurité pour surveiller votre maison et votre famille à partir de pratiquement n'importe où dans le monde.

Bruce Connew

Design Agency/
Sons & Co.

Creative Direction/
Timothy Kelleher

Team Members/
Matthew Arnold, Bruce Connew, Catherine Griffiths, Matthew Wilson

Client/
Bruce Connew

URL/
http://www.bruceconnew.com

Bruce Connew is a photographer based in New Zealand. His central projects have been shown as solo exhibitions in most public art galleries in New Zealand. This website serves as a portfolio archive for the photographer. The page can be horizontally scrolled to check the posts in the main page. When click into the subpages, users can vertically scroll to check the details. Each page is designed with a concise layout in which each image is generally three times larger than the descriptions. It allows users to browse the site to focus on photographs, and in each scroll, users can appreciate the works like reading a photography magazine.

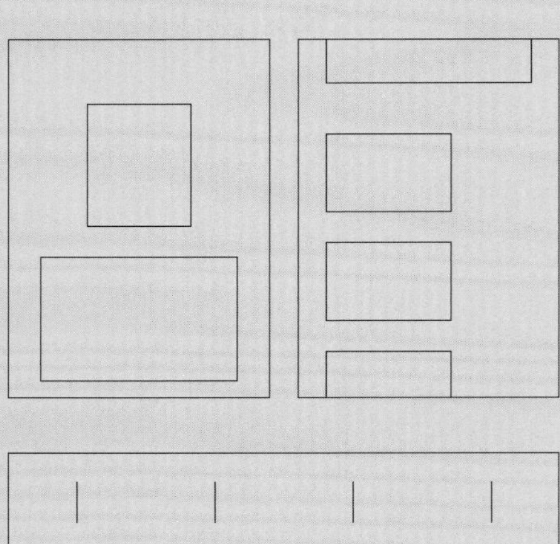

bruce connew →　projects →　books & →　writings →

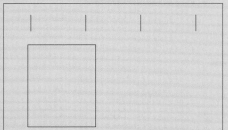

archive

On the way to an ambush

Burma, 1989

"... the two teenagers moved quickly together, entwining their arms for a photograph they must have known they would never see."

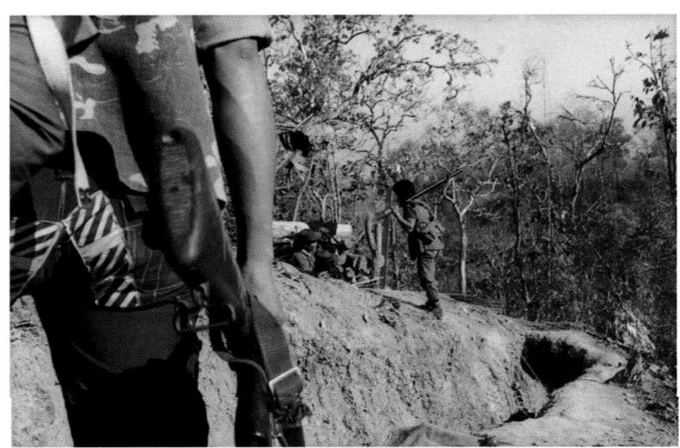

book

'On the way to an ambush' was published by Victoria University Press, Wellington, New Zealand, and launched 22 April 1999 to a generous crowd at Unity Books, Wellington, the best bookshop in New Zealand.
"This is his record of time spent looking and thinking about what has been seen and what it might mean. Through a process I can only describe as an unfurling or unravelling, this war in Burma becomes a metaphor for Connew's own life." Peter Turner, past-editor, Creative Camera magazine.
The final copies of 'On the way to an ambush' have been numbered and signed. Each book is accompanied by a signed pigment print of the cover image, 100x150mm, on Hahnemuhle Photo Rag, and a DVD of a contemporary recording of a slide show/narration of 'On the way to an ambush', first presented at Te Papa Tongarewa, Wellington, New Zealand, August 1998.

$195.00 NZD

exhibition

'On the way to an ambush' was a 40-image exhibition at War Photo Ltd, Dubrovnik, Croatia, May-July, 2008. The work was almost an exhibition in 1999 at the National Library Gallery, Wellington, New Zealand, but fell foul of institutional re-structuring.

related writings

On the way to an ambush, Peter Turner, April 1999 (texts)

'On the way to an ambush', Bruce Connew, April 1999 (texts)

view all 87 works

On the way to an ambush #39 / A Karen soldier dresses in the trenches, Mae La, Burma, 1989

'A random act', a review by Stephen Stratford, May 1999

Stephen Stratford, now Quote Unquote bolg, wrote the following review of 'On the way to an ambush' for now defunct Grace magazine, May 1999. It gives some context to the book and its story.

'A random act'

In his moving book, Bruce Connew reflects on the ambushes that lie in wait for all of us.

Bruce Connew's 'On the way to an ambush' began as a photo essay about his time in 1989 with the Karen independence fighters in Burma, but in the 10 years since, as he mulled it over, it turned into a meditation on the randomness of death.

In 1987, his wife Barbara, from whom he was separated, was killed in a car accident while taking their son Tim and three friends to school. This painful story and its aftermath is interwoven through the story of the Karen's war.

bruce connew →
projects →
books & →
writings →

Press Escape to Cancel

Kosova, 1999

archive

"The destruction in Peja was staggering. I walked around and around while loose spouting rang a dirge against itself, and oscillating reflections off plate glass windows, broken and barely attached to their frames, caught my eye, startling me, as they swayed in the breeze."

book

'Press Escape to Cancel' appeared as an essay of photographs and writing inside and on the covers of SPORT 24, Summer 2000, a New Zealand literary journal published by Victoria University Press publisher, Fergus Barrowman. The essay wove the madness of immediate post-war Kosova with the clinical madness of a Kosova asylum. I entered Kosova from Macedonia on 19 June 1999, seven days after Nato troops, and hitchhiked about for eight days during the early return of Kosovar Albanian refugees.

exhibition

'Press Escape to Cancel' was exhibited first at te tuhi, Auckland, New Zealand, March-April 2002, and toured through 2002-2003 to Rotorua Museum, Rotorua and Sarjeant Gallery, Whanganui.

related writings

Street wise, ART NEWS, Winter 2003 (publications)

'Press Escape to Cancel', Bruce Connew, 2000 (texts)

view all 43 works

Press Escape to Cancel #33 / Sign stabbed to the door of a home: behave or we'll be back, Sojeva, June 1999

"My blood is probably even more mixed, but I don't have time to explore it ... being different brought my father a bullet in the head in 1992 in Stolac." Jabir Derala

I entered Kosova from Macedonia on 19 June 1999, seven days after Nato troops, and hitchhiked about for eight days during the early return of Kosovar Albanian refugees.

The following is one of seven, brief texts, which accompany the images in 'Press Escape to Cancel'.

'Press Escape to Cancel', the title of this essay, is a repeating line from one of Jabir Derala's love poems. Jabir is a Macedonian poet, writer and journalist. The other day, I asked him, amongst other things, to describe his ethnicity: "My father is mixed Albanian and Turkish. My mother is mixed Turkish, Croat (Dalmatian) and (a bit) Iraqi. My blood is probably even more mixed, but I don't have time to explore it . . . it's not a jarring question. I find it very exciting. But, not extraordinary, because we on the Balkans, as the rest of the world, have mixed blood more than we are ready to admit. Somewhere it's a starting point for beautiful achievements, and somewhere it's a reason for bloodshed . . . I was raised as a cosmopolitan, a citizen of the world, with love for people, regardless of their backgrounds. I am proud to be different. I am completely aware that it brings trouble very often. Almost always, when we mention Balkans (and, not only) . . . being different brought my father a bullet in the head in 1992 in Stolac. Killed by a Croat. Should I hate Croats, then?! I am a bit of a Croat (25%), too. So, I have to hate a part of myself."

BRUCE CONNEW / 01.2000

the complete seven texts

Press Escape to Cancel #5 / Possessions in a wheelbarrow, Ferizaj, June 1999

view all 43 works →

bruce connew →
projects →
books & →
writings →

briefs

2015-01-29

Alice Connew / Bruce Connew, January 2015

A link to an interview between Alice Connew and Bruce Connew for Photobook Melbourne.

archive

Daniel Boetker-Smith, of Photobook Melbourne fame, Asia-Pacific Photobook Archive and much more, saw a photograph of Alice and me in a Berlin elevator posted on Alice's Instagram feed. One of my books is in the Asia-Pacific Photobook Archive, which piloted Daniel to a eureka moment of father/daughter recognition.

He emailed Alice to ask whether she and I would interview each other for Photobook Melbourne's news blog, exclusively I might add, in time for the magnificent Photobook Melbourne, 12-22 February 2015.

Of course, we agreed.

BRUCE CONNEW / 01.2015

BAAS Arquitectura

Design Agency/
Clase Bcn

Design Direction/
Daniel Ayuso

Design/
Héctor Sos

Client/
BAAS Arquitectura

URL/
http://www.baas.cat/ca

BAAS Arquitectura is an architecture, urban planning, and interior design studio formed by an expert team of architects and designers who work along with an extensive network of highly-specialized consultants.

Héctor Sos was invited to make the responsive website for the studio. He used a strict layout to reflect the philosophy of BAAS that simply but also sophisticatedly constructs useful and appropriate buildings.

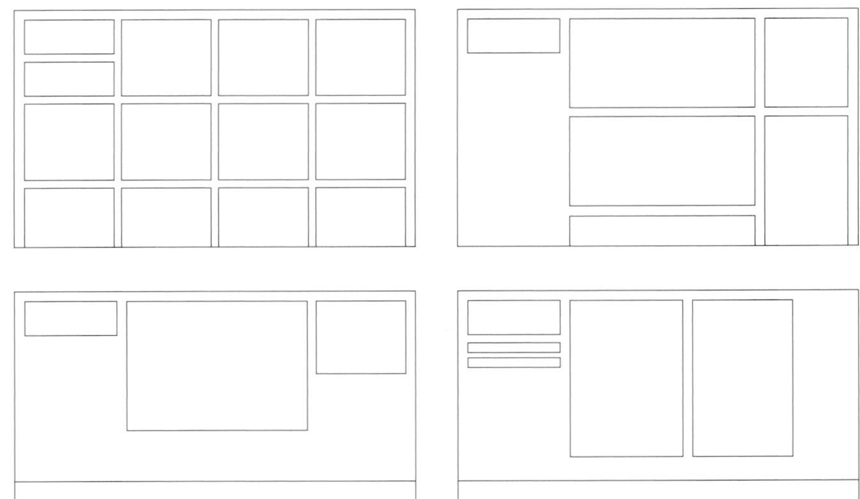

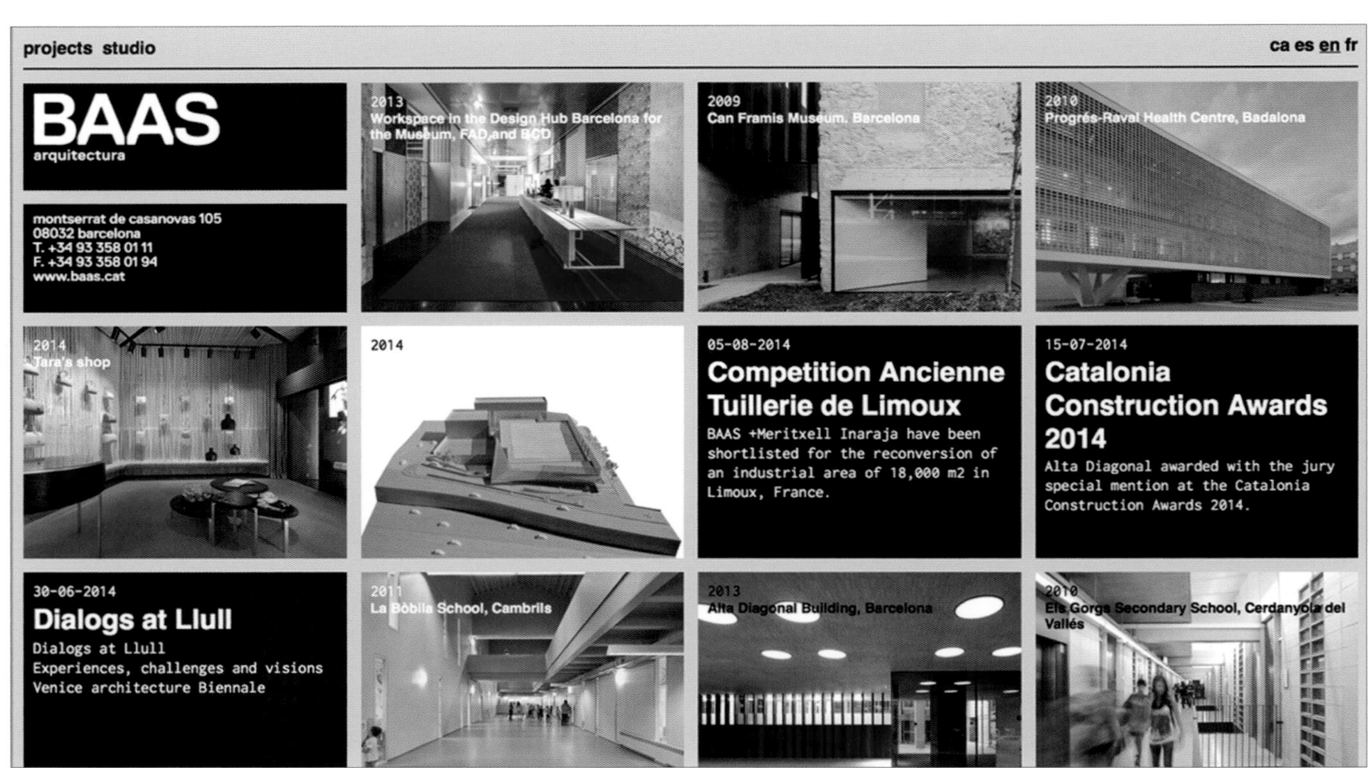

projects public buildings offices housing planning & landscape design temporary **studio** ca es en fr

BAAS
arquitectura

municipal funeral services, león

This building is fronted with an expansive lawn and a lake thus blending in with the natural environment and the nearby residential area.

The waiting room looks out onto an ivy-covered ledge surrounded by birches, and made of varnished wood. Carpeting and indirect lighting create a comfortable atmosphere. Vigil rooms are illuminated with natural light coming from courtyards with water which suggest peace, quiet and privacy.

The only visible façade - the rooftop - reflects the magnificent sky of León, giving an analogy to death.

- León
- 1997-2001
- 3,200 m2

team

Architecture
Jordi Badia + Josep Val

Computation structures
Eduard Doce

Calculation facilities
Consulting Lluis Duart SL.

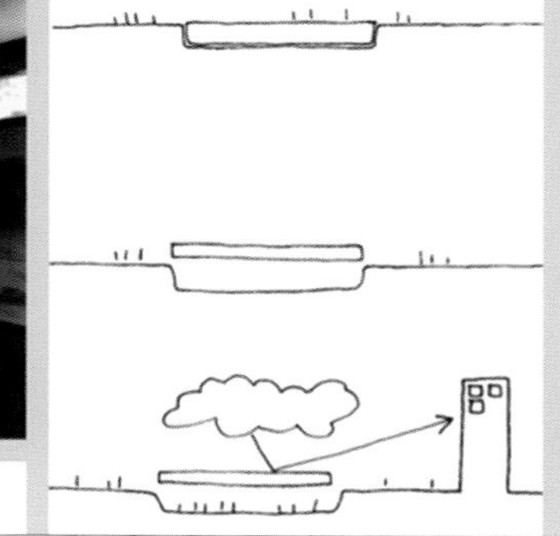

projects studio news practice profile jordi badia team clients awards bibliography contact ca es en fr

BAAS
arquitectura

BAAS arquitectura is an architecture, urban planning and interior design studio formed by an expert team of architects and designers who work along with an extensive network of highly-specialised consultants.

Founded in 1994, thanks to the many projects developed throughout these years the studio has gained vast experience that has earned it a host of prestigious Awards (FAD Awards, Ciutat de Barcelona 2009) and coverage in specialist journals (Architectural Review, El Croquis, A+U, Casabella, etc.)

The work carried out at BAAS arquitectura strive to meet and solve, simply but also sophisticatedly, the complex requirements that each project lays down by constructing useful and appropriate buildings to a high technical level and without eschewing the expressiveness and emotion that the finest architecture is capable of transmitting. Architecture that advocates the continuity of tradition and context whilst fully committed to respecting the environment.

On the past years BAAS arquitectura has acquired expertise in rehabilitation projects, both refurbishing existing office buildings as well as heritage listed constructions.

The studio divided into independent teams which carry out projects from the tender stage right through to their actual construction.

BAAS arquitectura has held ISO 9001 quality certification since 2007.

HIC> 10-10-2014
Anna & Eugeni Bach > Las afinidades electivas
read more

@BAASarch
Competition by BAAS & BOPBAA for Sant Salvador Pavilion in San Pau Hospital, Barcelona. #architecture @jordibadiabaas hhttp://t.co/C5g9PAhDUD

/BAASJordiBadia YouTube vimeo

contacto
Montserrat de Casanovas 105
08032 Barcelona
T. +34 93 358 01 11
F. +34 93 358 01 94
baas@baas.cat

POLAND
BAAS Abroad

projects studio news practice profile jordi badia team clients awards bibliography contact ca es en fr

BAAS
arquitectura

team
have worked with us
partners

- **Chairman:**
  - Jordi Badia,
- **Chief Executiver:**
- **Chief Financial Officer:**
  - Janette Velasco,
  - Isabel Cabrera,
- **Group leaders:**
- **Architecture group:**
  - Mireia Monràs
  - Mercè Mundet
  - David Bravo
  - Cristina Anglès
  - Andreu Egido
  - Eva Damià
  - Christian Schlanderer
  - Alba Azuara
  - Xavier Gracia
- **Head of Interior design department:**
- **Marketing and Communication:**
  - comunicacio@baas.cat,

HIC> 10-10-2014
Anna & Eugeni Bach > Las afinidades electivas
read more

@BAASarch
Competition by BAAS & BOPBAA for Sant Salvador Pavilion in San Pau Hospital, Barcelona. #architecture @jordibadiabaas hhttp://t.co/C5g9PAhDUD

/BAASJordiBadia YouTube vimeo

contacto
Montserrat de Casanovas 105
08032 Barcelona
T. +34 93 358 01 11
F. +34 93 358 01 94
baas@baas.cat

POLAND
BAAS Abroad

Container Artist Residency 01

Design Agency/
Project Projects LLC

URL/
http://www.containerartistresidency01.org

Curated by Prem Krishnamurthy with founder and director Maayan Strauss, Container Artist Residency 01 is a unique residency program that takes place on board commercial cargo ships as they navigate international trade routes.

Project Projects' graphic website conveys the industrial scale of international trade, while also referencing the sea as a metaphor for flows of capital. It uses full-bleed video of the sea and shipping ports as a dynamic background element, which will be updated periodically over the project's two-year lifespan.

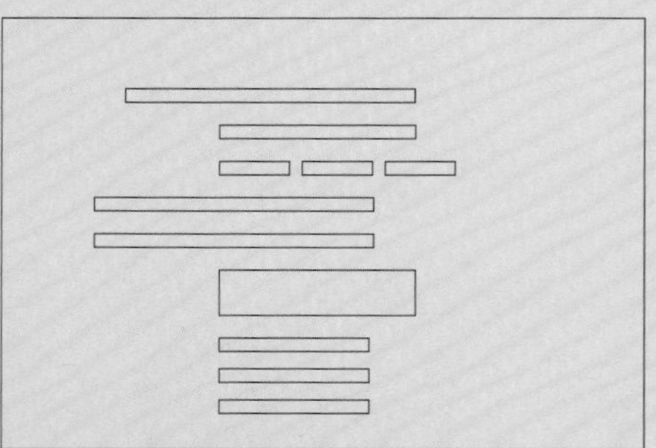

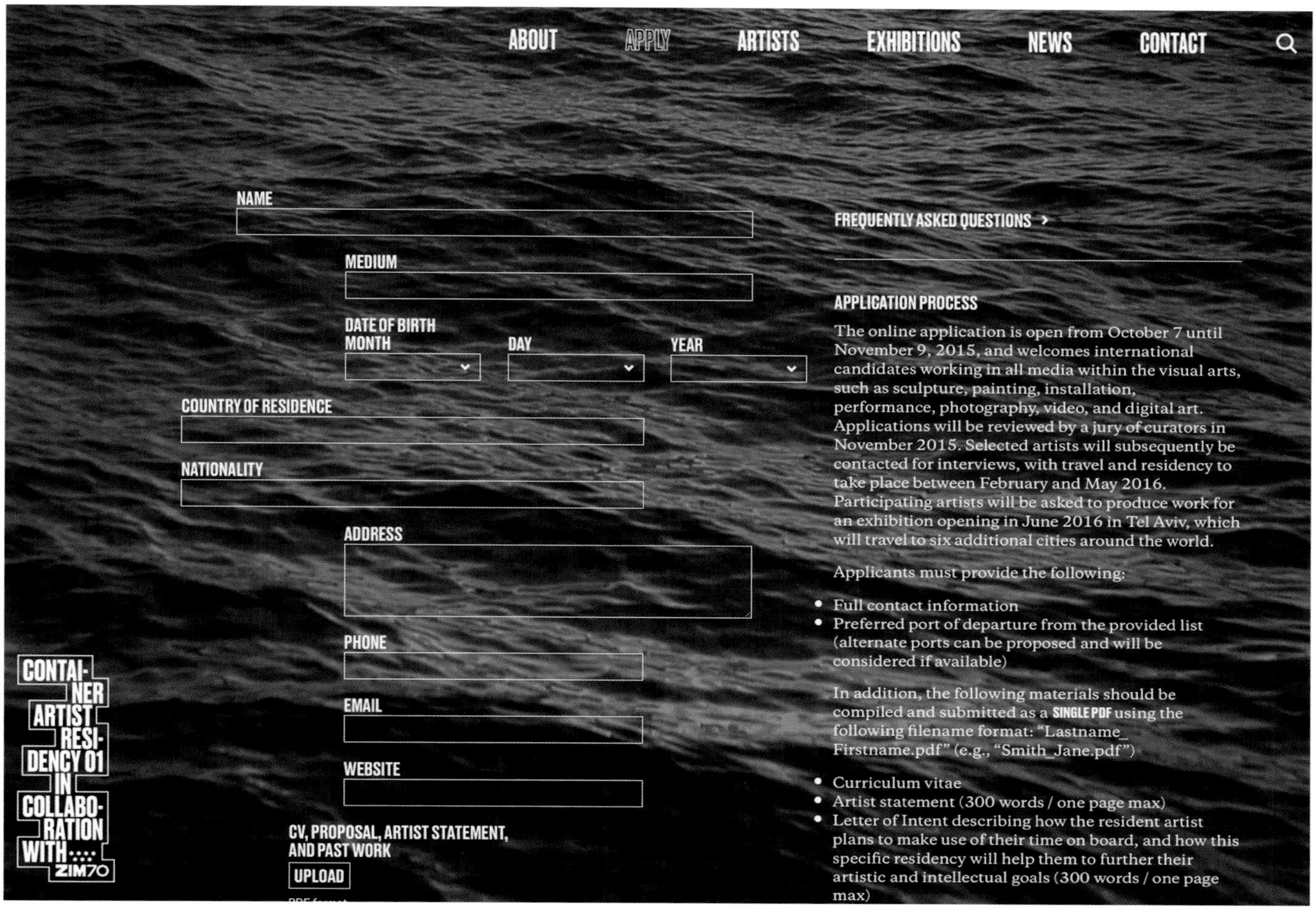

ABOUT APPLY ARTISTS EXHIBITIONS NEWS CONTACT

NAME

MEDIUM

DATE OF BIRTH
MONTH DAY YEAR

COUNTRY OF RESIDENCE

NATIONALITY

ADDRESS

PHONE

EMAIL

WEBSITE

CV, PROPOSAL, ARTIST STATEMENT, AND PAST WORK

UPLOAD

CONTAI-NER ARTIST RESI-DENCY 01 IN COLLABO-RATION WITH ZIM70

FREQUENTLY ASKED QUESTIONS >

APPLICATION PROCESS

The online application is open from October 7 until November 9, 2015, and welcomes international candidates working in all media within the visual arts, such as sculpture, painting, installation, performance, photography, video, and digital art. Applications will be reviewed by a jury of curators in November 2015. Selected artists will subsequently be contacted for interviews, with travel and residency to take place between February and May 2016. Participating artists will be asked to produce work for an exhibition opening in June 2016 in Tel Aviv, which will travel to six additional cities around the world.

Applicants must provide the following:

- Full contact information
- Preferred port of departure from the provided list (alternate ports can be proposed and will be considered if available)

In addition, the following materials should be compiled and submitted as a SINGLE PDF using the following filename format: "Lastname_Firstname.pdf" (e.g., "Smith_Jane.pdf")

- Curriculum vitae
- Artist statement (300 words / one page max)
- Letter of Intent describing how the resident artist plans to make use of their time on board, and how this specific residency will help them to further their artistic and intellectual goals (300 words / one page max)

Uniform

Design Agency/
Somewhere Else

URL/
www.theuniform.com.sg

Uniform is a communications, content, and branding studio, where they craft bespoke brand stories and tailor unique identities.

A new site that is both responsive and expressive of Uniform's brand personality loaded with multiple customized templates which provides flexibility for their different forms of content was designed and built. The seemingly traditional layout is given exciting elements and a ruler-like headline and breaths refreshing images.

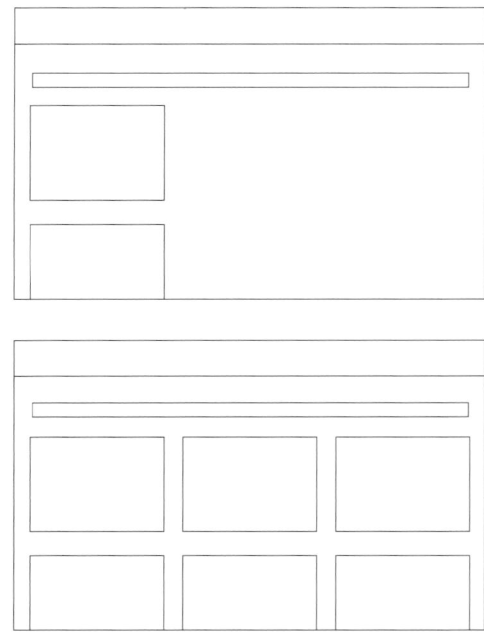

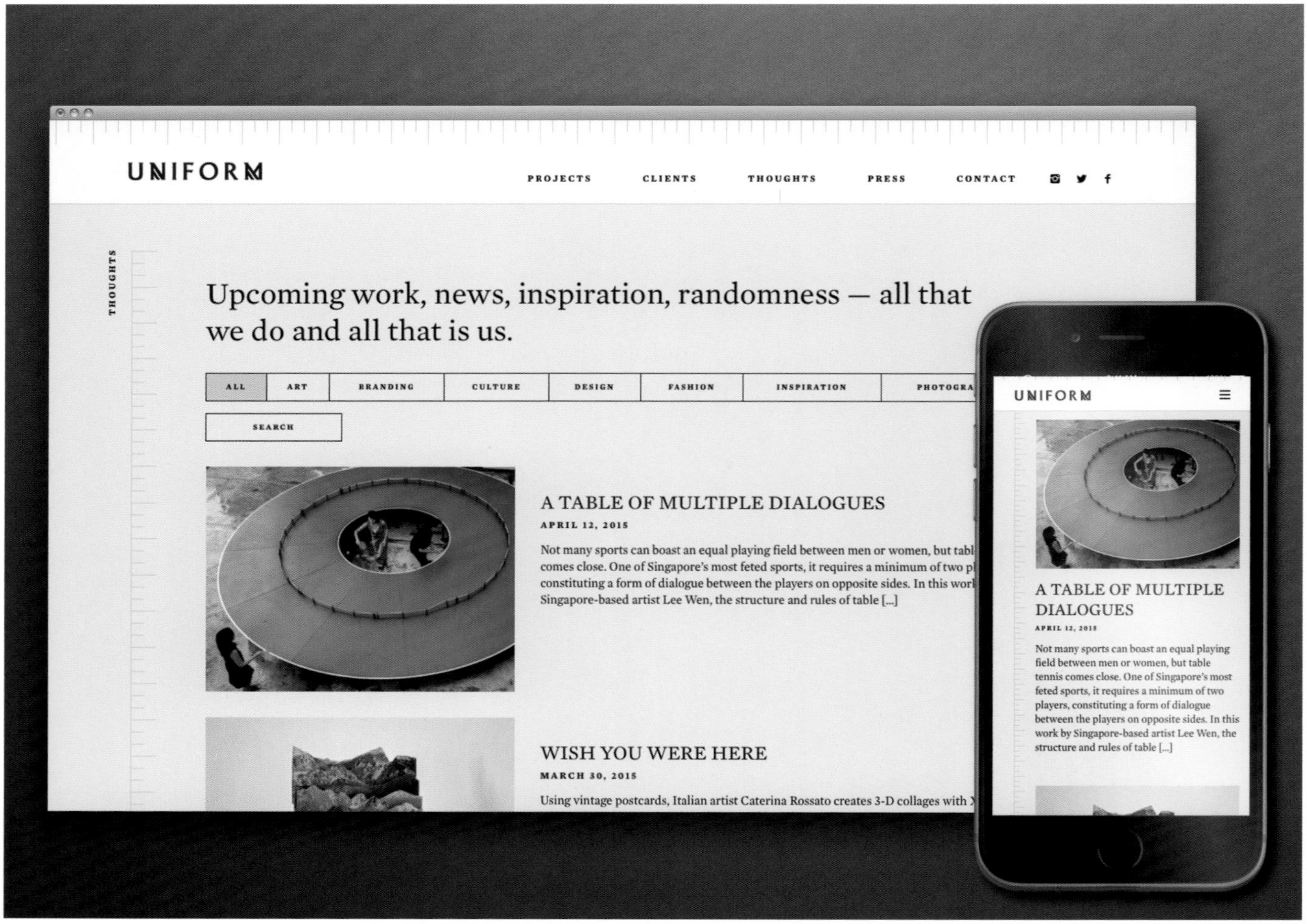

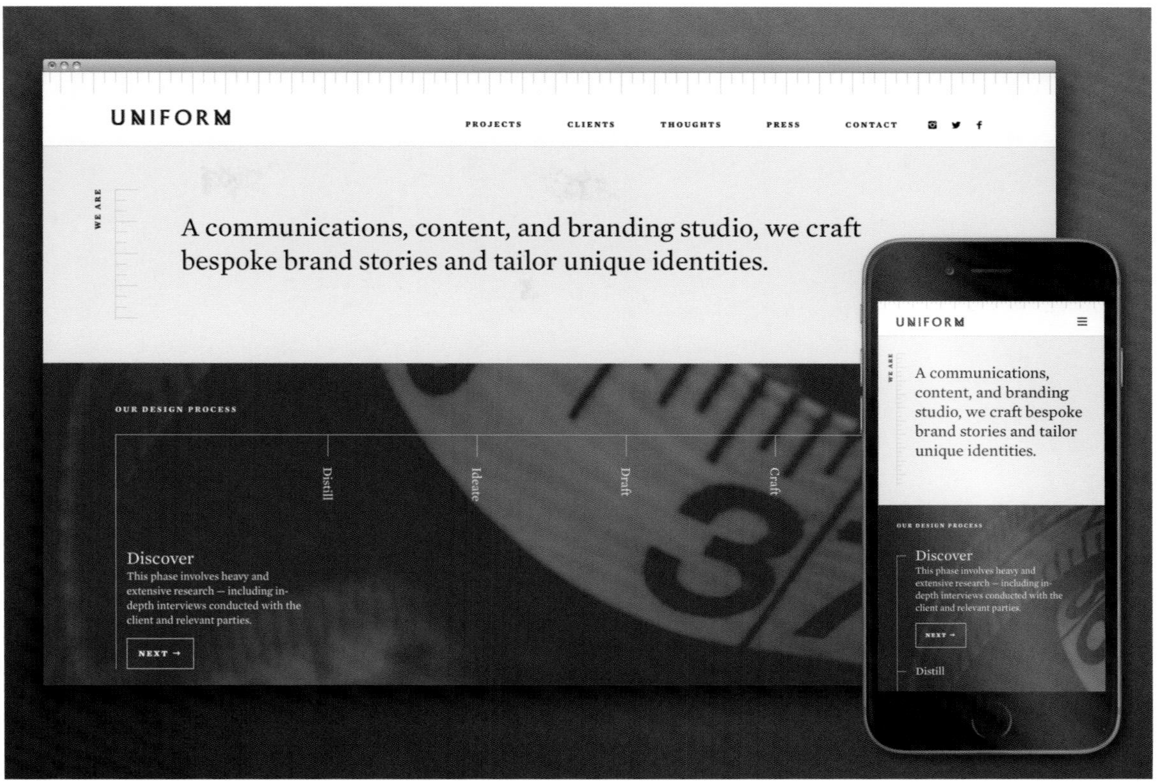

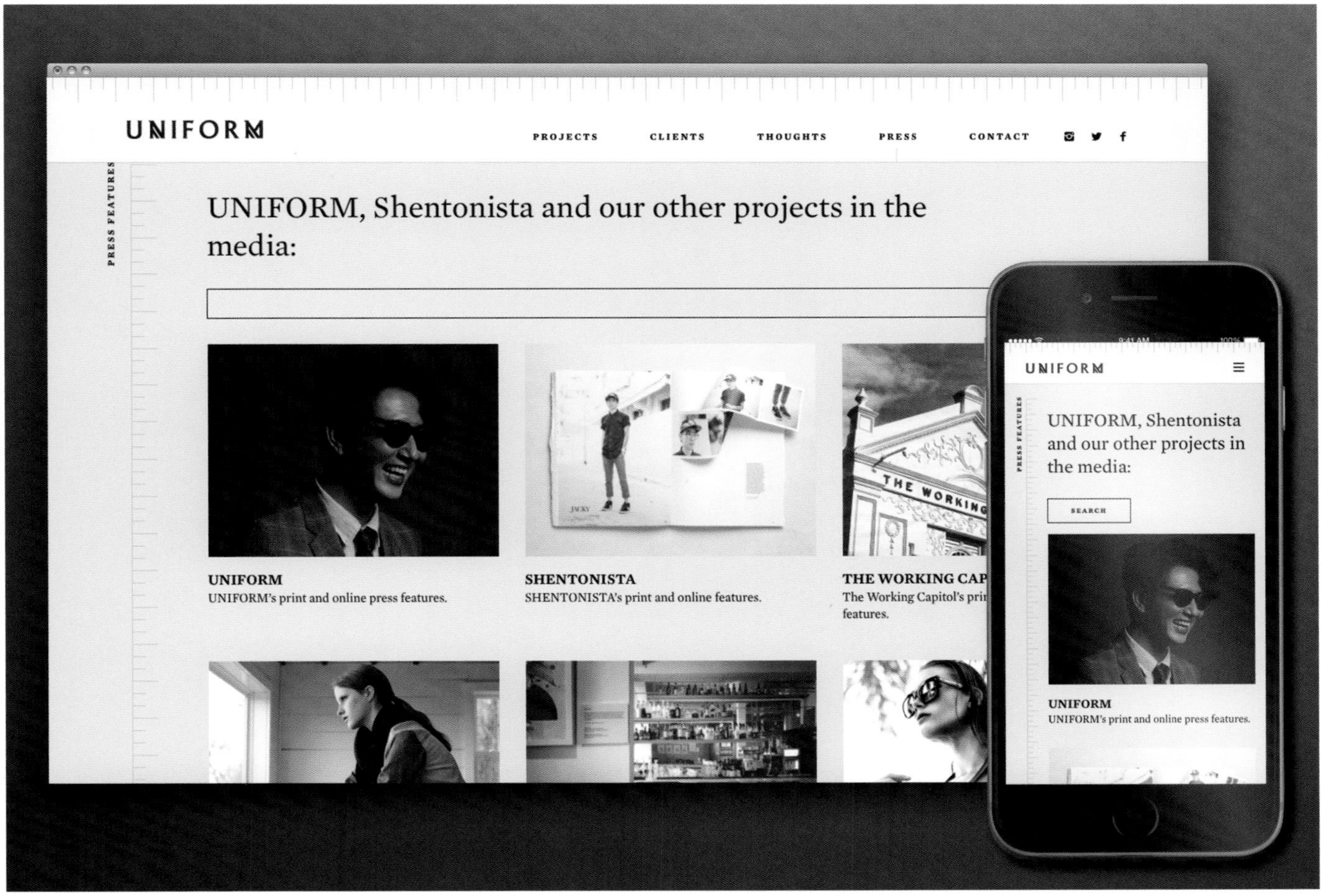

UNIFORM
PROJECTS CLIENTS THOUGHTS PRESS CONTACT
PRESS FEATURES
UNIFORM, Shentonista and our other projects in the media:
UNIFORM
UNIFORM's print and online press features.
SHENTONISTA
SHENTONISTA's print and online features.
THE WORKING CAP
The Working Capitol's pri features.
UNIFORM
PRESS FEATURES
UNIFORM, Shentonista and our other projects in the media:
SEARCH
UNIFORM
UNIFORM's print and online press features.

ANNE DE GRIJFF

Design Agency/
Mainstudio

Art Direction/
Edwin Van Gelder, Adriaan Mellegers

Design/
Edwin Van Gelder, Adriaan Mellegers

Copywriting/
Mo Veld

Photography/
Koos Breukel, Diana Scherer

URL/
http://annedegrijff.com

Anne de Grijff is a Dutch fashion designer. She creates capsules for each of what she has termed, "characters." The brand's identity is centered upon the concept of made-to measure, using leather and jerseys, pure wool, luxurious synthetics, and fine silks. Reflecting that material palette is a flexible grid incorporating the shapes: a square, circle, cross, and plus sign. The framing bold lines of the identity's graphics can be deconstructed and reconfigured into countless compositions to create an infinite number of such shapes. The site's landing page extends vertically in Roman numerals to structure its navigation: characters, wardrobe, salon, curriculum, and contact, while Dutch photographer Koos Breukel captures De Grijff's characters in the core of the brand's digital communication.

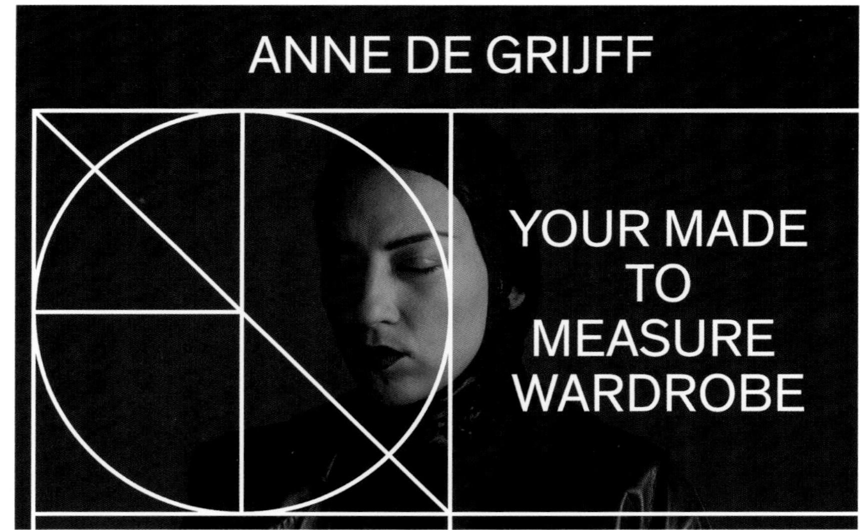

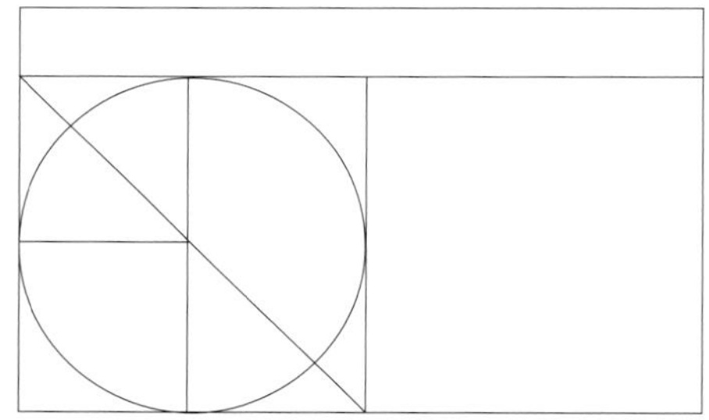

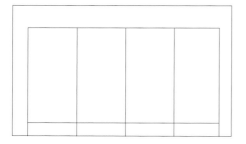

annedegrijff.com

Unfold

× Cut in front blazer navy blue fleece wool

× Cut in cross trousers navy blue fleece wool

× Basic top black polyester

annedegrijff.com

Salon Amsterdam

Salon Amsterdam

Anne de Grijff's approach to fashion is a plea for personal

42 | 54
Belgian Sportswear

Design Agency/
Codefrisko & Irradié

Photography/
Thomas Sweertvaegher

URL/
https://www.4254sport.com

42 | 54 is a new Belgian sport brand created by two Olympic champions. The e-commerce website gives prominence to the photography with full bleed images on product and shop pages that allow the user to see every detail in the clothes. The art direction is minimalist and matches the black and white products.

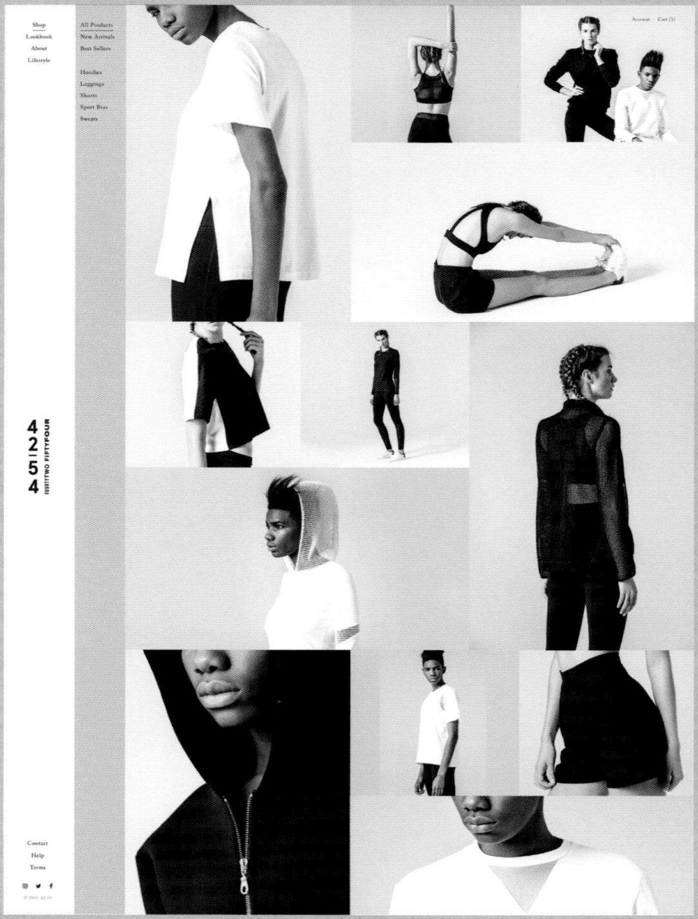

Shop
Lookbook
About
Lifestyle
Stockist
We are all heroes!
Shop
Lifestyle
Contact
Help
Terms

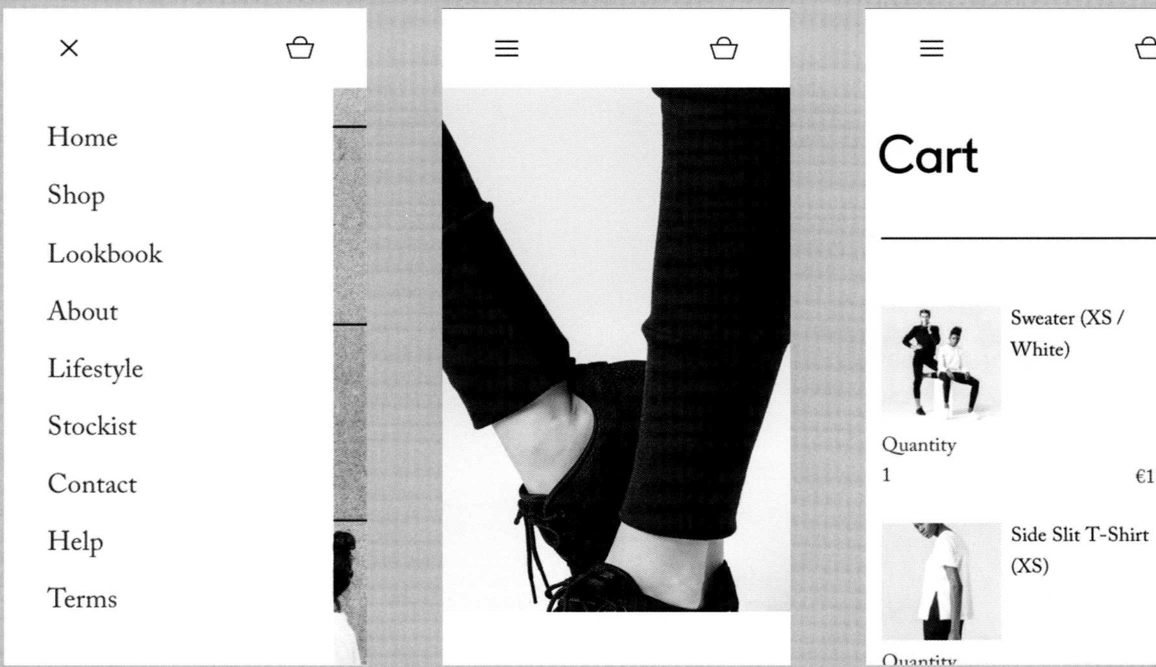
Home
Shop
Lookbook
About
Lifestyle
Stockist
Contact
Help
Terms
Cart
Sweater (XS / White)
Quantity
Price
1
€130.00
Side Slit T-Shirt (XS)

Sixpence Store Fighter Microsite

Design/
Du Haihang

Photography/
Mo Studio

Client/
Sixpence Store

Sixpence is an independent label and a store with stylized and crafted hand-sewn apparels. It was established in 2014 by two independent designers Yan Xiao and Vito. Fighter was featuring the debut collection from the duo.

The traditional, yet modern structure, achieved by artistic touches and new graphical language, resembles window-displays that infuse vintage taste. The blank spaces for information and pictogram create appropriate pause for visitors to temporarily break out from the boring scroll.

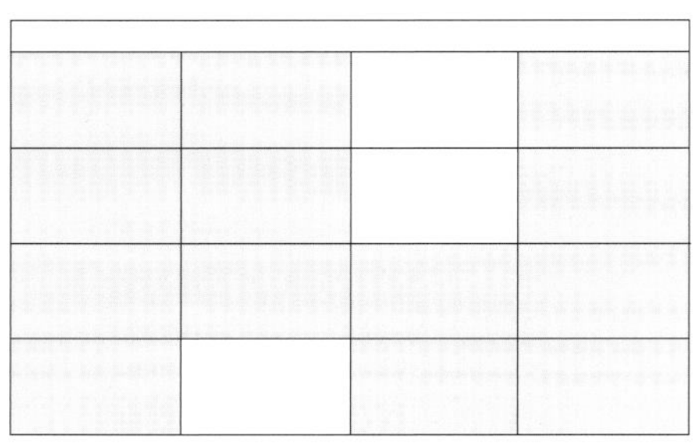

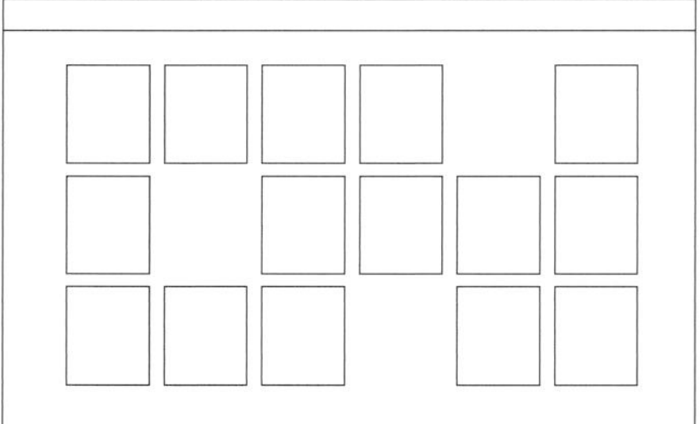

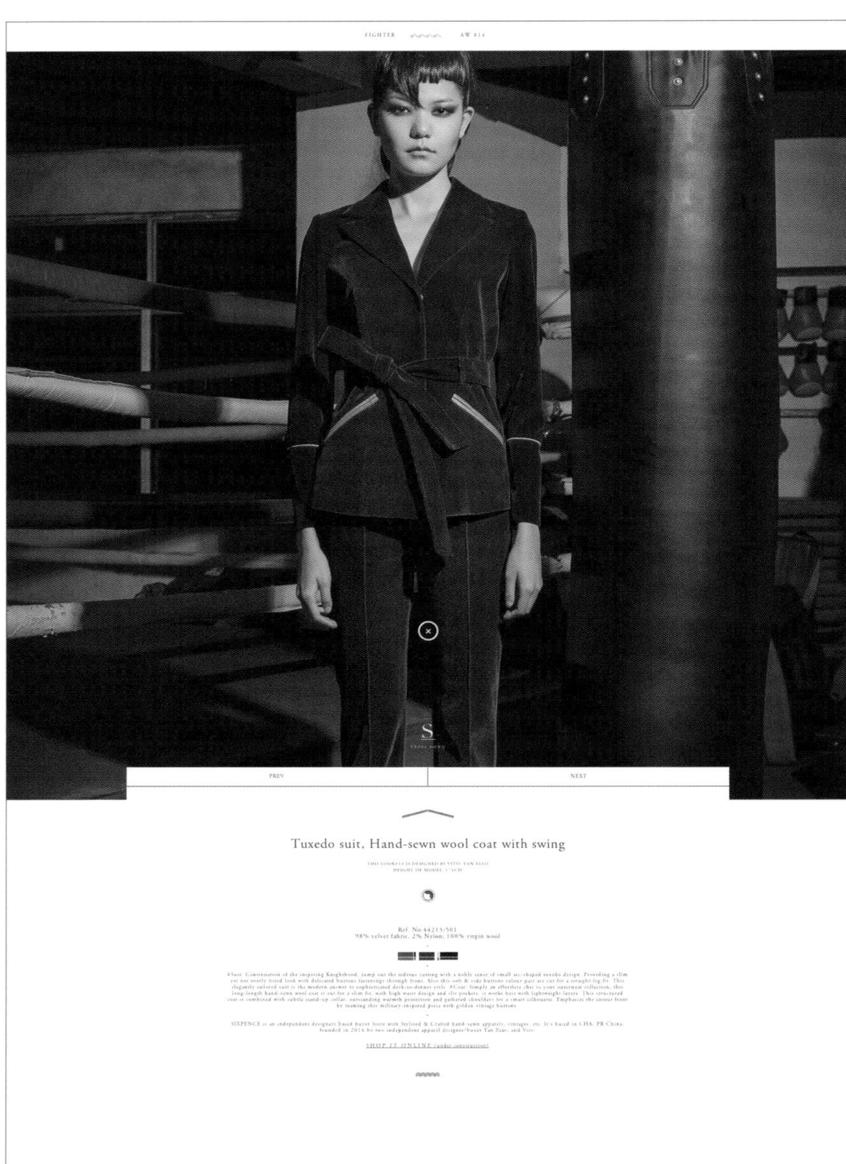

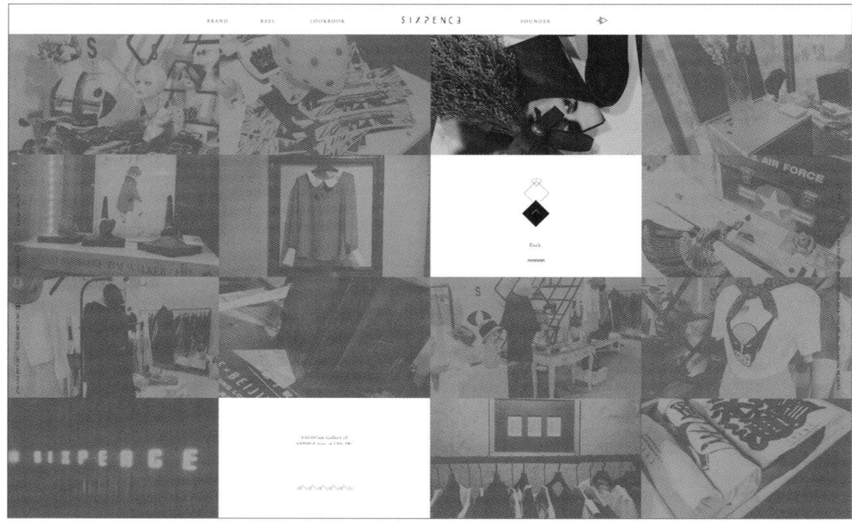

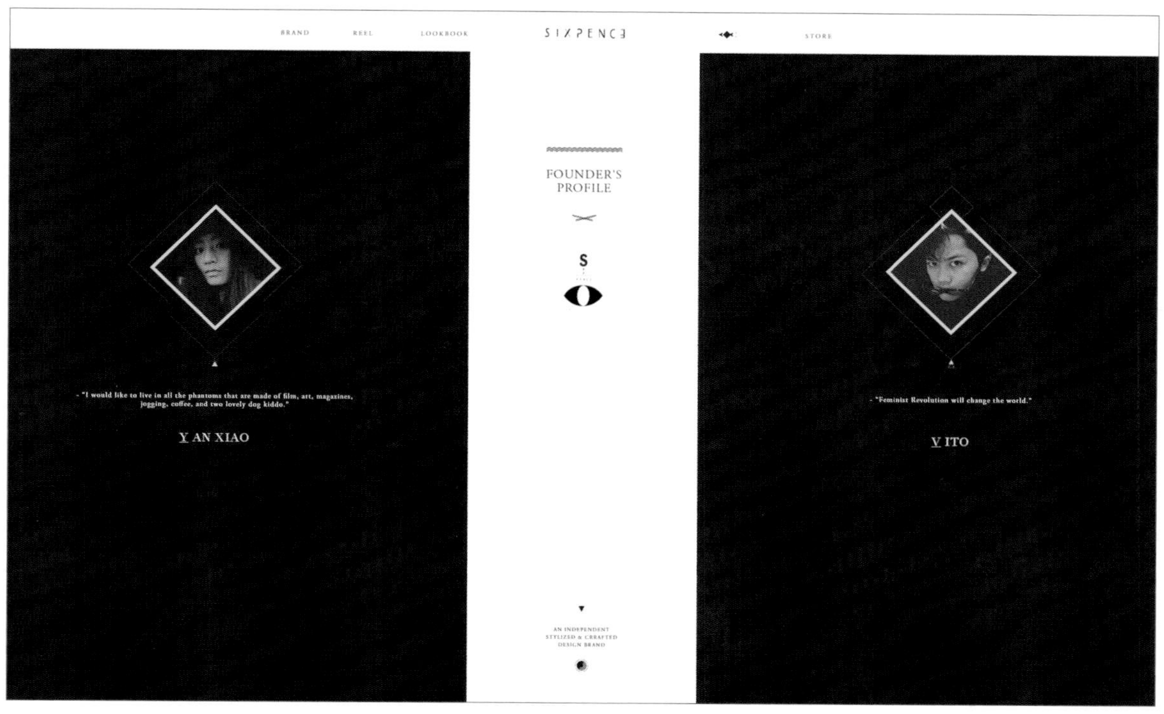
BRAND
REEL
LOOKBOOK
STORE
FOUNDER'S PROFILE
- "I would like to live in all the phantoms that are made of film, art, magazines, jogging, coffee, and two lovely dog kiddo."
Y AN XIAO
- "Feminist Revolution will change the world."
V ITO
AN INDEPENDENT STYLIZED & CRAFTED DESIGN BRAND

BRAND REEL SIXPENCE FOUNDER STORE

The debut work

SIXPENCE fighters seasonal series, one of which is named, inspired, and designed from the uncompromised fighters & knighthood, get dressed well for an inspiring winter.

Fighter

SIXPENCE 2014 A/W

206 BAI CHAO HUI, WEST JIEFANG ROAD, TIAN XIN Dist., CHANGSHA, PR CHINA.

W&CO Company Website

Design Agency/
W&CO

Development/
W&CO

URL/
http://winfieldco.com

As a design and development exercise, every two years W&CO updates their company website. This year they gave themselves a limit of 48 hours to design, develop, and deploy the site. This iteration relied on a 4 column grid layout and utilized dynamically sized and placed modules to add visual variety to the page layouts. The website was built using customized versions of Django, React JS, and Sass.

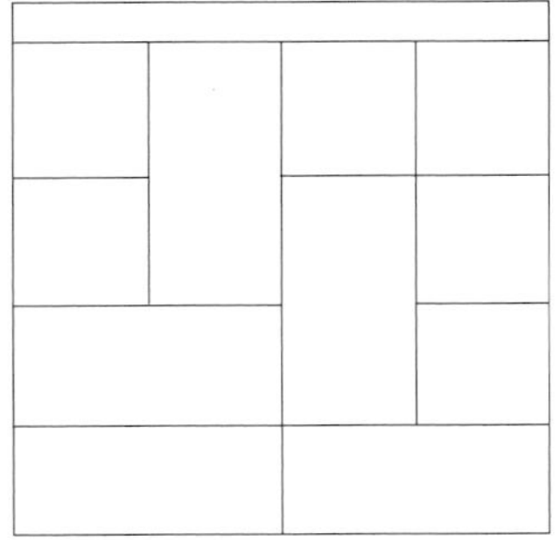

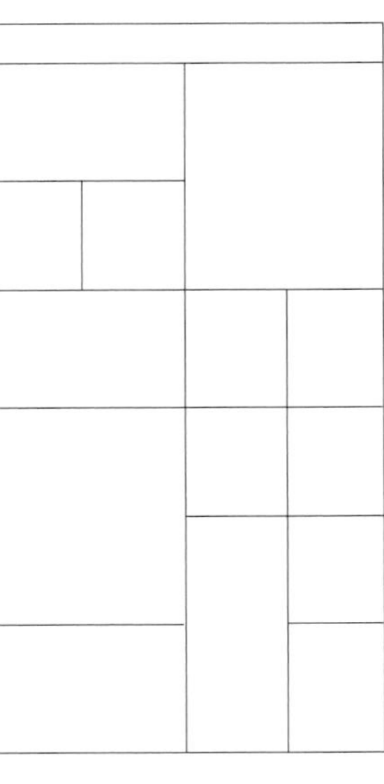

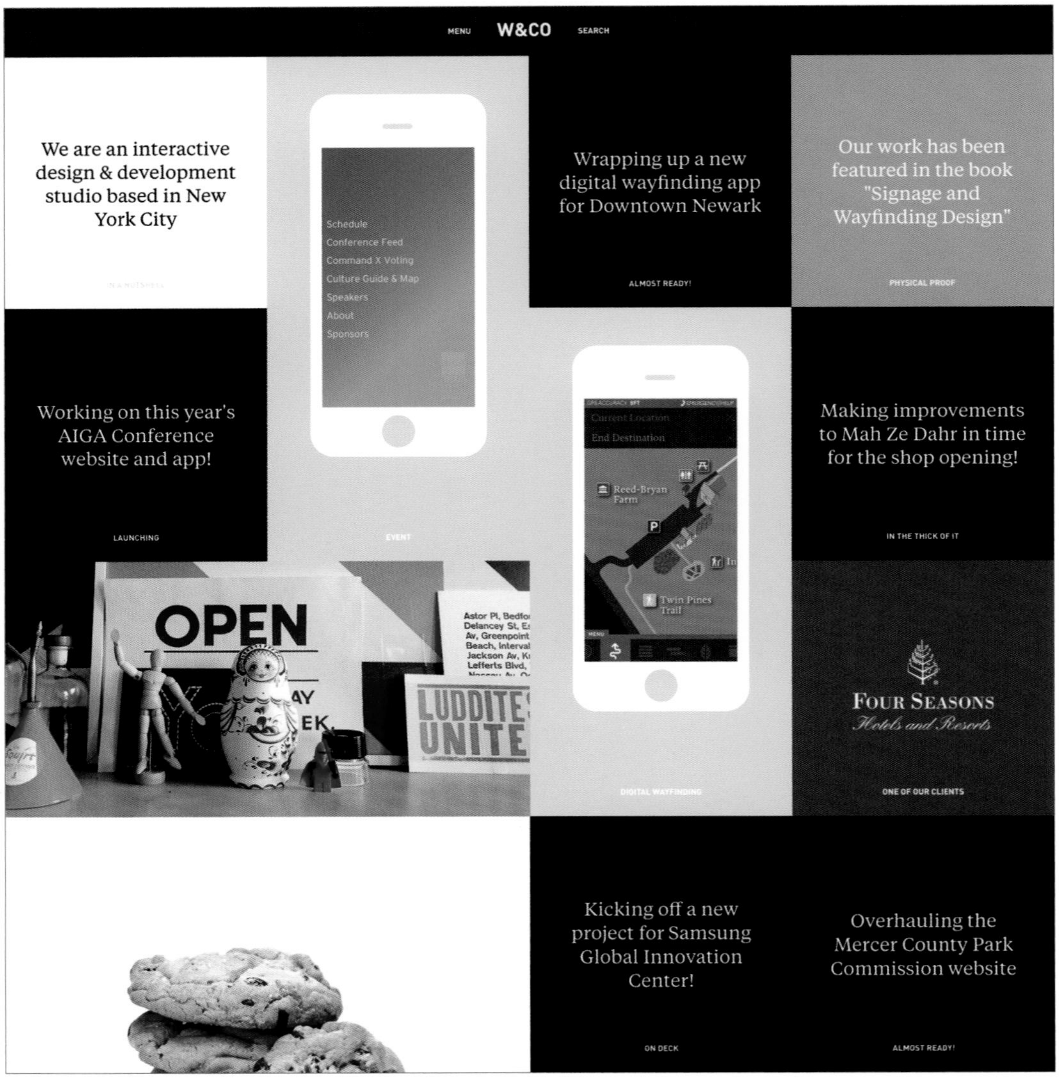

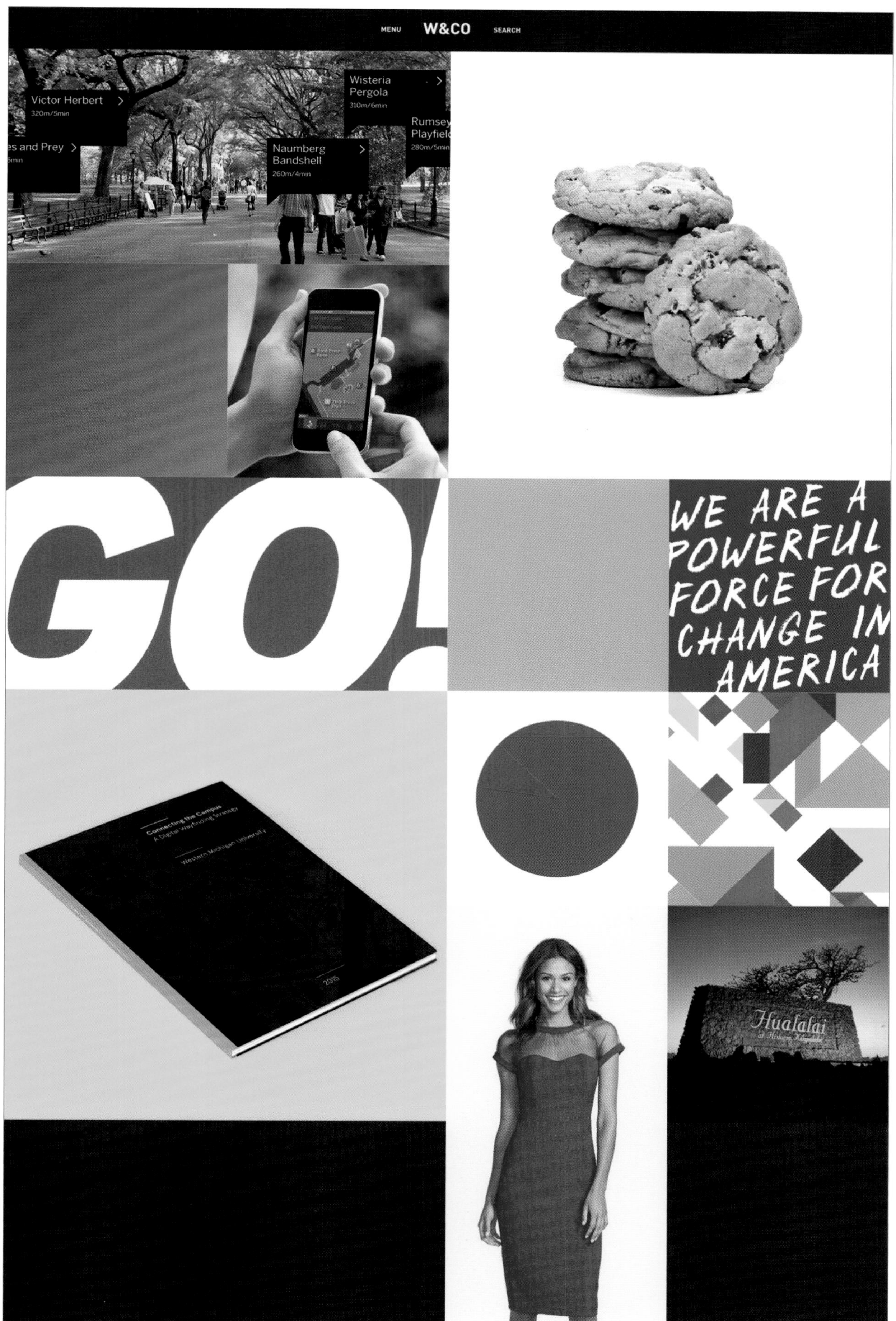
MENU
W&CO
SEARCH
Victor Herbert
320m/5min
Wisteria
Pergola
310m/6min
Naumberg
Bandshell
260m/4min
GO!
WE ARE A
POWERFUL
FORCE FOR
CHANGE IN
AMERICA
Connecting the Campus
A Digital Wayfinding Strategy
Western Michigan University
2015
Hualalai

FOLIO.2

Design/
Madelyn Bilsborough

Folio.2 is part of a series of Adobe Muse portfolio templates. The template is based around online portfolio for freelance creative's or studios/agencies. The design features a minimal layout with overlaying text and images, and simple and elegant details. Keeping the design to a minimum allowed Madelyn to focus on creating a sleek, quality look and feel through basic animation and movement.

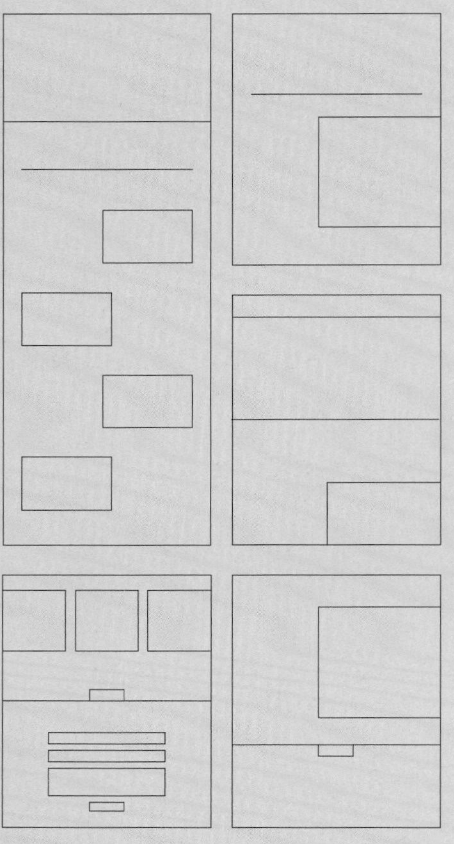

B – G

PROJECTS

Integer tristique erat non aliquet vestibulum. Aenean tempor sed tellus a mollis. Curabitur pulvinar risus sit amet.

03. *Project Name*

Integer tristique erat non aliquet vestibulum. Aenean tempor sed tellus a mollis. Curabitur pulvinar risus sit amet mi gravida luctus. Nunc ac malesuada magna.

VIEW PROJECT

B – G

PROJECT NAME

04.

Project Name

Integer tristique erat non aliquet vestibulum. Aenean tempor sed tellus a mollis. Curabitur ligula quis molestie. Suspendisse ante risus, consectetur ut eros vitae, tempus pretium diam. Vivamus laoreet tincidunt ligula non pellentesque. Pellentesque non ante consectetur, ornare enim sit amet, vulputate turpis.

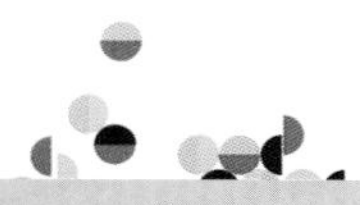

02. *Project Name*

03. *Project Name*

04. *Project Name*

SEE PROJECTS

Get in touch...

Integer tristique erat non aliquet vestibulum. Aenean tempor sed tellus a mollis. Curabitur pulvinar risus sit amet.

NAME

EMAIL

MESSAGE

SUBMIT

B – G

ABOUT

About

Integer tristique erat non aliquet vestibulum. Aenean tempor sed tellus a mollis. Curabitur pulvinar risus sit amet mi gravida luctus. Nunc ac malesuada magna. In porta eleifend massa, posuere faucibus sapien suscipit quis. Pellentesque tellus turpis, gravida vel magna quis, pulvinar facilisis libero. Sed nulla enim, aliquet nec augue a, volutpat tincidunt eros. Duis a vestibulum neque, ultricies vulputate nisi.

CLIENTS

belle

GUZMAN Y GOMEZ

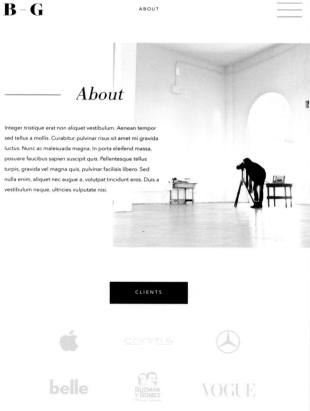

VOGUE

HAY

Design/
Emanuele Cecini

HAY was founded in 2002 and the furniture collection was launched at IMM Cologne in 2003. HAY's ambition is to encourage Danish furniture design's return to the innovative greatness of the 1950's and 1960's in a contemporary context.

HAY operates in the field between architecture and fashion bringing the statics from architecture and the dynamics from fashion.

This is a proposal for a new website.

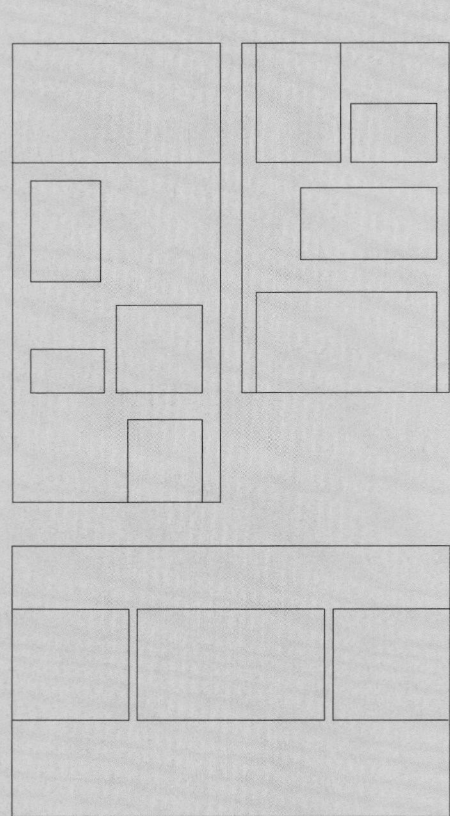

HAY has invited Ronan and Erwan Bouroullec to design a new collection of furniture for the redesigned University of Copenhagen (KUA). The collection includes a wooden chair, a bar stool and several tables.

We have attempted to create a range of educational furniture, which in form and identity has a clear dating in our age, and with it's compelling manner uncovers the current functional needs of a university. It has also been our aspiration, to distance ourselves from the slightly institutional expression of traditional educational furniture and create furniture with greater originality and a more domestic expression.

CPH30 is characterized by its slanted legs very suitable for dining room tables or

DIMENSIONS
L 200 x D 90 x H 74 cm
L 250 x D 90 x H 74 cm
L 300 x D 90 x H 74 cm
L 250 x D 120 x H 74 cm
L 300 x D 120 x H 74 cm
L 140 x D 140 x H 74 cm
L 200 x D 80 x H 105 cm

MATERIALS
Frame: Clear lacquered oak

COLOURS
Oak, clear lacquer
Oak, soaped
Black, stained

LINOLEUM COLOURS
Black
Grey
Green
Off white

WE LOVE WHAT WE DO

Show more →

HAY operates in the field between architecture and fashion bringing the statics from architecture and the dynamics from fashion.
We are ambitious in the field of innovation and the use of cutting edge technology.
HAY celebrates the uncomplicated design and strives to stay solid, straight-forward, joyful and functional.

HAY AND WH
EXHIBITION IN MILAN

Show more →

HAY and Wrong for Hay have moved to Milan for one week exhibiting in Via Ciovassino during Salone del Mobile. It is the first time since 2008 that HAY has exhibited in here and it is the Milanese debut for Wrong for Hay.

As a key feature of the installation, an edited selection of products will be sold in the HAY Mini Market, an on-site pop-up shop that will allow visitors, both trade and public, to purchase HAY and Wrong for Hay accessories and textiles.

COLLECTION

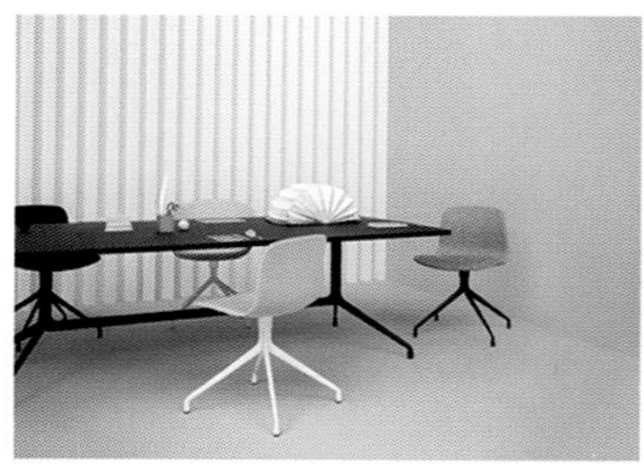

CHAIRS

LOUNGE

TABLES

STORAGE

OFFICE

RUGS

DECORATION

MIRRORS

OTHERS

HAY

DESIGNERS

RONAN & ERWAN BOUROULLEC

Born in 1971/1976

Ronan (born 1971) and Erwan Bouroullec (born 1976) are brothers and designers based in Paris. They have been working together for about fifteen years bonded by diligence and challenged by their distinct personalities.

Designs of the Bouroullecs are part of select international museums' permanent collections such as the Musée National d'Art Moderne Centre Pompidou and the Musée des Arts Décoratifs in Paris, the Museum of Modern Art in New York, the Art Institute of Chicago,

STORES

HAY HOUSE

Oestergade 61, 2nd-3rd Floor
DK - 1100 Copenhagen K
DENMARK

Phone: +45 42 820 820
Mon-Fri 10-18
Sat 10-17

HAY CPH

Pilestraede 29-31
DK - 1112 COPENHAGEN K
DENMARK

Phone: +45 42 820 820
Mon-Fri 10-18
Sat 10-17

Brands&People

Design Agency/
FACE

Design Direction/
Rik Bracho, Gerardo Ortiz

Art Direction/
Rik Bracho, Gerardo Ortiz

Design/
Rik Bracho

Photography/
Salvador Hernández Cueva

URL/
http://www.brands.mx/

Brands&People is a brand-centric company focused on mobilizing commercial brands in Latin America with over 20-year experience. During their renaming, the agency commissioned FACE to design a new identity and communication, focus, and visual language. FACE worked in collaboration with Gerardo Ortiz and Emmanuel Moreau on this project. The aim was to have a commercial but smart approach by mixing elements such as pop culture, a modular identity system, and sharp design elements. From the color code to the typography, everything was measured to have a coherent, strong, yet appealing visual identity.

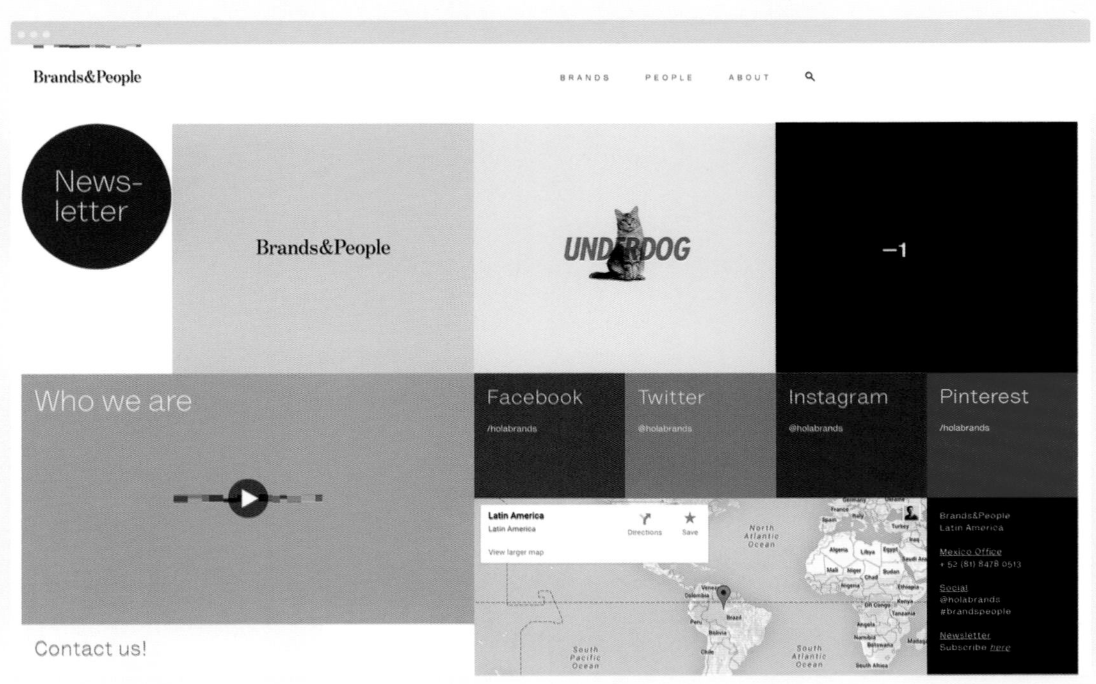

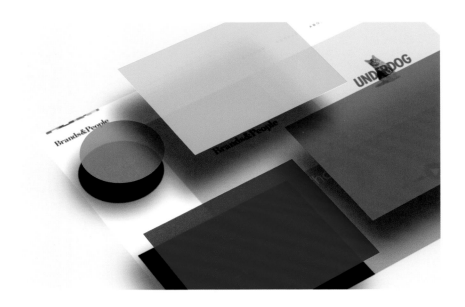

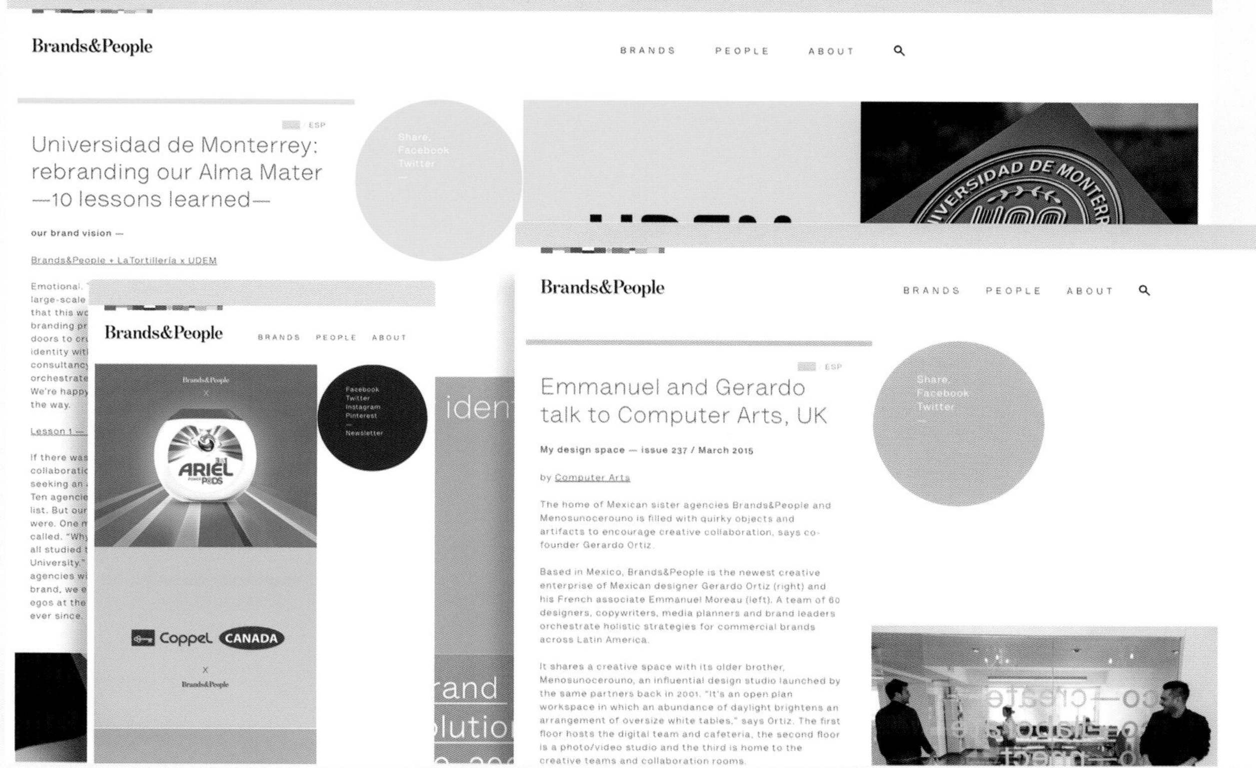
Brands&People
BRANDS PEOPLE ABOUT
Universidad de Monterrey: rebranding our Alma Mater —10 lessons learned—
our brand vision —
Brands&People + LaTortillería x UDEM
Emmanuel and Gerardo talk to Computer Arts, UK
My design space — issue 237 / March 2015
by Computer Arts
The home of Mexican sister agencies Brands&People and Menosunocerouno is filled with quirky objects and artifacts to encourage creative collaboration, says co-founder Gerardo Ortiz.
Based in Mexico, Brands&People is the newest creative enterprise of Mexican designer Gerardo Ortiz (right) and his French associate Emmanuel Moreau (left). A team of 60 designers, copywriters, media planners and brand leaders orchestrate holistic strategies for commercial brands across Latin America.
It shares a creative space with its older brother, Menosunocerouno, an influential design studio launched by the same partners back in 2001. "It's an open plan workspace in which an abundance of daylight brightens an arrangement of oversize white tables," says Ortiz. The first floor hosts the digital team and cafeteria, the second floor is a photo/video studio and the third is home to the creative teams and collaboration rooms.

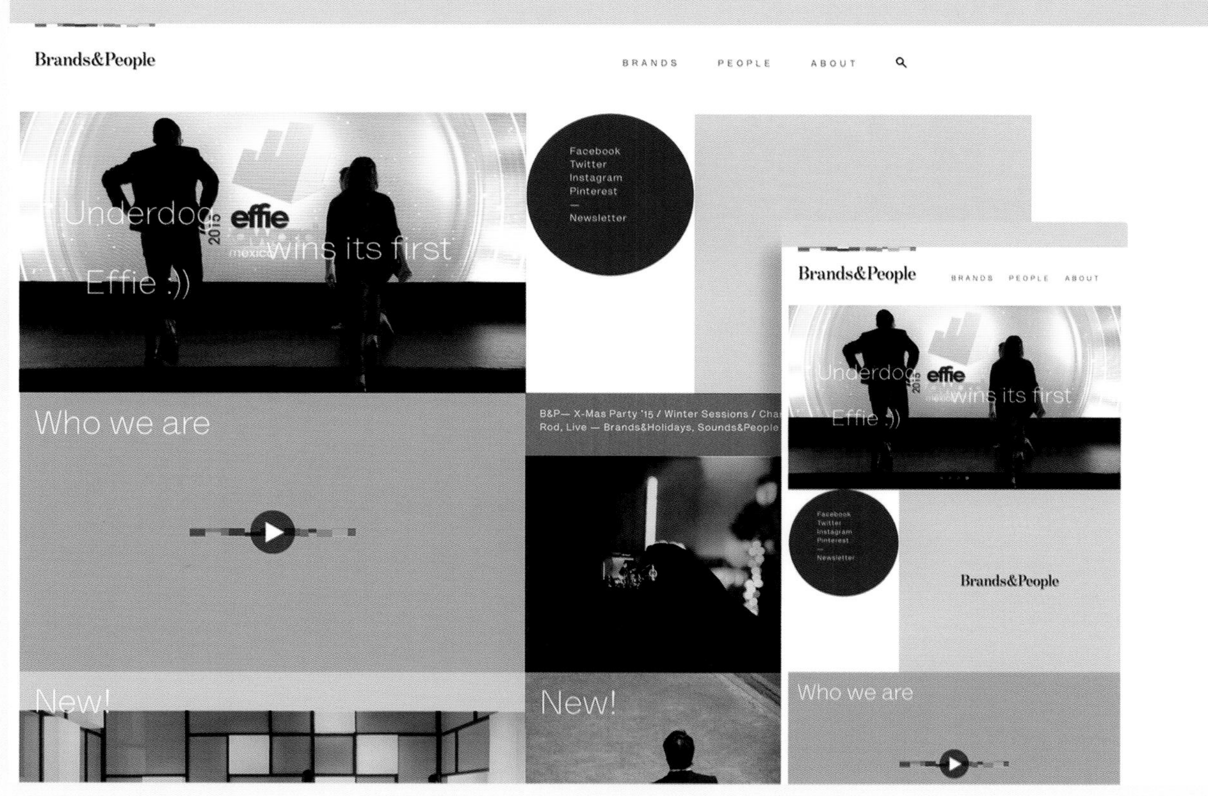
Brands&People
BRANDS PEOPLE ABOUT
Underdog wins its first Effie :))
Facebook
Twitter
Instagram
Pinterest
Newsletter
Who we are
B&P— X-Mas Party '15 / Winter Sessions / Cha
Rod, Live — Brands&Holidays, Sounds&People
New!
New!
Who we are

JH.ZANE

Design/
Florent Gomez

URL/
https://j-h-zane.myshopify.com

JH.ZANE is a fashion label based in London run by creative director and chief fashion designer Juhao Zeng. Florent Gomez balances functionality and aesthetic with artistic values based around an openness and unconventional structure that unites the brand values and aesthetic sensitivities.

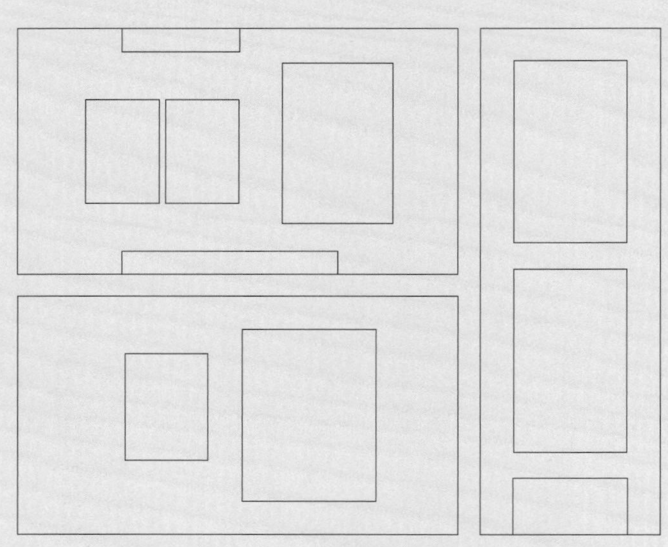

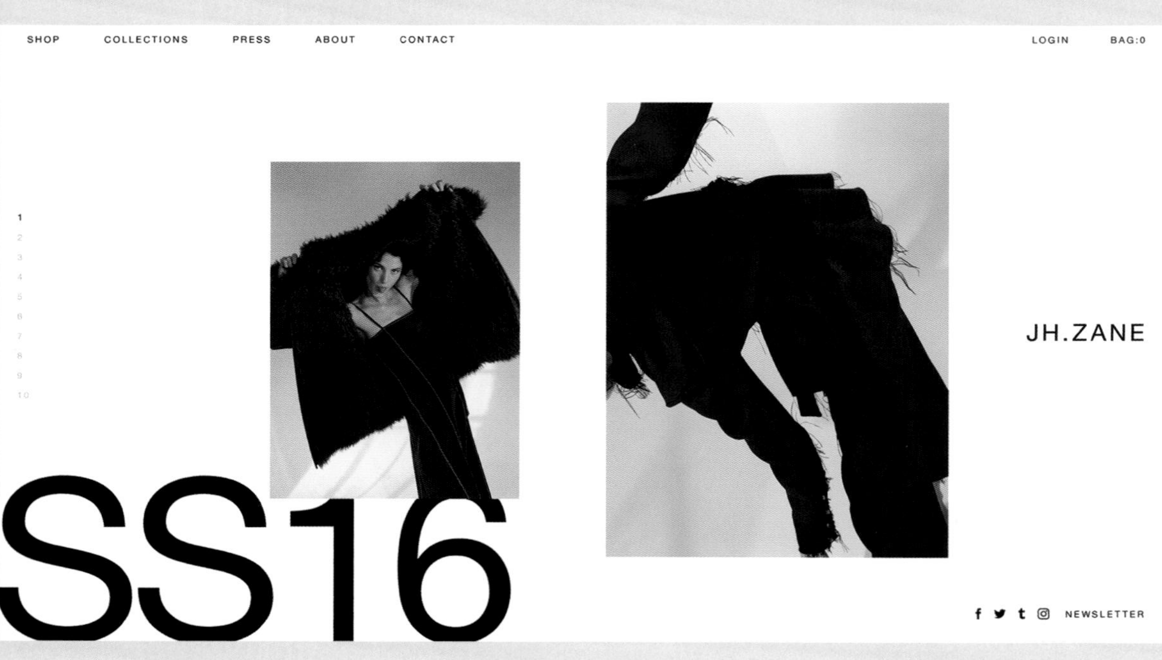

SHOP COLLECTIONS PRESS ABOUT CONTACT

ALL AW15
TOP SS15
SHIRT AW16
SKIRT SS16
TROUSERS
DRESS
OUTWEAR
SALE

DRESS

SHOP
ALL
TOP
SHIRT
SKIRT
TROUSERS
DRESS
OUTWEAR
SALE

COLLECTIONS
AW15
SS15
AW16
SS16

PRESS

ABOUT

CONTACT

LOGIN BAG:0

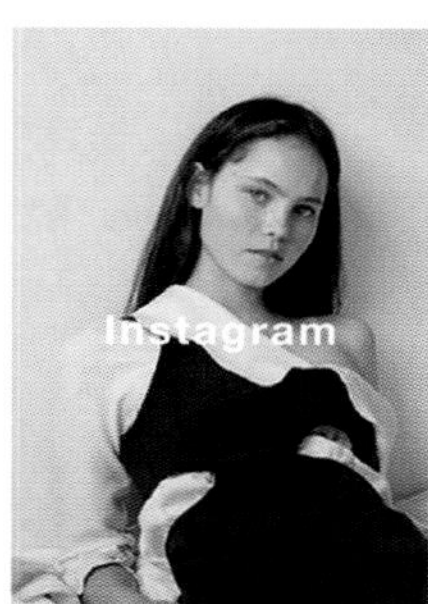

SCHÖN! MAGAZINE

JH.ZANE

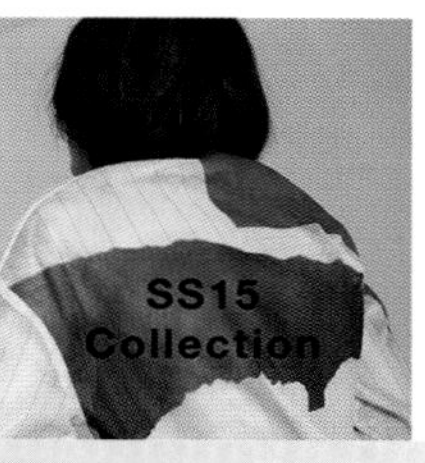

NEWSLETTER

SHOP
ALL
TOP
SHIRT
SKIRT
TROUSERS
DRESS
OUTWEAR
SALE

COLLECTIONS
AW15
SS15
AW16
SS16

PRESS

LOGIN BAG:0

ABOU

SALE

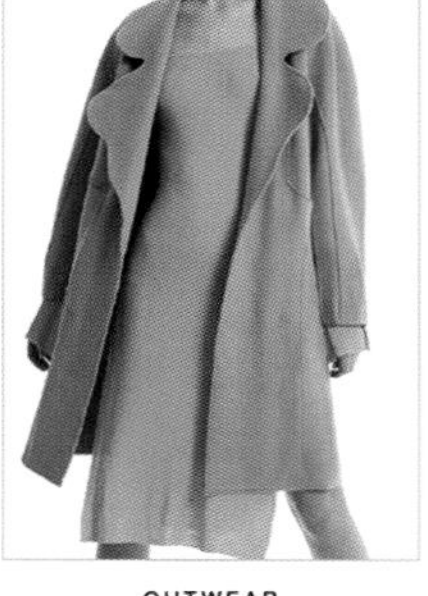

OUTWEAR

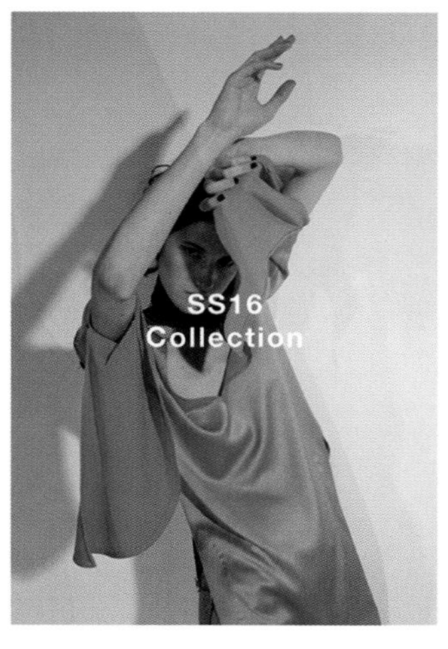

JH.ZANE

NEWSLETTER

JH.ZANE
Bag:0
SS16

JH.ZANE
Bag:0

Bag:0
PETRIe
Contributor Magazine

SS16
Collection
The Zournal
Instagram
Off Black Magazine
Press Updates
AW15
Collection
SS15
Collection
NEWSLETTER
Delivery
Sizing
Returns
Shipping
Terms&Conditions
Stockists

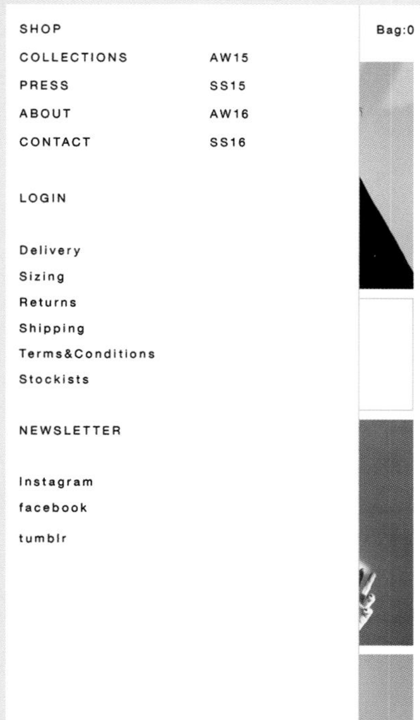
SHOP
COLLECTIONS
PRESS
ABOUT
CONTACT
AW15
SS15
AW16
SS16
LOGIN
Delivery
Sizing
Returns
Shipping
Terms&Conditions
Stockists
NEWSLETTER
Instagram
facebook
tumblr
Bag:0

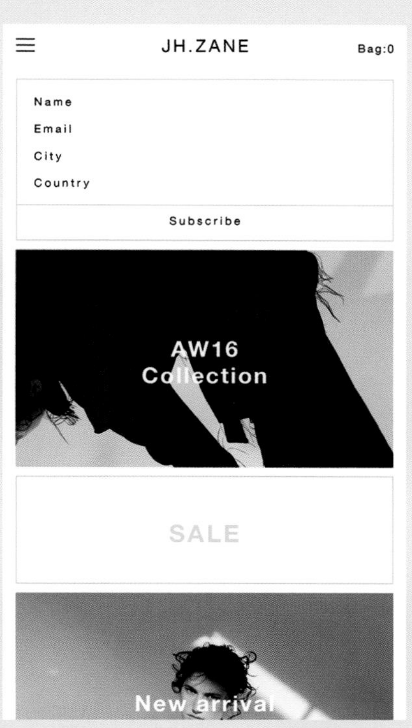
JH.ZANE
Bag:0
Name
Email
City
Country
Subscribe
AW16
Collection
SALE
New arrival

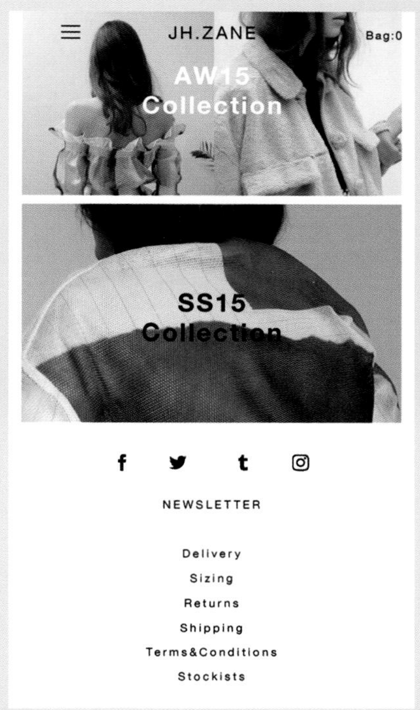
JH.ZANE
Bag:0
AW15
Collection
SS15
Collection
NEWSLETTER
Delivery
Sizing
Returns
Shipping
Terms&Conditions
Stockists

JH.ZANE
Bag:0
-30%
Sky Melted Long Coat
725.00 500.00 Gbp
Sky Melted Long Coat
500.00 Gbp
Sky Melted Long Coat
500.00 Gbp
Sky Melted Long Coat
500.00 Gbp

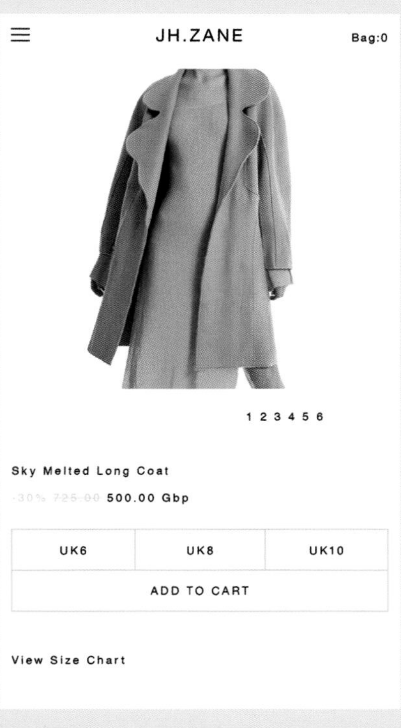
JH.ZANE
Bag:0
1 2 3 4 5 6
Sky Melted Long Coat
-30% 725.00 500.00 Gbp
UK6
UK8
UK10
ADD TO CART
View Size Chart

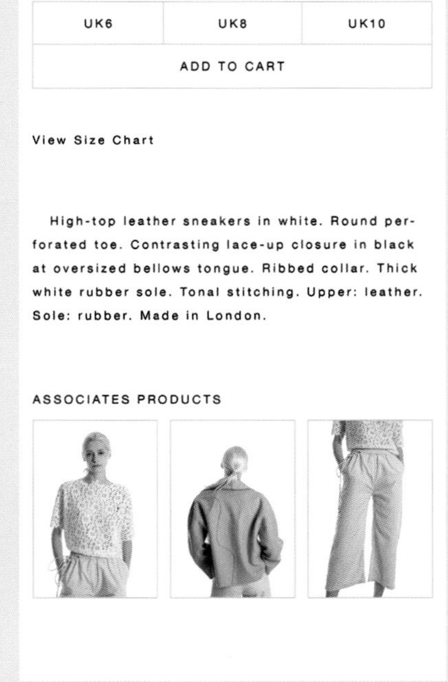
JH.ZANE
Bag:0
UK6
UK8
UK10
ADD TO CART
View Size Chart
High-top leather sneakers in white. Round perforated toe. Contrasting lace-up closure in black at oversized bellows tongue. Ribbed collar. Thick white rubber sole. Tonal stitching. Upper: leather. Sole: rubber. Made in London.
ASSOCIATES PRODUCTS

Energy University

Design/
Javier Arizu

This website was designed for Energy University, an educational center focused on the research and development of energy. The identity embraces an academic and neutral structure, which allows the faculty to identify and organize all its different activities. On the other hand, each of the areas explores a different way of representing energy, thus achieving its own personality regardless belonging to the same structure.

By combining an academic structure together with an expressive visual language Javier Arizu and his team embrace the university's education approach: a fusion of all disciplines with energy at its center core.

Energy University
Focusing Future

University
Editions
Theatre
Festival 2013
Blog

Log in
Search
Contact

Energy University, is a non-profit learning institution in Silicon Valley whose stated aim is to assemble, educate and inspire a cadre of leaders who strive to understand and facilitate the development of exponentially advancing technologies and apply, focus and guide these tools to address humanity's grand challenges on energy.

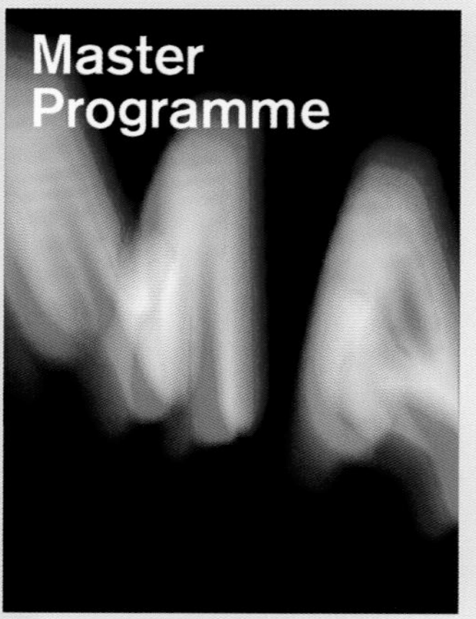

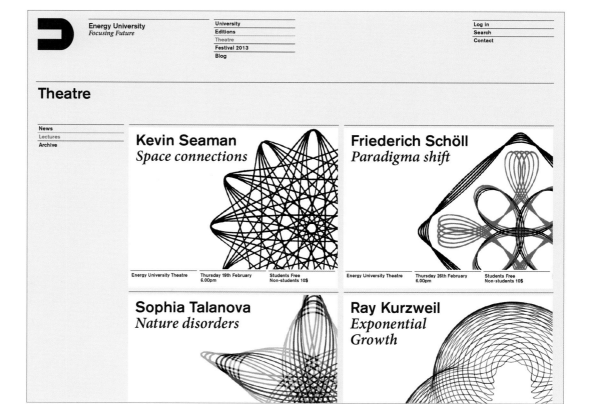

Energy University
Focusing Future

University
Editions
Theatre
Festival 2013
Blog

Academics
Admissions
Faculty
Alumni

Log in
Search
Contact

Faculty

Filter by
BA
MA
Biotechnology
Political Managment
Neurophysics
Sustainability
Renewable energies
Ecologic Systems
Event Horizon
Focusing Future

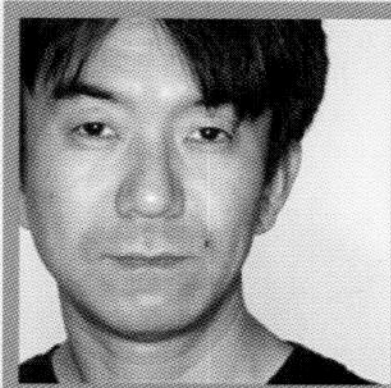

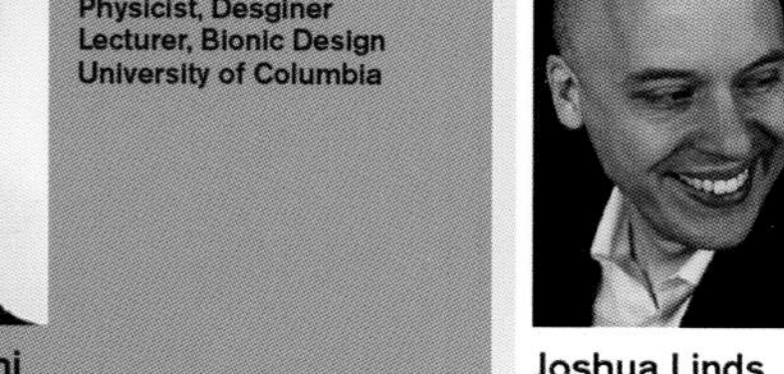

Nagano, 1958
Physicist, Desginer
Lecturer, Bionic Design
University of Columbia

Hideshi Yamaguchi
Biotechnology

Since 1975 he has been senior designer, consultant, and has maintained a professional practice with an extensive roster of built work ranging from public structures (Federal Reserve Bank 3C Region, Remington Park, Moore College of Art Auditorium Renovation) to social work and investigation, He is principal of Bionic World, in Philadelphia. He has taught at the University of Pennsylvania, Yale University, Tel Aviv University, and others. Here at Energy University, he has held seminars on Tectonics and on Bionics, and has taught design studios in the undergraduate, graduate and thesis programs, continuously since 1972.

site: www.bionicworld.com
twitter: @Hideshi_Yamaguchi ×

Joshua Linds
Renewable energies

Thomas Reuter
Focusing future

Robert Donovan
Biotechnology

Victoria Gillespie
Event Horizon

Bryan Doyle
Social energies

Himano Kokoro
Ecologic systems

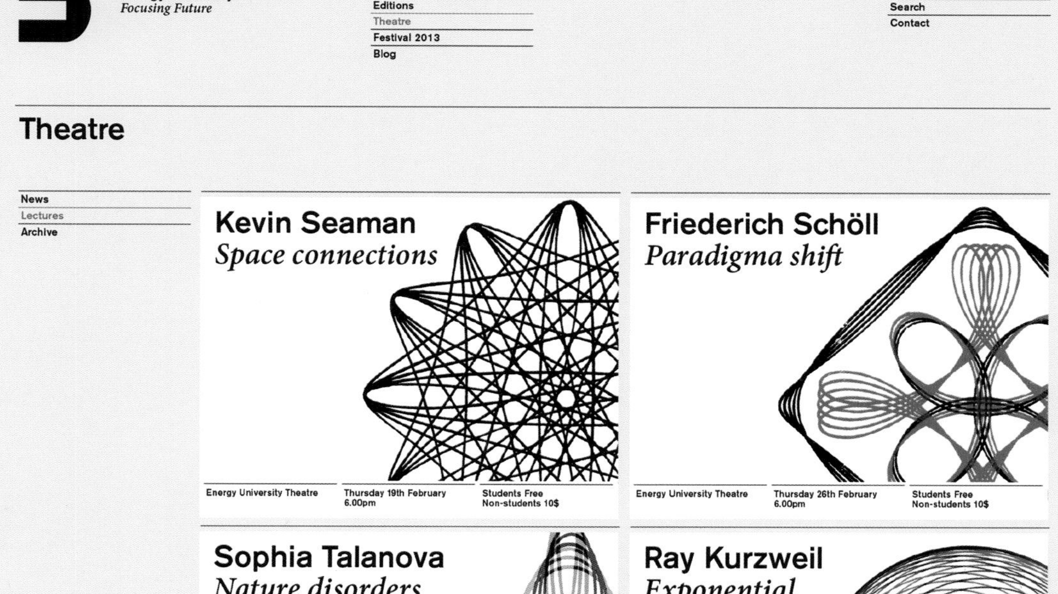

Enter the Museum

Design/
Manon Moreau

Texts & Photos/
Natural History Museum of Nantes

The site is a conceptual project for Natural History Museum of Nantes.

With refreshing and bold frameworks, the site is systematically organized and generates narrative by impressive images and titles. The grid, being the skeleton of the site, interprets the adventurous spirit of the museum to its visitors.

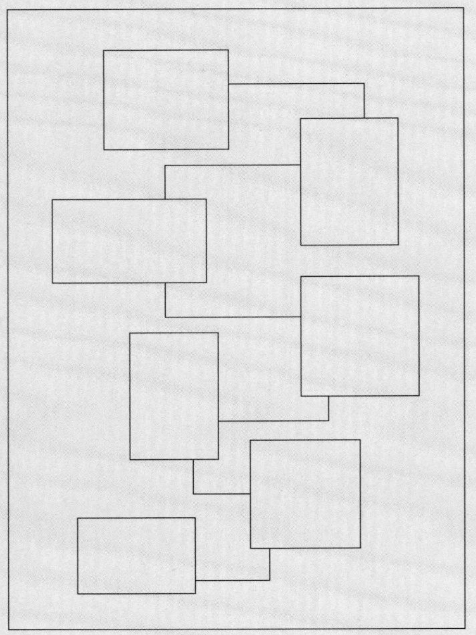

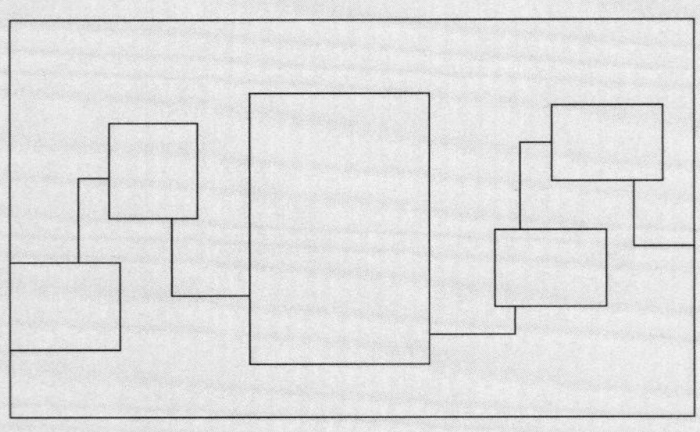

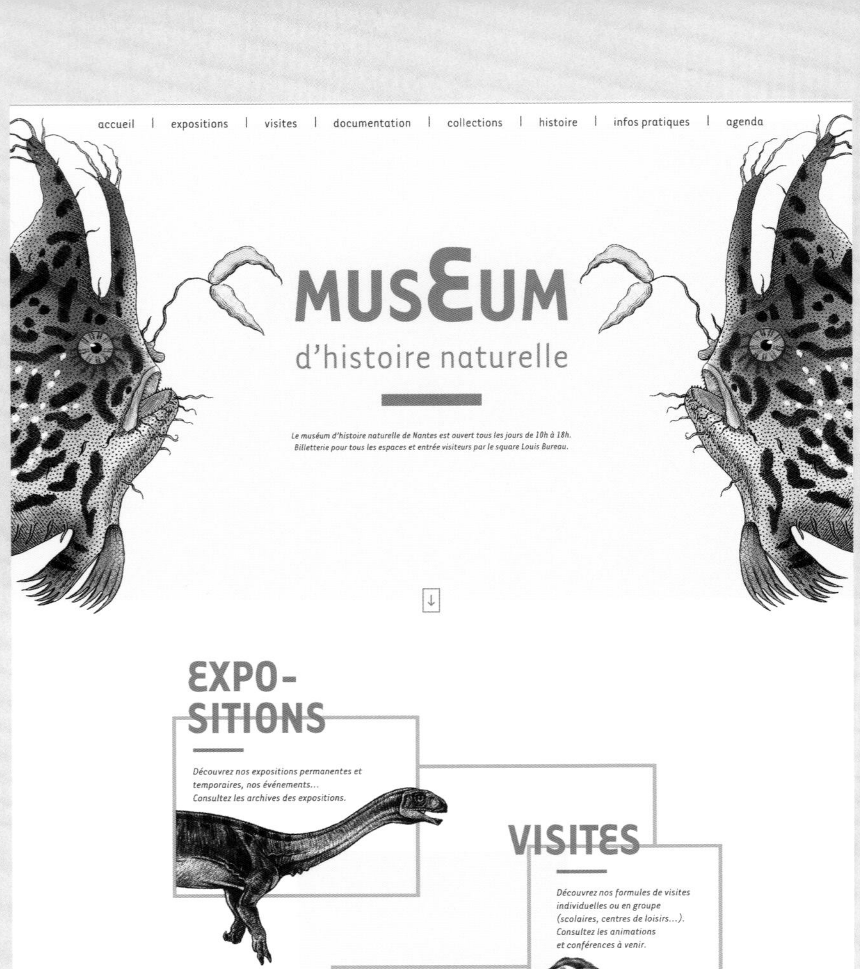

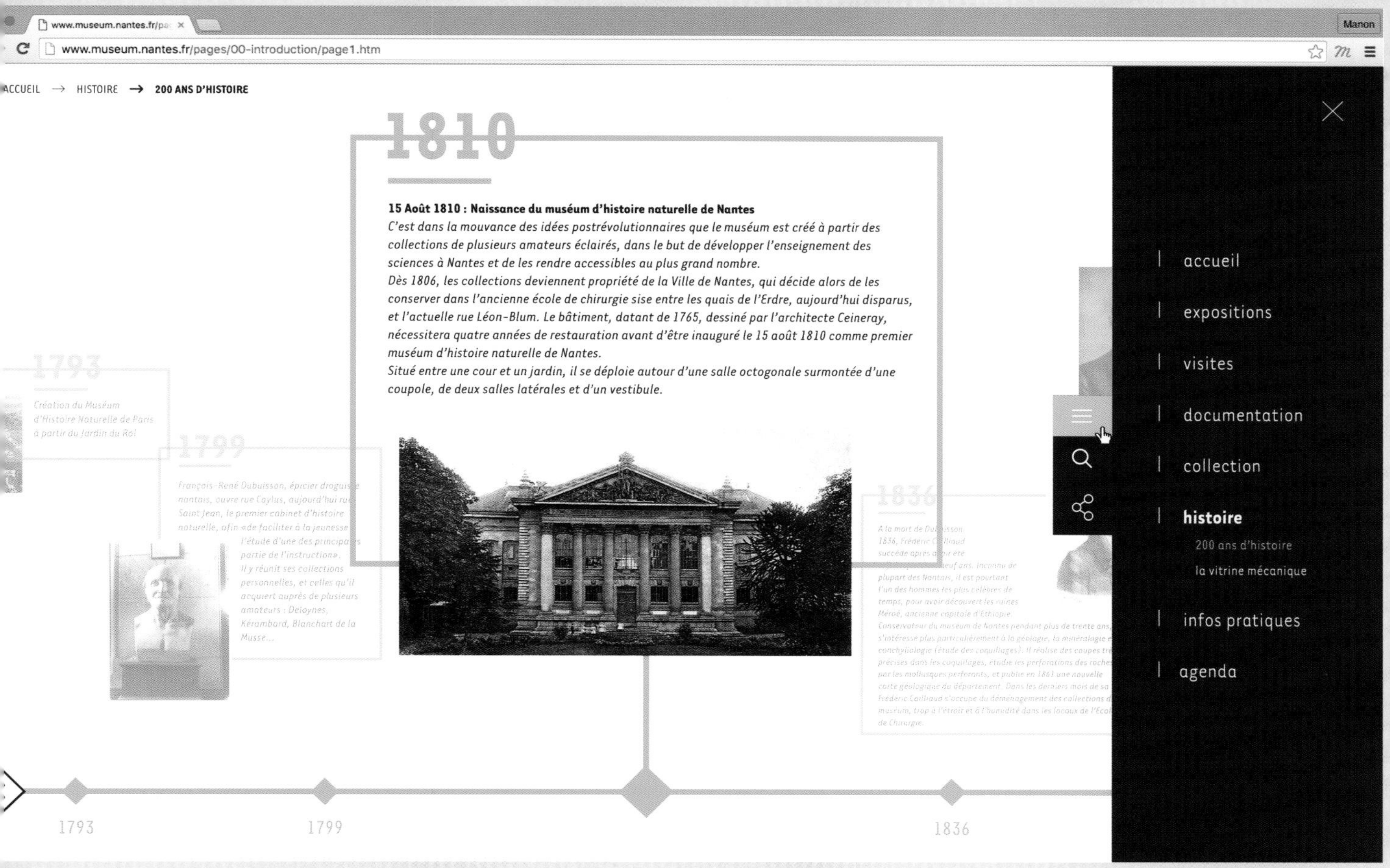

www.museum.nantes.fr/pages/00-introduction/page1.htm

ACCUEIL → HISTOIRE → **200 ANS D'HISTOIRE**

1810

15 Août 1810 : Naissance du muséum d'histoire naturelle de Nantes

C'est dans la mouvance des idées postrévolutionnaires que le muséum est créé à partir des collections de plusieurs amateurs éclairés, dans le but de développer l'enseignement des sciences à Nantes et de les rendre accessibles au plus grand nombre.
Dès 1806, les collections deviennent propriété de la Ville de Nantes, qui décide alors de les conserver dans l'ancienne école de chirurgie sise entre les quais de l'Erdre, aujourd'hui disparus, et l'actuelle rue Léon-Blum. Le bâtiment, datant de 1765, dessiné par l'architecte Ceineray, nécessitera quatre années de restauration avant d'être inauguré le 15 août 1810 comme premier muséum d'histoire naturelle de Nantes.
Situé entre une cour et un jardin, il se déploie autour d'une salle octogonale surmontée d'une coupole, de deux salles latérales et d'un vestibule.

1793

Création du Muséum d'Histoire Naturelle de Paris à partir du Jardin du Roi

1799

1836

1793 1799 1836

- accueil
- expositions
- visites
- documentation
- collection
- **histoire**
  - 200 ans d'histoire
  - la vitrine mécanique
- infos pratiques
- agenda

www.museum.nantes.fr/pages/00-introduction/page1.htm

ACCUEIL → COLLECTIONS → ZOOLOGIE → **MONSTRES**

Veau Bos taurus
Squelette à 2 pattes
MHNN.Z.019720

Starlet Makeup Studio

Direction/
Creation

Design/
Vadim Kukin

Photography/
Starlet Makeup Studio

Client/
Starlet Makeup Studio

URL/
http://www.starletstudio.lv

Starlet Makeup Studio is a professional school which helps the students to master all the aspects of becoming a make-up artist. Starlet also offers a variety of services that associated with make-up.

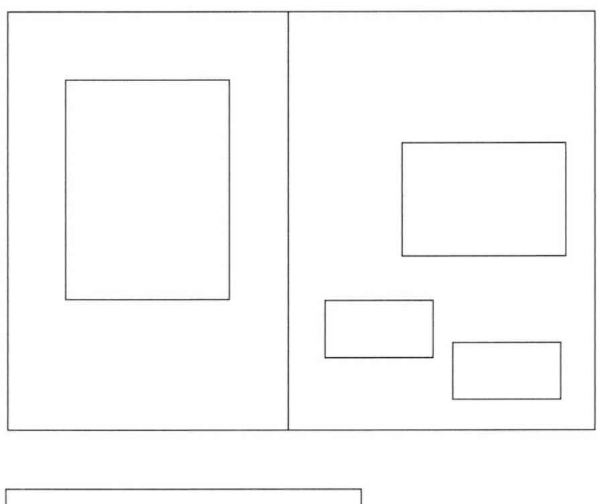

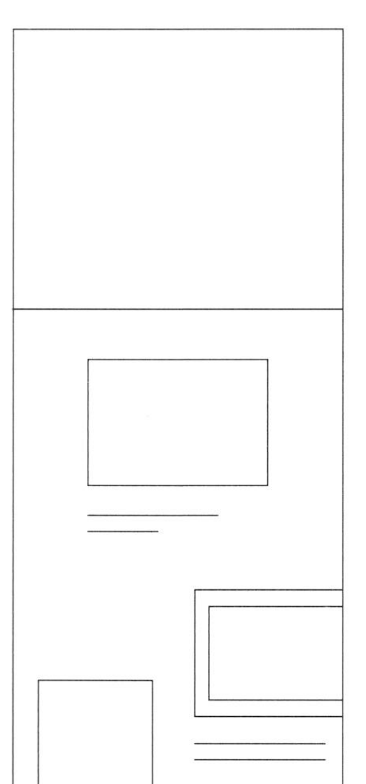

Портфолио

Мы открыты для сотрудничества с фотографами, студиями и модельными агенствами.

Фея. Фотограф Андрис Криштабанс.

Студийная фотосъемка. Фотограф Настя Фелини.

© 2015 Starlet Studio SIA

www.starletstudio.lv

Студия профессионального макияжа

E. Melngaiļa 5, Riga, LV-1011
info@starletstudio.lv +371 26414072

f

Школа Starlet – это освоение в совершенстве всех тонкостей профессии визажиста.

Макияж для студийной съемки. © Ирина Иванова.

НОВОСТИ

12 сентября
L'Oréal Professionnel на Латвийской Неделе Моды Riga Fashion Week

ШКОЛА

2 сентября
Начался набор новой группы для обучения по программе «Вечерний макияж»

starlet
STUDIO
LAT
© 2015 Starlet Studio SIA
www.starletstudio.lv
Студия профессионального макияжа
E. Melngaiļa 5, Riga, LV-1011
info@starletstudio.lv +371 26414072
f
Все об уходе за волосами
Этот семинар для всех, кто желает узнать о правильном уходе за волосами на дому. Вы научитесь подбирать себе шампунь, маску, лак и другие средства, которые сохранят здоровье ваших волос и будут при этом выглядеть потрясающе.
12 августа
11⁰⁰-13⁰⁰
25-30 €
Язык Русский
Лектор Ирина Иванова
визажист, преподаватель школы макияжа Starlet Studio
ЗАПИСАТЬСЯ
Вы также можете записаться позвонив по телефону +371 26414072 или написав нам на почту info@starletstudio.lv

◇◇◇◇◇◇◇◇◇◇◇◇◇◇◇◇◇◇◇◇◇◇◇◇◇◇◇◇◇◇◇

Alice Mourou

Design/
Alice Mourou

URL/
http://alicemourou.com

Alice Mourou is a digital designer and creative director based in Hong Kong. Also, she is local Behance community leader and international Awwwards jury.

She developed this site for her project archive. Embraced simplicity and elegance, the website is clean in structure, yet filled with artistic elements.

◇◇◇◇◇◇◇◇◇◇◇◇◇◇◇◇◇◇◇◇◇◇◇◇◇◇◇◇◇◇◇

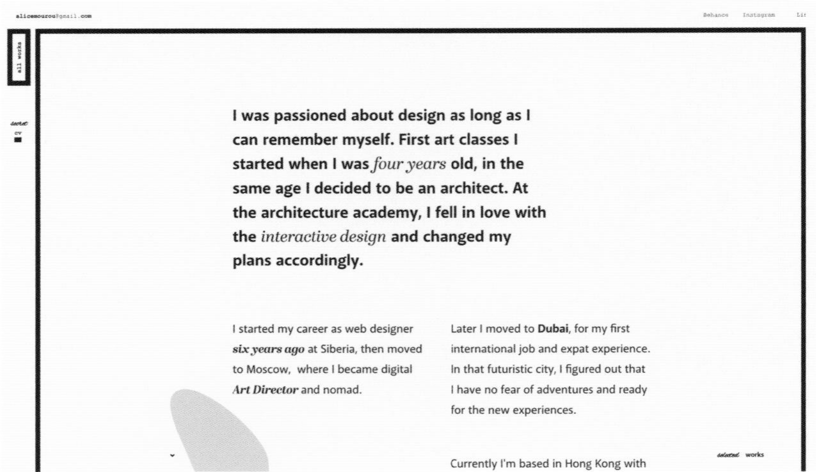

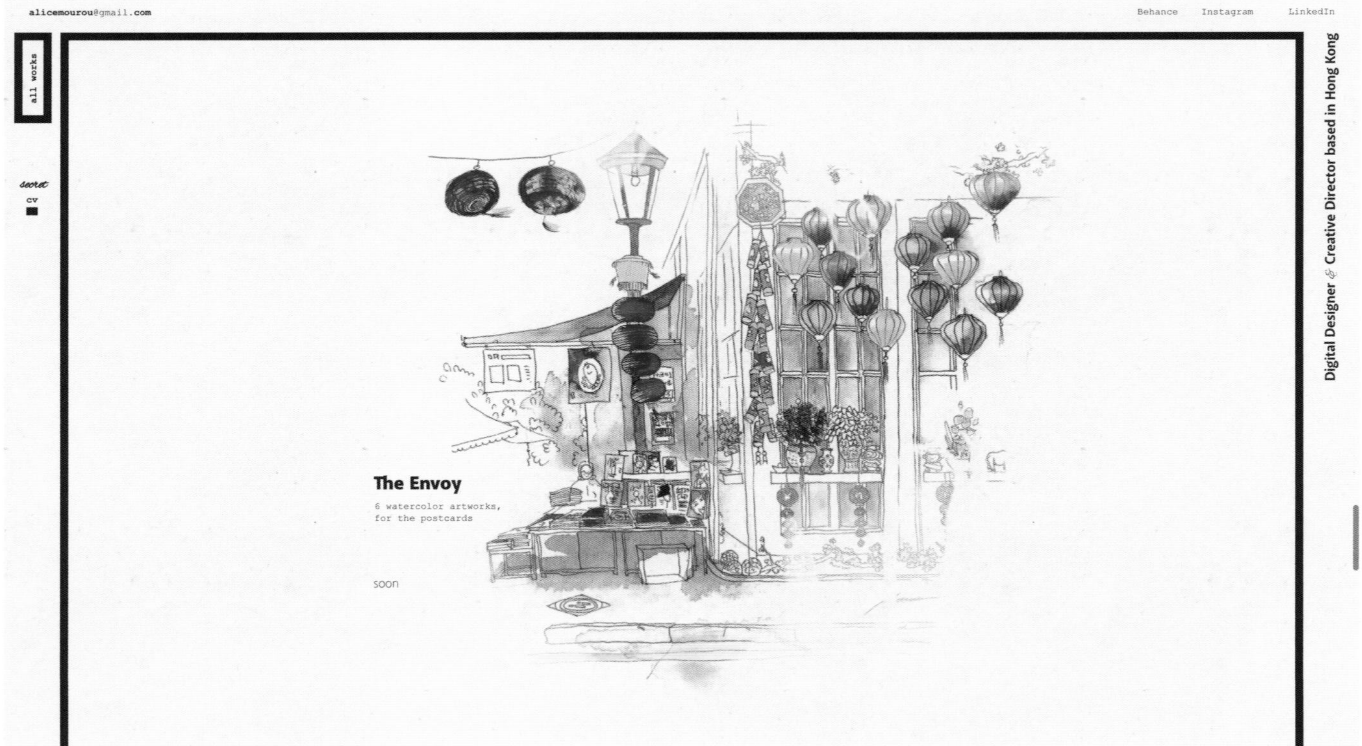

alicemourou@gmail.com
Behance
Instagram
LinkedIn
all works
secret
cv
Digital Designer & Creative Director based in Hong Kong
elesac
Alexander McQueen
let me know about the launch
Elesac
Art Direction, aesthetic, wireframes, landing page design
Elesac
elesac
We guarantee authenticity and safety!
An online platform for artistic and intelligent ladies to rent and share designer bags
Manifesto
How it works
Contacts
let me know about the launch
Facebook
Instagram

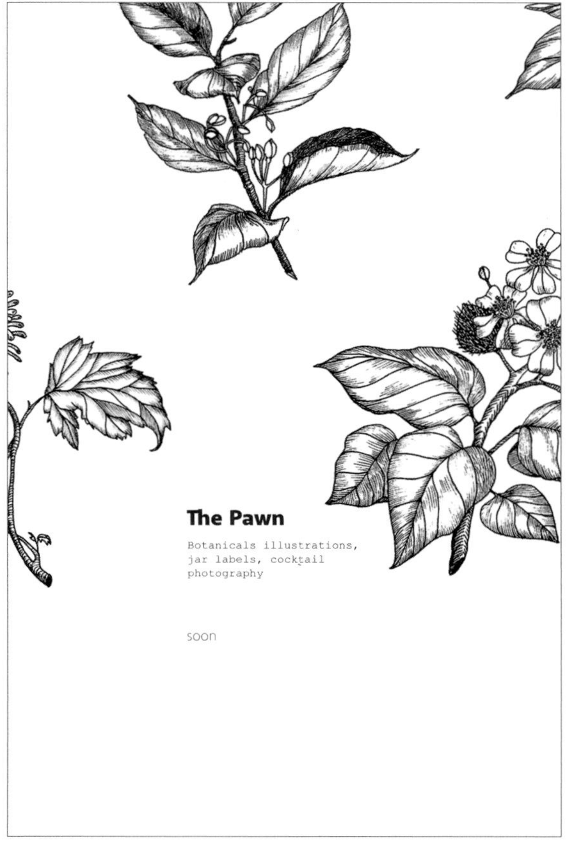
The Pawn
Botanicals illustrations, jar labels, cocktail photography
soon

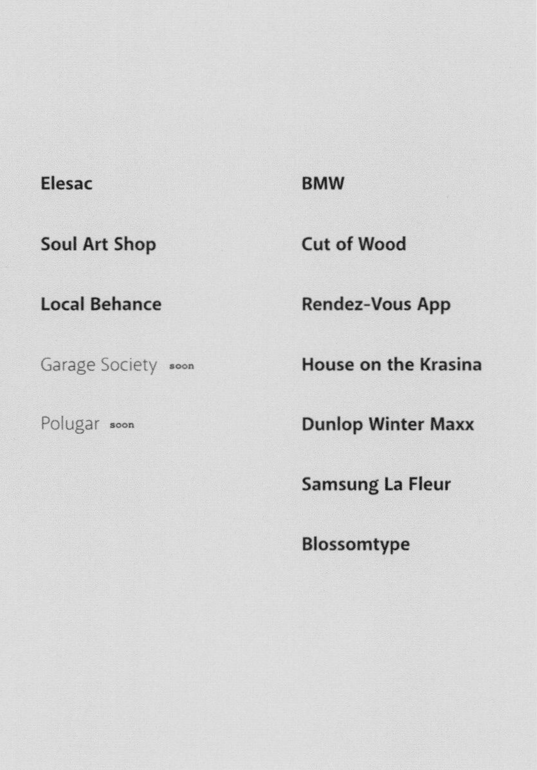
Elesac
Soul Art Shop
Local Behance
Garage Society soon
Polugar soon
BMW
Cut of Wood
Rendez-Vous App
House on the Krasina
Dunlop Winter Maxx
Samsung La Fleur
Blossomtype

Le Salón

Design Agency/
INBALOZA graphic design

Design Direction/
Inbal Lapidot Vidal

Photography/
Rotem Rachel Chen

Client/
Le Salón Agency

Website design for alternative model agency Le Salón.

Le Salón was established to provide an answer to several requirements: photography, models, graphic design, fashion and styling. Their love for design, art, and creative thinking are instilled into the website designed by Inbal Lapidot, to represent the all-in-1 agency with its versatile abilities and a focus on fashion, graphic design, art, and culture.

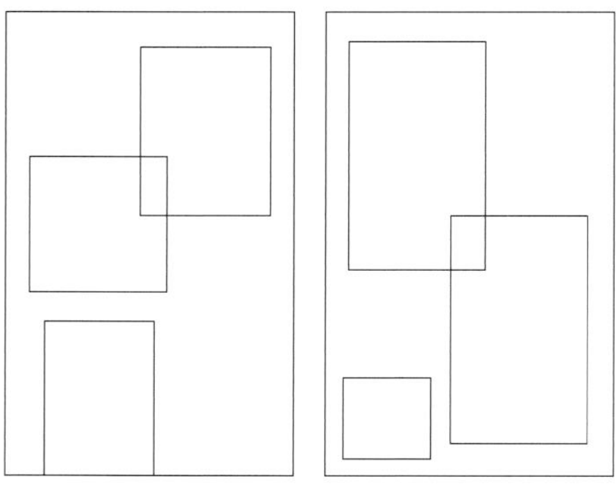

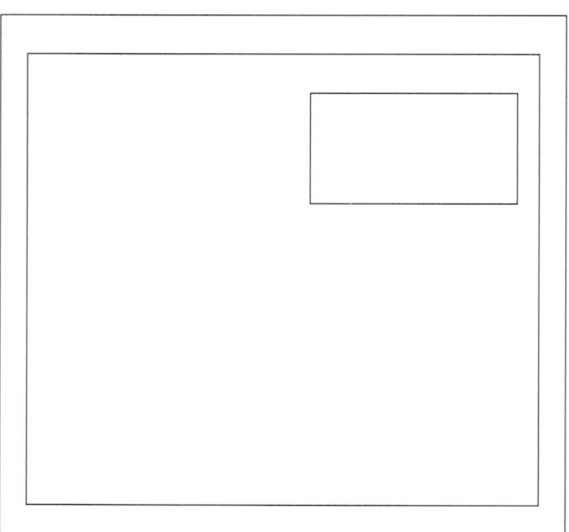

about models contact
LE SALÓN
f
LE SALÓN
WELCOME
ROTEM
WE ARE
A fashion agency.
Le Salon provides an answer to several requirements: photography, models, graphic design, fashion and styling.
Our love to design, art and creative thinking makes it possible to work for various fields such as commercial, graphic and cultural.
L
DALYA
E

about
models
contact
LE SALÓN
LE SALÓN
Fashion Agency
N
"THE ONLY REAL ELEGANCE IS IN THE MIND; IF YOU HAVE GOT THAT, THE REST REALLY COMES FROM IT."
Diana Vreeland

about
models
contact
LE SALÓN
NATALI
height 172 cm
hips 89 cm
waits 64
bust 69
shirt small
dress 36
shoes 38
eyes brown
hair brown

about
models
contact
LE SALÓN
NATALI
A
L

about
models
contact
LE SALÓN
CONTACT US
SEND
× close

NorthSide 2014

Identity Design/
Sandra Gutkin

Web Development/
Morten Lybech

Client/
Northside Festival

The site was designed for NorthSide Festival 2014, which is a Danish music festival. The festival has a mission statement focused on innovation, sustainability, and user involvement.

NorthSide required a new and modern web design that could express the level and image that the festival has achieved. Focused on key words such as clean, urban, tight, cool, and modern, Morten Lybech designed a website with Scandinavian colors, bold typography, and organized and clear layout.

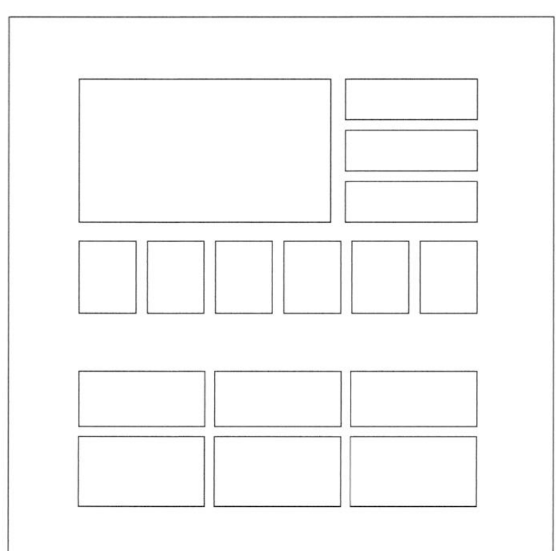

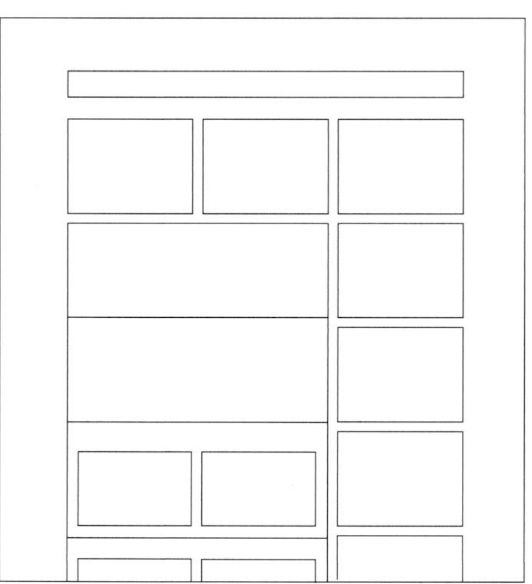

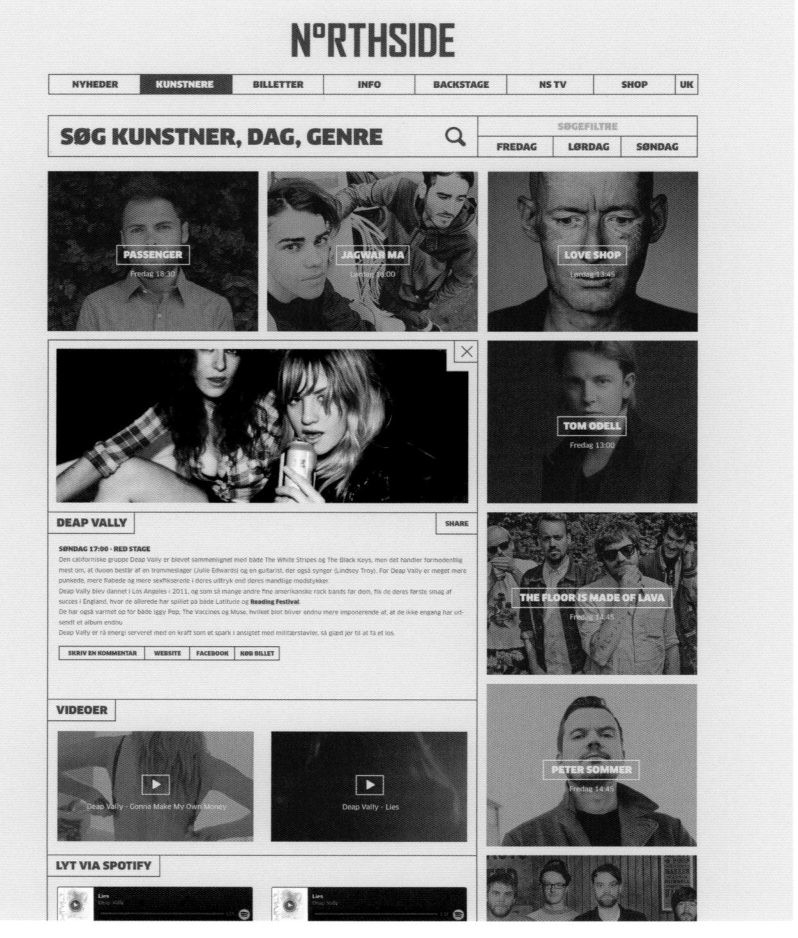

N°RTHSIDE

NYHEDER | KUNSTNERE | BILLETTER | INFO | BACKSTAGE | NS TV | SHOP | UK

BILLETTER

PARTOUTBILLET – ALLE TRE DAGE **1095,-**

Prisen er gældende indtil d. 30. april. 1. maj stiger prisen til 1.395,- kroner plus gebyr. Obs! UDSOLGT

KØB BILLET

ENDAGSBILLET – FREDAG **695,-**

Giver adgang til NorthSide om fredagen. Obs! Begrænset antal.

KØB BILLET

ENDAGSBILLET – LØRDAG **1095,-**

Prisen er gældende indtil d. 30. april. 1. maj stiger prisen til 1.395,- kroner plus gebyr. Obs! UDSOLGT

KØB BILLET

ENDAGSBILLET – SØNDAG **695,-**

UDSOLGT

NORTHSIDE/SPOT-KOMBIBILLET **1095,-**

Prisen er gældende indtil d. 30. april. 1. maj stiger prisen til 1.395,- kroner plus gebyr. Obs! UDSOLGT

KØB BILLET

EARLY BIRD-BILLET **695,-**

Giver adgang til NorthSide om fredagen. Obs! Begrænset antal.

KØB BILLET

NORTHSIDE TWEETS

Vi har indgået samarbejde med **@Tuborg** for de kommende fem år **http://t.co/XhGcJeC0AX**

SENEST TILMELDTE TIL NORTHSIDE

TILMELD DIG HER

N°RTHSIDE

NYHEDER | KUNSTNERE | BILLETTER | INFO | BACKSTAGE | NS TV | SHOP | UK

VÆRDIER

Vi vil skabe Danmarks mest innovative og bæredygtige musikbegivenhed – for og med vores gæster, kunstnere og samarbejdspartnere. For at gøre det arbejder NorthSide med tre kerneværdier, som fungerer som rettesnore for alt, hvad vi gør:

MUSIK
Musikken har førsteprioritet hos NorthSide! Det er musikken, vi skaber festivalen omkring, og det er musikken, som er grunden til, at NorthSide blev etableret.
Vi tilstræber at præsentere en række større, internationale kunstnere, samt det bedste fra den danske musikscene.

INNOVATION
Vi ønsker ikke at lave en hvilken som helst festival, men at udvide begreberne for, hvordan man opfatter en musikbegivenhed som NorthSide. Der er eksempelvis ikke camping på NorthSide. For hele tiden at udvikle os, samarbejder vi med bl.a. Aarhus Universitet, World-Perfect og Culture Works. Vi har ligeledes etableret en udviklingsenhed, NorthSiders, som har engageret sig i udviklingen af NorthSide som publikumsinddragende event.

BÆREDYGTIGHED
På NorthSide ønsker vi at arbejde aktivt for at belaste miljøet mindre. Som udgangspunkt har en musikbegivenhed over tre dage et stort forbrug, og dette faktum tager vi aktivt stilling til. Frem mod 2013-udgaven af NorthSide har vi fokus på affaldshåndtering, energiforbrug og økologi. Det er ikke en nem opgave at få 20.000 festglade mennesker til at tænke på miljøet, men vi gør forsøget! Og det er indtil videre vores oplevelse, at NorthSides publikum er meget engagerede i og positive overfor dette arbejde. Det er på samme måde et krav til alle leverandører og boder, at der tilbydes økologiske produkter til publikum.

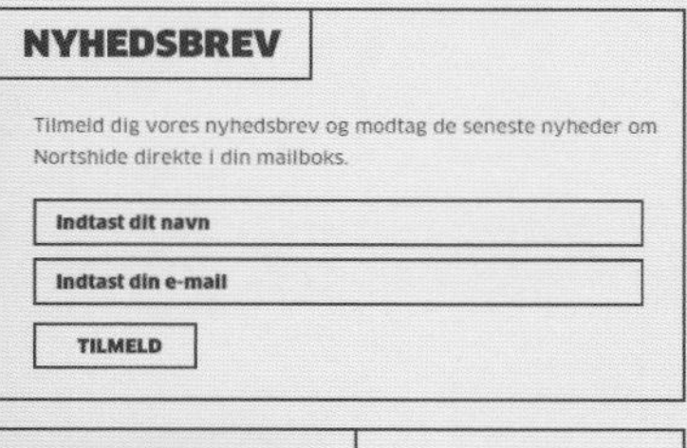

NYHEDSBREV

Tilmeld dig vores nyhedsbrev og modtag de seneste nyheder om Northside direkte i din mailboks.

Indtast dit navn

Indtast din e-mail

TILMELD

NORTHSIDE APP

Du kan nu hente vores smartphone app, hvor du kan planlægge dit program inden du kommer til festivallen og meget mere...

ITUNES | GOOGLE PLAY

KONTAKT

Har du spørgsmål eller brug for at kontakte Northside, kan du kontakte os via nedenstående link

KONTAKT

Design for Screen — ❸

Icon Applicaton

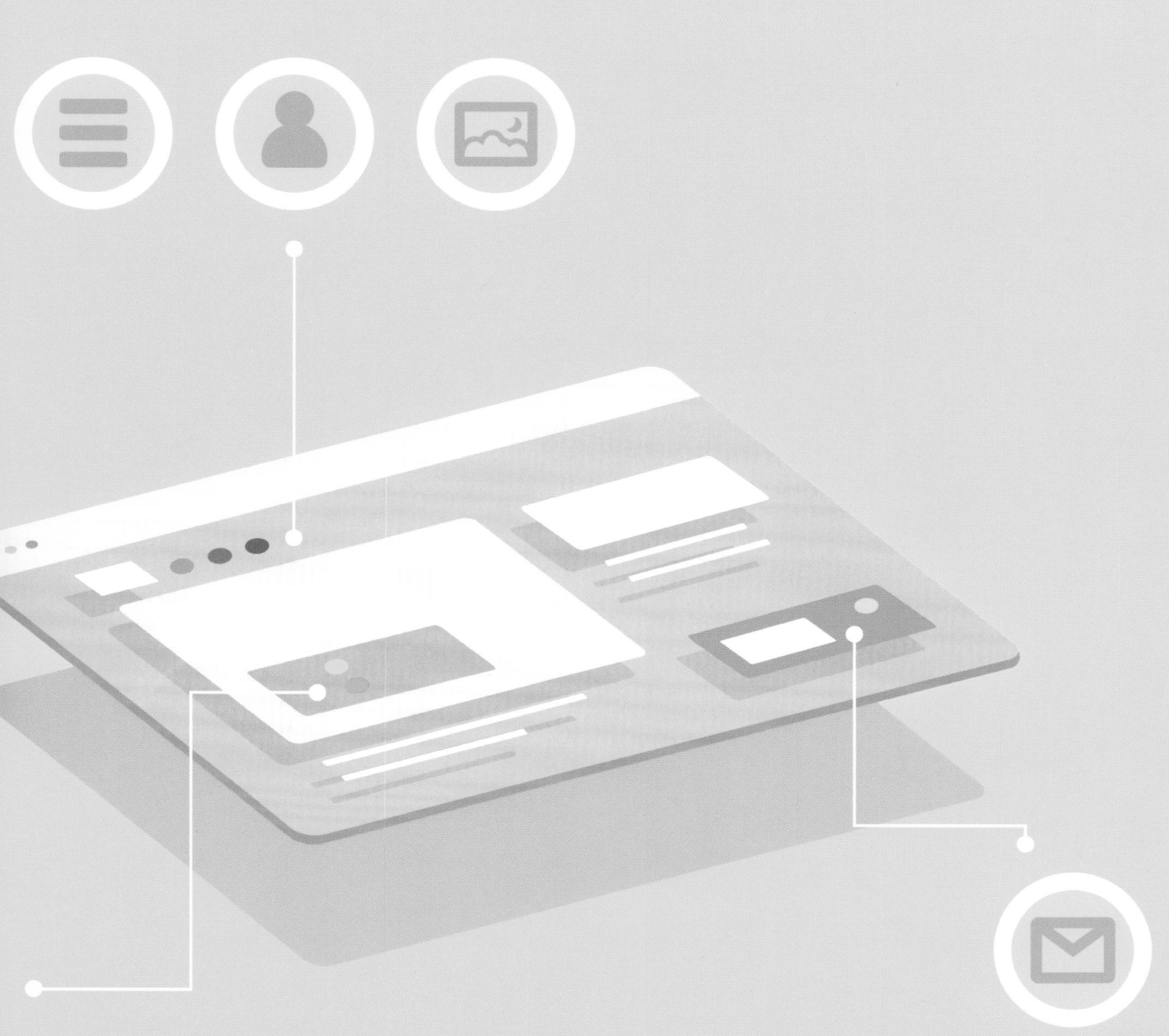

Interview with
Current Haus

Current Haus focuses on creating digital experiences that connect brands with culture to inspire, entertain, and produce results. They are a team of multi-skilled specialists hungry for new challenges with a passion for great design. Working with clients all over the globe, their mission is to turn fresh ideas into bold brands and polished digital products.

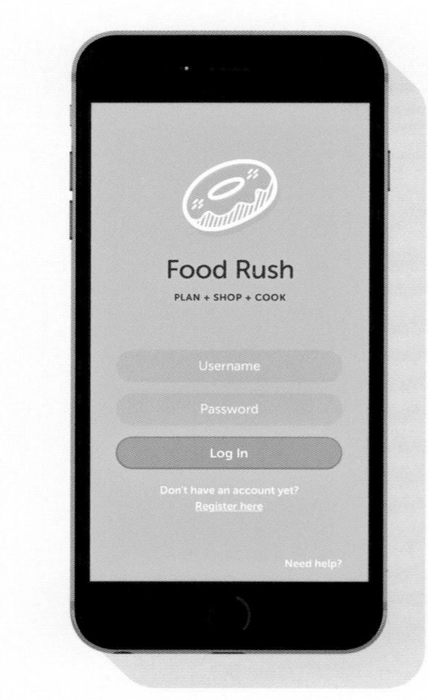

1 **PLAN**
Decide how much you want to spend on food, how many meals you want to eat and tell us about your taste.

2 **SHOP**
Based on your taste, we create a full menu for you and put together a shopping list.

3 **COOK**
Based on ingredients you've selected, we put together a set of recipes for each day of the week.

◊ Q1 ◊ Can you tell us a little bit about your background and how you came about to be doing web design?

The idea of Current Haus is to bridge the free flowing nature of European design with an American marketing business approach. The studio was founded by Kalina Giersz, art director from Poland who graduated with honors in graphic design from the Warsaw Academy of Arts, and Drew Polk, Managing Director from California, an expert in integrated marketing. When we first started working together, we were mostly focused on web design, but we quickly shifted towards creating apps. We realized that it is an exciting moment for the industry which is driven by progress and innovation.

◊ Q2 ◊ Please kindly describe your design process: Is there a specific routine/technique that you adhere to?

First and foremost, our design process revolves around the user. Who will be using the app or website? How will they interact with it? Why would they need it? Finding answers for these questions helps us to start creating an individual visual language of the product.

For us, the crucial part of design is wireframing the flow of the product. After wireframes are signed off, we move to the design and coding phase. In our studio, designers and developers work together and in parallel. We try to avoid the approach of completing a design and handing it over to the coding team. Working in tandem forces designers and developers to think of each other when making decisions.

◊ Q3 ◊ A lot of web designs might look beautiful but not friendly to users. How do you take a complex chunk of information and make sense out of it?

Usability and readability are always the main objective. Aesthetics add value and uniqueness, but a good design is much more than being pretty. That's why we put so much stress on wireframing in our process. By creating a hierarchy of information, we can control how the content is presented to the user.

◊ Q4 ◊ What makes a good icon design?

Well-designed icons become a symbol that serves a specific purpose. Usually, this is communication and the key is simplicity and a clear message. For example, at the airport, people from all over the globe use a pictogram communication system to find their way around. It all depends on the intention. With Food Rush, our icons were made to convey fun and give the app personality and charisma.

◊ Q5 ◊ Pictograms and icons are a keystone of nonverbal and multicultural communication. How do you think of the function of icon in web design?

The language of icons is becoming an independent form of communication that evolves separately and faster from actual verbal languages. Look at the 'hamburger' menu icon—it wasn't until the iPhone 3Gs when people started to get familiar with it. Now it's a commonly understood symbol by users all over the globe.

Overall, the advantage of icons is to communicate ideas quickly. Users mostly spend only a few seconds glancing through a website, so pictograms have a higher chance of capturing their attention. However, sometimes they are being overused in a way that does not add value. An overload or generic treatment of icons ironically hinders the message.

◊ Q6 ◊ Comparing to the icons on print matters, what are the properties of icons for screen? What are your design strategies?

Icon design is a very fun visual process for us. We try not to overthink about it, just put our ideas on paper. For both print and web, we start with sketches that are turned into vector illustrations. It is important to keep proportions and a good balance of strokes. If icons will be used for the web, we export clean SVGs. In addition, digital design allows us to take icons one step further by adding movement and creating fun animations.

◊ Q7 ◊ The icons in your project are very sophisticated and organized. What was your initiative to design these icons?

When we were designing the icons for the Food Rush app, first of all, Kalina was very hungry. Second of all, we were thinking about the overall vibe—an original approach that would stand out. There were already similar app ideas on the market, but their UI design was generic. There seemed to be a niche for this kind of product.

◊ Q8 ◊ What are the target audience of this App? Do they affect your design strategy?

We definitely wanted to appeal to a very specific target—millennial active iOS users. This group is most-likely willing to experiment with bold and original products without fear of trying new solutions. We could take more design risks with vivid color palette, custom UI elements, and animated interactions.

◊ Q9 ◊ How do you balance the readability and aesthetics in this project?

Typography, spacing, and hierarchy of information.

◊ Q10 ◊ I found that the stroke of your icons strike a perfect balance with the fonts. Could you share with us how do you make a balance between the elements?

First, we had an idea of an app and we needed a set of icons that would express the overall vibe that we were looking for. Typography was selected to match them. In this project we used Museo Sans Rounded—it has a nice, clean, fun feel with rounded glyphs that also complements the strokes of icons.

Food Rush App

Design Agency/
Current Haus

Design/
Kalina Giersz

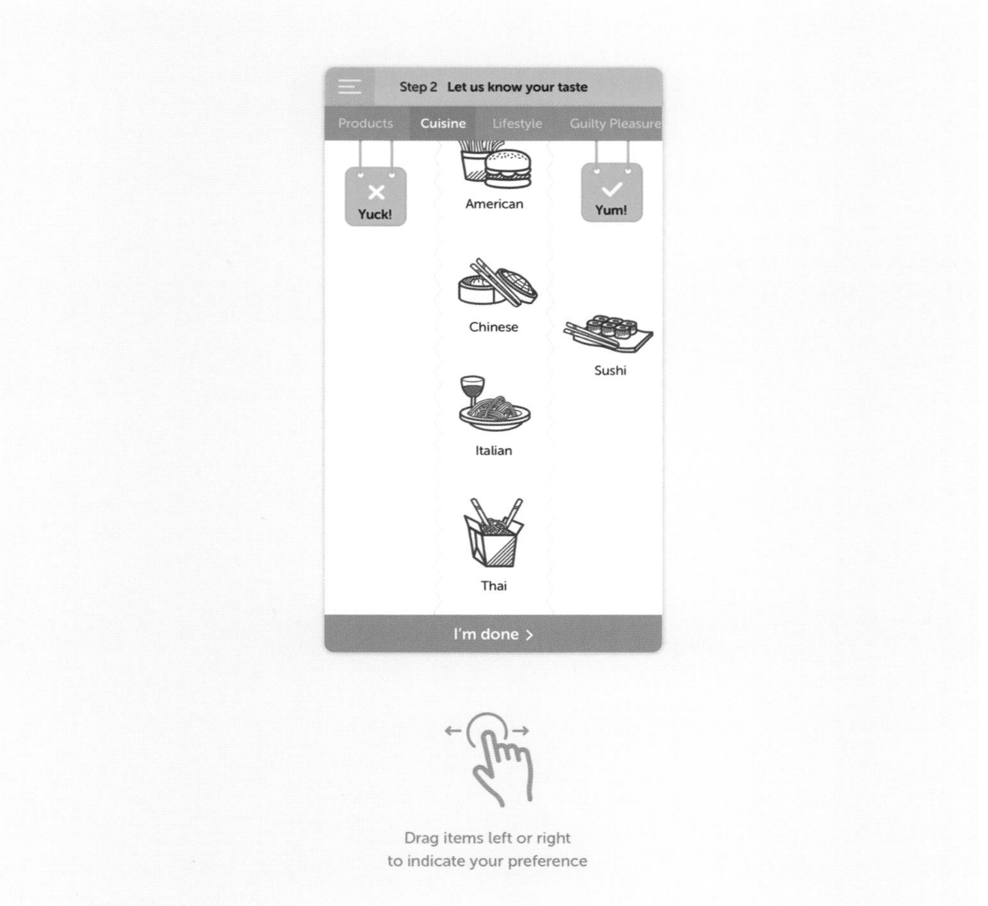

Food Rush is your personal assistant application that takes meal planning off your back. In three easy steps, indicate your eating preferences and habits. Food Rush takes care of the rest providing recipes and grocery lists to satisfy your tastes while not breaking the bank. You can save meals you love for future cooking and create weekly schedules – all while having the flexibility to plan for an entire party, or just for one.

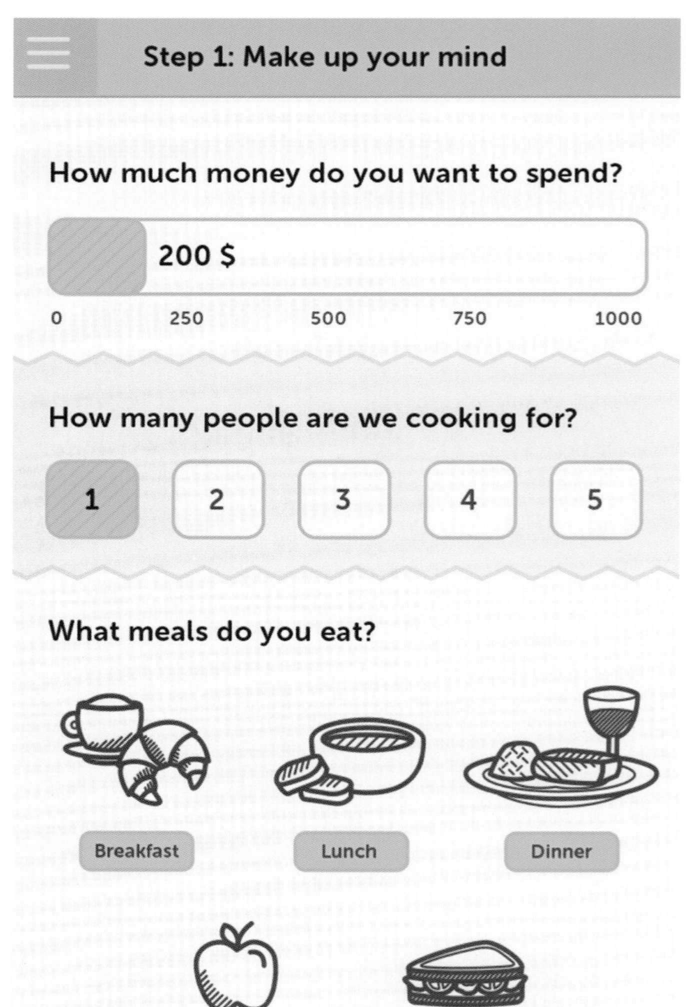

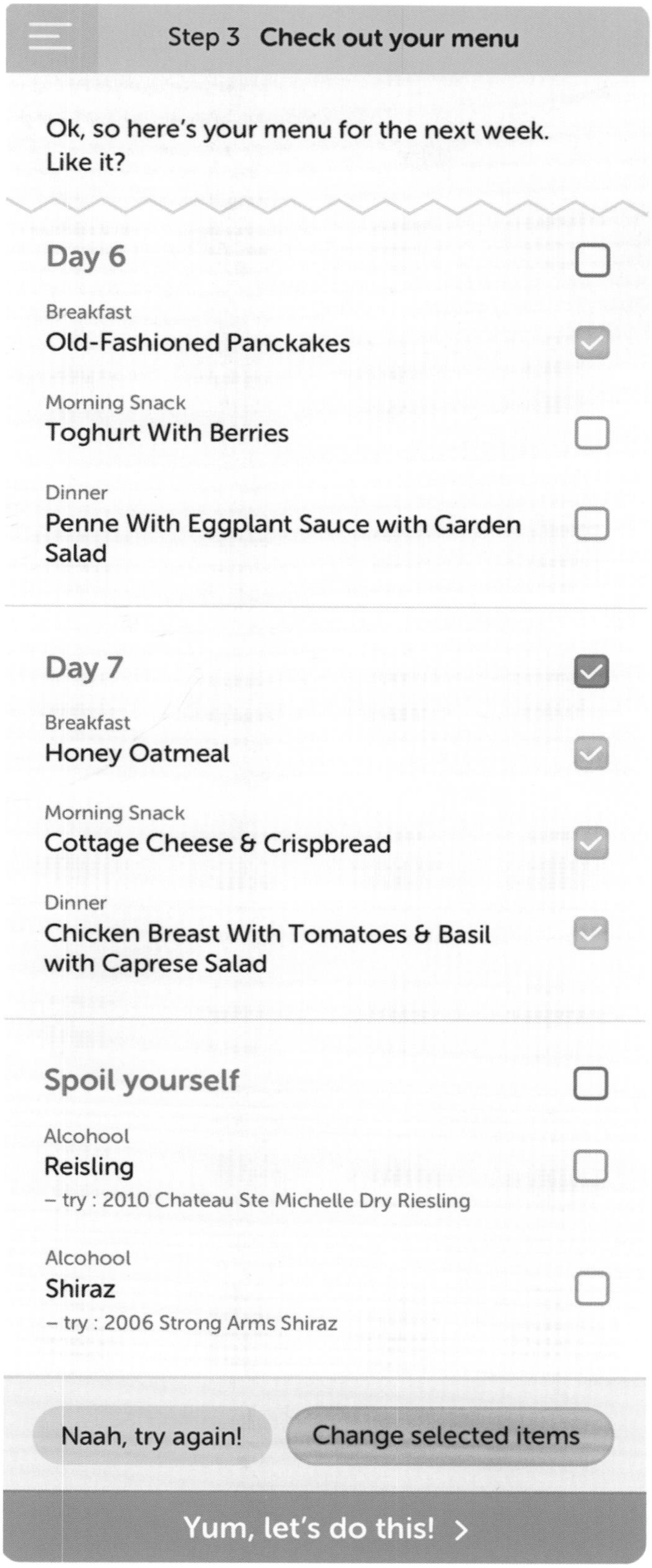

Step 3 **Check out your menu**

Ok, so here's your menu for the next week. Like it?

Day 6

Breakfast
Old-Fashioned Panckakes

Morning Snack
Toghurt With Berries

Dinner
Penne With Eggplant Sauce with Garden Salad

Day 7

Breakfast
Honey Oatmeal

Morning Snack
Cottage Cheese & Crispbread

Dinner
Chicken Breast With Tomatoes & Basil with Caprese Salad

Spoil yourself

Alcohool
Reisling
– try : 2010 Chateau Ste Michelle Dry Riesling

Alcohool
Shiraz
– try : 2006 Strong Arms Shiraz

Naah, try again! | Change selected items

Yum, let's do this! >

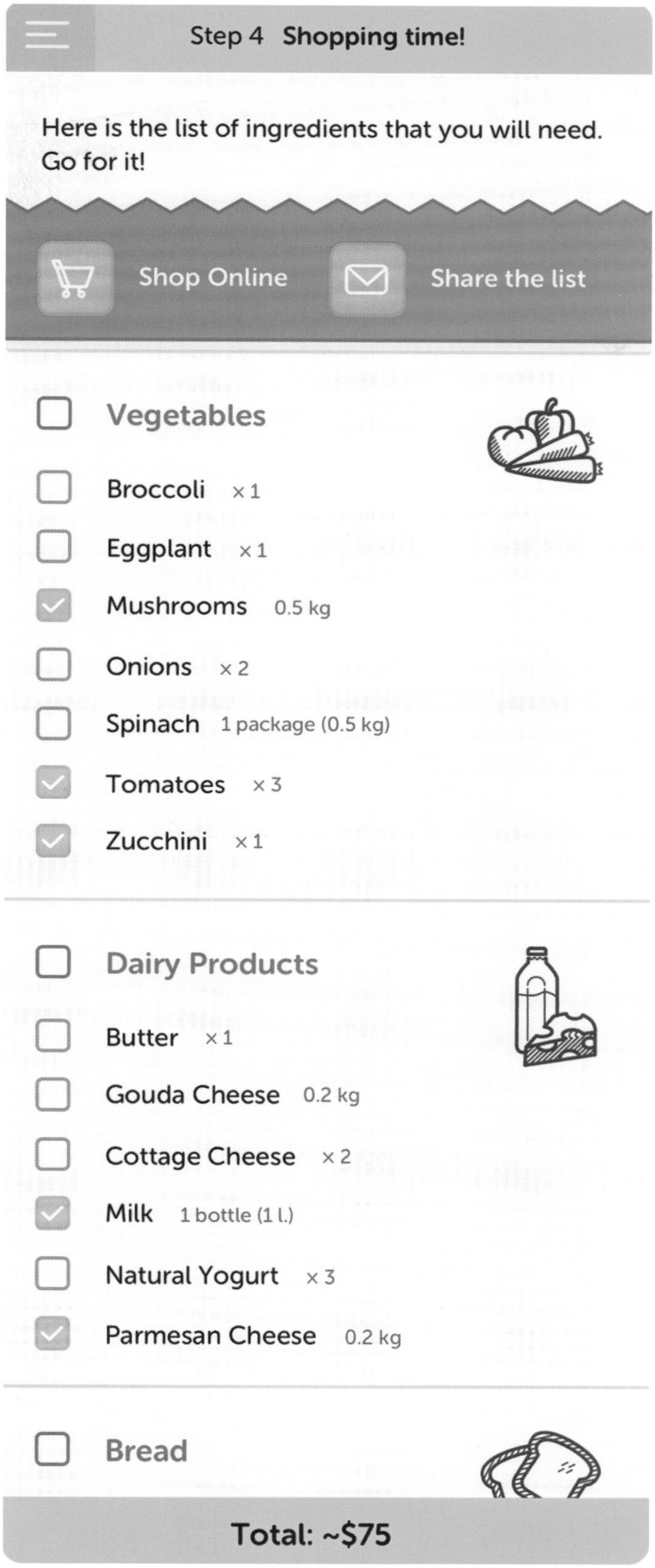

Step 4 **Shopping time!**

Here is the list of ingredients that you will need. Go for it!

Shop Online | Share the list

Vegetables

- Broccoli × 1
- Eggplant × 1
- Mushrooms 0.5 kg
- Onions × 2
- Spinach 1 package (0.5 kg)
- Tomatoes × 3
- Zucchini × 1

Dairy Products

- Butter × 1
- Gouda Cheese 0.2 kg
- Cottage Cheese × 2
- Milk 1 bottle (1 l.)
- Natural Yogurt × 3
- Parmesan Cheese 0.2 kg

Bread

Total: ~$75

Interview with

Oddds

Oddds was founded in 2013 by Reinold Lim and Sarah Tan. Their focuses are in branding, art direction, illustration, graphic design, packaging, to name a few. Oddds incorporates the study and evolution of cultures into their philosophy and attitude as their work reflects significantly on behaviors and futurism. They believe in aesthetics about how it draws attention and influences people.

◇ Q1 ◇ Can you tell us a little bit about your background and how you came about to be doing web design?

The team is consisted of Reinold Lim, art director & designer from Penang, and Sarah Tan, design director and designer from Singapore. Oddds started in 2013, out of a means of creative self-expressionism and to realize our views and perspectives on design and art. Our focuses are mainly in art direction, branding, packaging and graphic design. Intrigued by behaviors and futurism, Oddds has grown over the past few years where our body of work has evolved to an array of identities, lifestyle brands to clothing brands for unique individuals and startups from a mix of international clientele from the US, the UK, Canada, Germany, Vietnam, Australia, and abroad. Web design and layout was something that we've encountered and meddled around with amidst our past working experiences that has since been introduced into our field of work.

◇ Q2 ◇ Please kindly describe your design process: Is there a specific routine/technique that you adhere to?

Firstly, we believe in researching and experimenting different methodologies of design as one of our crucial processes: Research – Think/Conceptualization – Think Again – Work/Execution – Refine.

◇ Q3 ◇ A lot of web designs might look beautiful but not friendly to users. How do you take a complex chunk of information and make sense out of it?

We believe in minimalism. Segmenting and extracting the important messages to its viewers allows them to get the messaging they need and in the meantime, they can enjoy the visual aesthetic and be engaged with the website. The designing of interfaces and to understand its functionalities is most important to the brand or product at first glance.

◇ Q4 ◇ What makes good icon designs?

In our opinion, a good icon is clever and simple yet able to draw attention from the viewers.

◇ Q5 ◇ Pictograms and icons are a keystone of nonverbal and multicultural communication. How do you think of the function of icon in web design?

Visually expressed and understood by viewers almost immediately. Similarly, recognized like in an Ad, it takes a few seconds for a viewer to register what he/she sees through its communication or messaging.

◇ Q6 ◇ Comparing to the icons on print matters, what are the properties of icons for screen? What are your design strategies?

The difficulty stems from how we make a difference when we have to design and simplify such that it becomes something for a general usage or into everyday objects.

Also, we meet difficulties such as the understanding on how people view objects differently and to singularly design an icon that is able to capture and represent an object well.

◇ Q7 ◇ Icons, being a pictogram narrative, on one hand offer user an intuitive image. On the other hand, they might generate misunderstandings. How do you make them convincing and easy to understand?

It would be best, if the information aligns with the icon design. Or we can bring in a narrative by tapping into a person's subconscious that is vaguely recognized.

◇ Q8 ◇ The icons in your project is very sophisticated and organized. What was your initiative to design these icons?

The rebranding proposals and concepts that initiated the design of these icons were inspired by the logo and personality of the brand. Given its quirky nature, we translated this into the brand hence the bold outlines and colors were introduced.

◇ Q9 ◇ What are the target audience of this App? Do they affect your design strategy?

Our concept for the menu was to provide a informative yet engaging menu, proposed within an tablet format rather than a printed form inline to the fresh and lively approach proposed.

◇ Q10 ◇ How do you balance the readability and aesthetics in this project?

Enabling clear readability and segmentation of information.

◇ Q11 ◇ I found that the logic of this app is mostly lead by the icons rather than words. How do you guide the users and keep the site informative?

The functionality of the menu was designed in such a manner of being led by the icons was to create movement as the eye leads itself to other pages within. The icons are surrounded by copy which allows another form of communication.

PIK NIK

Design Agency/
Odds

Design Direction/
Sarah Tan

Art Direction/
Reinold Lim

Design/
Reinold Lim, Sarah Tan

Photography/
Sarah Tan

PIK NIK is a rebranding project for a cafe that gives a modern spin to their proposed logo and concept. Callouts and descriptive words are used throughout the menu to bring out random quirks about the food and the cafe's unique selections. Each section shows the different options of available food or drinks. A combination of graphical icons, lines, bold strokes, and circles, and a baring-it-all approach were conceptualized and developed for PIK NIK.

THE ULTIMATE WAFFLE BURGER

SAUSAGE UP........................RM14.90
GARLIC BUTTERED...............RM14.90
ALA BEEF............................RM18.90

EVERYTHING COMES WITH:
SUNNY SIDE EGG + BACON + SALMON + SALAD

SIGNATURE WAFFLES

SMOKED SALMON..................RM12.90
TURKEY BACON....................RM12.90
FLUFFY FRENCH..................RM12.90
BAKED BRUNCH....................RM18.90

WITH SUNNY SIDE EGG + BACON + SALAD

SWEET WAFFLE

BUTTERMILK........................RM6.90
GERMAN APPLE...................RM8.90
CINNAMON...........................RM8.90

WAFFLE ICE-CREAM
('NEW ZEALAND NATURAL' PREMIUM)

APPLE SAUCE.............RM12.90
PECAN WALNUT...........RM12.90
GINGER BREAD...........RM12.90

SWEET SELECTIONS

RED BLUEBERRY CAKE........RM6.90
APPLE CIDERNOG................RM6.90
BANANA WHITE....................RM6.90

What 's Where

Design/
Marija Erjavec, Pia Sissala

Tutor/
Mikko Mutanen

The UI design is part of a wayfinding system proposal. With multiple icons and five colors of each floor, the app indicates at which floor you are and shows you the way to the destination using beacons on your device.

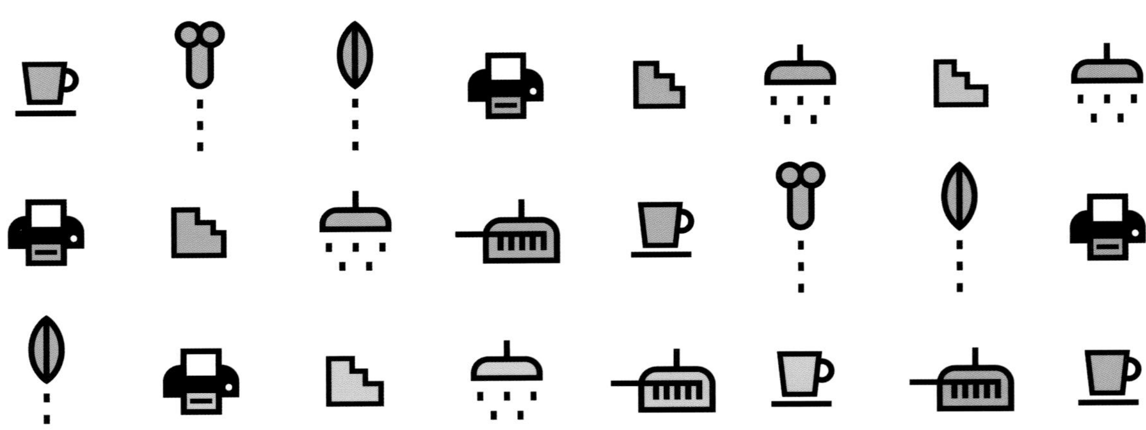

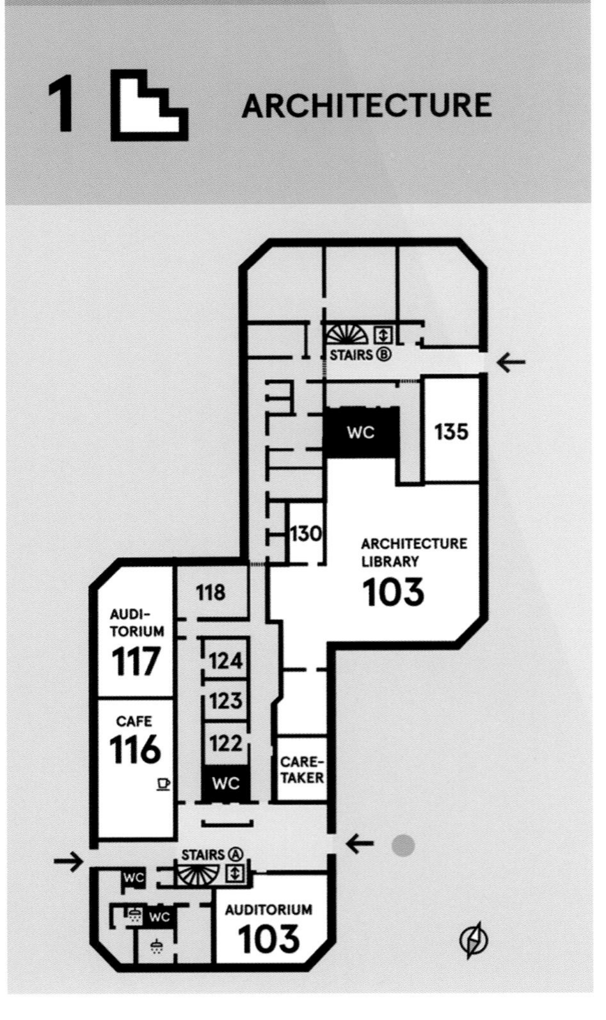

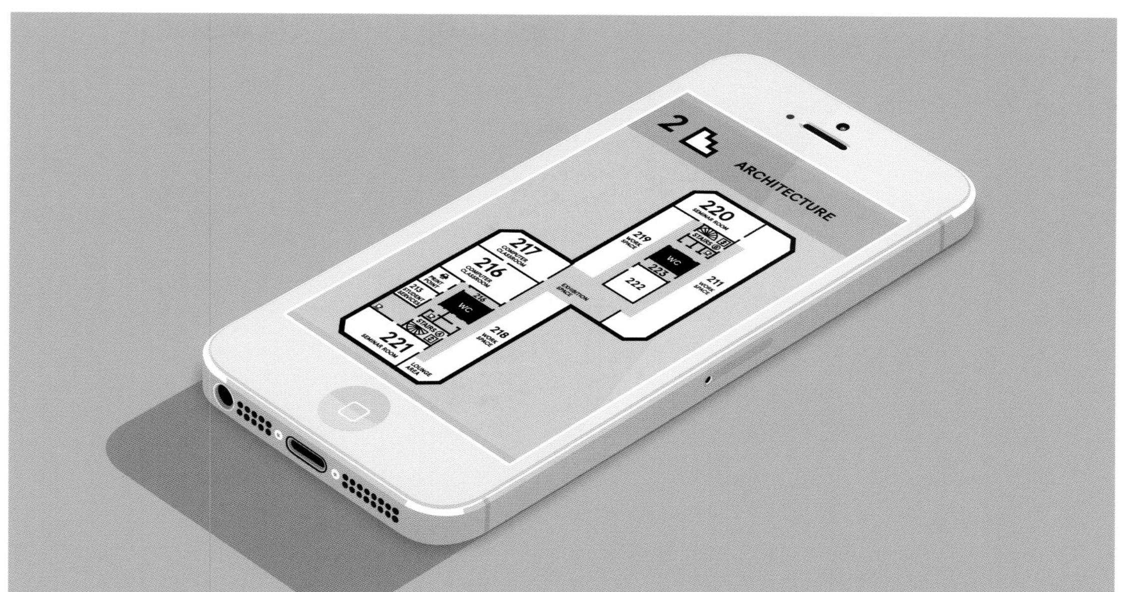
2
ARCHITECTURE
220
SEMINAR ROOM
217
COMPUTER CLASSROOM
216
COMPUTER CLASSROOM
219
WORK SPACE
WC
223
222
211
WORK SPACE
EXHIBITION SPACE
221
SEMINAR ROOM
218
WORK SPACE
LOUNGE AREA

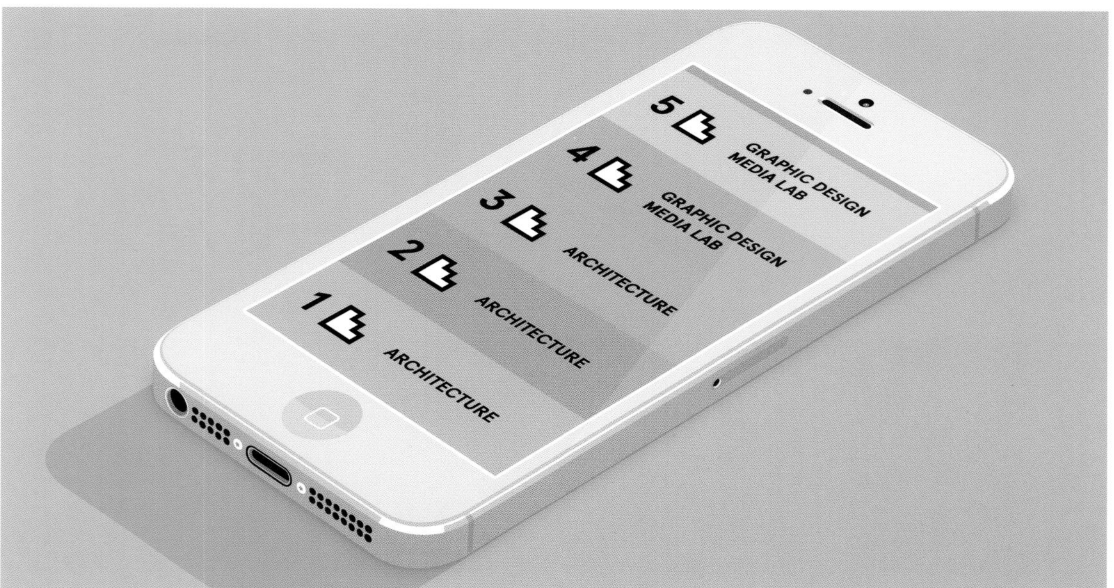
5
GRAPHIC DESIGN
MEDIA LAB
4
GRAPHIC DESIGN
MEDIA LAB
3
ARCHITECTURE
2
ARCHITECTURE
1
ARCHITECTURE

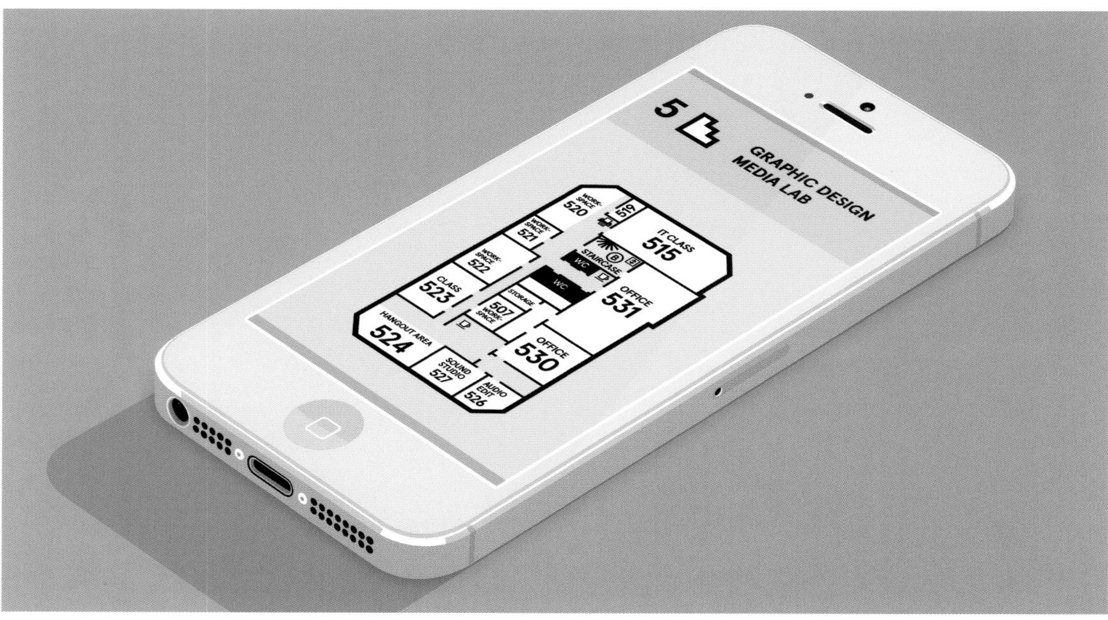
5
GRAPHIC DESIGN
MEDIA LAB
WORK SPACE
520
521
522
IT CLASS
515
STAIRCASE
WC
OFFICE
531
CLASS
523
STORAGE
507
WORK SPACE
HANGOUT AREA
524
OFFICE
530
SOUND STUDIO
527
AUDIO EDIT
526

Eat to be_

Design Agency/
The Woork Co

Client/
Eat to be_

The Woork Co was approached to create naming, branding, and website design for a mobile application served as a nutrition coach and monitor. Personal trainers, nutritionists, yoga teachers, and herbalists alike could use the app to offer personal coaching to their followers and clients.

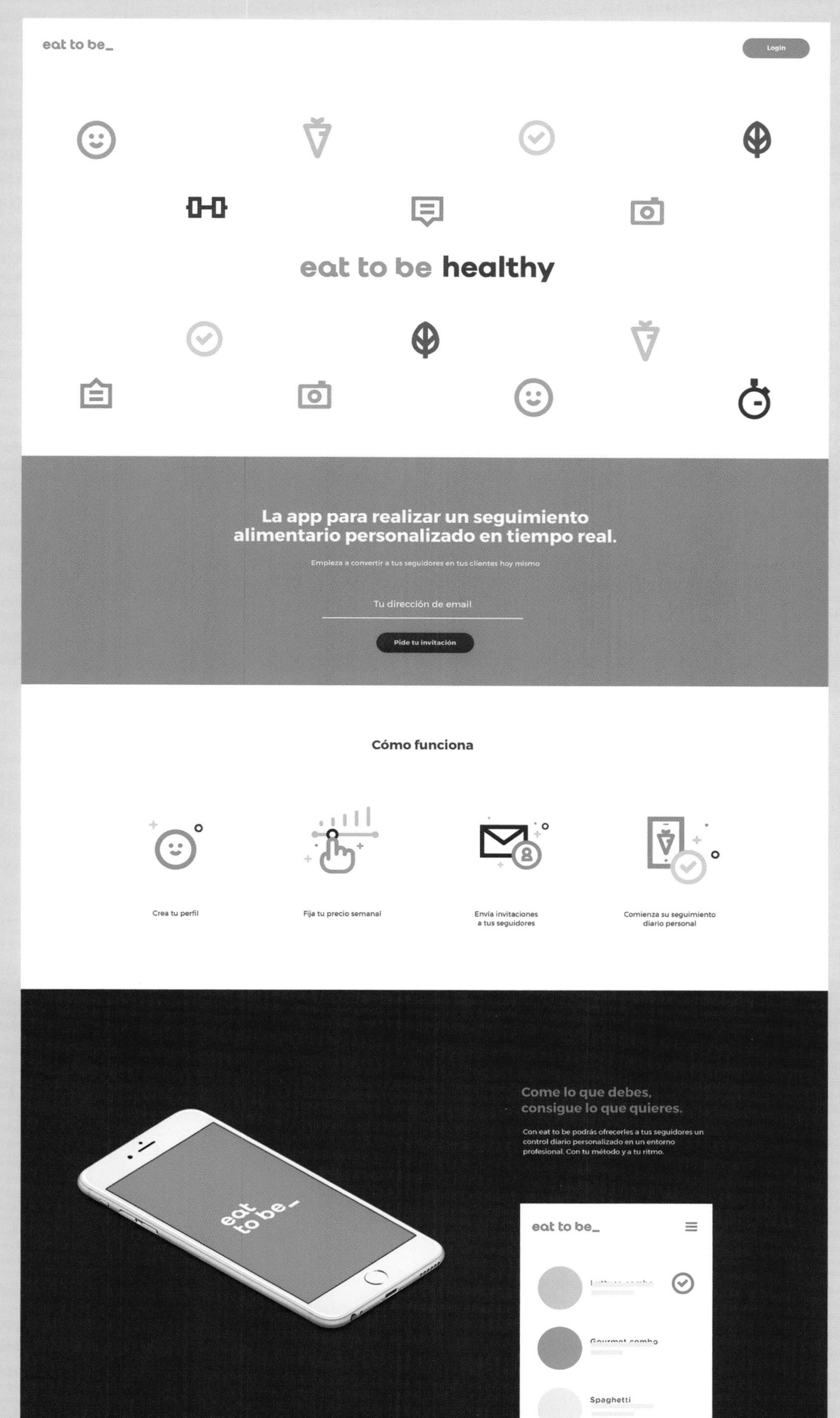
eat to be_
Login
eat to be healthy
La app para realizar un seguimiento alimentario personalizado en tiempo real.
Empieza a convertir a tus seguidores en tus clientes hoy mismo
Tu dirección de email
Pide tu invitación
Cómo funciona
Crea tu perfil
Fija tu precio semanal
Envía invitaciones a tus seguidores
Comienza su seguimiento diario personal
Come lo que debes, consigue lo que quieres.
Con eat to be podrás ofrecerles a tus seguidores un control diario personalizado en un entorno profesional. Con tu método y a tu ritmo.
eat to be_
eat to be_
Spaghetti

Planner App

Design/
Carmen Nácher

Planner App is a time management app proposal to help people manage their daily activities in a cleaner and more customizable way. The most notable advantage of this app is the icon families designed to link with 24 hours of the day. The user can create a personal schedule by linking names and descriptions to certain icons, which are developed to connect directly to the most common activities in a regular day. The application also allows users to save their activities or schedules for days, weeks, or months.

Icon set

04:00 PM
100%
01:00 -
02:00 Work
03:00
04:00 Pick up -...
05:00 -
+
06:00 Gym
07:00 -
08:00 -
09:00 Drinks w-..

04:00 PM
100%
04:00 PM
Now
Pick up order
Go to the store to pick up the order and stop by the library.

04:00 PM
100%
06:00 PM
Gym
-
SET ALARM

04:00 PM
100%
06:00 PM
SET ALARM

04:00 PM
100%
13. May. 2015
MAY
Mo Tu We Th Fr Sa Su
1 2 3
4 5 6 7 8 9 10
11 12 13 14 15 16 17
18 19 20 21 22 23 24
25 26 27 28 29 30 31

02:05 PM
100%
About
Planner App helps you organize your daily tasks in the most simple and direct way.

Styria Digital

Design Agency/
moodley brand identity

Direction/
Mike Fuisz

Design/
Kurt Glänzer

Client/
Styria Media Group

Styria Media Group works to improve internet business. moodley was invited to develop a website that simplified the complex. This website enables ad placements within the Styria-Portfolio much easier. Clear language and calm colors make the world of "1 and 0" a walk through the possibilities of the web. The focus is not on the technology, but on the potential of the Styria network. With a family of sophisticated icons and symbols, the site is embedded with flexibility and dynamic functionality. After all, there is still a lot of personality to be found behind high-tech applications.

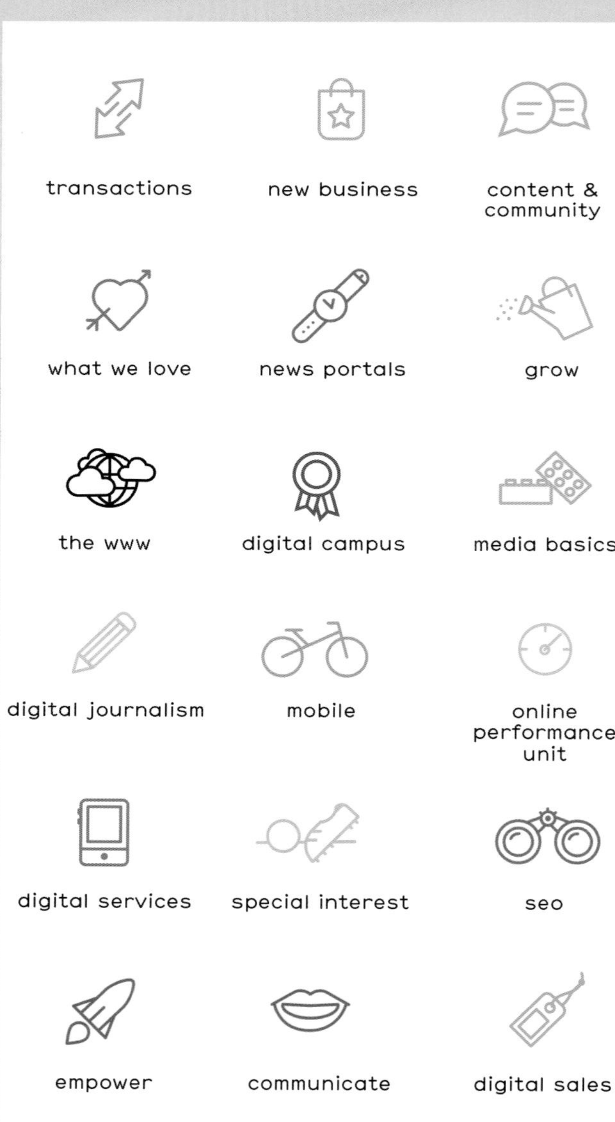

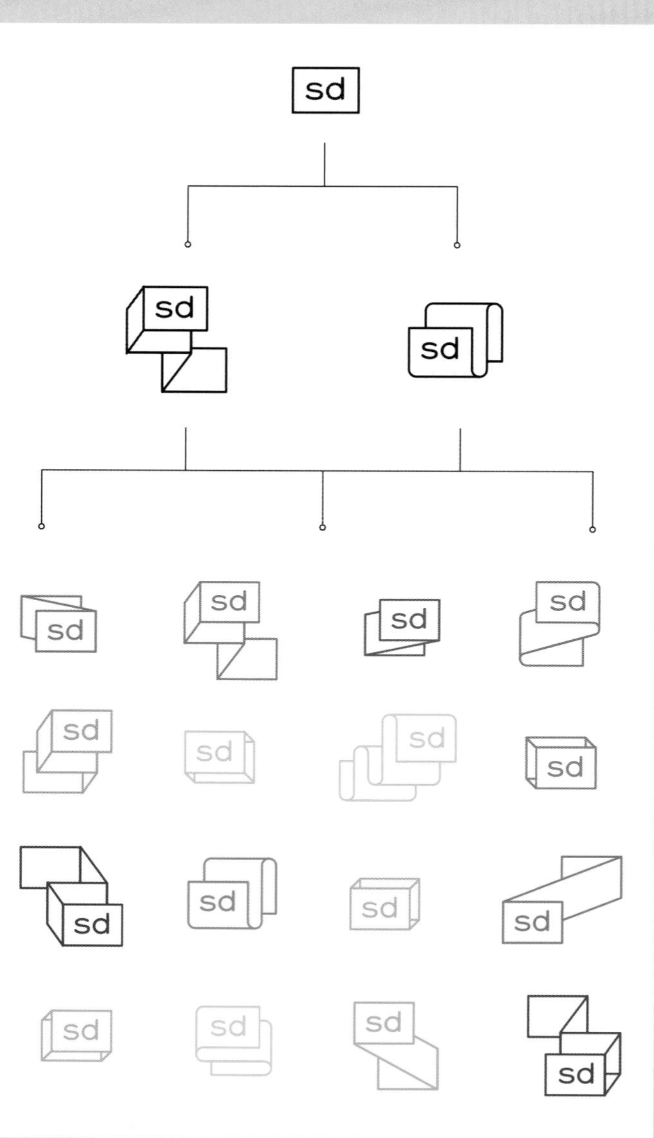

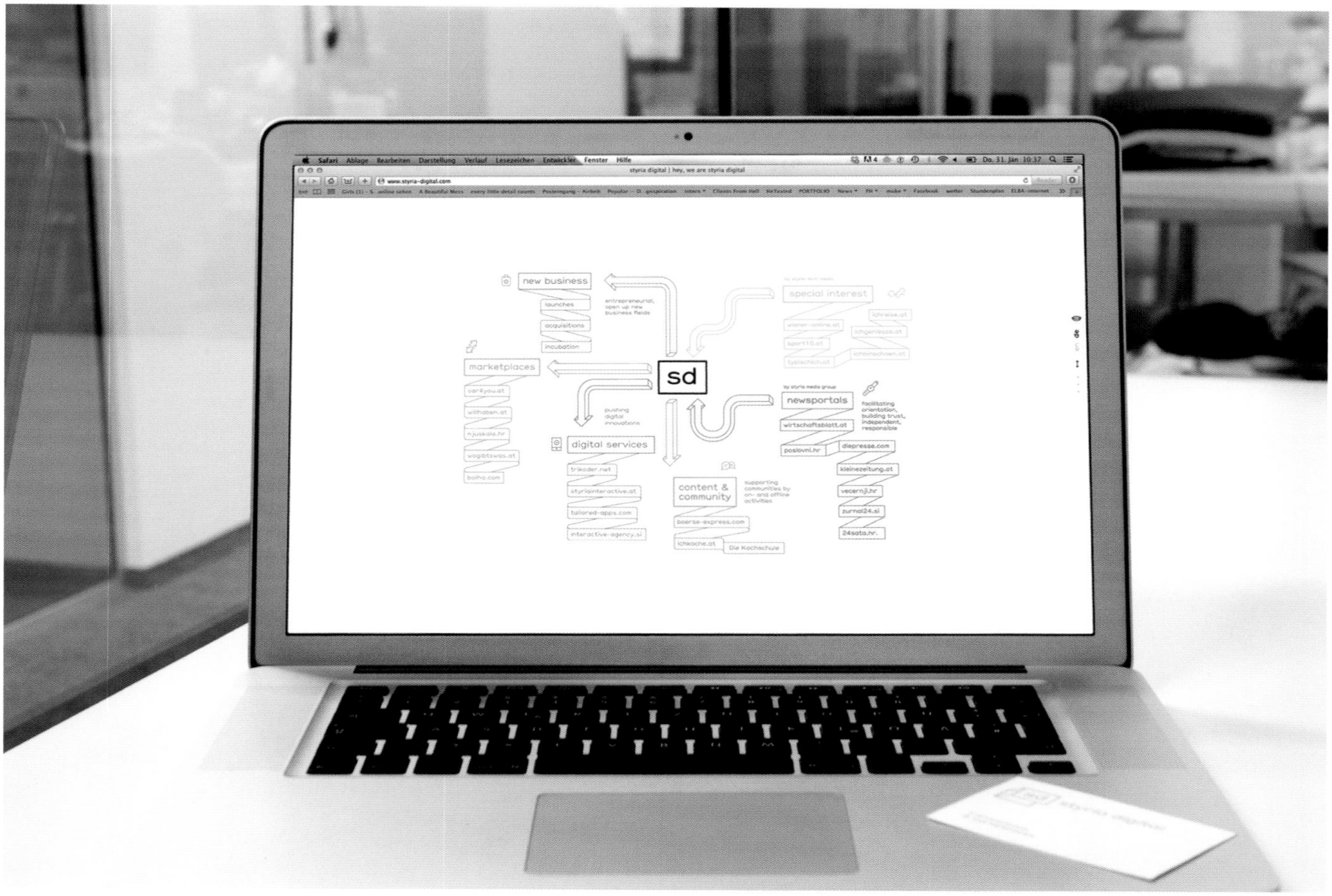

styria digital
hey, we are
styria digital
Wir sind Teil der Styria Media Group. Unsere
Leidenschaft: Wir finden und entwickeln

we help to grow
we empower
Head of Digital Services

Peter Travel Blog

Design/
Natalia Maltseva

Peter Travel Blog is a website designed to showcase the travel addict's travel notes. For this blog, Natalia Maltseva developed a set of travelling icons for the blogger to share his entertaining stories and useful tips from his travels around the world. Rather than describing the physical facts with wordy descriptions, pictograms make it easier to be understood.

HI!

My name is Peter and I'm a travel addict.

Join me as I share entertaining stories and useful tips from around the world...

To some, travel means sunbathing on the deck of a cruise ship while getting a massage. That's nice, but it's not for me!

To me... travel isn't just about relaxing; it's also about venturing out into the unknown, following your own path, and pushing beyond your comfort zone. It means trying new food, experiencing other cultures, and doing silly things sometimes. At its best, travel lets you view the world with a sense of awe and wonder.

40 COUNTRIES | 28620 KMS | 50 000 PHOTO | 7000 M | 52 °C | -35 °C

BLOG

20 FEB 2015

Crazy meet the grizzly bears
Canada, Yukon, National Park

Grizzly bears are majestic symbols of the wild. Bears live in and use a variety of habitat types, playing important roles in each one.

This makes them an "umbrella species," meaning that when we protect them and their habitat we also protect many species. Grizzly bears can also help ecosystems by distributing seeds and nutrients through their scat, and occasionally regul [...]

READ MORE »

Babel—Universal Language Exhibition

Design/
Alex Alessi, Daniele Caldari, Marco Fabbri, Filippo Ventura

Teacher/
Cristina Chiappini

Teaching Assistant/
Matteo Stocco

Babel is a utopian project of a future ruled by a total universality of one language. In 1936 Eric Gill tried to highlight in his book "An essay on typography" the vision of a thought typographical unitary given by the analogy between sign and phonetic. The Babel website was based on an exhibition which enabled audiences to integrate and interact with the project to create significant and necessary future expression symbols. On this site, visitors can draw new signs for this new language from what they heard.

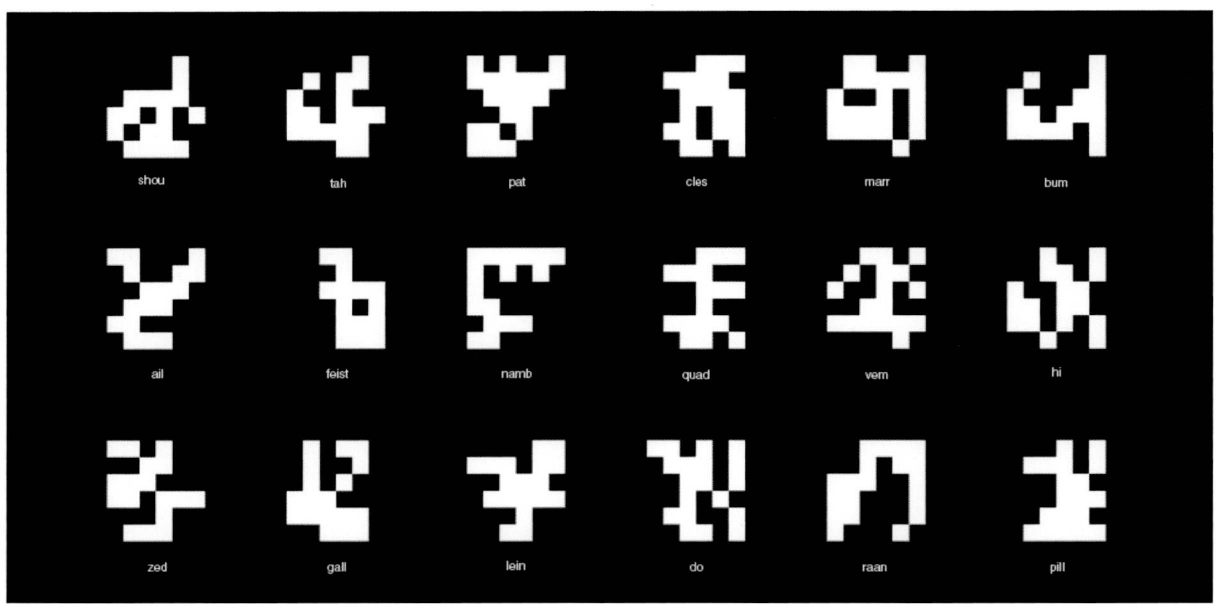

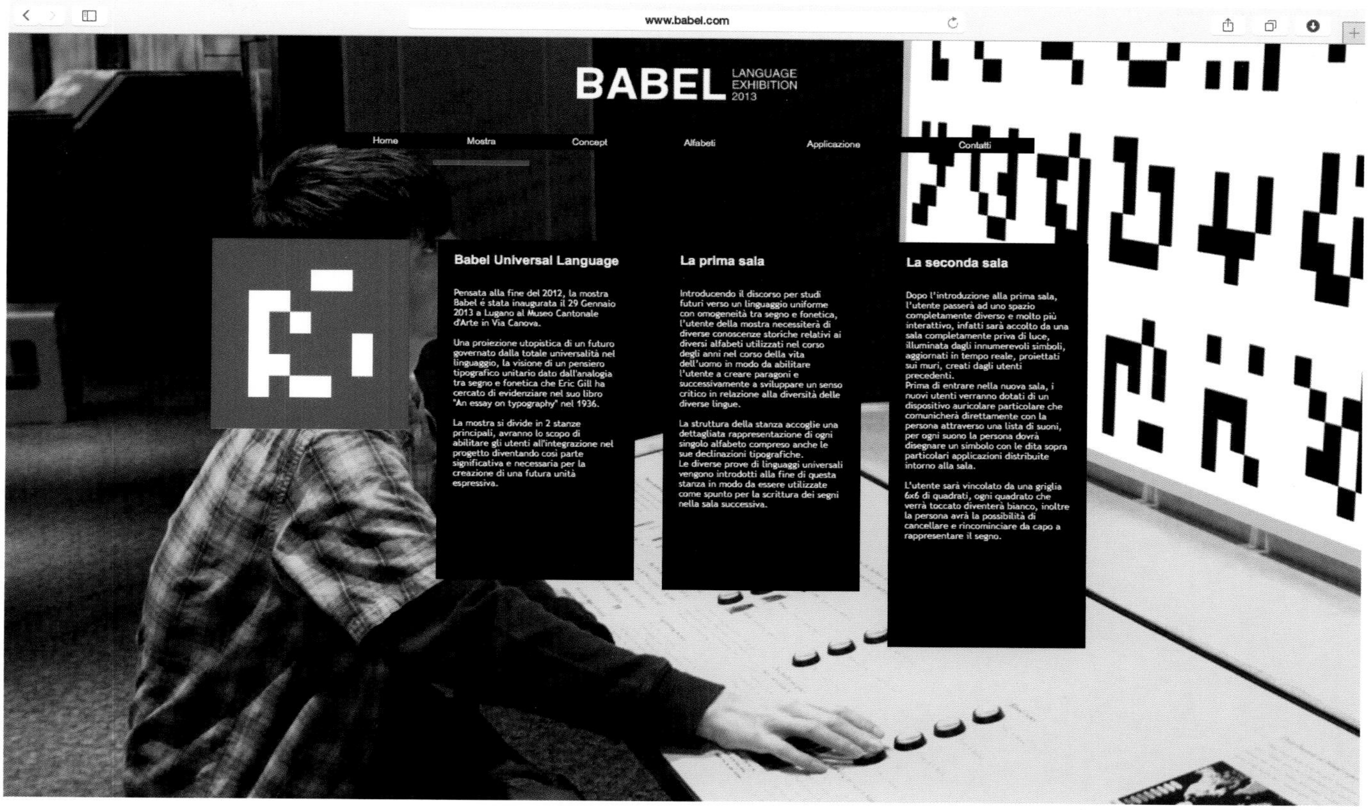

www.babel.com

BABEL LANGUAGE EXHIBITION 2013

Home Mostra Concept Alfabeti Applicazione Contatti

Babel Universal Language

Pensata alla fine del 2012, la mostra Babel é stata inaugurata il 29 Gennaio 2013 a Lugano al Museo Cantonale d'Arte in Via Canova.

Una proiezione utopistica di un futuro governato dalla totale universalità nel linguaggio, la visione di un pensiero tipografico unitario dato dall'analogia tra segno e fonetica che Eric Gill ha cercato di evidenziare nel suo libro "An essay on typography" nel 1936.

La mostra si divide in 2 stanze principali, avranno lo scopo di abilitare gli utenti all'integrazione nel progetto diventando così parte significativa e necessaria per la creazione di una futura unità espressiva.

La prima sala

Introducendo il discorso per studi futuri verso un linguaggio uniforme con omogeneità tra segno e fonetica, l'utente della mostra necessiterà di diverse conoscenze storiche relativi ai diversi alfabeti utilizzati nel corso degli anni nel corso della vita dell'uomo in modo da abilitare l'utente a creare paragoni e successivamente a sviluppare un senso critico in relazione alla diversità delle diverse lingue.

La struttura della stanza accoglie una dettagliata rappresentazione di ogni singolo alfabeto compreso anche le sue declinazioni tipografiche.
Le diverse prove di linguaggi universali vengono introdotti alla fine di questa stanza in modo da essere utilizzate come spunto per la scrittura dei segni nella sala successiva.

La seconda sala

Dopo l'introduzione alla prima sala, l'utente passerà ad uno spazio completamente diverso e molto più interattivo, infatti sarà accolto da una sala completamente priva di luce, illuminata dagli innumerevoli simboli, aggiornati in tempo reale, proiettati sui muri, creati dagli utenti precedenti.
Prima di entrare nella nuova sala, i nuovi utenti verranno dotati di un dispositivo auricolare particolare che comunicherà direttamente con la persona attraverso una lista di suoni, per ogni suono la persona dovrà disegnare un simbolo con le dita sopra particolari applicazioni distribuite intorno alla sala.

L'utente sarà vincolato da una griglia 6x6 di quadrati, ogni quadrato che verrà toccato diventerà bianco, inoltre la persona avrà la possibilità di cancellare e rincominciare da capo a rappresentare il segno.

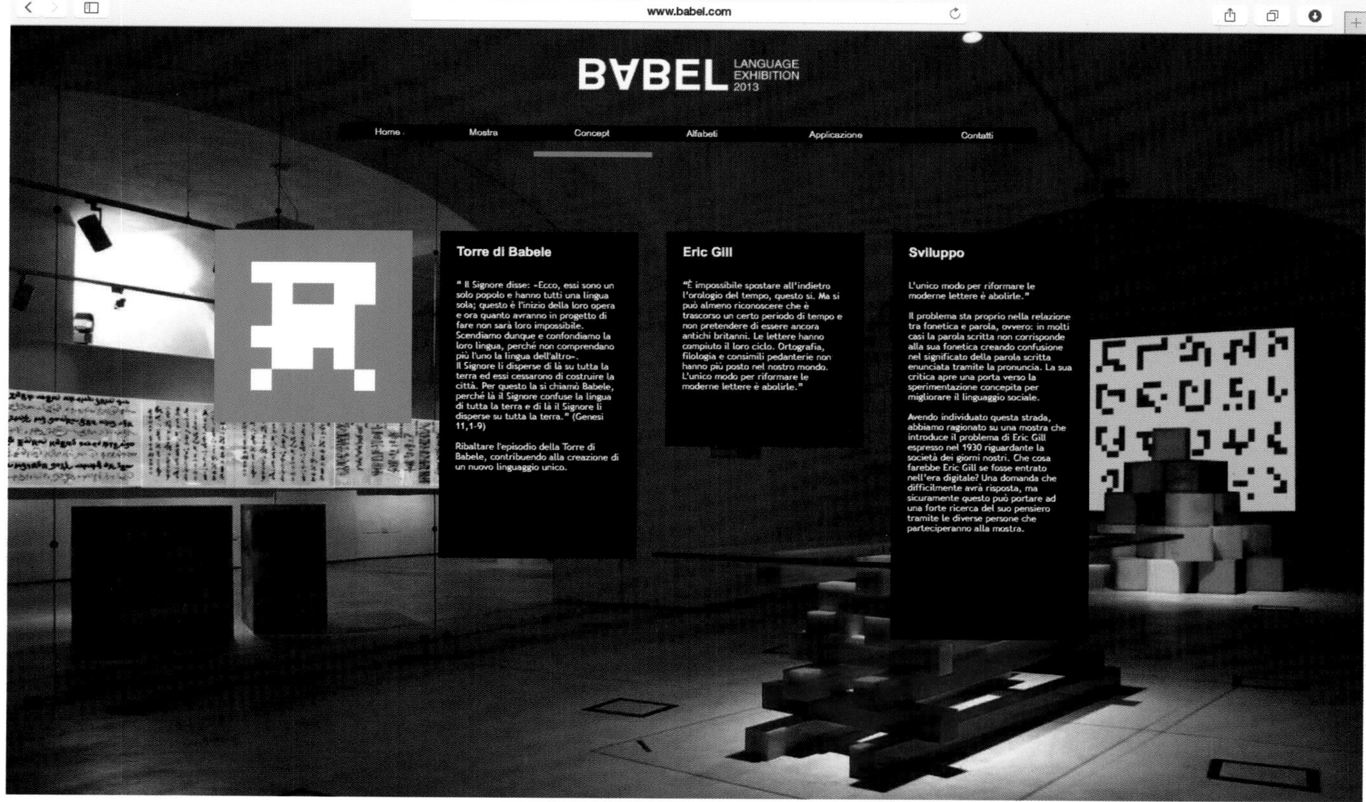

www.babel.com
BABEL LANGUAGE EXHIBITION 2013
Home
Mostra
Concept
Alfabeti
Applicazione
Contatti
Torre di Babele
" Il Signore disse: -Ecco, essi sono un solo popolo e hanno tutti una lingua sola; questo è l'inizio della loro opera e ora quanto avranno in progetto di fare non sarà loro impossibile. Scendiamo dunque e confondiamo la loro lingua, perché non comprendano più l'uno la lingua dell'altro-.
Il Signore li disperse di là su tutta la terra ed essi cessarono di costruire la città. Per questo la si chiamò Babele, perché là il Signore confuse la lingua di tutta la terra e di là il Signore li disperse su tutta la terra." (Genesi 11,1-9)
Ribaltare l'episodio della Torre di Babele, contribuendo alla creazione di un nuovo linguaggio unico.
Eric Gill
"È impossibile spostare all'indietro l'orologio del tempo, questo si. Ma si può almeno riconoscere che è trascorso un certo periodo di tempo e non pretendere di essere ancora antichi britanni. Le lettere hanno compiuto il loro ciclo. Ortografia, filologia e consimili pedanterie non hanno più posto nel nostro mondo. L'unico modo per riformare le moderne lettere è abolirle."
Sviluppo
L'unico modo per riformare le moderne lettere è abolirle."
Il problema sta proprio nella relazione tra fonetica e parola, ovvero: in molti casi la parola scritta non corrisponde alla sua fonetica creando confusione nel significato della parola scritta enunciata tramite la pronuncia. La sua critica apre una porta verso la sperimentazione concepita per migliorare il linguaggio sociale.
Avendo individuato questa strada, abbiamo ragionato su una mostra che introduce il problema di Eric Gill espresso nel 1930 riguardante la società dei giorni nostri. Che cosa farebbe Eric Gill se fosse entrato nell'era digitale? Una domanda che difficilmente avrà risposta, ma sicuramente questo può portare ad una forte ricerca del suo pensiero tramite le diverse persone che parteciperanno alla mostra.

Lawrence Boone Selections

Design Agency/
Phoenix the Creative Studio

Design Direction/
Louis Paquet

Design/
Louis Paquet, Phoenix Team

Account Management/
Fouad Mallouk

URL/
https://booneselections.com

Lawrence Boone Selections discovers and imports the finest wines from those of the most renowned wine regions in the world to those of the most obscure. They only import sustainably produced wines that are true expressions of their terrain.

For Boone Selections, the problem of the wine industry is that everything always looks the same: traditional, classy, and often boring. The client demanded an identity that would differentiate him from the other companies in the industry. He needed new communications that would be in line with his vision of the wine world. The logo symbolizing grapes, elegant website, and icons related to wine are therefore a result.

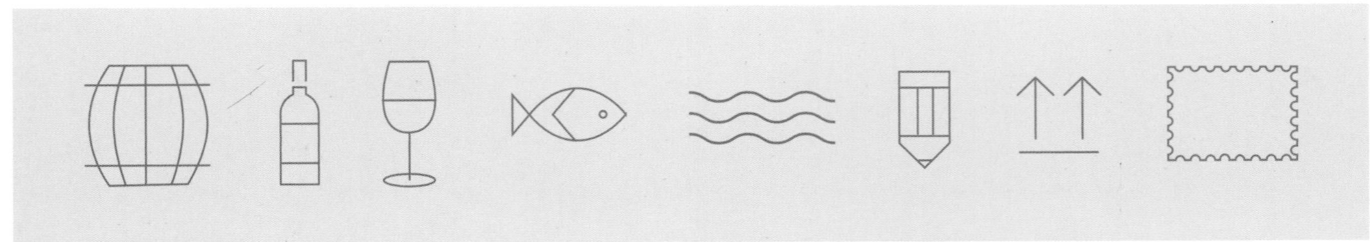

PREV
FLOW 2009
NEXT
SOTA ELS ÀNGELS
BOONE
LAWRENCE BOONE SELECTIONS
DESEA
2009
PRODUCERS
SOTA ELS ÀNGELS
REGION
EMPORDÀ, SPAIN
Handpicked and selected at the optimal ripeness. Hand harvested in small 15kg boxes. After cooling, grapes are de-stemmed and placed in stainless-steel tanks. Cold soaked for 5 days at 6ºc, followed by alcoholic fermentation at 18ºc. Medium maceration for 10-15 days. Aged 12 months in lightly toasted French Allier oak barrels.
2009
REDWINE
750ml
13.8%
desea
75CL

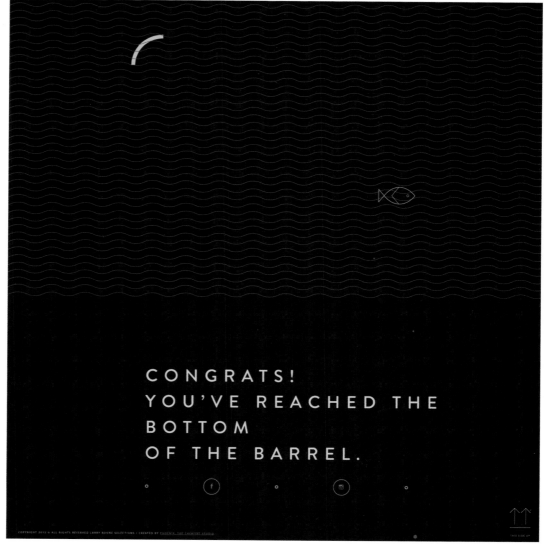

CONGRATS!
YOU'VE REACHED THE BOTTOM
OF THE BARREL.

Sonder 6

Design Agency/
CTDL GAMES

Design/
Piotr Buczkowski, Krzysztof Domaradzki, Tomasz Lassota, Maciej Mach

Sonder 6 is an endless runner game with engaging visuals and immersive music. The goal of the game is simple: tap to rotate and hold to speed up in order to go through as many gates as possible. Beat your friends' scores and show them who the best player is. The characters are pixelated to create a totally brand-new experience.

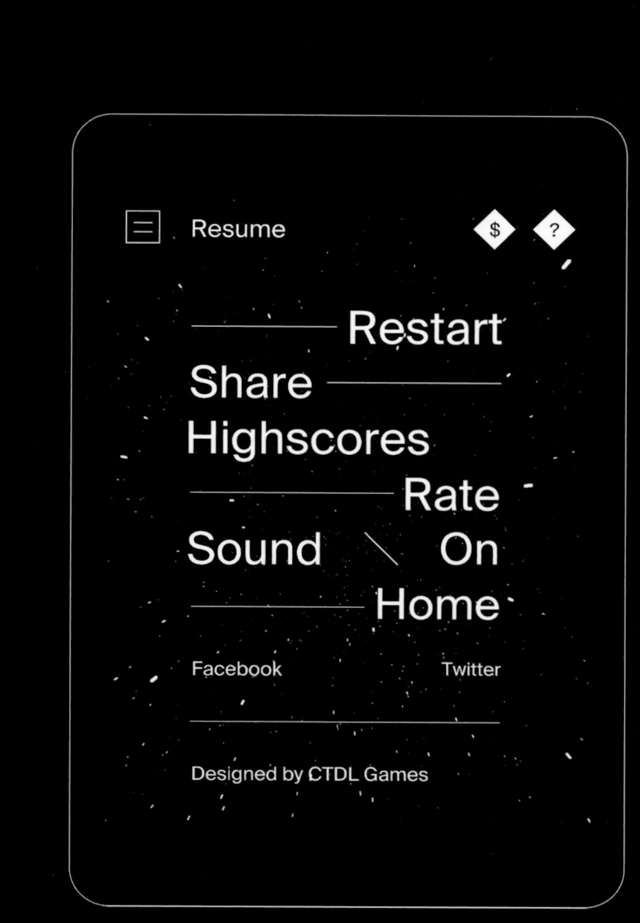
Resume
$
?
Restart
Share
Highscores
Rate
Sound
On
Home
Facebook
Twitter
Designed by CTDL Games

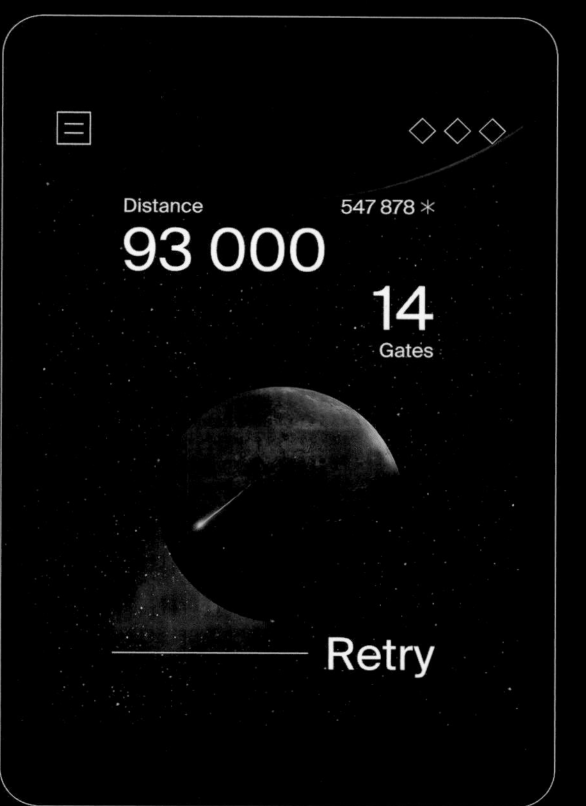
Distance
547 878 *
93 000
14
Gates
Retry

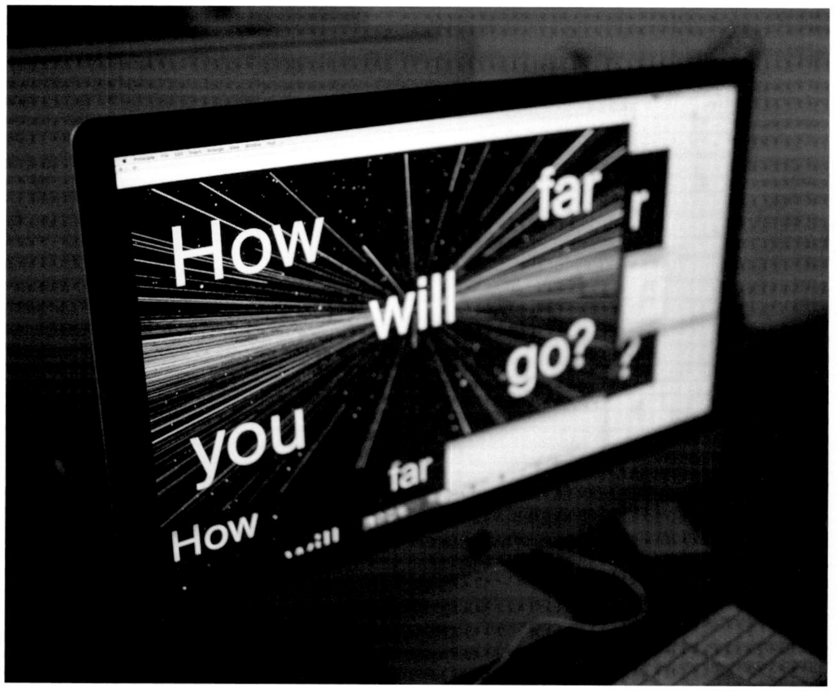
How
far
will
go?
you
far
How

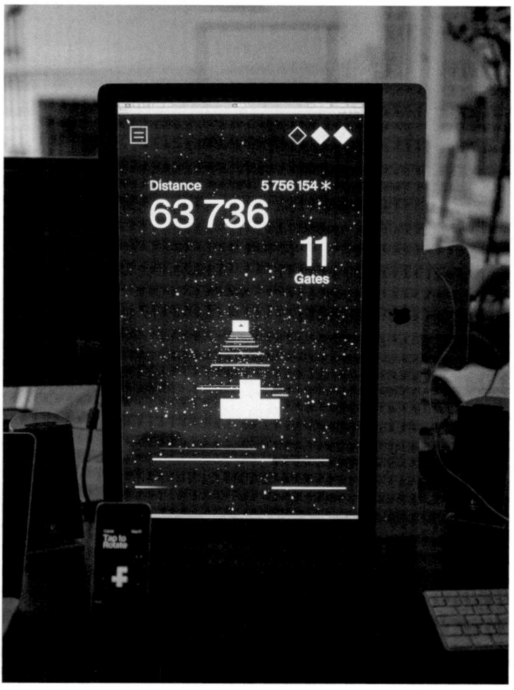
Distance
5 756 154 *
63 736
11
Gates

STRADA CAFE

Design/
Nino Mamaladze, Nick buturishvili, Nick Kumbari, Levan Ambokadze

The Strada project revolved around the idea that a restaurant could deliver an engaging and interactive experience even before you arrived at the premises. The designers wanted to use simplicity to communicate this to its consumers with instantly recognizable icons. At a glance, visitors could make quick decisions without the typical over-complicated menu system.

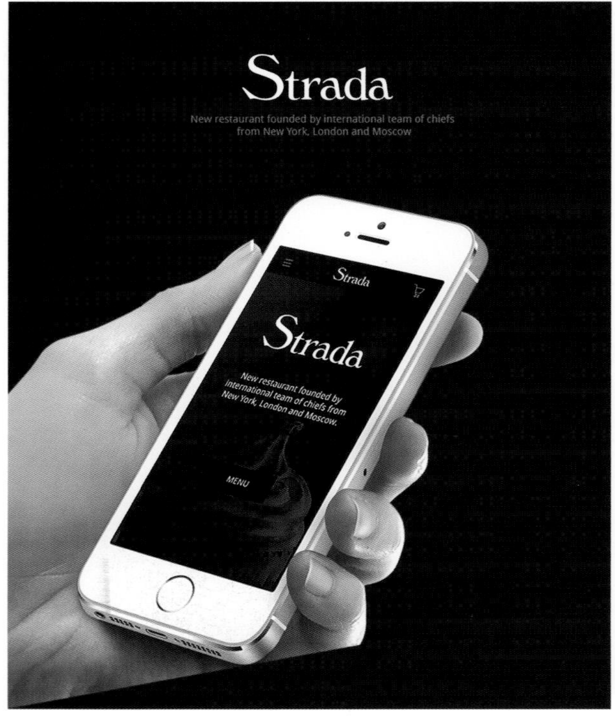

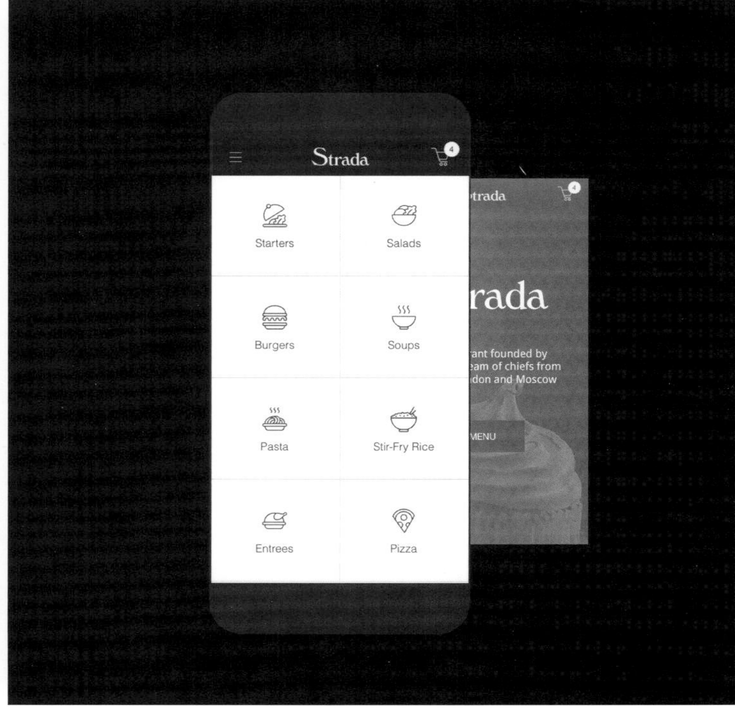

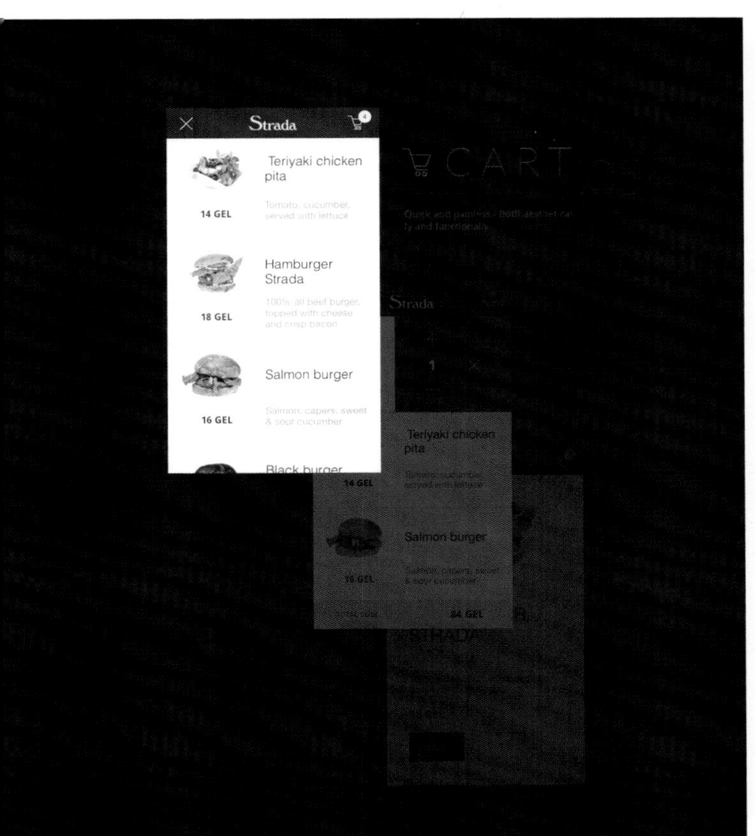

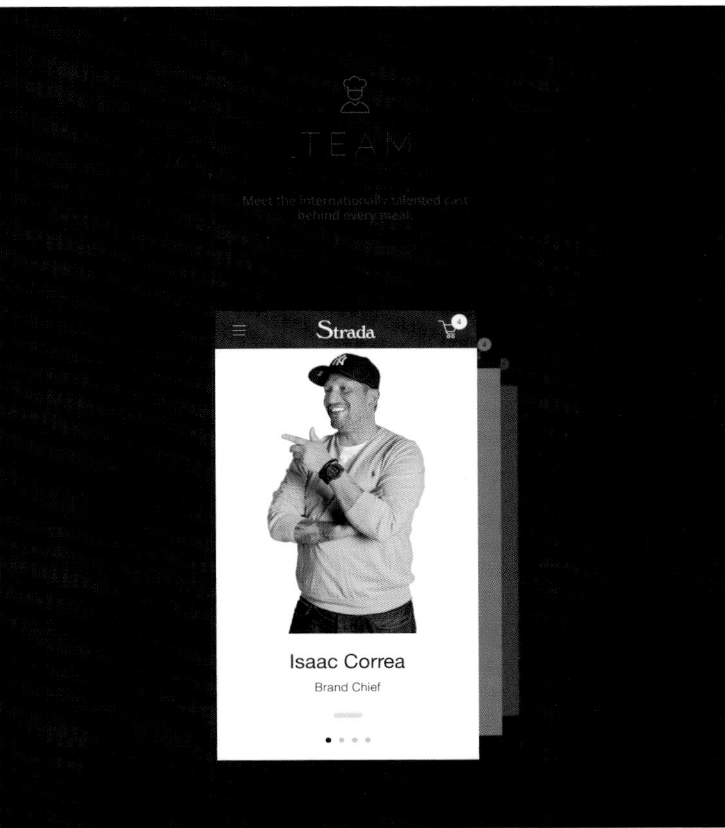

Strada

Great people at Strada cook the best damn food in Tbilisi. We had no other option but to design a website to match the culinary excellence of Strada chefs - a literal treat for your eyes. Bon appétit!

Design for Screen — 4

Text & Typography

Line Heigh

TLE FONT

38px

Contents

16px

Interview with

Sons & Co.

Sons & Co. is a small-scale website design studio in New Zealand yet with high productivity and outstanding qualities that endow them great fames and multiple awards. They talk less, without even a studio website, but their works speak for themselves.

◇ Q1 ◇ Can you tell us a little bit about your background and how you came about to be doing web design?

We're a team of four from varied backgrounds: graphic design, advertising, computer science, and law. The common thread is an interest in design and technology and the web as a medium for both. In 2008 we came together, designers and developers sitting at the same table, to develop a way of working that values design, simplicity, and good humor above all else.

◇ Q2 ◇ Please kindly describe your design process: Is there a specific routine/technique that you adhere to?

We don't have an overly strict or complicated process; we just show up each day, pour some coffee and get to work. In the middle of the day there's a break for food, some more coffee and then straight back to it. As far as we can tell, that's the way it's been done for centuries and we see no reason to mess with the recipe.

To us, "creative" feels like the antithesis of "process," like everyone we have habits, but all projects have their own personality. Ultimately we're focused on the outcome and how we get there varies job-to-job. We love the informality of the design studio and the freedom it provides and would hate to turn into a Gantt Chart.

◇ Q3 ◇ A lot of web designs might look beautiful but not friendly to users. How do you take a complex chunk of information and make sense out of it?

Our views are pretty simplistic: good design is good design and you know it when you see it or use it. We can rationalize with the best of them, but to paraphrase E. B. White, analyzing design is like dissecting a frog: few people are interested and the frog dies in the process.

◇ Q4 ◇ How do you determine the line height and letter spacing for a website?

It's completely contextual, but we have written some very nerdy custom code to dynamically set values so they're relative to the font size, but use a sliding scale to maintain good proportions. We tweak from there.

◇ Q5 ◇ How do you think of the function of color in web design?

It's. You have composition, proportion.

◇ Q6 ◇ Which fonts would you recommend in web design? Or do you have any preference?

You get what you pay for and young type foundries like Klim, Swiss and Grilli are doing great things for print and web designers.

◇ Q7 ◇ It is said that there is no bad typeface but only improper use of typeface. Do you agree? Is it true in web design?

There are bad typefaces, but a good typeface is no guarantee of a good outcome. In the end, typefaces are tools and you can wield them like a scalpel or like an axe.

◇ Q8 ◇ The typography in your project for Tennent Brown is very impressive. What was your inspiration to make the title so intriguing and in optical illusion?

Alt Group developed the beautiful identity, which included the folded type elements, and we brought it to life on the screen. It's an optical trick created using three duplicate text elements. Each element is masked to reveal a single line of text, then skewed and rotated on different planes. On scroll, it gives the illusion of a single element with text flowing over a stepped path.

◇ Q9 ◇ Who was the target audience for this design? How did it impact your work?

It's a portfolio site. The aim was to bring people's attention to the designs of Tennent Brown, but also to illustrate the way they think and work. Hugh and Ewan are particularly interested in how a good building can uplift a person's quality of life and wellbeing. A large part of the site is given over to Hugh and Ewan's clients telling their own stories, which is a nice gesture on behalf of the architects.

◇ Q10 ◇ How do you balance the readability and aesthetics in this project?

I think they go hand-in-hand. In part, it's an editorial website so readability is important and we lean on good examples publication design, rather than web design, for inspiration.

◇ Q11 ◇ How many fonts did you use on this website? What was your purpose?

Just one font — Neue Haas Grotesk —it's all that was required.

Tennent Brown Architects

Design Agency/
Sons & Co.

Creative Direction/
Timothy Kelleher, Dean Poole

Design/
Matthew Arnold, Paul Bright, Nicole Stock, Katarina Mrsic, Jinki Cambronero, Greg Brown

Client/
Tennent Brown

URL/
http://tennentbrown.co.nz

Ngā Purapura delivers a new type of building that aims to deliver sports, nutrition and lifestyle learning in an environment that embraces the wider community and gives expression to Tikanga Māori.

The building incorporates two indoor sports courts, a cardio gym, nutrition training kitchen, classrooms, administration and academic offices.

The whakatauki (proverb) that underlies Te Wānanga -"E kore au e ngaro he kakano i ruia mai i Rangiatea" (I will never be lost, the seed which was sown from Rangiatea) - is also expressed in the nohopuku (reflective) space, being in the form of a kakano (seed). This space is also for developing new kawa (protocols) in support of the kaupapa (purpose) of the facility.

The holistic model of Māori health 'Te Whare tapa Wha' (the four sides of the house) – addresses the need for physical (tinana), mental and emotional (hinengaro), spiritual (wairua), and social (whanau), aspects of life - all to be in balance for wellbeing. The design represents this model with a four folded roof, creating spaces with associated functions leaning against the neutral form of the sports hall.

The Kaupapa panels, sandblasted into the external sports hall walls were designed by Te Wānanga O Raukawa students.

AWARDS

2013 NZIA Branch Award

2013 Best Design Awards Ngā Aho

2013 Best Design Awards Purple Pin

2013 Interior Awards Finalist - Civic

2013 Interior Awards Finalist - Craftmanship

2012 Sustainability Awards Excellence in Concrete for the Community

PUBLICATIONS

Architecture NZ July/ Aug 2012

Art of the Architect 2014

Interior June/ Aug 2013

Interior Dec/ Feb 2012/ 2013

Font: Neue Haas Grotesk \ ***Font-Kerning:*** 1px \ ***Line Height:*** 28.1px

The project is ambitious in its vision – to create a 'community space that fosters the connection between nature, wellness, and humanity's need for transition to a regenerative existence'. The sustainability aspirations of the Aro Ha project are equally ambitious. Aro Ha is designed to be able to operate the facility for periods with-out connection to the grid and reliance on fossil fuels. Maximum on site food production based on Permaculture principles, to fulfil the self-sufficiency ethos also define the project. This vision and the scale, make it unique in New Zealand.
AROHA

Tennent Brown is an architecture company based in New Zealand. With a humanity care in the effect of buildings and environments may affect people, they design to uplift the quality of life, work, play, and wellbeing of those the buildings serve.

Sons & Co. was commissioned to create the official website to illustrate their philosophy and showcase their works. This is effectively realized through the eye-catching title with vivid characteristic as architectures, a modern and responsive website, clear structure, and minimal concept. The typography is also evoking its aesthetic through Neue Haas Grotesk to convey a modern look.

Connection and separation are themes that run throughout this house. Inspired by the eroding channels in the rocks and cliffs far below the house, the interior has been thought of like carved lines through the topography. Clefts and cliffs are etched into the plan of the house like in the separation of the upstairs bedrooms, and sun is grabbed wherever it can be.
At the top of the stairs, just outside Rona's room, is an anteroom with a deep window seat. It is one of those spaces that would be labelled sketchily on the plans with some vague notation of 'nook' or alcove'. It, like the adjoining hall-cum-sitting space, is flexible, neither bedroom nor lounge nor study, and yet is all of those things.
Matt's large study is on the lowest floor and Alyson had reservations about this 'man cave' being so separated from the rest of the house. She was gratified then, when she found Hugh had understood her concerns and designed the edge of the stairs to be open, allowing Alyson to call down from her own study and the two to talk comfortably while still being in their own spaces.
The site sits on the edge of a 45m cliff facing south over Taputeranga Island in Island Bay with magnificent views of the harbour entrance, Cook Strait and the South Island Kaikouras. The clients desired a large family home that responded to the dramatic views, was spacious, low maintenance, warm and able to accommodate their large collection of New Zealand paintings and ceramics.
An appreciation of the weather is seen in small details: zinc was selected as cladding for its low maintenance, durability and weathertightness in the face of extreme salt laden winds from the south; the covered vestibule that allows wind-ravaged

FIVE
PERSPECTIVES

ISLAND BAY HOUSE | ARO HĀ RETREAT | ASB SPORTS CENTRE | VICTORIA UNIVERSITY | NGĀ PURAPURA | ALL PROJECTS | STUDIO & CONTACT | LOGIN

2016

WAIMEA ESTUARY, TASMAN BAY

TOREA STUDIO

ACCOMMODATING GUESTS AND FRIENDS

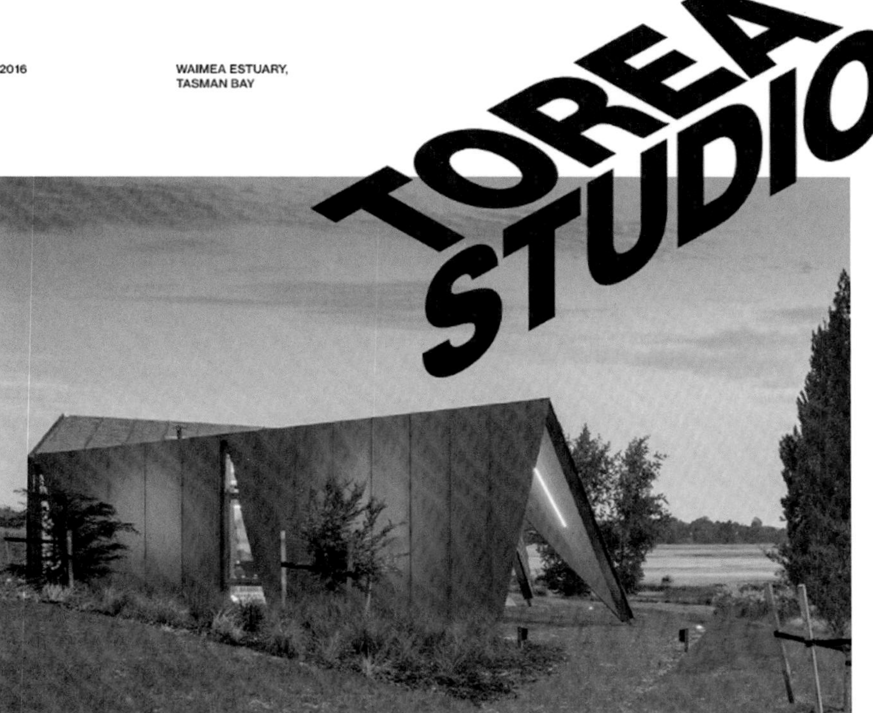

Torea studio is a study and meeting space, plus guest accommodation. Following the design language of the main Torea house, the studio draws on the metaphor of two Torea (oystercatchers) walking down the site to the Waimea estuary.

The building is composed from 'folded' triangular cross-laminated-timber (CLT) panels clad in charcoal coloured seamed zinc, that form both the enclosure of the building and a series of protected outdoor spaces beneath the 'wings'. The interior is a series of simple cave-like rooms with the interior of the CLT panels exposed, which lends a calm unity to the spaces, despite the dynamic angles of wall and roof.

An outdoor terrace is carved from the surrounding paddock with two local fieldstone walls, a contrast to the crisp metal cladding.

This construction has only been possible due to XLAM NZ's sophisticated new CNC bridge machine that has enabled precise cutting of each CLT panel direct from a computer model.

AWARDS

2016 NZIA Branch Award

Interview with

Pierre Nguyen

With rich experience in digital design, Pierre Nguyen, also known as Monsieur Caillou, is a widely-recognized French digital art director and UX designer based in Paris. He is a freelance designer working for agencies like AKQA, BETC, and Spintank. His design often draws inspiration from magazine, and he forms his special style: unusual layout, typographic passion, and composition of images.

◊ Q1 ◊ Can you tell us a little bit about your background and how you came about to be doing web design?

I studied graphic design in art school and at Gobelins, a school focused on digital design and animation, and print media, and video and sound, in Paris. At first, I studied print design, but I soon turned to web design for my fascination to screen design. Today I work mainly on web design, app design, and branding.

◊ Q2 ◊ Please kindly describe your design process: Is there a specific routine/technique that you adhere to?

It is all about user experience. My first question is who my target user is; what they want to do with it; and how to give them fabulous user experience. When I come up with the answers, the solution gradually comes into realization. Besides, my projects are mainly inspired by print design and video game design.

◊ Q3 ◊ A lot of web designs might look beautiful but not friendly to users. How do you take a complex chunk of information and make sense out of it?

As I mention above, user experience is always my priority. It is necessary to listen carefully to users and meet their requirements.

◊ Q4 ◊ How do you determine the line height and letter spacing for a website?

I define the line height for the best readability as possible and I love to give breathe to the design. That's why I am used to playing with blank spaces.

Concerning letter spacing, it is basically depended on one's design style. But in that case again, readability is essential. Only in some exceptions I will use very large letter spacing.

◊ Q5 ◊ How do you think of the function of Typography in web design?

Essential! Typography conveys a lot of information about the brand and for most of users. It is imperceptible. This is about subconscious.

◊ Q6 ◊ Which fonts would you recommend to web designers? Or do you have any preference?

I really like the fonts of commercial type, such as Grilli and Hoefler.

◊ Q7 ◊ The interactivity allows users to make a more direct contact with the content than print design, what does it influence typography on screen?

Indeed, typography can also play a role in navigation. It needs to be clear, well-understand, and invites users to interact on it with a minimum of information.

◊ Q8 ◊ It is said that there is no bad typeface but only improper use of typeface. Do you agree? Is it true in web design?

Yes I agree. But I consider letter as a graphic shape, so it is interesting when some rules are not respected even in type design.

◊ Q9 ◊ The typography in your project of Monsieur Caillou is very impressive. What was your initiative to use the type in a bold manner?

I wanted to make a real and great impact when the visitor comes to my website. So I quickly chose to make a minimal design with a huge emphasis on font. I chose the Druk font because she fits perfect with what I imagined for my site.

◊ Q10 ◊ This website, being your portfolio, showcases your aesthetic inclination and pursuit. What do you want to convey to your readers? How do fonts and typography manage to do it?

I started to design my website with the idea that it should reflect my fascination to magazine and create titles and images as in magazines. The use of oversized titles helps to give this direction.

◊ Q11 ◊ How do you balance the readability and aesthetics in this project?

More typography, less images!

◊ Q12 ◊ How many fonts did you use on this website? What was your purpose?

I used only two fonts. Druk for the title, and Graphik for body text. Druk is perfect for impressive design, while Graphik is used for the function to secure the readability.

Monsieur Caillou

Design/
Pierre Nguyen

URL/
http://www.monsieurcaillou.com

Title: Druk \ ***Contents:*** Graphik \ ***Font-Kerning:*** Normal \ ***Line Height:*** 16px

Monsieur Caillou is the nickname of Pierre Nguyen. The website is his personal online portfolio, composed of 6 projects, a dedicated icon page, and short archive.

Awarded with both Fwa and Awwwards, the website is mainly inspired by magazine. His passion for magazine and typography instills the moderate yet overwhelmingly impressive type to this site. The bold types, all capitalized and every project name of a specific color, work with artistic shades to embody it with a strong personality.

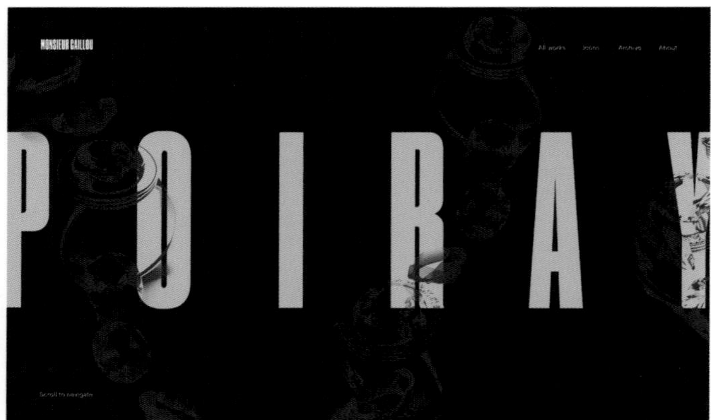

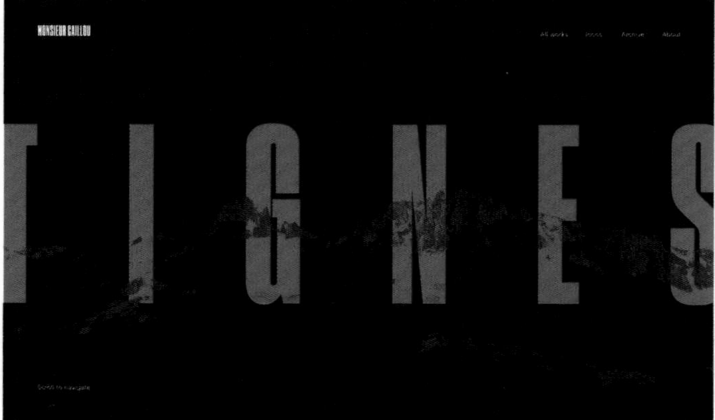

Back to home

All works Icons Archive About

MAJE

DATE 2014

BETC DIGITAL AGENCY

ROLE ART DIRECTION

UX DESIGN

LET'S SCROLL

Bonne Marque

Design Agency/
Bonne Marque

URL/
https://bonnemarque.se

Through the wild fire of their Born Makers rebrand, Bonne Marque created a smooth and immersive experience of an online archive. The dark landing page begins with twelve words within a 3x4 grid. The words within this responsive brand statement light sporadically, forming separate sentences that define their characters and crafts. Case study titles are represented by intimidating monolith-esque letters, over which stands a brief description of the project. All writing is composed by a novelist and poet, and the case studies make the best use of their writer's skills. Combined with Alexander Engzell's design, masterfully balancing his unique eye for minimalism and inventive thinking, the result is worthy of a visit.

Font: Sentinel; 18px \ ***Font-Kerning:*** Normal \ ***Line Height:*** 28.8px

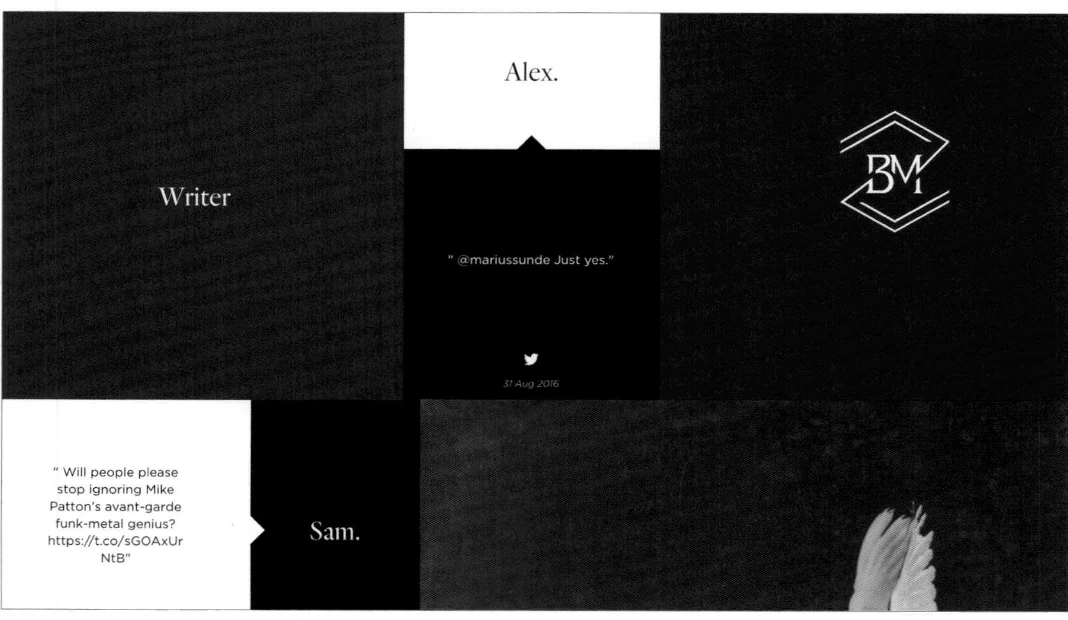

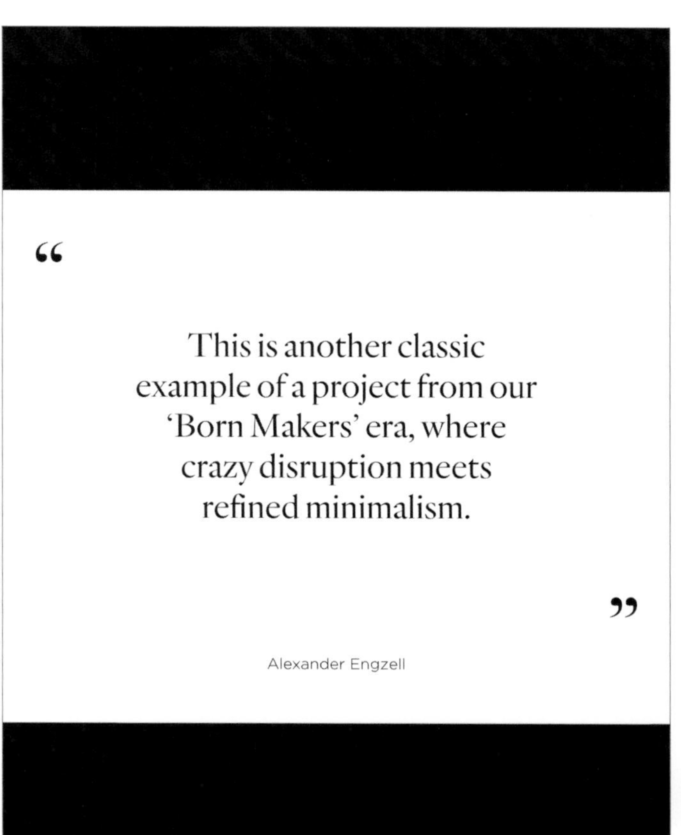
“
This is another classic example of a project from our ‘Born Makers’ era, where crazy disruption meets refined minimalism.
”
Alexander Engzell

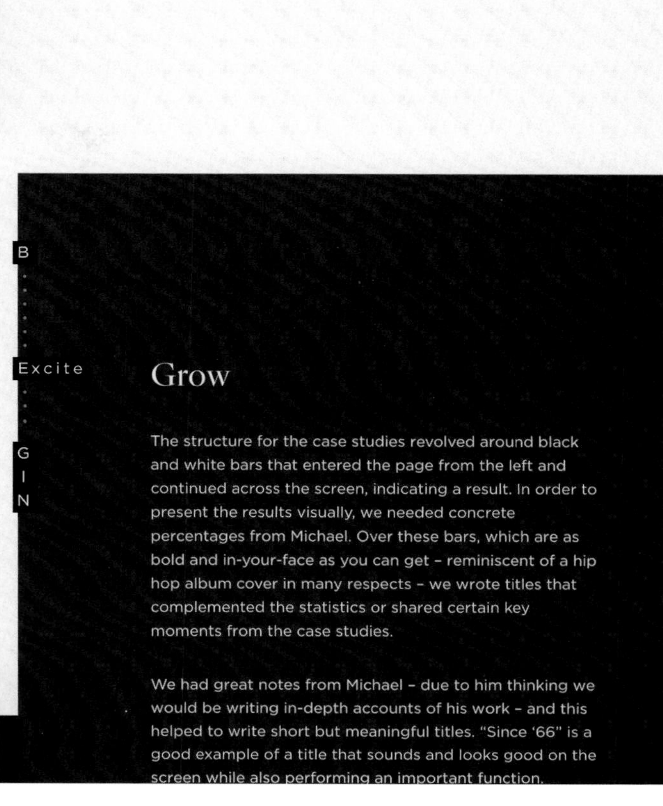
B
Excite
G
I
N
Grow
The structure for the case studies revolved around black and white bars that entered the page from the left and continued across the screen, indicating a result. In order to present the results visually, we needed concrete percentages from Michael. Over these bars, which are as bold and in-your-face as you can get – reminiscent of a hip hop album cover in many respects – we wrote titles that complemented the statistics or shared certain key moments from the case studies.
We had great notes from Michael – due to him thinking we would be writing in-depth accounts of his work – and this helped to write short but meaningful titles. “Since ‘66” is a good example of a title that sounds and looks good on the screen while also performing an important function.

ME
NU
An introduction to the team that made this happen.
HUNTER FARMER

Long Life Wood

Design Agency/
M—2—H

Web Design, UI/UX/
Alexander Laguta

Animation/
Alexey Smolkin

M—2—H was engaged to give a fresh look for the website and brand identity of Long Life Wood, a manufacturer of thermally solid wood. They were asked to showcase the production and its applications, provide assistance and process purchase orders.

The team used animation to bring accent to the most important bits of information and gave the brand a fresh new look it deserved. New logo reflects company's product in a simplified minimalistic manner and attracts audiences' attention to the quality of the product itself.

Font: Gotham; 16px \ ***Font-Kerning:*** Normal \ ***Line Height:*** 25.6px

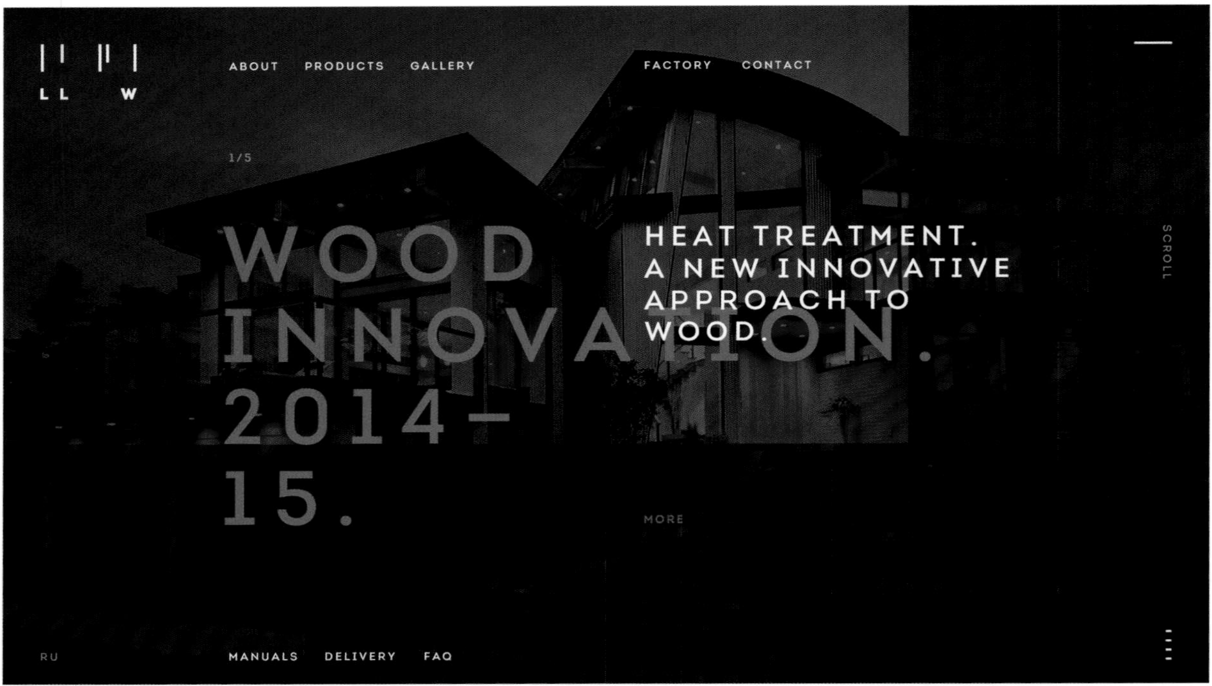

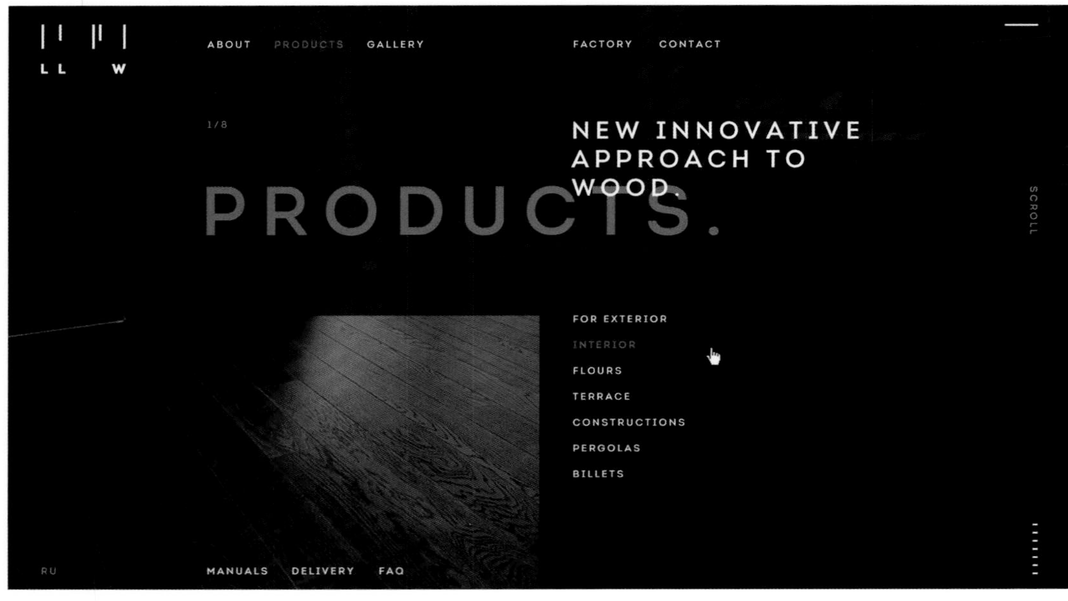

ABOUT PRODUCTS GALLERY FACTORY CONTACT

1-4/42

BEST EUROPEAN QUALITY. 2014.

INTERIOR.

SCROLL

PLANEN WOO

NEO SOLID 22MM

MORE

YASEN BLACK

OAK SOLID

RU

MANUALS DELIVERY FAQ

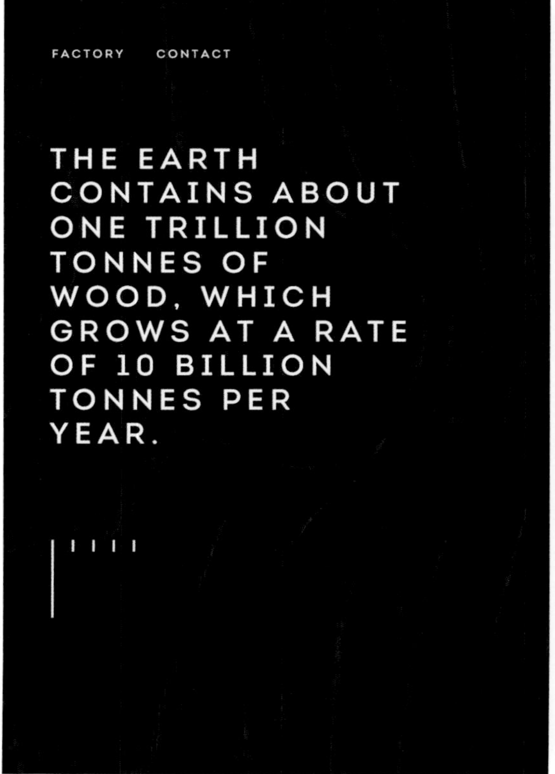

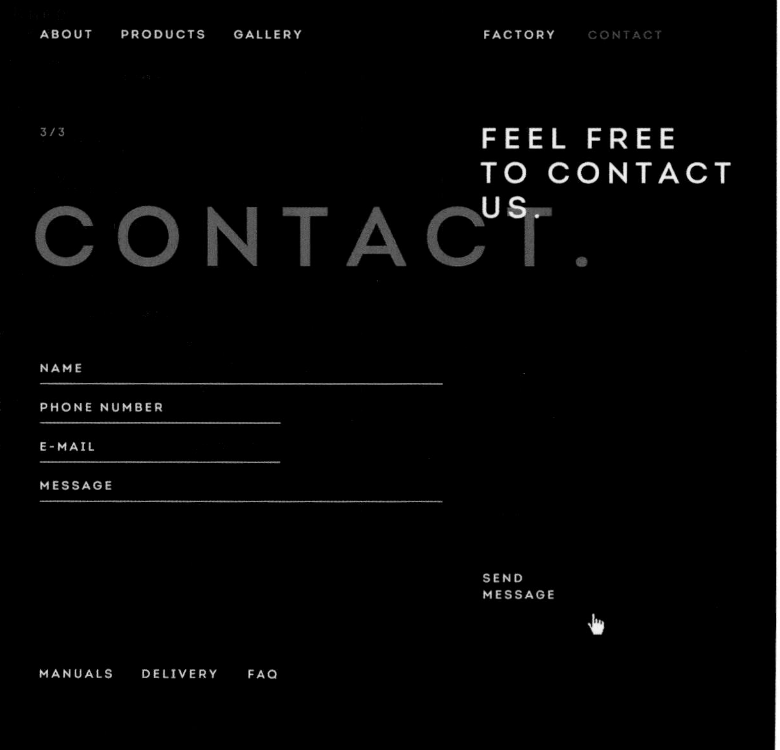

Irregular Noise Audio Reactive

Design/
Du Haihang

URL/
http://www.irregularnoise.com

The site is a visualization of an interactive audio experiment that cross various platform based on web audio api and web real time communication technologies known as WebRTC, which can work across modern browsers and devices. In each page, designer used a unique and elegant type, both English and Chinese, to be paired with the audio sequence.

Title: Helvetica \ ***Contents:*** Arial; 11px \ ***Font-Kerning:*** 1px \ ***Line Height:*** Normal

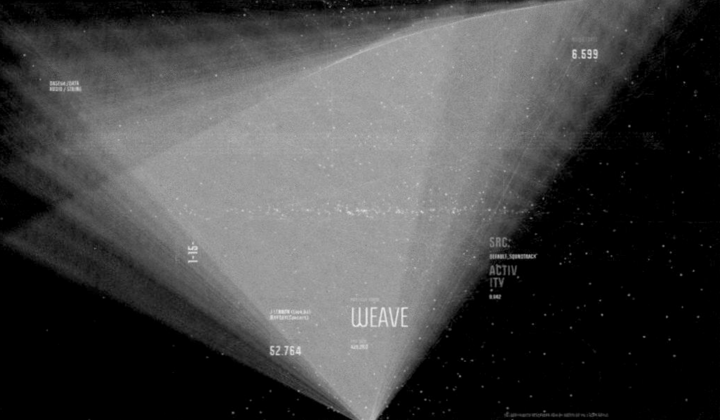

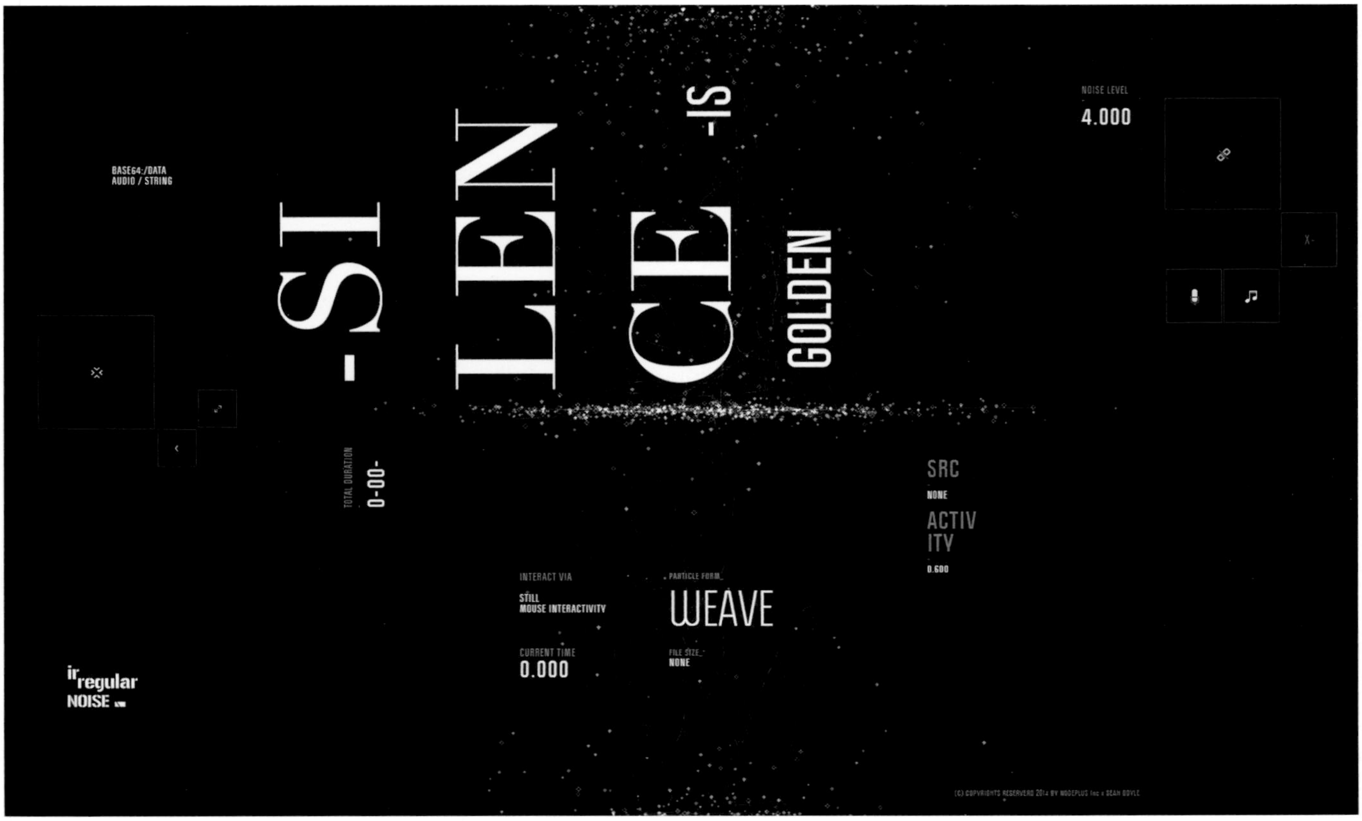

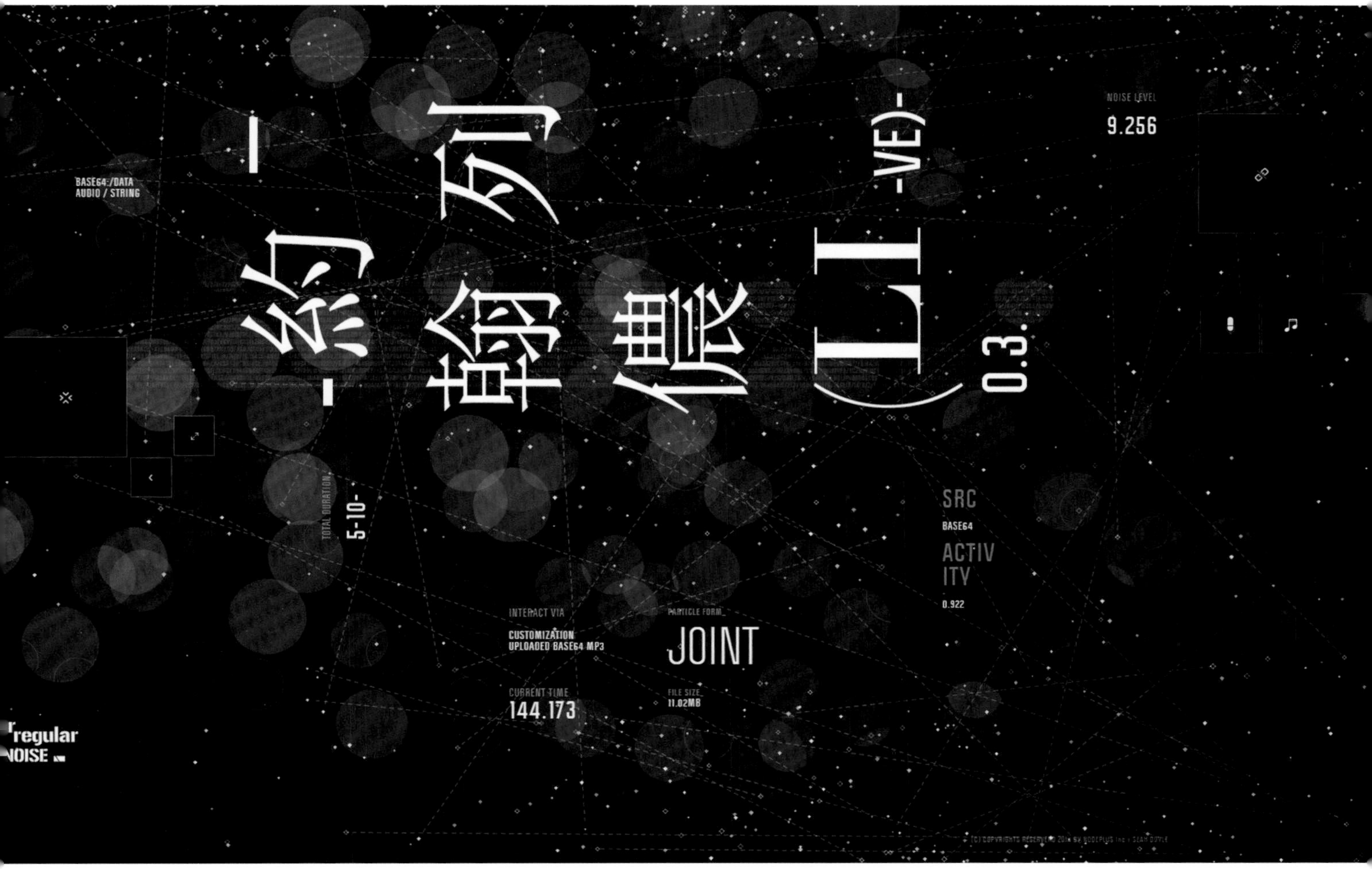

NOISE LEVEL
9.256

BASE64:/DATA
AUDIO / STRING

TOTAL DURATION
5-10-

SRC
BASE64
ACTIV
ITY
0.922

INTERACT VIA
CUSTOMIZATION
UPLOADED BASE64 MP3

PARTICLE FORM
JOINT

CURRENT TIME
144.173

FILE SIZE
11.02MB

regular
NOISE

irregular
NOISE

NOISE LEVEL
5.955

TOTAL DURATION
4-01-

SRC
BASE64
ACTIV
ITY
0.574

INTERACT VIA
CUSTOMIZATION
UPLOADED BASE64 MP3

PARTICLE FORM
SWIRL

BASE64:/DATA
AUDIO / STRING

CURRENT TIME
58.770

FILE SIZE
9.21MB

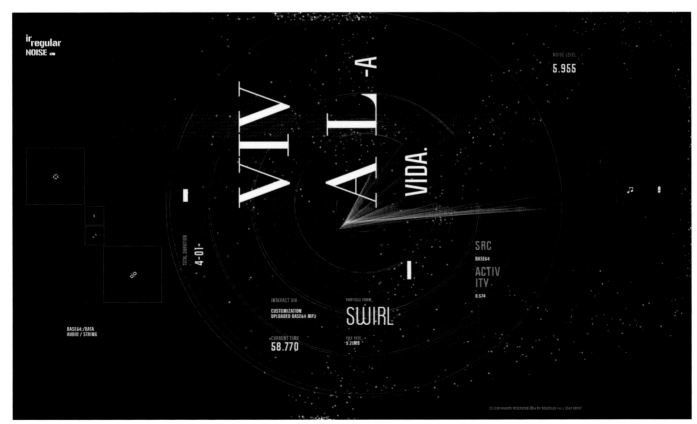

HOUSE OF BOREL

Design Agency/
Immersive Garden

Direction/
Dilshan Arukatti

Design/
Flavien Guilbaud, Dilshan Arukatti

Photography/
Günther Gheeraert

Client/
House of Borel

House of Borel is a new luxury brand that required a digital experience to be introduced to the world. As distinguishing and precious as House of Borel, Immersive Garden had conceived a visually appealing and high standard setting to express the values and reveal the nature of the brand. The mysterious yet intuitive navigation leads customer through the secrets through several sequences of promotional videos showing its elegance. The animations and smart transitions enhance the journey when they discover the rich contents from the experience.

Title: Crimson Text; (Bold) \ ***Contents:*** ProximaNova-Light; 16 px \ ***Font-Kerning:*** 1px \ ***Line Height:*** 1.5px

FROM USING
ORGANIC LEATHERS
TO INVESTING
IN SMALL

04

FAMILY-OWNED BUSINESSES, HOUSE OF BOREL WISHES TO CONTRIBUTE TO MAKING THE WORLD A BETTER PLACE BY CAREFULLY CHOOSING HOW OUR PRODUCTS ARE MADE AND SELECTING WHERE THE COMPONENTS COME FROM.

04

CLOSE

Blacknegative

Design Agency/	Direction/	Design/	Photography/	Client/	Url/
Immersive Garden	Dilshan Arukatti	Dilshan Arukatti	Camille Marotte, Günther Gheeraert	Blacknegative	http://blacknegative.com

The visual setting of Blacknegative features a mysterious and dark ambience with a pure design up to the standards of its own productions. The objective was to create from scratch a groundbreaking website that featured all the productions of Blacknegative. The approach was to present in a smart and simple way several case studies by creating an immersive experience that strikes visitors' attention and offers them a diverse exploring experience.

Title: Helvetica, Arial \ ***Contents:*** Helvetica, Arial; 12px \ ***Font-Kerning:*** Normal \ ***Line Height:*** Normal

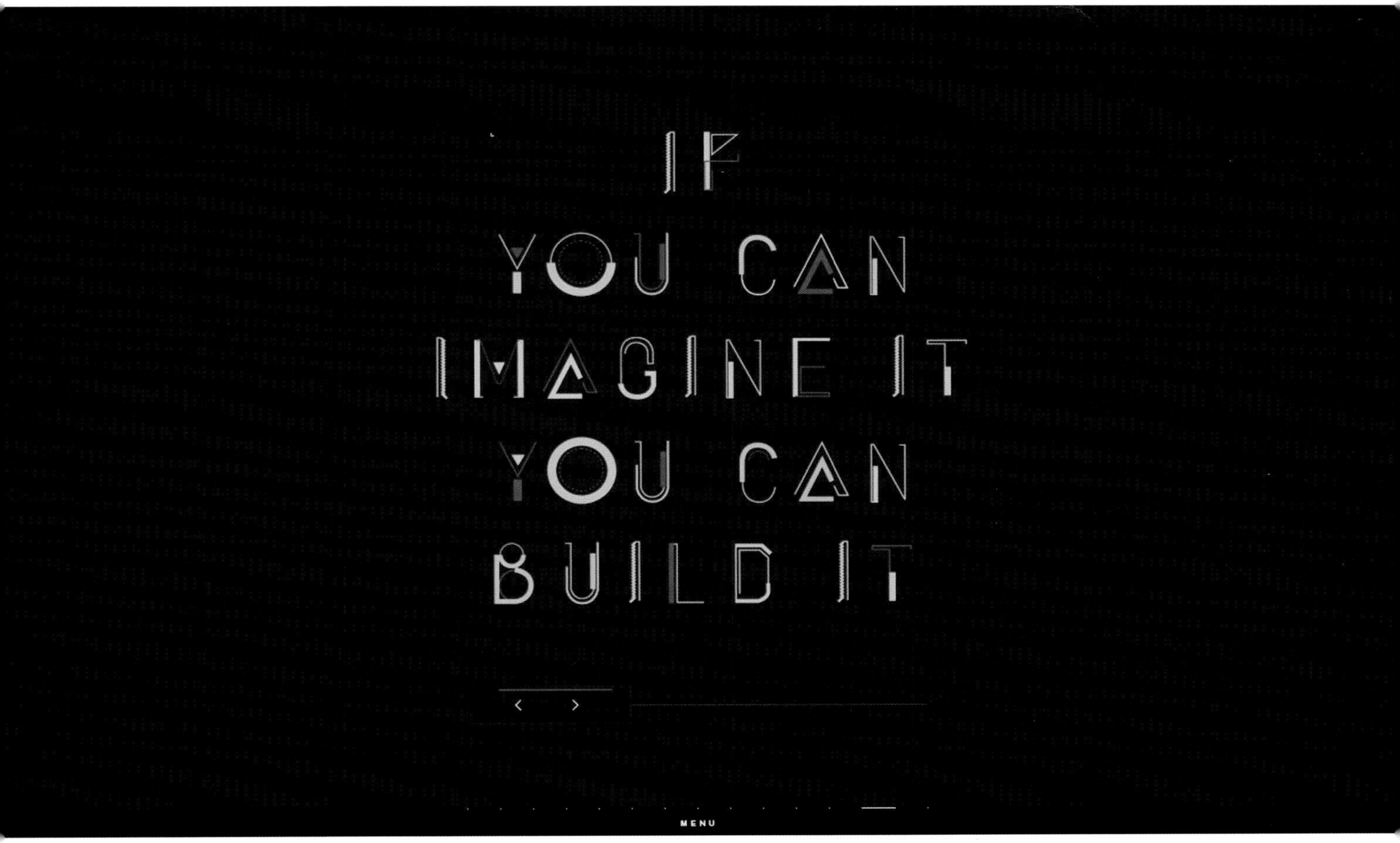

IF
YOU CAN
IMAGINE IT
YOU CAN
BUILD IT

MENU

WE TRY
TO

M A K E
T H E - E B
A - B E T T E R
P L A C E

Robert Downey Junior

Direction/
Firman Suci Ananda

Design/
Firman Suci Ananda

Client/
Smash Urban Media, New York

This is a conceptual project to redesign the website for Robert Downey Junior. To develop a new personal website for Robert Downey Jr., Firman Suci Ananda aimed to create a simple and elegant word mark giving audiences the feeling of the monochrome style.

Contents: PT Mono \ ***Font-Kerning:*** 25px \ ***Line Height:*** 48 ~ 61.3px

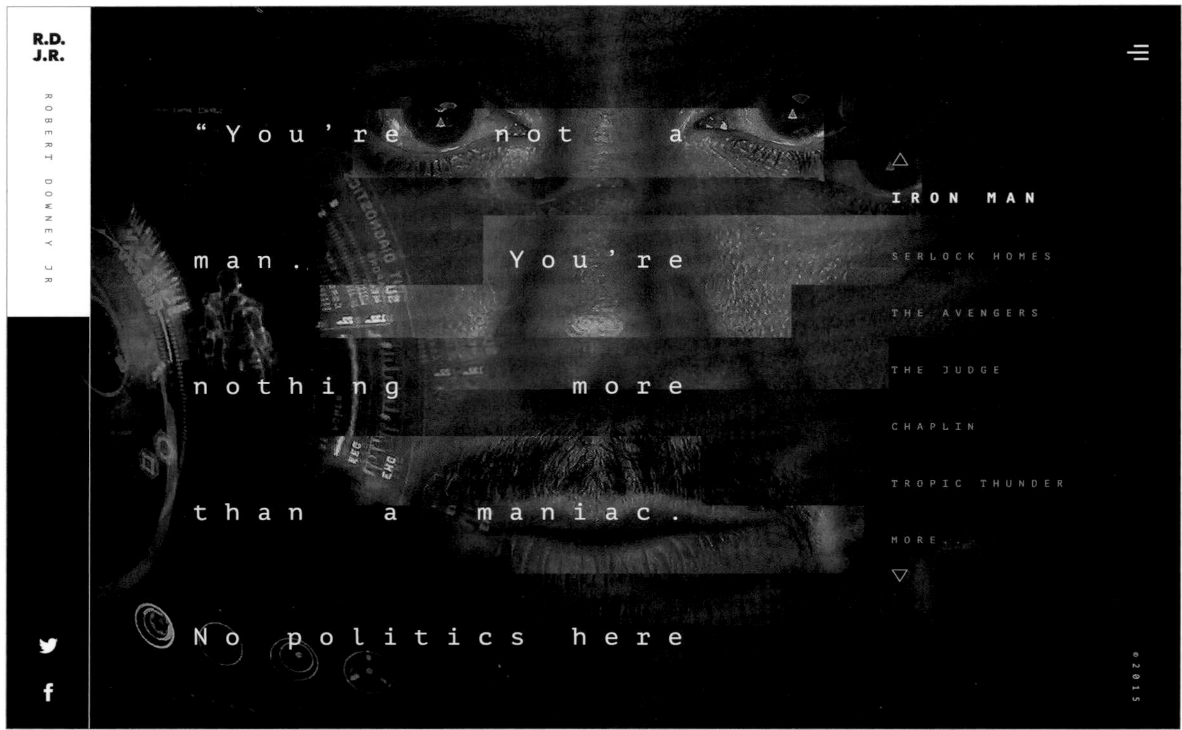

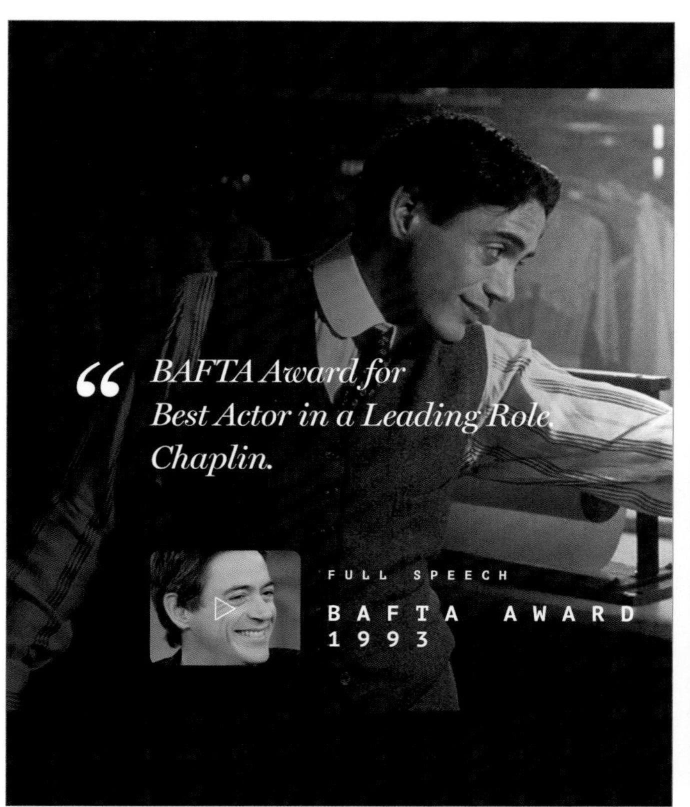

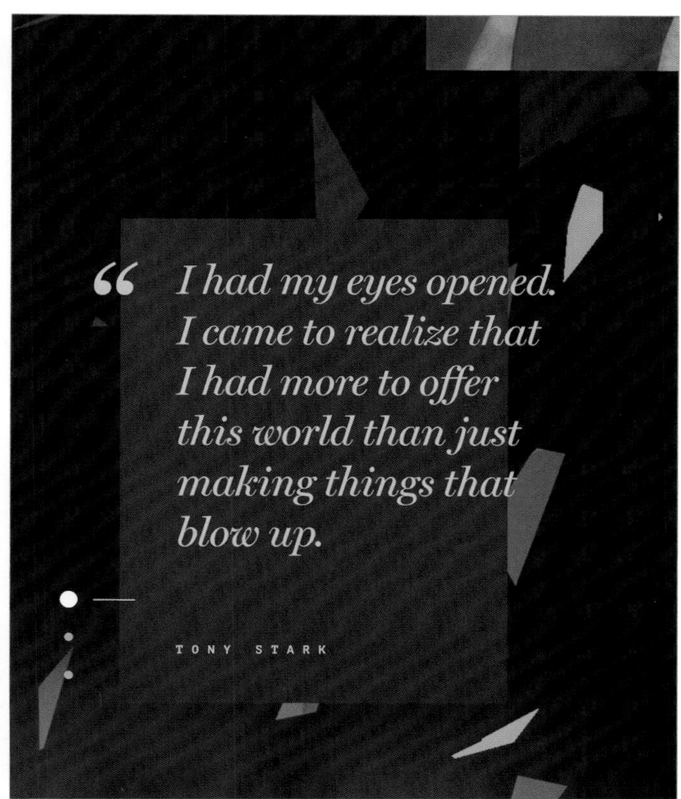

“ I had my eyes opened.
I came to realize that
I had more to offer
this world than just
making things that
blow up.
TONY STARK

INTERVIEW
VIDEOS

TV • 1:34

ROAD TO RECOVERY

TV • 2:51

LESS THAN ZERO

TV • 2:02

EARLY LIFE

TV • 3:07

DRUG ABUSE

Studio Chevojon

Design Agency/ Mashvp
Photography/ Yoan Chevojon
Client/ Yoan Chevojon
URL/ http://www.studiochevojon.com

The site is a folio for a photographer. Although the client gave Mashvp a free rein, he also had very specific demands about the framing. Since the popular grids and layouts were hard to appeal to the photographer, Mashvp created this simple and more nuanced user experience, but with dynamic borders when zooming and no cropping related to web standards. The burger menu seemed to be a great opportunity to place the most important information when clicked, such as the horizontal scrolling important to Yoan Chevojon. Particular care was taken during the development stage, such as respecting the "smooth" style given to animations, scrolling, and many other elements to be discovered.

Title: MN; 120px \ ***Contents:*** MN; 74px \ ***Font-Kerning:*** Normal \ ***Line Height:*** 60px

12.02.16

Valmeinier

RETOUR

→

09.02.16

l'Escale et
La Praya

→

José Morraja

Design Agency/
Play&Type Studio

Client/
José Morraja

URL/
http://josemorraja.com

José Morraja is a photographer and film director based in Spain, famous for the hedonism, humor, tension, and rebellion spirits in his works. His films and images are a tool that allows him to express openly, without fear, with attitude. The website designed by Play&Type Studio cherishes the same values. The dynamic navigation and the layout give a visual break and entrance into the projects. The page is mainly occupied by full-screen images, while the text, which is in large scale neon green and use Montserrat, express a bold and personalized style of the owner, where hedonism, humor, tension and rebellion all play their part.

Title: Montserrat \ ***Contents:*** Helvetica Neue; 14px \ ***Font-Kerning:*** Normal \ ***Line Height:*** 20 px

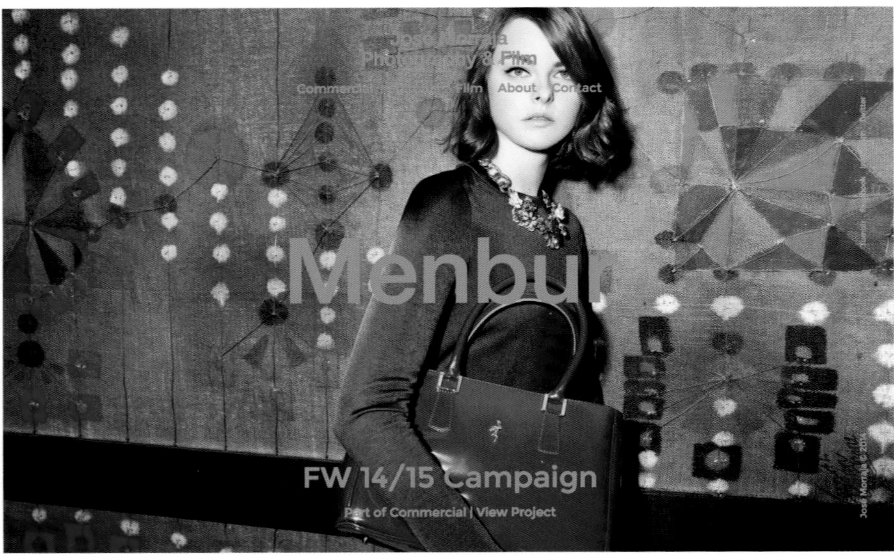

José Morraja
Photography & Film

Commercial Editorial Films About Contact

The Hunter Neo2

Styled by Jorge Olmedo
Make up & Hair by Lolita
Digital Retouching by Leticia Jiménez
Models Dima Dionesov & Eva Lois

Back | Share

Tumblr Facebook Instagram Twitter

José Morraja
Photography & Film

Commercial Editorial Films About Contact

The Hunter Neo2

Styled by Jorge Olmedo
Make up & Hair by Lolita
Digital Retouching by Leticia Jiménez
Models Dima Dionesov & Eva Lois

Back | Share

Tumblr Facebook Instagram Twitter

Klimov Design

Design/
Alex Yurkov

URL/
https://klimov.agency

Alex Yurkov has developed a design of website for Klimov Design, a design agency based in Russia. He worked with Klimov Design to initiate a site that could reflect their stylish and bold projects in the digital world.

Title: Futura-pt \ ***Contents:*** Futura-pt; 14px \ ***Font-Kerning:*** Normal \ ***Line Height:*** 50px

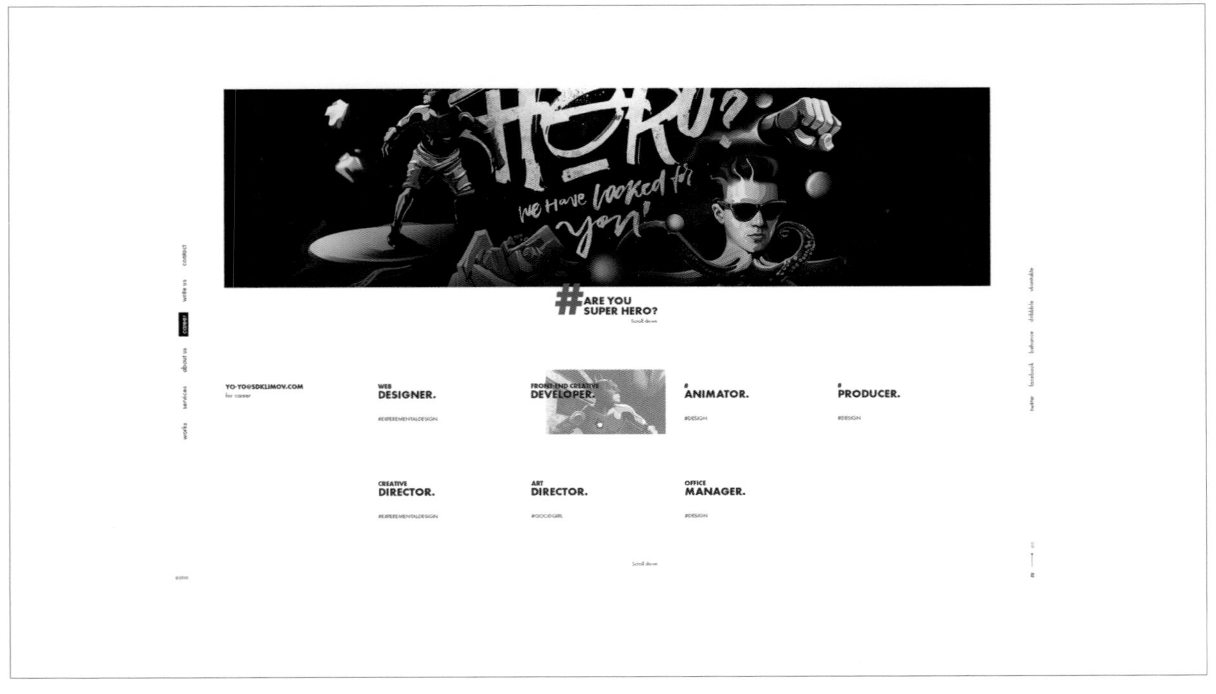

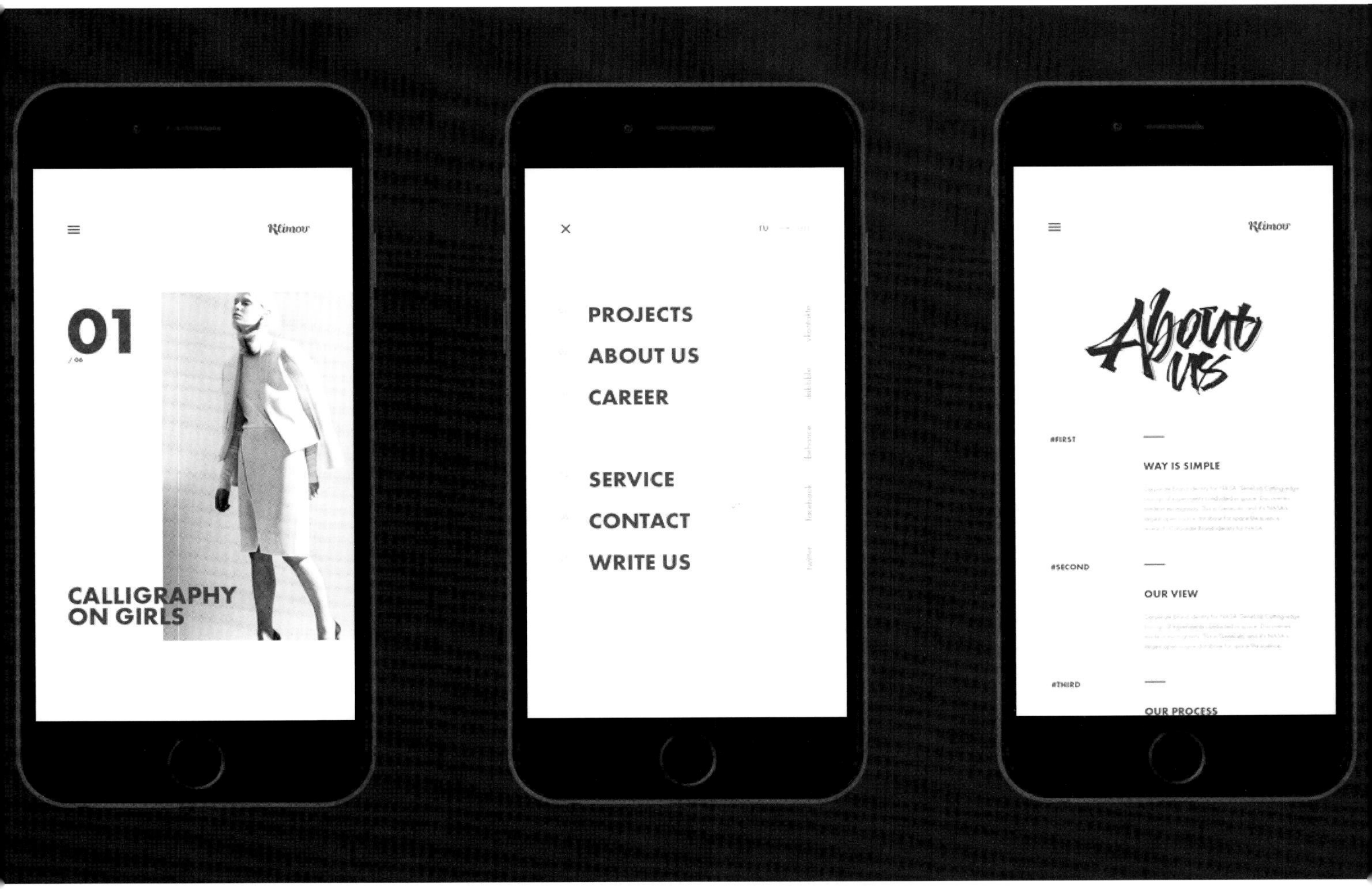

Maeva Barrière

Design Agency/
Mashvp

Photography/
Sylvie Romieu, DDM, KAROLINA B, Maeva Barrière

Client/
Maeva Barrière

URL/
http://maevabarriere.com

First culinary artist ever, Mashvp explored many different trails concerning user experience. The starting brief evoked a very simple website, quite dynamic, and soft at the same time. Within the website, they applied techniques such as TweenMax, webgl 2D, transitions between the pages of the website, and animated typographies. Also, these techniques lead to a traditional agency-folio structure for this website. Indeed, the content is highlighted by the familiar web tree and the sober style. The typographic research has naturally been oriented towards a "grotesque" one (Neue House / milieugrotesque.com) for its easiness but also to refine the set.

Title: Neue Haas Grotesk; (Bold) \ ***Contents:*** MaisonNeue-Demi; 14px \ ***Font-Kerning:*** Normal \ ***Line Height:*** Normal

Goûtons Voir
Ô Raison Rose
Je Madonne
MB
Poult
Rêver le goût et la couleur
Accueil
Installation comestible
Recherche & théorie
Actualités
Je Madonne
Installation comestible

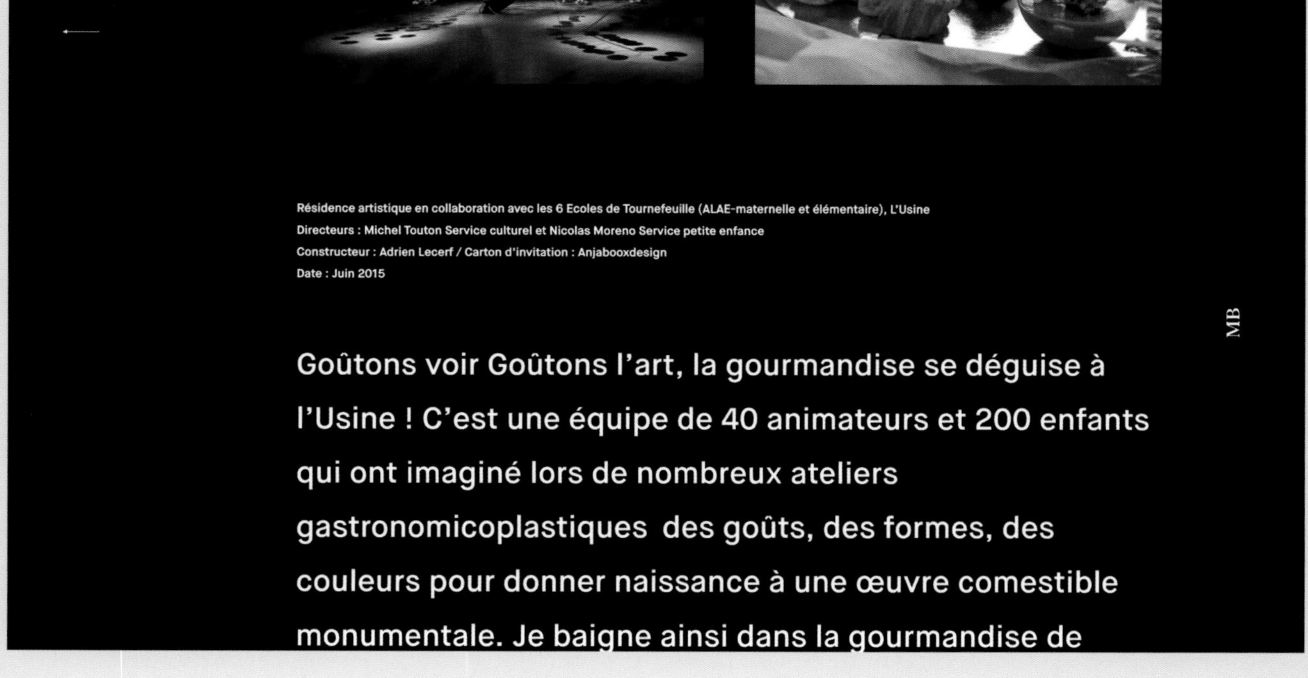
Résidence artistique en collaboration avec les 6 Ecoles de Tournefeuille (ALAE-maternelle et élémentaire), L'Usine
Directeurs : Michel Touton Service culturel et Nicolas Moreno Service petite enfance
Constructeur : Adrien Lecerf / Carton d'invitation : Anjabooxdesign
Date : Juin 2015
MB
Goûtons voir Goûtons l'art, la gourmandise se déguise à l'Usine ! C'est une équipe de 40 animateurs et 200 enfants qui ont imaginé lors de nombreux ateliers gastronomicoplastiques des goûts, des formes, des couleurs pour donner naissance à une œuvre comestible monumentale. Je baigne ainsi dans la gourmandise de

Down the Long Driveway, You'll See It

Design Agency/
Sons & Co.

Creative Direction/
Timothy Kelleher

Design/
Matthew Arnold, Greg Brown, Mary Gaudin, Duncan Forbes

Client/
Mary Gaudin

URL/
http://downthelongdriveway.com

The project is a small scale website for a book of pictures of modernist New Zealand homes. The idea for the project wasn't so much to document the houses in purely architectural terms, but to give an idea of the way these houses were and are lived in, as well as showing details of the designs and the materials used in their construction. Designers adopted a minimalist concept and developed a website with a clear structure.

Title: HelveticaNeueW01-55Roma \ ***Contents:*** Helvetica Neue; 12px \ ***Font-Kerning:*** Normal \ ***Line Height:*** 1.7px

Down
the long
driveway,
you'll see it

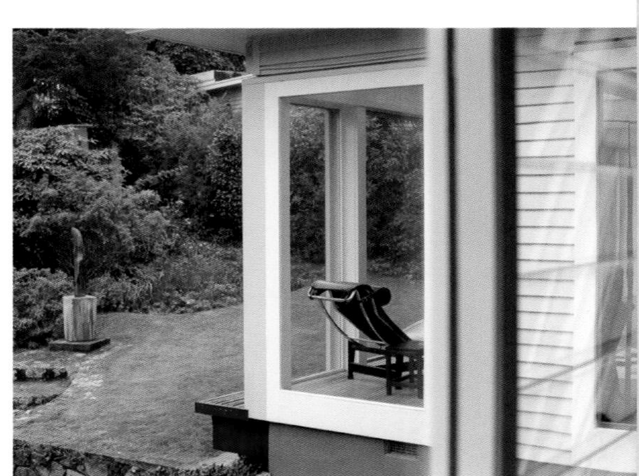

This is a book of pictures of modernist New Zealand homes.

These houses aren't new, they're old and lived in. They can be a little dusty, slightly worn around the edges and all have what antique dealers like to call "patina". But they're perfect in the minds of the people who live in them because of what they represent, which when designed, was a better way of living.

Down the long driveway, you'll see it

Einhorn House 1950 Helmut Einhorn

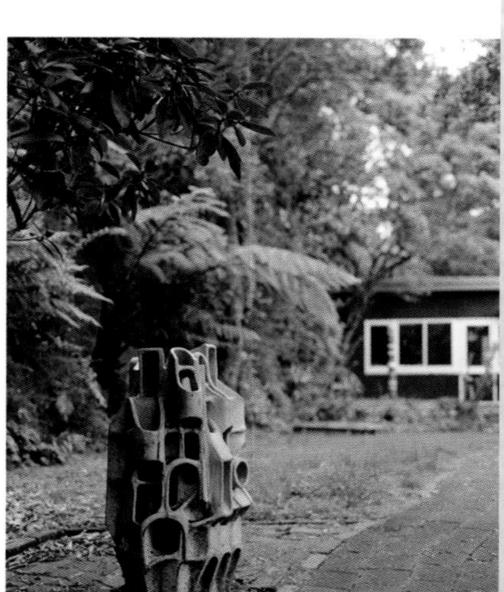

Mary Gaudin & Matthew Arnold

Design The International Office

33 23

This is a book of pictures of modernist New Zealand homes.

These houses aren't new, they're old and lived in. They can be a little dusty, slightly worn around the edges and all have what antique dealers like to call "patina". But they're perfect in the minds of the people who live in them because of what they represent, which when designed, was a better way of living.

Down the long driveway

Henderson House	1950	Ernst Plishke
Einhorn House	1950	Helmut Einhorn
Lang House	1953	Ernst Plischke
Sellars House	1954	Guy Sellars
McKenzie House	1958	Cedric Firth
Ballantyne House	1959	Warren & Mahoney
Manning House	1960	Jack Manning
Sutton House	1961	Tom Taylor
Alington House	1963	William Alington
Fletcher House	1964	Hall & Mackenzie
Orr-Walker House	1965	Mark Brown and Fairhead
Munro House	1968	Warren & Mahoney
Martin House	1971	John Scott
Wood House	1974	Ted Wood

Down the long driveway,
you'll see it

Photography, Mary Gaudin
Text, Matthew Arnold
Design, The International Office

65 NZD

Free shipping
worldwide.
Dispatched from France.

buy

Fletcher Systems

Design Agency/ Sons & Co.
Creative Direction/ Timothy Kelleher
Design/ Matthew Arnold, Greg Brown, Matthew Wilson
Client/ Fletcher Systems
URL/ http://fletcher-systems.co.nz

Established in 1999 by New Zealand designer Fletcher Vaughan, Fletcher Systems is recognized and respected throughout New Zealand and internationally for its creative and highly original furniture.

The logic of the website is leading by texts of different types of furniture. In the subpages, Sons & Co. designed a perfect layout for the pictograms and information, making it very sophisticated yet comfortable for audiences to check through.

Title: HelveticaNeueW01-55Roma \ ***Contents:*** Helvetica Neue; 14px \ ***Font-Kerning:*** Normal \ ***Line Height:*** 1.7px

Portrait
Seating.

29
pcs.

6pcs Modular

The multi-talented seating system

8pcs Lumber

Ash dowel timber

4pcs Breakout

For doing.
Or doing nothing.

Details

In-use

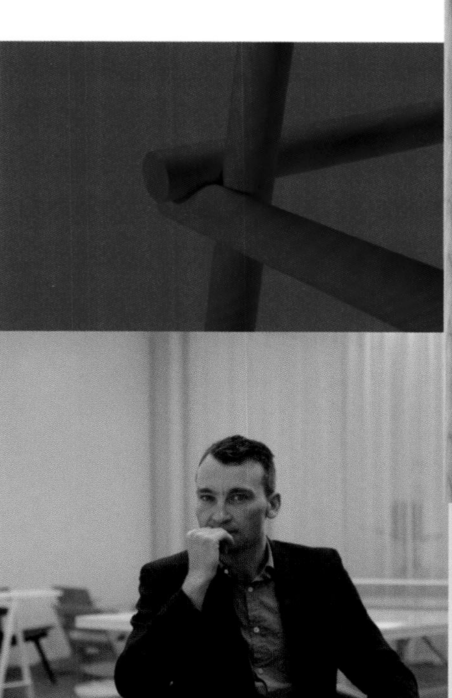

The Lumber easy chair, side table and stool are inspired by the construction of traditional log cabins. They obtain their strength through the clever three-way interlocking knuckle-joints.

The beauty of the joint is that it requires very little mechanical fastening, and the connections are self tightening - so any movement in the frame actually pulls the connections tighter together.

8
pcs.

Baby Lumber Stool
Lumber Chair
Lumber Easy Chair
Lumber Side Table
Lumber Stool
Lumber Table
Petrel Shelf
Twig

Jamie McLellan,
Designer.

These pieces are designed from simple components to create a playful, robust and enduring family that has a strength that far exceeds their visual lightness. Solid ash dowels and hand-construction make beautiful babies.

inty ++

Design Agency/
M—2—H

Web Design, UI/UX/
Alexander Laguta

Animation/
Alexey Smolkin

URL/
http://inty.pro

M—2—H was asked to digitalize the story of interactive installations and presentations by studio inty++ to showcase its projects and abilities for desktop and mobile audience.

They focused on absolutely essential and trashed everything else. This approach allowed them to add more air and simplify the interface of Inty++. The site becomes easier to understand and navigate, and led to better user experience and customer satisfaction.

Title: Helvetica Neue cyrillic; 24 px \ ***Contents:*** Helvetica Neue cyrillic; 20 px \ ***Font-Kerning:*** Normal \ ***Line Height:*** 24px

++ PROJECTS ART SOLUTIONS ABOUT CONTACT

Nike
ACG Flyknit
Trainer Chukka.
All Conditions
Gear.
Promotion
2015.

NIKE
CITY WEAR NEW
GENERATION.

JUNE 2015

Scroll

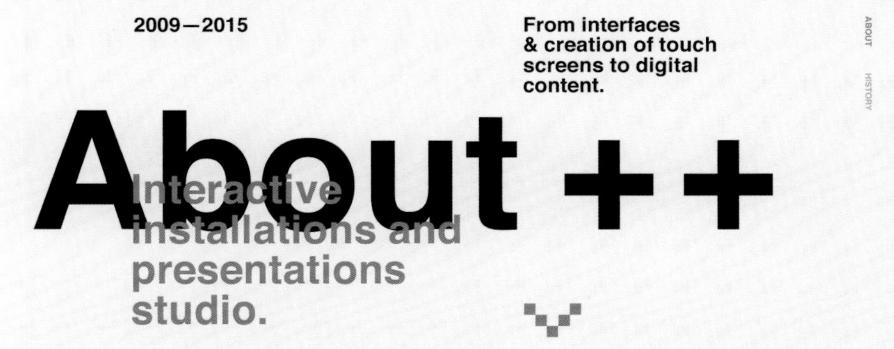

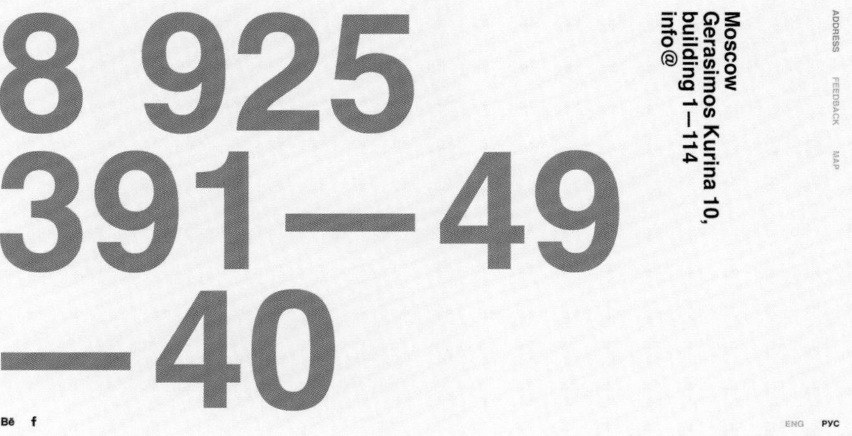

ABCo.

Design Agency/	Design Direction/	Art Direction/	Design/	Photographer/
Oddds	Sarah Tan	Reinold Lim	Reinold Lim, Sarah Tan	Sarah Tan

Notably regarded with simplicity and functionality together with processes and ratio, brewing parameters to precision control derives a unique product. The Auroma One, that a coffee science machine invented and campaigned on Kickstarter, consisted of a team of scientist, engineers, and ardent lovers of coffee. The visual identity is created methodically from rudiments of science and coffee brewing techniques. The branding collaterals expand and convey the message of "Science and Experiential Playfulness." Clean infographics were constructed from the basis of Auroma's intelligence, capabilities, and minimalism.

Fonts: Arcon & Thingbats Mono

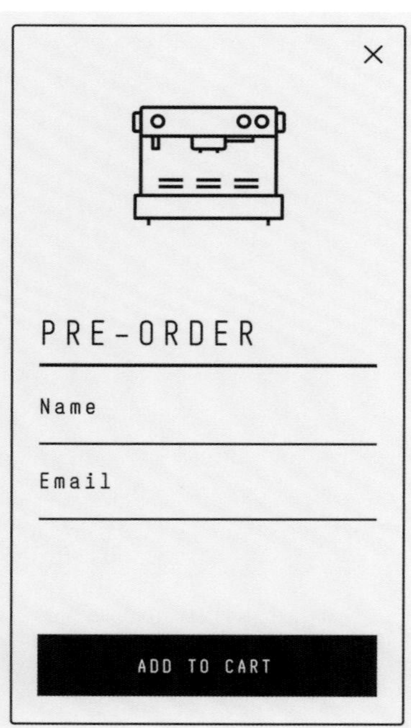

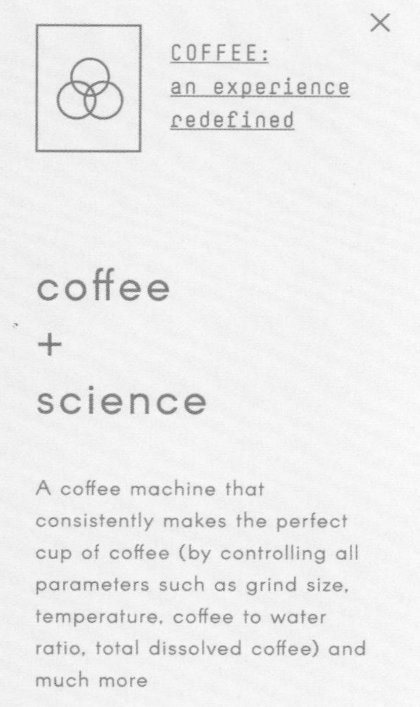

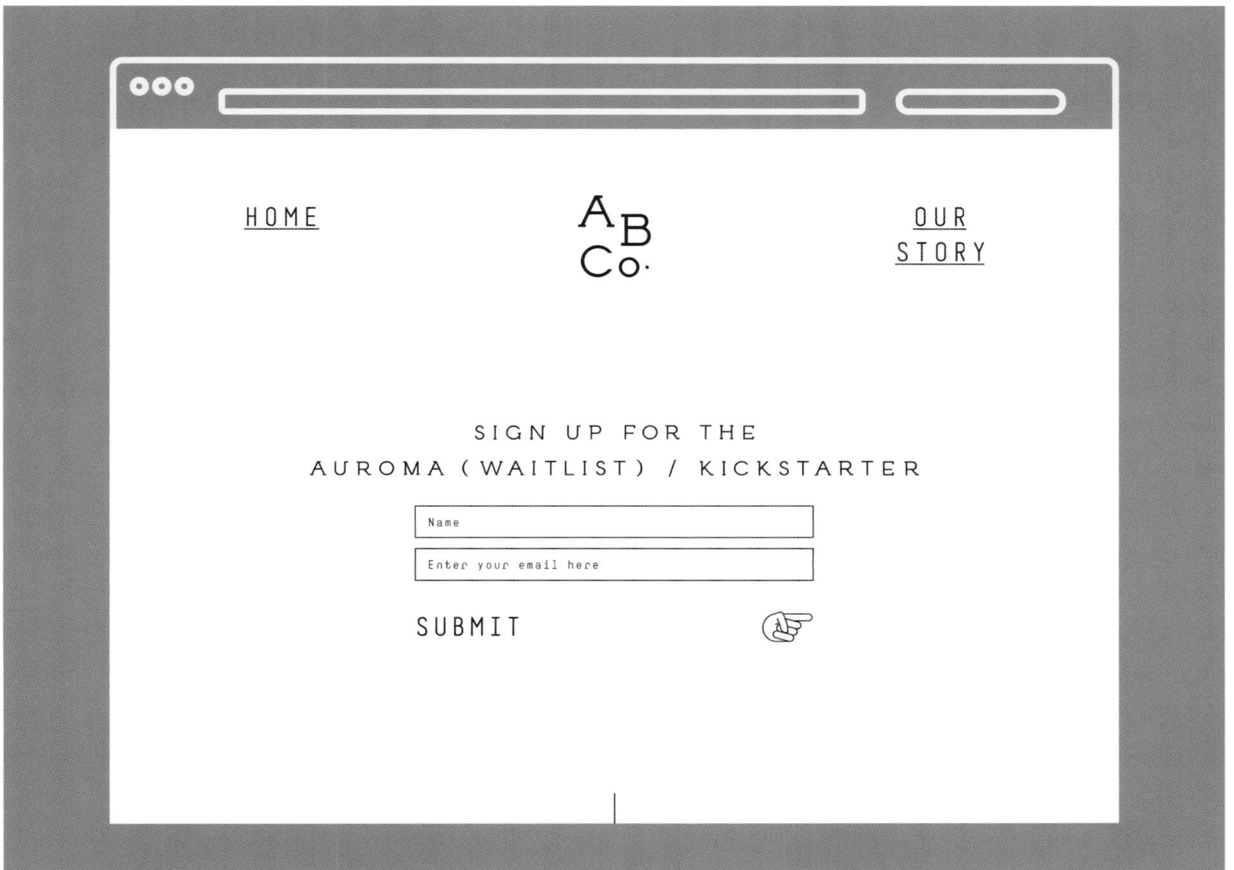

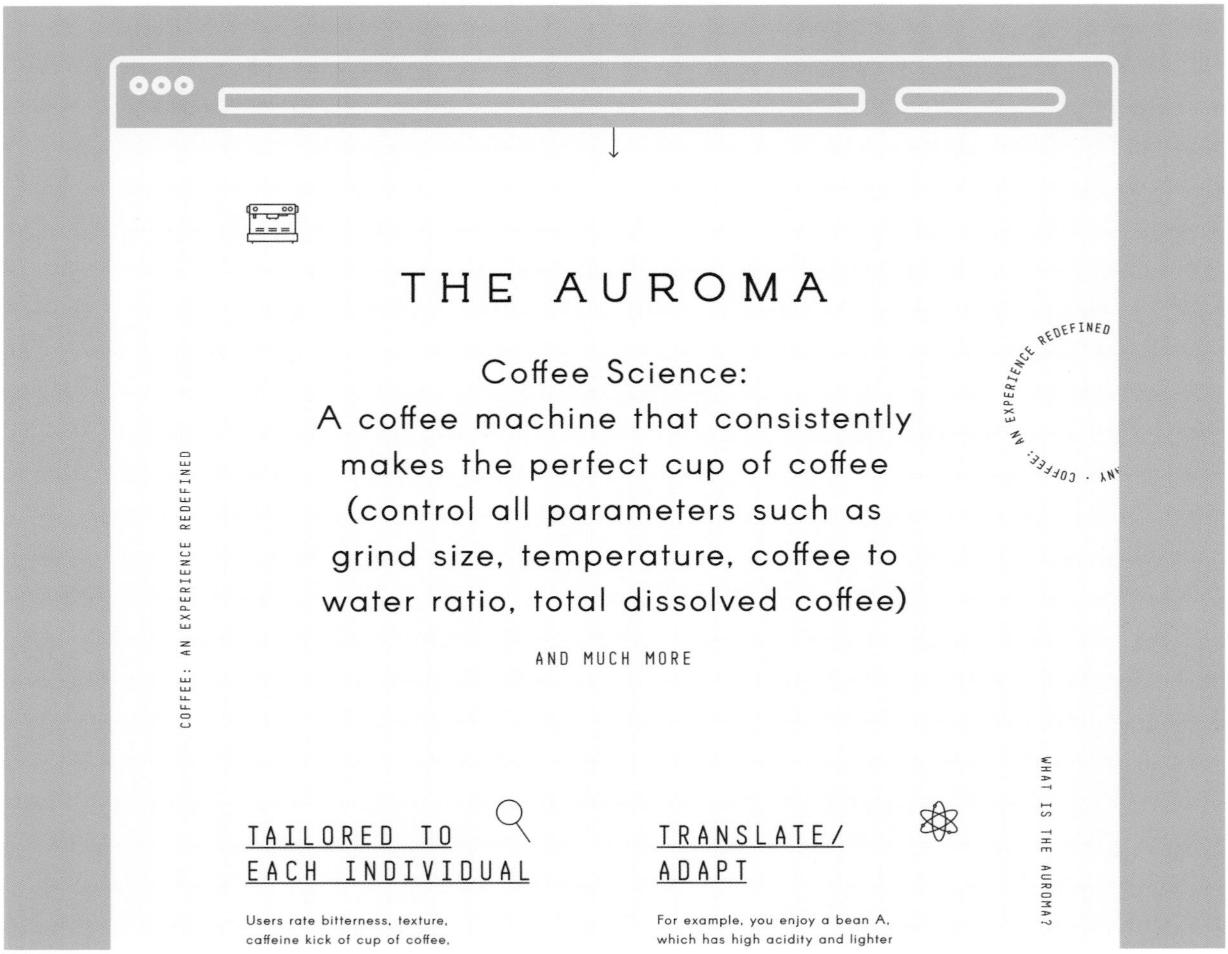

THE AUROMA

Coffee Science:
A coffee machine that consistently makes the perfect cup of coffee (control all parameters such as grind size, temperature, coffee to water ratio, total dissolved coffee)

AND MUCH MORE

COFFEE: AN EXPERIENCE REDEFINED

COFFEE: AN EXPERIENCE REDEFINED

WHAT IS THE AUROMA?

TAILORED TO EACH INDIVIDUAL

Users rate bitterness, texture, caffeine kick of cup of coffee,

TRANSLATE/ ADAPT

For example, you enjoy a bean A, which has high acidity and lighter

KÒNIC THTR—KÒNICLAB

Design/
Héctor Sos

Client/
KÒNIC THTR

URL/
http://koniclab.info

Corporate web design for the art collective Kònic THTR, which is an artistic platform based in Barcelona dedicated to contemporary creation at the confluence between arts, new technologies, and science. Héctor Sos employed overlapping elements to make the site as dizzy as an avant-garde digital world.

Title: Comfortaa \ ***Contents:*** Questrial; 20px \ ***Font-Kerning:*** 3px \ ***Line Height:*** 25px

KÒNIC THTR–KÒNICLAB

English

HOME PROJECTS ABOUT CONTACT

Rosa Sánchez & Alain Baumann are leading the conceptual, creative and technological developments in Kònic (Thtr&Lab).

KÒNIC THTR–KÒNICLAB

English

HOME PROJECTS ABOUT CONTAC

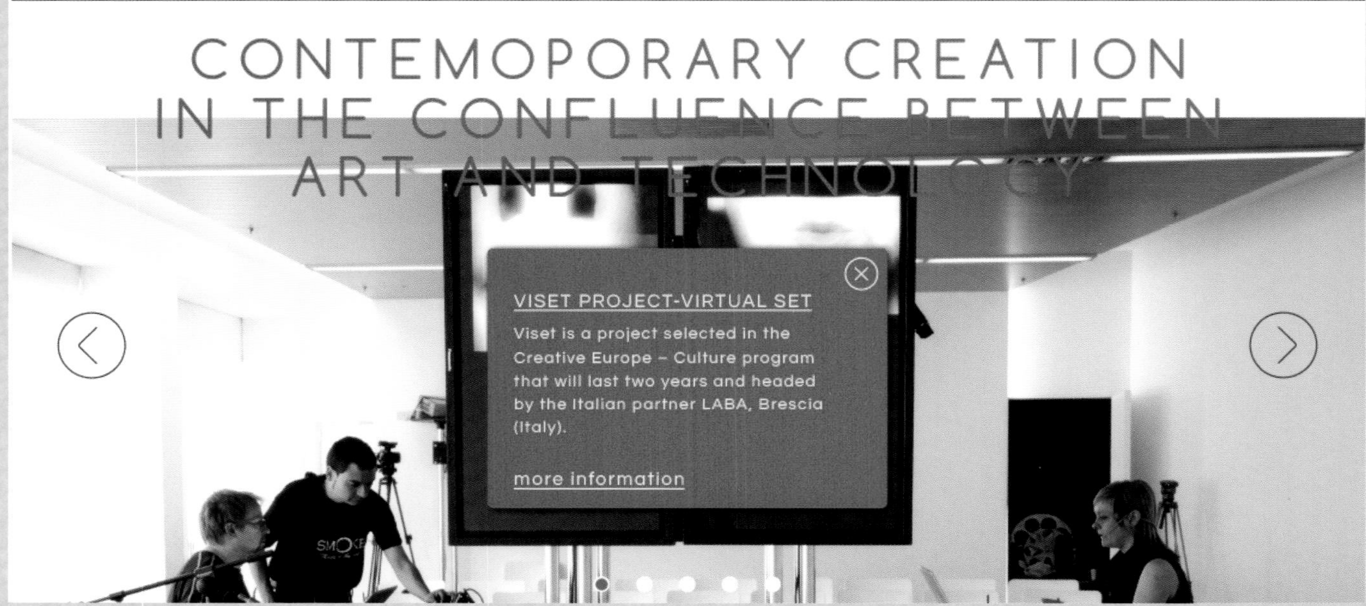

CONTEMOPORARY CREATION
IN THE CONFLUENCE BETWEEN
ART AND TECHNOLOGY
VISET PROJECT-VIRTUAL SET
Viset is a project selected in the Creative Europe – Culture program that will last two years and headed by the Italian partner LABA, Brescia (Italy).
more information

ECC Architectural

Design Agency/
Sons & Co.

Creative Direction/
Timothy Kelleher

Design/
Matthew Arnold, Luke Cossey, Brendon Muschamp

Client/
ECC Lighting

URL/
http://eccarchitectural.co.nz

ECC Architecture is the world's leading lighting brand, exclusive to New Zealand architects and designers. They specialize in lighting for residential, office and commercial, retail and hospitality and street and urban projects.

Title: Helvetica Neue LT W04_45 Light \ ***Contents:*** HelveticaNeueW01-75Bold; 18px \ ***Font-Kerning:*** Normal \ ***Line Height:*** 25px

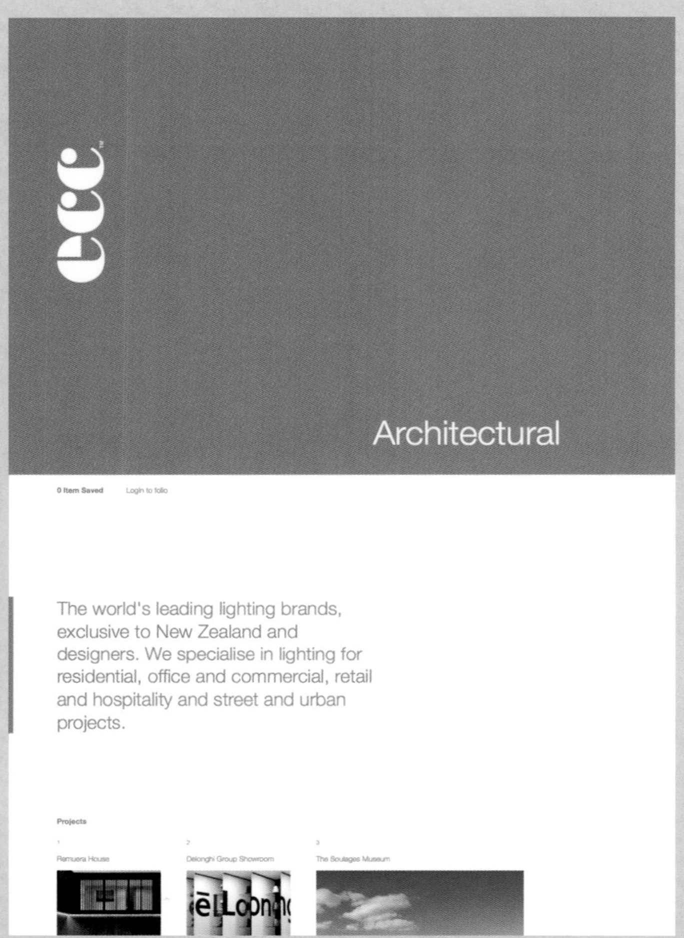

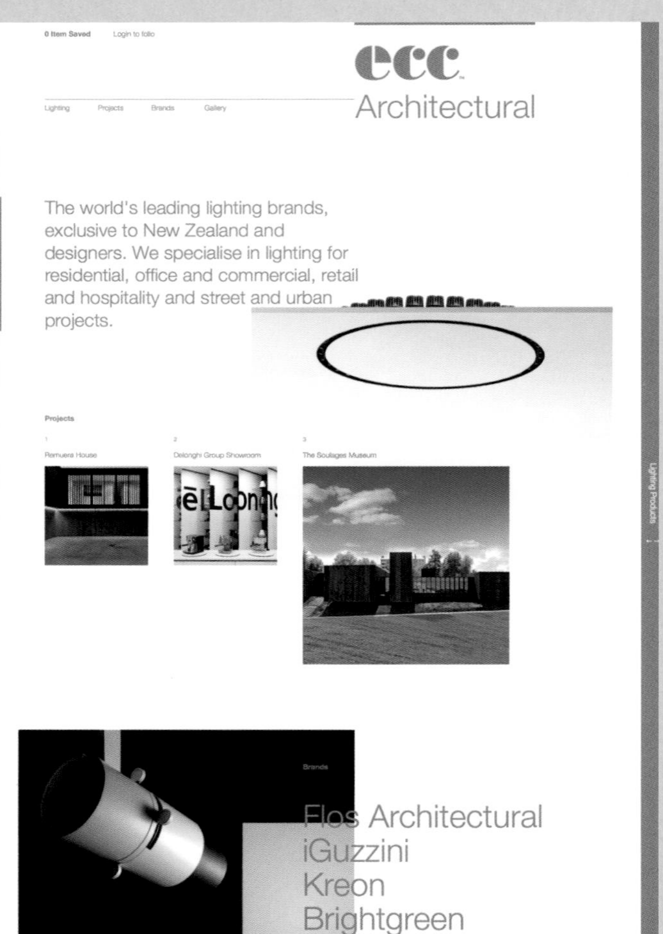

0 Item Saved Login to folio

Lighting Projects Brands Gallery

ecc
Architectural

Lighting Products

Flos Architectural.
Kap 105 Round.

Luminaire for recessed mounting on ceilings for halogen, metal halide and LED lamps.

The Kap version incorporates body injected in aluminium with liquid paint finish. It is available in two sizes: 105 mm and 145 mm.

Main view made of anodized gloss aluminium with diffuser element made in borosilicate glass.

Lampholders with heatsink element in injected aluminium and embedment ring of the optical body in thermoplastic material.

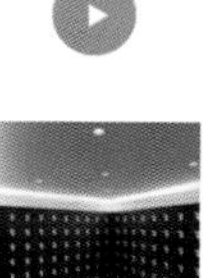

FLOS Archit

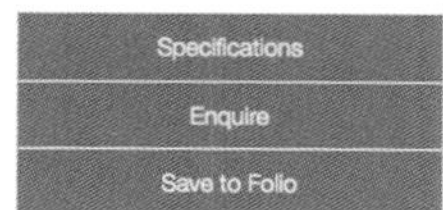

Architectural

Lighting Projects Brands Gallery

"Architecture is the masterly, correct and magnificent play of volumes brought together in light."

- Le Corbusier.

Retail

Lighting Products

Gallery

Filippa K New York

Aesop Emporium Melbourne

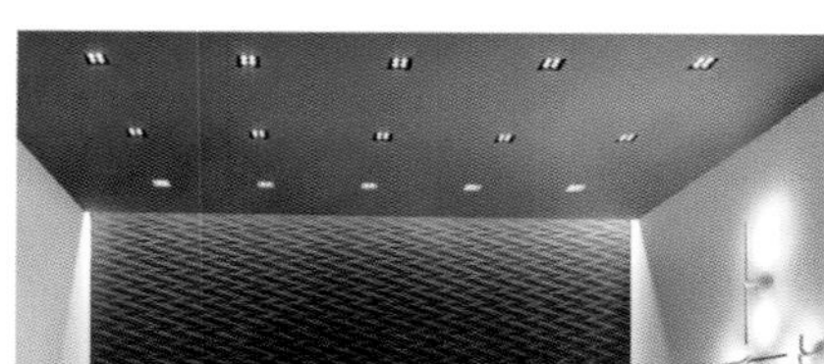

NuDD x Oddity @ MakerHive

Design/
Mourou

URL/
http://nudd.odditystudio.com

Nudd is an experimental life drawing and performance group in Hong Kong. They work with different creative groups to host unique social experience. NuDD collaborate with Oddity and the maker-hive to invite all painters and makers in town for next session. By using the digital technology Alice experimented with human body shape, lines, and proportions and destroy acceptable ordinary model to move it forward to the future.

Title: Brandon Grotesque \ ***Contents:*** Brandon Grotesque; 11px \ ***Font-Kerning:*** 0.6px \ ***Line Height:*** 24px

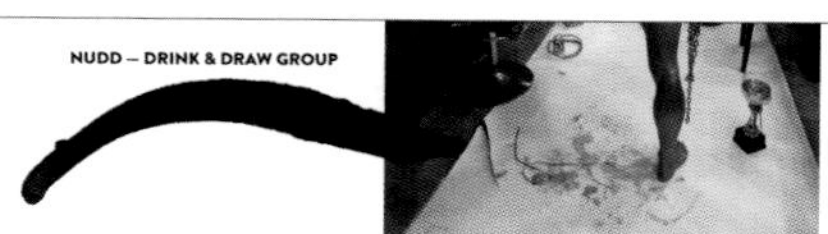
NUDD – DRINK & DRAW GROUP

FACEBOOK INSTAGRAM

260 FOR MEMBERS
360 REGULAR
380 WALKINGS

DRINKS AND DRAWING MATERIALS INCLUDED

NUDDHK@GMAIL.COM

COUNT ME IN!

NUDD – DRINK & DRAW GROUP
A MAKER SESSION
FACEBOOK INSTAGRAM
NUDDHK@GMAIL.COM

NUDD – DRINK & DRAW GROUP
NUDD COLLABORATE
WITH ODDITY & THE MAKERHIVE TO INVITE
ALL PAINTERS AND MAKERS IN TOWN
FOR OUR NEXT SESSION.
BY USING THE DIGITAL TECHNOLOGY WE WILL
EXPERIMENT WITH HUMAN BODY SHAPE, LINES AND
PROPORTIONS AND DESTROY ACCEPTABLE
ORDINARY MODEL TO MOVE IT FORWARD TO THE
FUTURE. LET'S ENJOY THE ODD BEAUTY AND DREAM
ABOUT THE POSSIBLE HUMAN'S EVOLUTIONS.
FACEBOOK INSTAGRAM
NUDDHK@GMAIL.COM
15:00 17:30

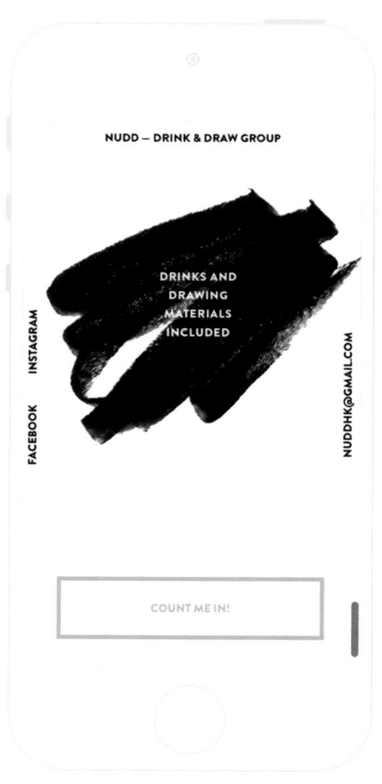
NUDD – DRINK & DRAW GROUP
DRINKS AND
DRAWING
MATERIALS
INCLUDED
FACEBOOK INSTAGRAM
NUDDHK@GMAIL.COM
COUNT ME IN!

BNY

Design/
Andrew Aden

Photography/
Anton Repponen

Client/
Creative Soldier

Brooklyn Navy Yard is a property based in New York City, offering offices and high quality apartments for rent or sale. Designer used a slightly changing blue through its logo and titles to reflect its maritime background.

Title: Roboto \ ***Contents:*** Roboto; 11px \ ***Font-Kerning:*** 0.6px \ ***Line Height:*** 24px

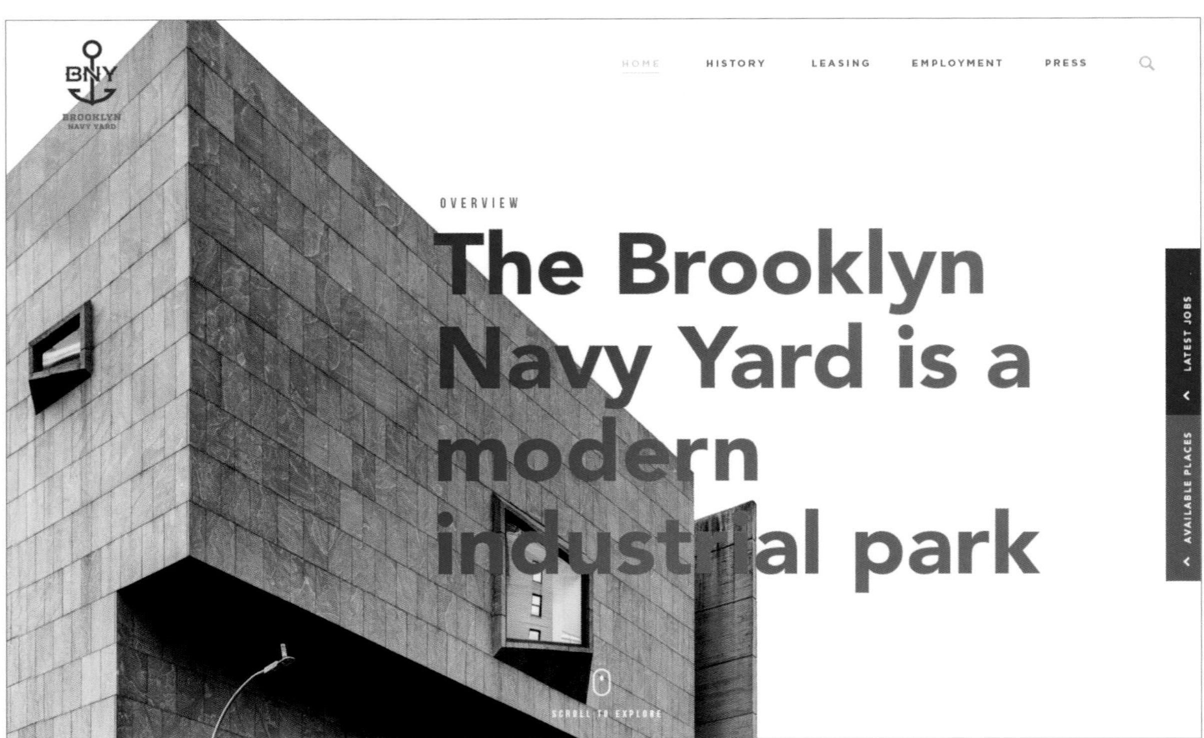

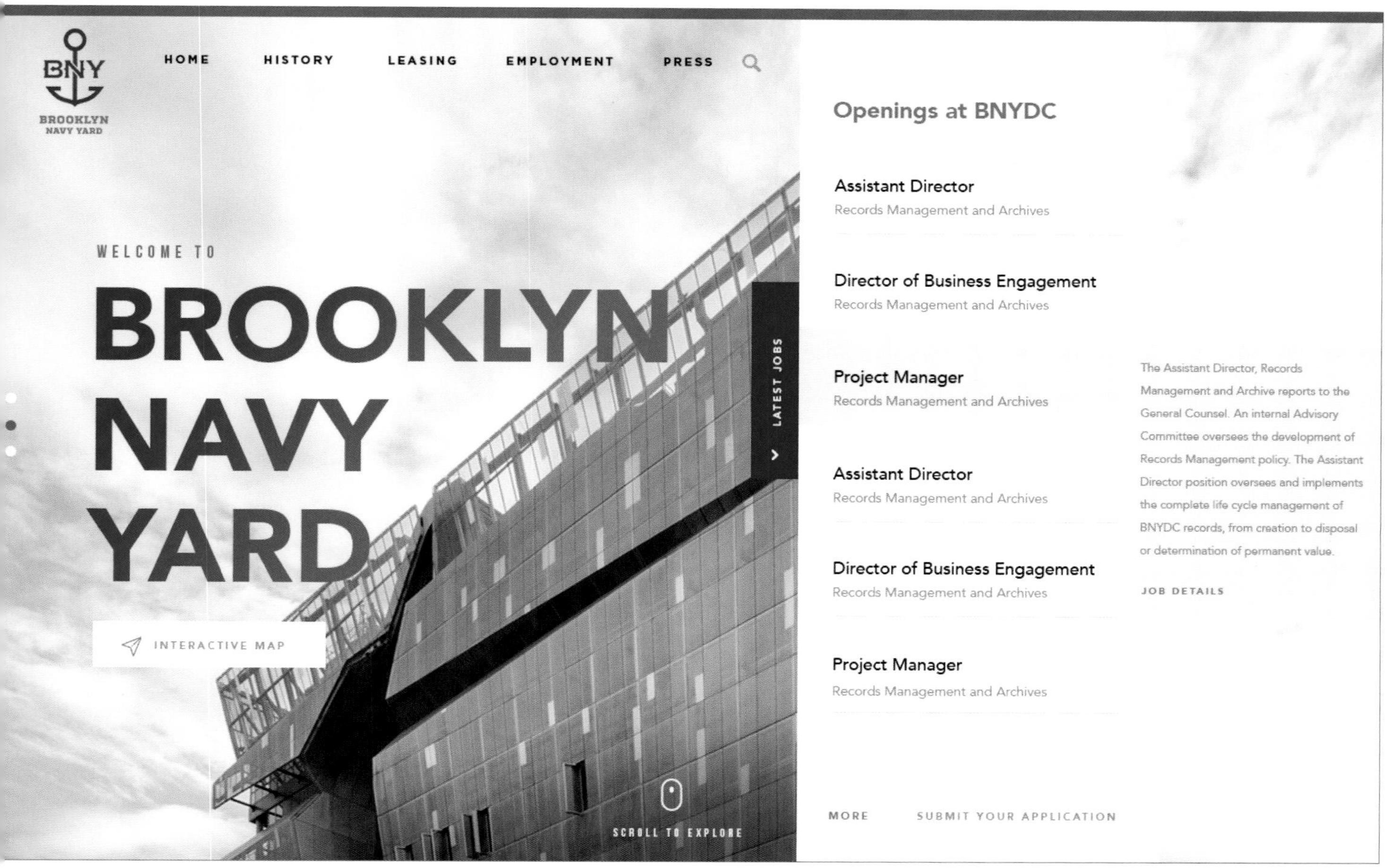

BROOKLYN NAVY YARD

HOME HISTORY LEASING EMPLOYMENT PRESS

WELCOME TO

BROOKLYN NAVY YARD

INTERACTIVE MAP

LATEST JOBS

SCROLL TO EXPLORE

Openings at BNYDC

Assistant Director
Records Management and Archives

Director of Business Engagement
Records Management and Archives

Project Manager
Records Management and Archives

Assistant Director
Records Management and Archives

Director of Business Engagement
Records Management and Archives

Project Manager
Records Management and Archives

The Assistant Director, Records Management and Archive reports to the General Counsel. An internal Advisory Committee oversees the development of Records Management policy. The Assistant Director position oversees and implements the complete life cycle management of BNYDC records, from creation to disposal or determination of permanent value.

JOB DETAILS

MORE SUBMIT YOUR APPLICATION

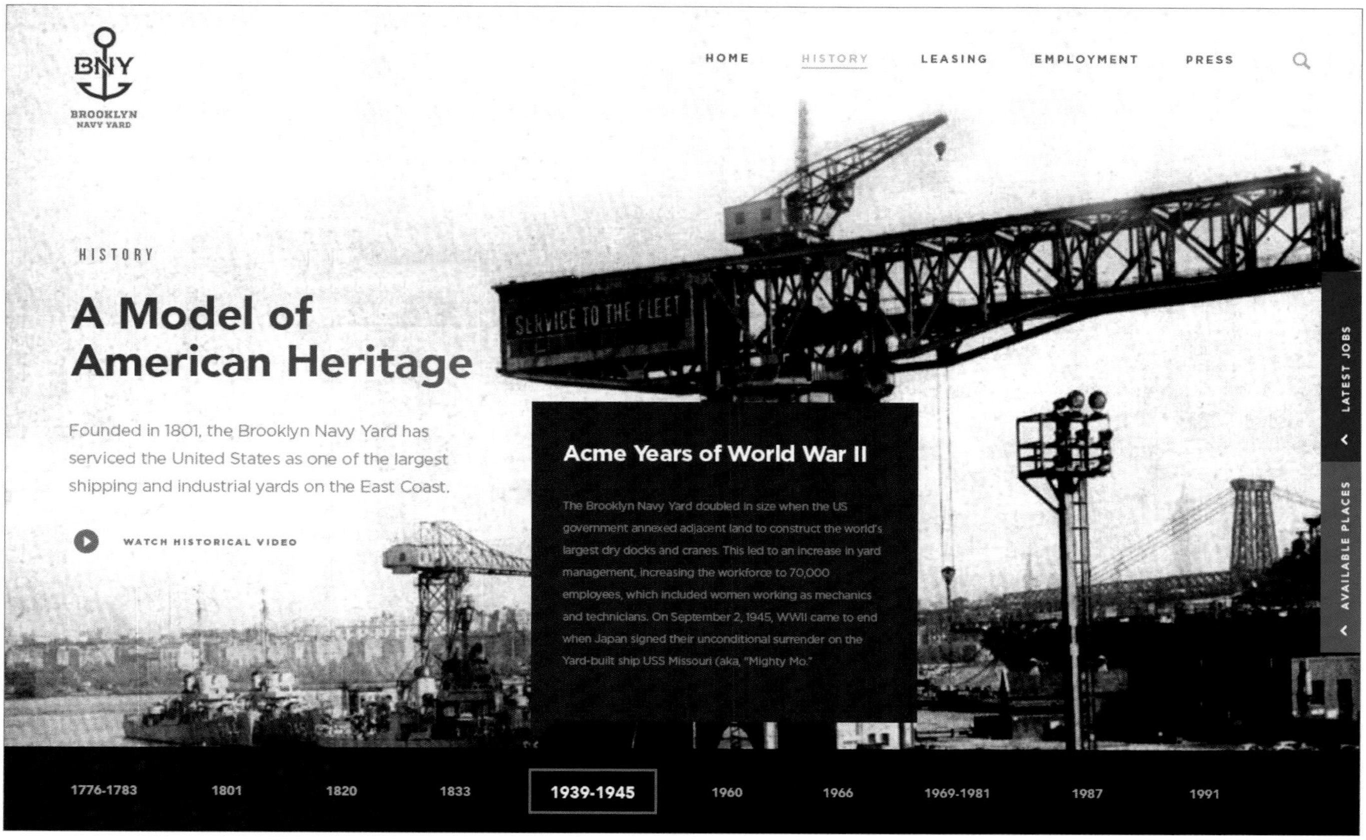

BROOKLYN NAVY YARD

HOME HISTORY LEASING EMPLOYMENT PRESS

HISTORY

A Model of American Heritage

Founded in 1801, the Brooklyn Navy Yard has serviced the United States as one of the largest shipping and industrial yards on the East Coast.

WATCH HISTORICAL VIDEO

SERVICE TO THE FLEET

Acme Years of World War II

The Brooklyn Navy Yard doubled in size when the US government annexed adjacent land to construct the world's largest dry docks and cranes. This led to an increase in yard management, increasing the workforce to 70,000 employees, which included women working as mechanics and technicians. On September 2, 1945, WWII came to end when Japan signed their unconditional surrender on the Yard-built ship USS Missouri (aka, "Mighty Mo."

LATEST JOBS

AVAILABLE PLACES

1776-1783 1801 1820 1833 1939-1945 1960 1966 1969-1981 1987 1991

ACME

Design Agency/
Immersive Garden

Direction/
Dilshan Arukatti

Design/
Mathieu Boulet, Dilshan Arukatti

Photography/
Multiple

Client/
ACME

URL/
http://acme-experience.com

Born 40 years ago when Dubai was only a desert, ACME is today one of the most competitive storage solutions provider worldwide. The goal was to create a breathtaking experience for the ACME's 40 years. In order to illustrate the complexity of creating smart storage solutions, Immersive Garden used smooth animated combinations of pictures that rebuild themselves and change on each page of the website. The Heritage part is conceived entirely in WebGL to allow user to be immersed in an emotional way in Acme's story.

Title: MFRED \ ***Contents:*** FF DIN Web Pro; 16 px \ ***Font-Kerning:*** Normal \ ***Line Height:*** 1.56px

CLEVER
SPACES
Acme has been providing pallet and case storage as well as handling solutions adapted for a wide variety of industries.
SCROLL TO CONTINUE

×

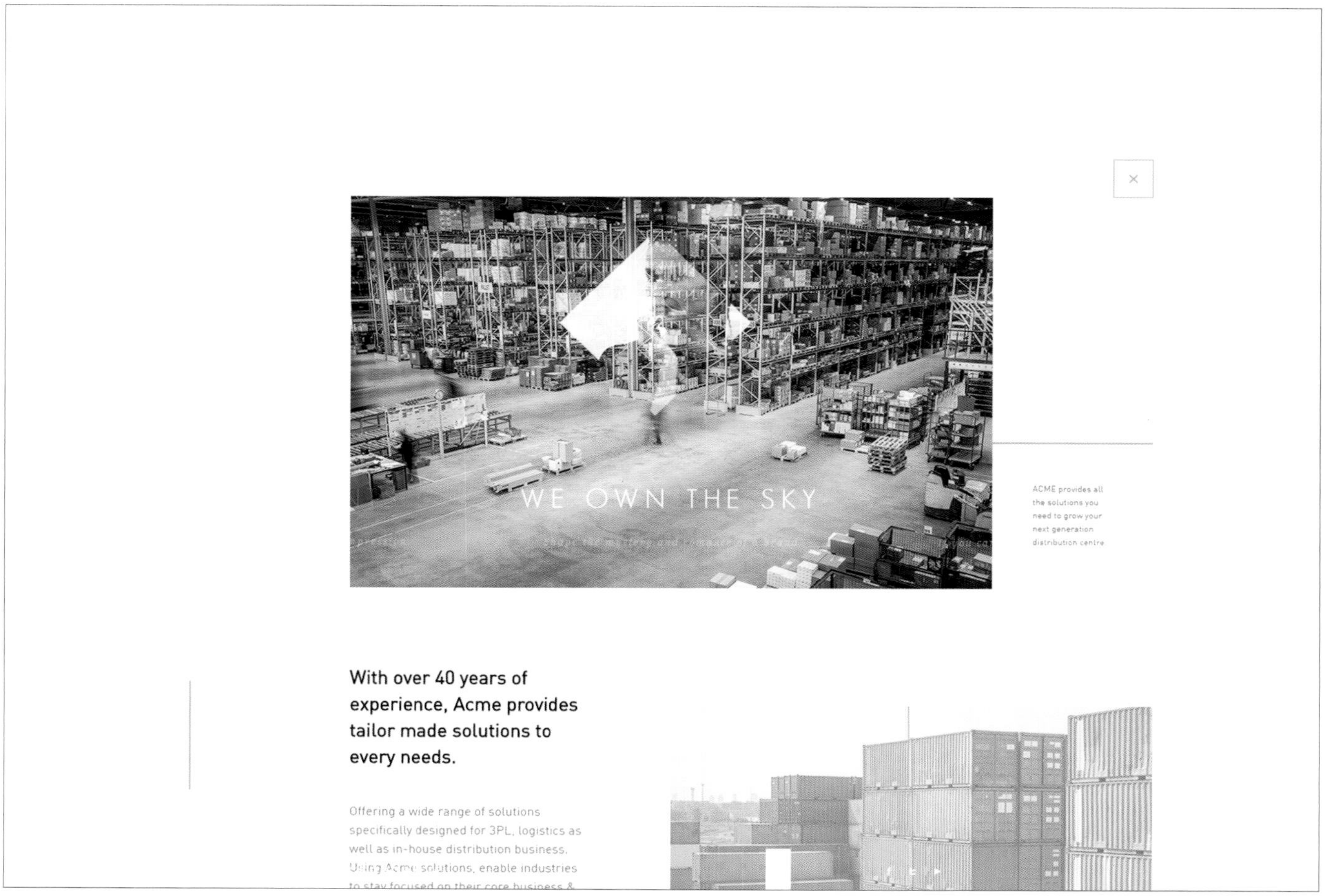

WE OWN THE SKY

ACME provides all the solutions you need to grow your next generation distribution centre

With over 40 years of experience, Acme provides tailor made solutions to every needs.

Offering a wide range of solutions specifically designed for 3PL, logistics as well as in-house distribution business. Using Acme solutions, enable industries to stay focused on their core business &

Petas

Design Agency/ AQuest S.r.l.
Direction/ Tomas Baruffaldi
Design/ Roberto Campara
Client/ Petas
URL/ http://www.petas.it

Petas is a facility management company. The site features Parallax plus soft and smooth animations. AQuest believes that human motivation is fuel and a key element in organization.

Title: FuturaStdBook(Bold); 50px \ ***Contents:*** Futura Std (Bold); 14px \ ***Font-Kerning:*** 3px \ ***Line Height:*** 23.3px

PETAS

ATTIVITÀ

Facility
Management

SETTORI

© PETAS . P.IVA IT 03374880239 . REA 331154

CONTATTACI . CREDITS

AD Magazine

Design/
Alex Yurkov

This project is a UI design for AD Magazine in order to create a smarter and more intelligent way to advertise brands. One can create and customize a unique campaign by using video-promos provided by this platform, and raise the brand to next level.

Title: Helvetica Neue Font; 66px \ ***Contents:*** Helvetica Neue Font; 16px \ ***Font-Kerning:*** Normal \ ***Line Height:*** 23.3px

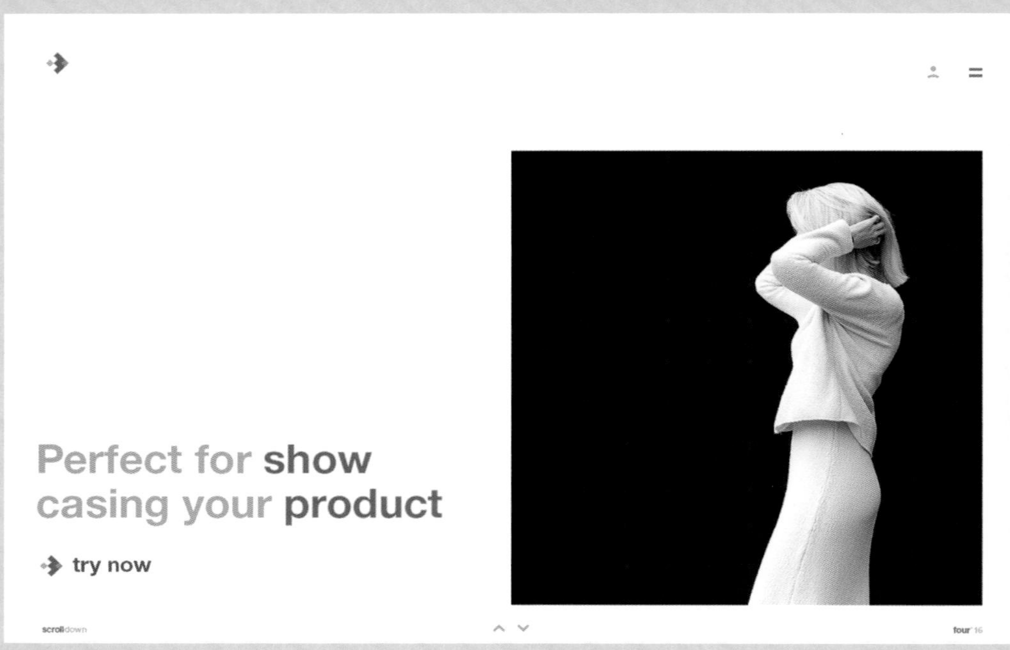

Beoplay A9 —
Floor-standing speaker/
wireless / original design
This webapp makes is easier for directors and brand advertisers to manage, publish and track your very own AD Channel. Create beautiful campaigns that generate more time on site, increase engagement and generate conversion!
play
scrolldown
one'16

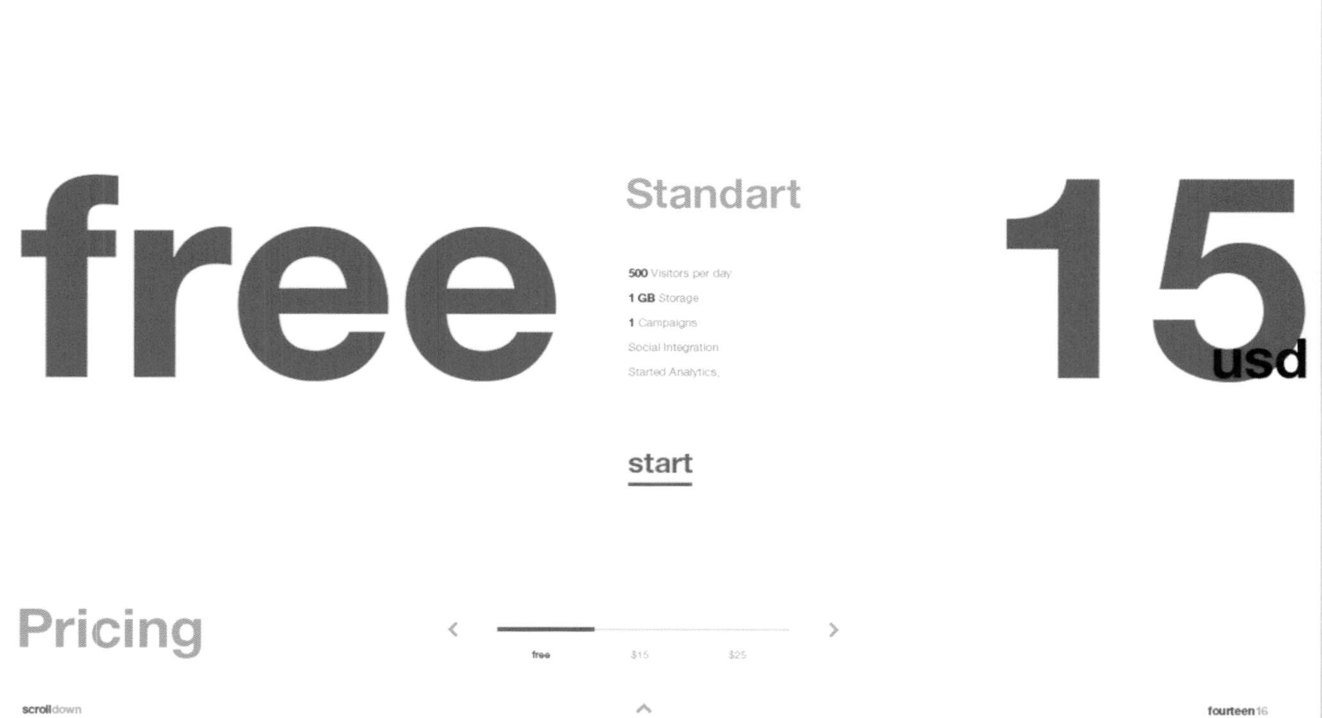
free
Standart
500 Visitors per day
1 GB Storage
1 Campaigns
Social Integration
Started Analytics,
15
usd
start
Pricing
free
$15
$25
scrolldown
fourteen16

Onirim

Design Agency/	Direction/	Design/	Photography/	Client/	URL/
Immersive Garden	Dilshan Arukatti	Flavien Guilbaud, Dilshan Arukatti	Onirim	Onirim	http://onirim.com

Onirim is a high standard production company focused on creating qualitative films for luxury brands. The challenge on this project was to offer an experience with a strong graphic identity that reflects ONIRIM's notoriety and standards, while also being a setting which is to enhance its productions and authors. The feeling conveyed is a smart, modern, and classy website that is completely administrable by the client. The artistic touch resides in the choices of composition, use of font, and color.

Title: MarkPro-Black; 90px \ ***Contents:*** MaisonNeue-Bold; 14px \ ***Font-Kerning:*** Normal \ ***Line Height:*** 14px

ONIRIM

directors photographers projects post-production about us

ONIRIM IS A CREATIVE PRODUCTION COMPANY. WE REPRESENT DIRECTORS AND PHOTOGRAPHERS. WE PRODUCE COMMERCIALS, BRAND CONTENT AND PHOTOS.

↓ SCROLL TO DISCOVER

FACEBOOK
TWITTER
LINKEDIN
INSTAGRAM

COPYRIGHT ONIRIM - LEGAL NOTICE -CREDITS -PRIVATE ACCESS

directors photographers projects post-production about us

↓ SCROLL TO DISCOVER

COPYRIGHT ONIRIM - LEGAL NOTICE -CREDITS -PRIVATE ACCESS

La Petite Reine

Design Agency/
Studio Gambetta

Client/
La Petite Reine

URL/
http://cafelapetitereine.ch

Graphic design and website for La Petite Reine, a coffee and bar located in Geneva. And a series of about 100 buffers logos were created as collaterals for the website.

Title: Custom (Bold) \ ***Contents:*** Verdana (Bold) \ ***Font-Kerning:*** 2px \ ***Line Height:*** 34px

cafelapetitereine.ch

HOME

Webdesign by Kafo-art & Benito

CASSE CROUTE

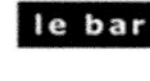

Casse Croute
Whisky
Fiorenzana Gazose
Coffee & Tea
Cocktails
Absinthe
Beers
Soft Drinks
Vins
Aperitifs
Shots
Club Mate

le bar

ADRESSE
Place de Montbrillant à coté de Genève roule!, 1201 Genève,
Voir plan d'accès

Crédits photo: ©Nicolas Haeni

le contact

la carte

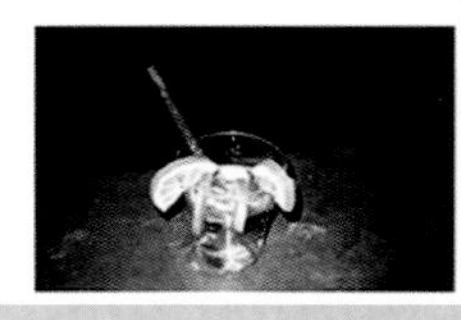

ORAIRES

00:00
me-je
11:00
01:00
ve
11:00
02:00
sa
17:00
02:00

Soupe 8/10 CHF
Empanada 6 CHF

cafelapetitereine.ch

HOME

Webdesign by Kafo-art & Benito

le contact

PR

Crédits photo: ©Nicolas Haeni

À la Petite Reine:
terrasse orientée sud-ouest...
soleil toute la journée!!

ADRESSE

Place de Montbrillant à coté
de Genève roule!, 1201 Genève,
Switzerland

la carte

le bar

HO-RAIRES

lu - ma:
11:00–00:00
me - je:
11:00–01:00
ve:
11:00–02:00
sa:
17:00–02:00

DNOVA

Design Agency/
TIMA INSTITUTE

URL/
http://www.dnova.com.cn

DNOVA is a black diamond brand based in Hong Kong. They reached out to TIMA INSTITUTE for a visual identity to empower the branding with cultural and aesthetic values.

The team decided to create an identity for the black diamond as mysterious as our universe. Based on the concept, the team designed a comprehensive solutions for the brand, including poster, website, leaflet, and E-platform. The website was developed with various special effects like Transitions and Flutter to offer a mysterious and playful user experience.

Title: DIN Alternate \ ***Contents:*** DIN Alternate; 14 px \ ***Font-Kerning:*** Normal \ ***Line Height:*** 20px

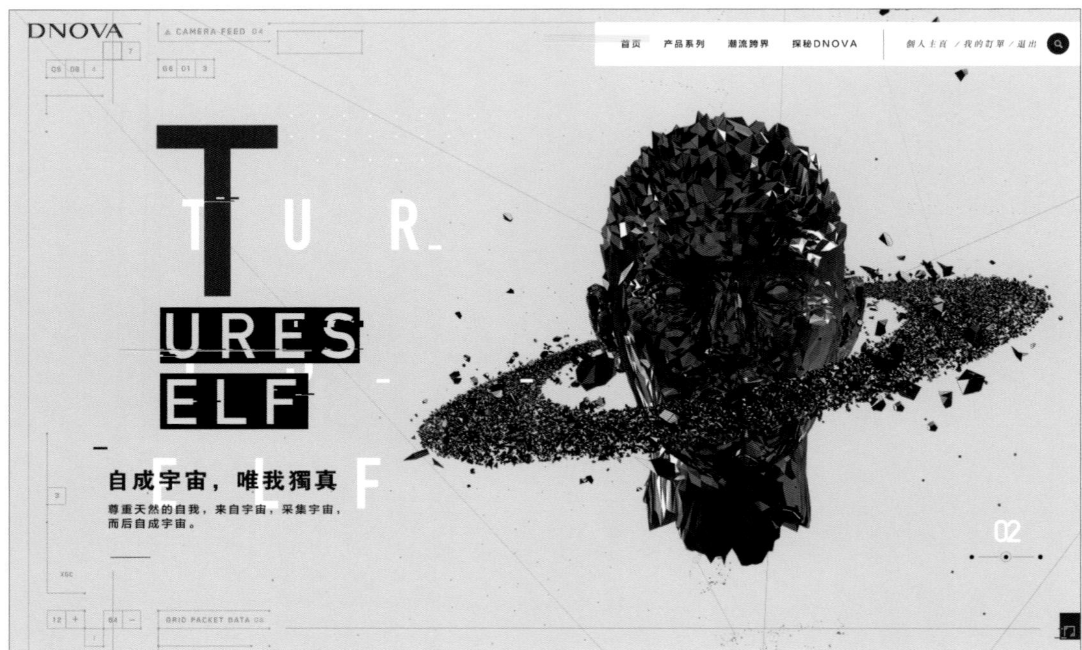

DNOVA

CAMERA FEED 04

首页　产品系列　潮流跨界　探秘DNOVA　個人主頁 / 我的訂單 / 退出

LIMIT

CROSSOVER

潮流跨界

在DNOVA的审美宇宙中，
一切都没有界限，
与各界设计师的跨界碰撞，激发出无限灵感，
用艺术，衍生生活。

01

GRID PACKET DATA

首页
产品系列
ORIGIN
起源
無以追溯的身世之謎。
是诞生于洪荒之时
地幔身处的自然宝藏？
还是天体分解后漂流至地球的宇宙遗迹？

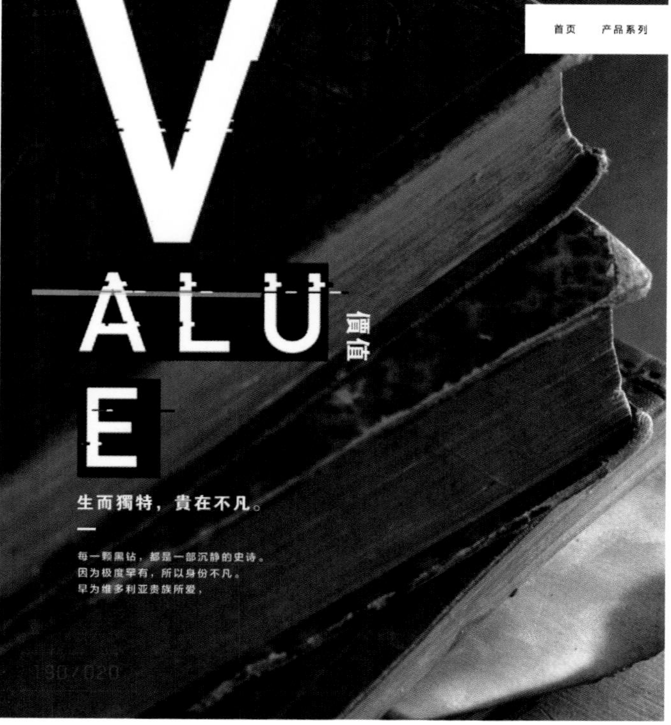

首页
产品系列
VALUE
價值
生而獨特，貴在不凡。
每一颗黑钻，都是一部沉静的史诗。
因为极度罕有，所以身份不凡。
早为维多利亚贵族所爱，

Papazian Jewelry

Design/
Kommigraphics Design Studio

Client/
Papazian Jewelry

URL/
http://www.papazian.gr

The company Papazian produces a great variety of jewelry mannequin and display bases. All of their creations share a common vision and have the ultimate aim to help their clients reach their audience. Based on this philosophy, Kommigraphics Design Studio designed a modern website that brings out the values of the company and its entire product catalog.

Inspired by the hand-crafted creation process, Kommigraphics created a custom video that is divided into four different chapters to introduce the company. The use of grey as well as the powder color was chosen in order to deliver the elegant character of the products, while the sweet orange connects the long experience with the modern design trends. All typography used embraces Papazian's new brand identity and its specific details highlight the special design of the products.

Title: Gotham (Bold) \ ***Contents:*** Gotham-Book; 13px \ ***Font-Kerning:*** Normal \ ***Line Height:*** 24px

SEARCH

MENU

HANDMADE JEWELRY DISPLAYS

VARTAN PAPAZIAN

SINCE 1963 VARTAN PAPAZIAN COMPANY IS ONE OF THE WORLD'S LEADING MANUFACTURERS OF LUXURY PACKAGING AND DISPLAY PRODUCTS.

During all these years, our professional team has created a variety of products for jewelry shops such as stands for showcases, boxes, risers, trays, drawers, rolls, folders, pouches, watch winders and many more.

We have been renowned for the high quality of our handmade products, the innovative ideas, the effective co-operation with clients around the world and the ability to tailor our services to each customer's needs surpassing their expectations.

We are always next to you, full of new ideas, determination and love, because we believe in what we do.

ABOUT US

WHERE THE RAW MATERIALS

WORK SHOP

BECOME ARTIFACTS

ABOUT PAPAZIAN

02

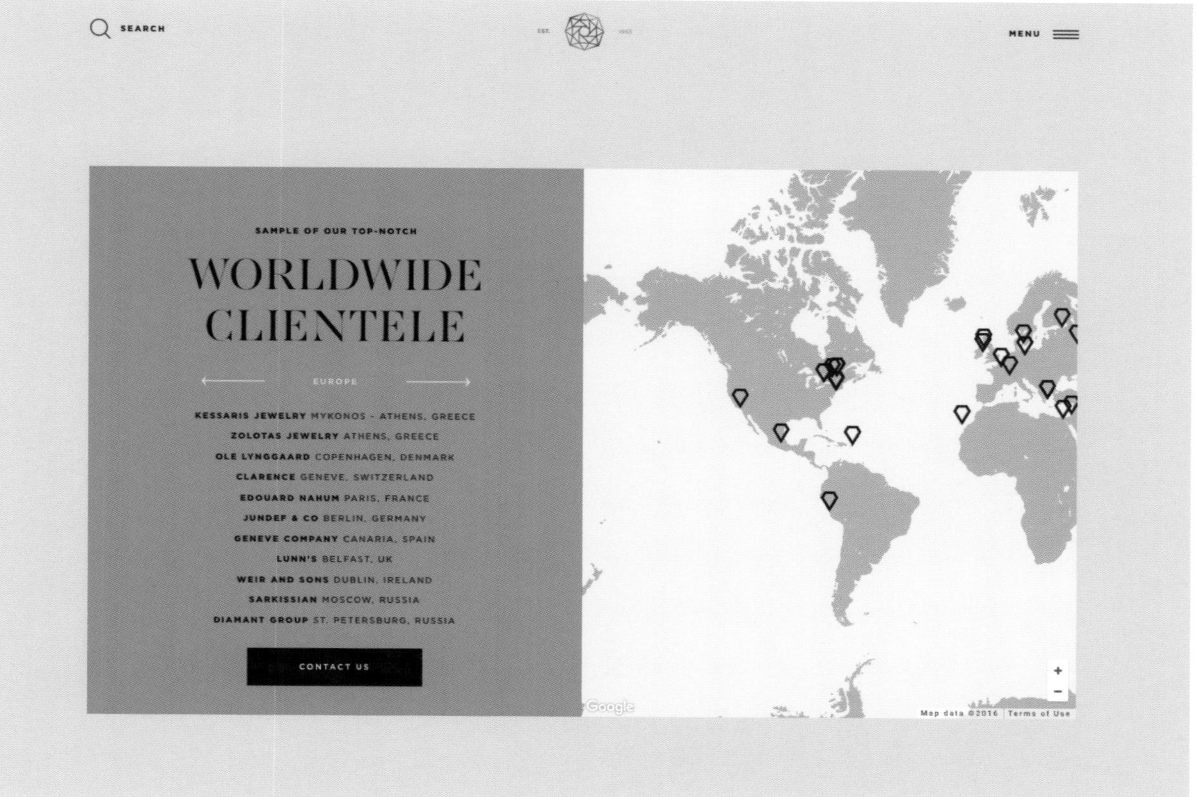

SEARCH
EST.
MENU
SAMPLE OF OUR TOP-NOTCH
WORLDWIDE CLIENTELE
EUROPE
KESSARIS JEWELRY MYKONOS - ATHENS, GREECE
ZOLOTAS JEWELRY ATHENS, GREECE
OLE LYNGGAARD COPENHAGEN, DENMARK
CLARENCE GENEVE, SWITZERLAND
EDOUARD NAHUM PARIS, FRANCE
JUNDEF & CO BERLIN, GERMANY
GENEVE COMPANY CANARIA, SPAIN
LUNN'S BELFAST, UK
WEIR AND SONS DUBLIN, IRELAND
SARKISSIAN MOSCOW, RUSSIA
DIAMANT GROUP ST. PETERSBURG, RUSSIA
CONTACT US
Google
Map data ©2016 | Terms of Use

Galvan Mobili

Design Agency/	Direction/	Design/	Client/	URL/
AQuest S.r.l.	Tomas Baruffaldi	Tomas Baruffaldi	Galvan Mobili	http://www.galvanmobili.it

The tradition and the innovation of decorations and product are in a single Italian name: Galvan Mobili. AQuest transformed their passion and dedication into this website to meet the needs and taste of contemporary world. They used Futura, which is characterized by simple lines and nearly perfect geometric forms, to represent Italian craftsmen's consistent pursuit of excellence and perfectness.

Contents: FuturaStd-Book; 15.4px \ ***Font-Kerning:*** Normal \ ***Line Height:*** 28.8px

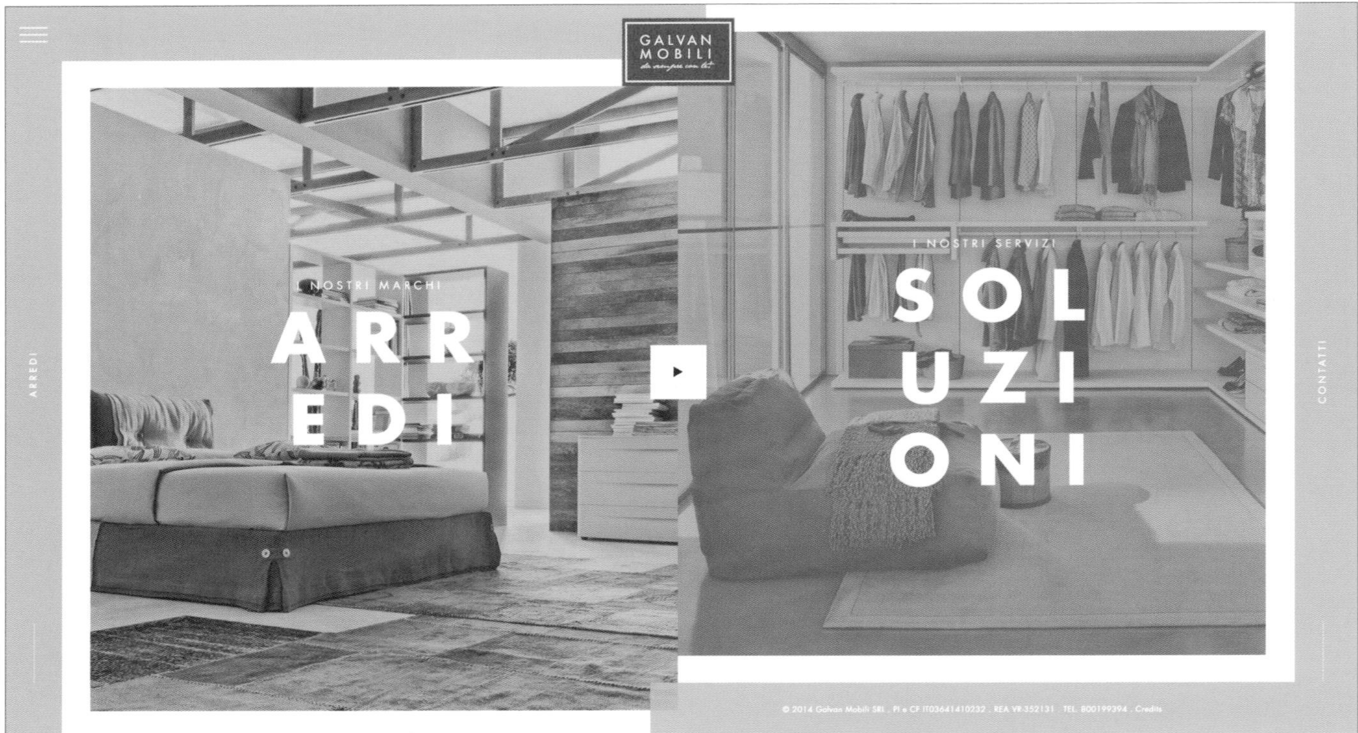

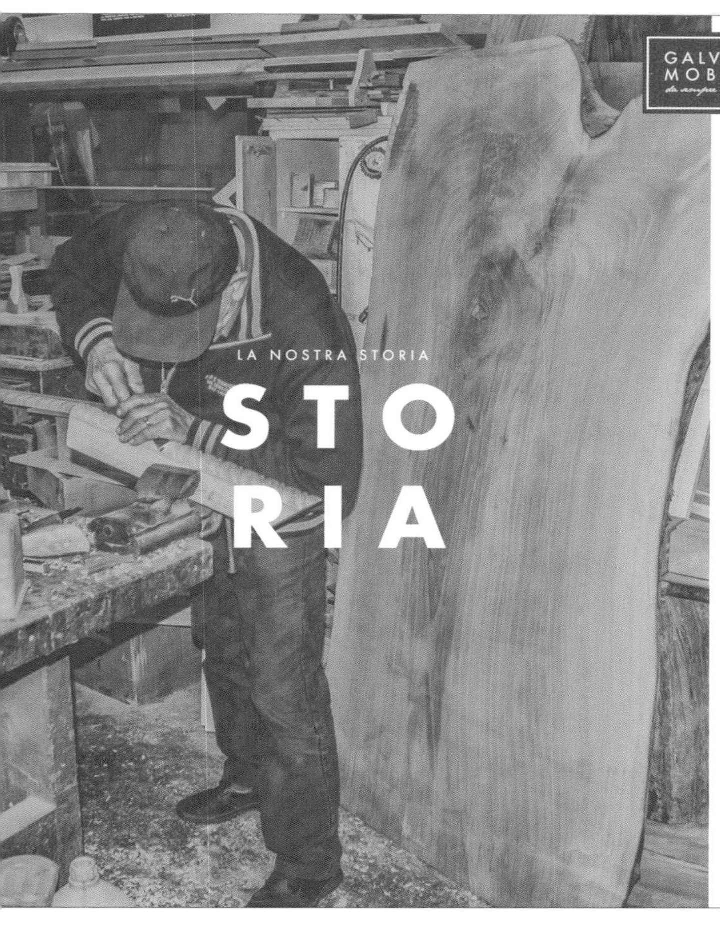

1962

NIENTE DI PIÙ SODDISFACENTE DELLA PASSIONE CHE ACCOMPAGNA LA PROPRIA PROFESSIONE IN UN PERCORSO LUNGO PIÙ DI CINQUANT'ANNI.

E' ciò che caratterizza Luigi Galvan, un uomo che ha reso celebre il suo nome grazie alla passione per l'arte della manifattura di mobili. Ed è dal 1962 che Luigi riesce a trasmettere questa passione di generazione in generazione sempre con l'aiuto della moglie Perlita e del figlio Giorgio, sempre al suo fianco.

1985

Nel 1985 si affianca, alla produzione di mobili, una sezione di vendita di mobili moderni di marchi veneti che troverà, poi, maggiore spazio nel 1990 con la costruzione del nuovo centro che tutt'oggi identifica Galvan Mobili.

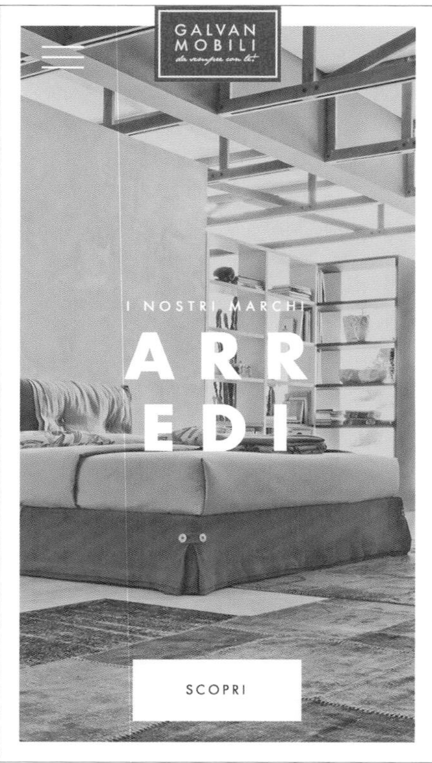

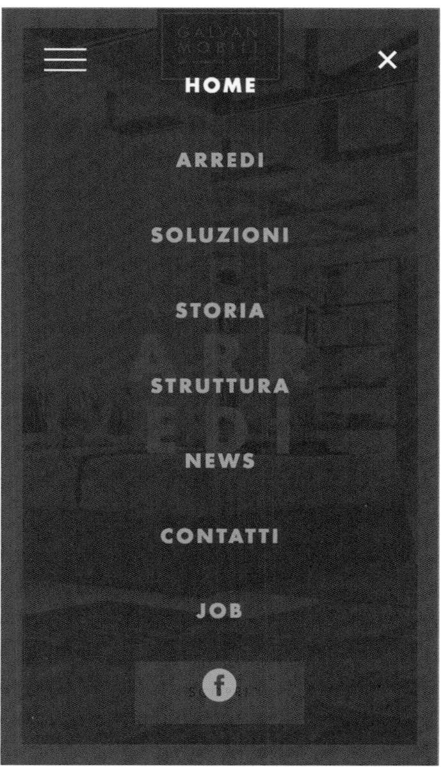

VENETA CUCINE

L'OTTAVA MERAVIGLIA È PIÙ VICINA DI QUANTO PENSI. GUARDA IN CUCINA!

CONTATTACI

A Verona Veneta Cucine è Galvan. L'esperienza, la creatività e l'attenzione all'innovazione del gusto, rendono Veneta Cucine in grado di realizzare progetti di vita per creare un unico ed emozionante spazio da vivere tutti i giorni con chi si ama. Il design diventa accessibile e arricchisce la vostra cucina in modo raffinato e personale.

Sapiegos

Design Agency/	Web Design, UI/UX/	Animation/	URL/
M—2—H	Alexander Laguta	Alexey Smolkin	www.vilniustechpark.com

This site for Sapiegos Tech Park was complicated for M—2—H as they had to build a digital-home for something that has yet to be built. They used metaphoric images to set the mood of creativity and define the growing Sapiegos community. Also, they created the platform in the concept of "evolution" which will grow and evolve with the project itself so the website can be expanded alternatively based on future demands.

Title: Din; 83.46px \ ***Contents:*** Din; 18.46px \ ***Font-Kerning:*** Normal \ ***Line Height:*** 16px

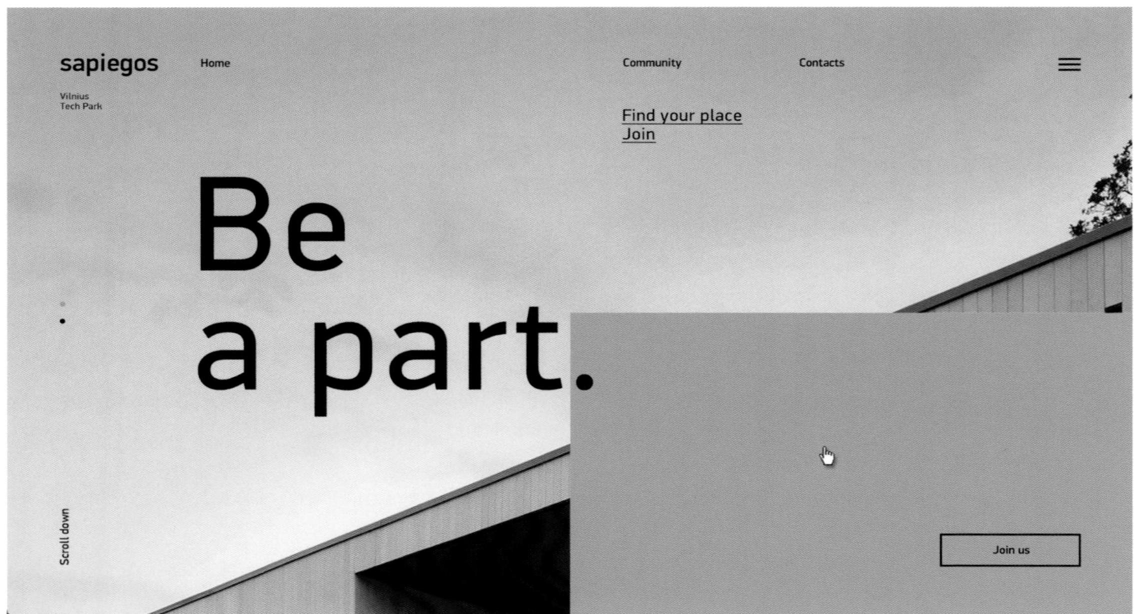

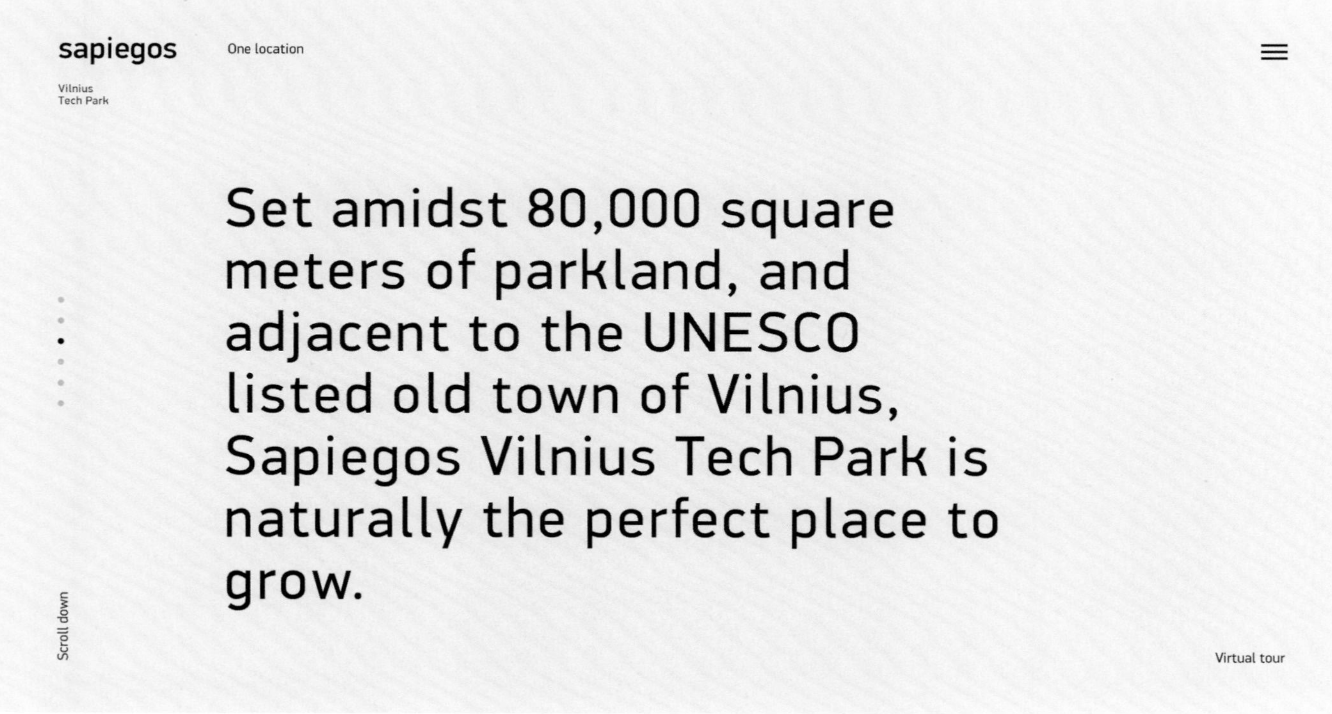

sapiegos

One location

Vilnius
Tech Park
Google Tech
Where nature
meets innovation,
where history meets the

One
location.

Scroll down

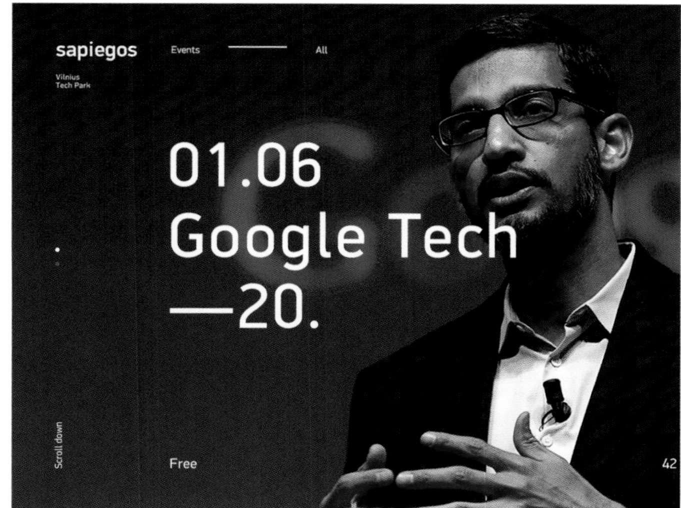

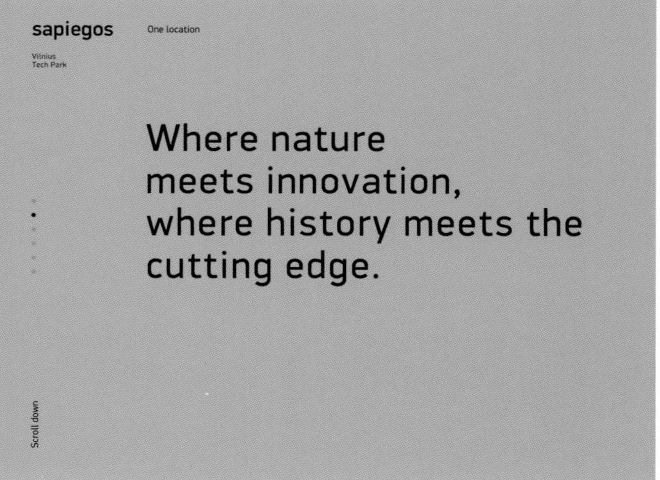

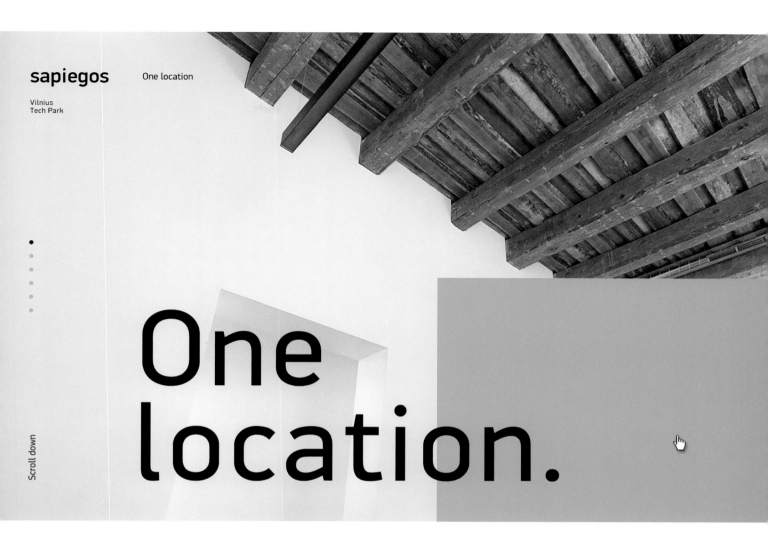

TOKYO TOKYO

Design/
Florent Gomez

TOKYO TOKYO is a new monthly Web Magazine about the world of fashion in Japan. Florent Gomez adopted a simplicity layout, use of Japanese Katakana, and clean and white background to illustrate its Japanese aesthetics. In the title, he reversed the type to improve its artistic effects. The entire design is fresh and classic.

Contents: FuturaStd-Book; 15.4px \ ***Font-Kerning:*** Normal \ ***Line Height:*** 28.8px

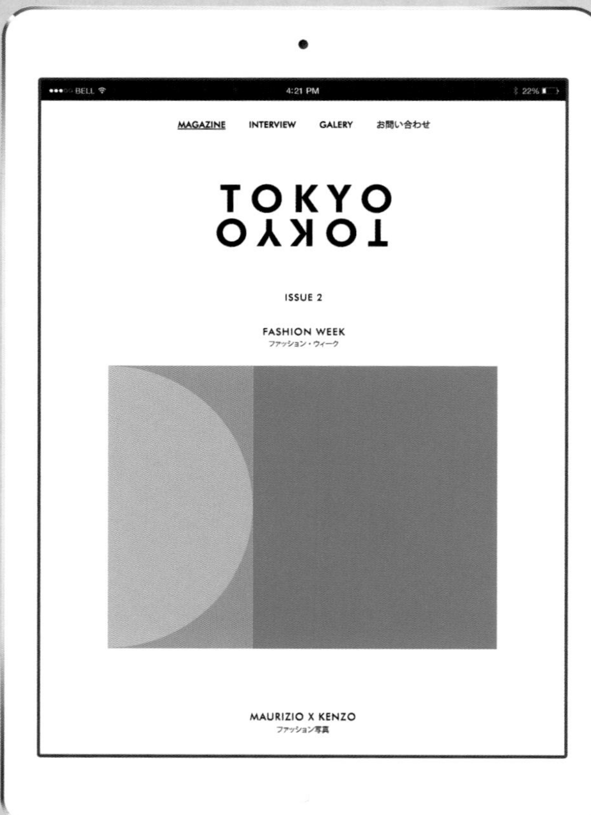

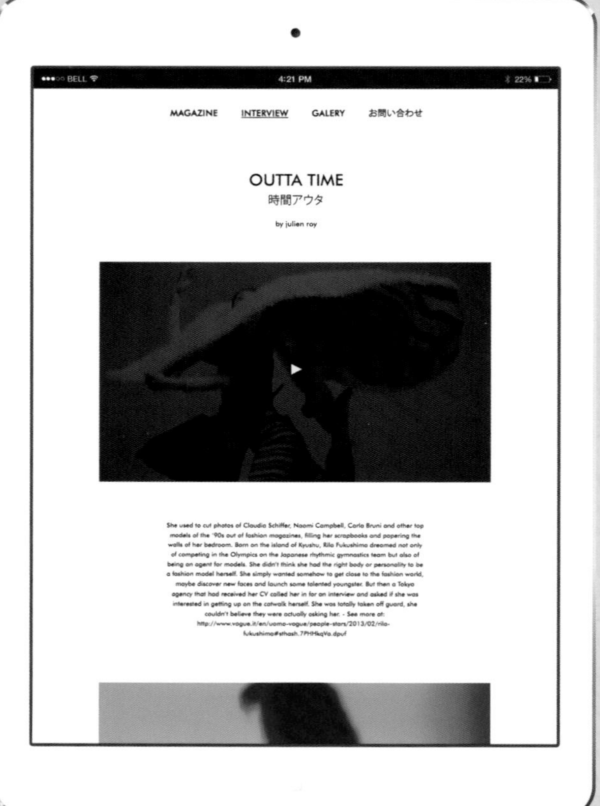

MAGAZINE INTERVIEW GALERY お問い合わせ

ISSUE 2

GALERY
ゲーラリー

⟵ ⟶

MAGAZINE INTERVIEW GALERY お問い合わせ

9:00 PM

ゲーラリー

THE NEW WAVE OF JAPAN
日本の新しい顔

RILA FUKUSHIMA

She used to cut photos of Claudia Schiffer, Naomi Campbell, Carla Bruni and other top models of the '90s out of fashion magazines, filling her scrapbooks and papering the walls of her bedroom. Born on the island of Kyushu, Rila Fukushima dreamed not only of competing in the Olympics on the Japanese rhythmic gymnastics team but also of being an agent for models. She didn't think she had the right body or personality to be a

issue 2
新しい号が利用可能

Du Haihang Portfolio 2016

Design/
Du Haihang

URL/
http://www.duhaihang.com

The site serves as Portfolio 2016 of interactive designer and developer Du Haihang. The site features a group of WebGL typeface animations to lead the design. Visitors can drag, swipe, and scroll to experience the site.

Title: Simsun; 16px \ ***Contents:*** Conduit; 12px \ ***Font-Kerning:*** Normal \ ***Line Height:*** 13px

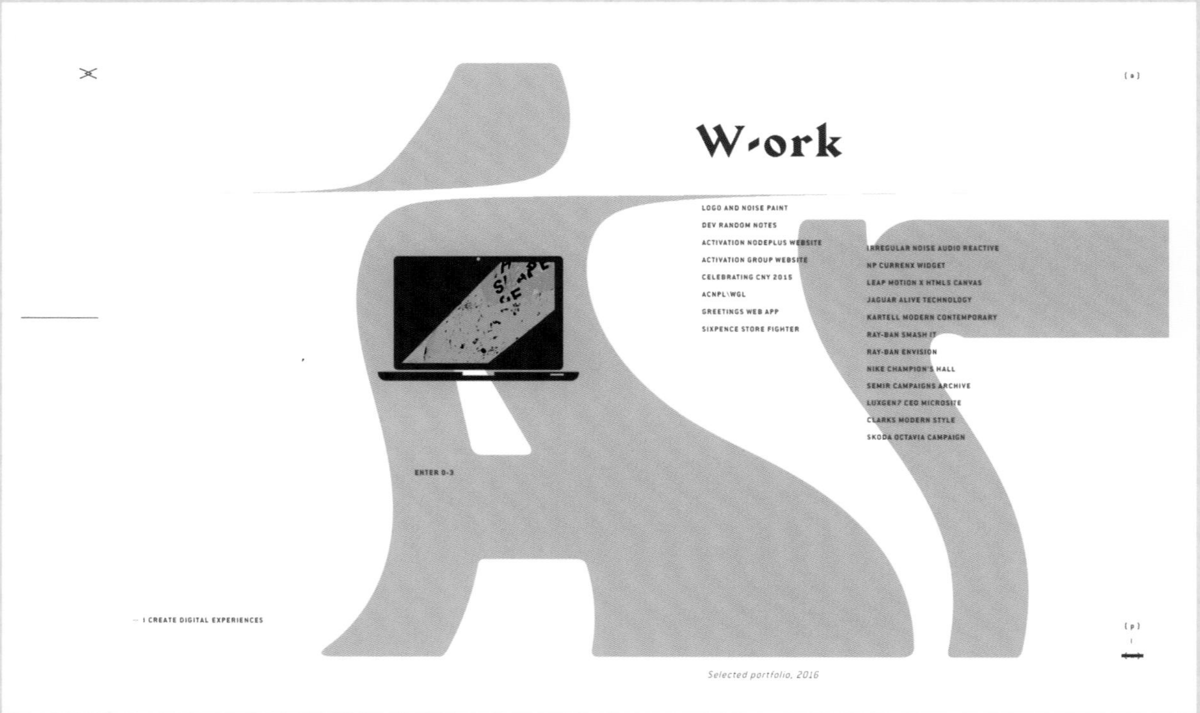

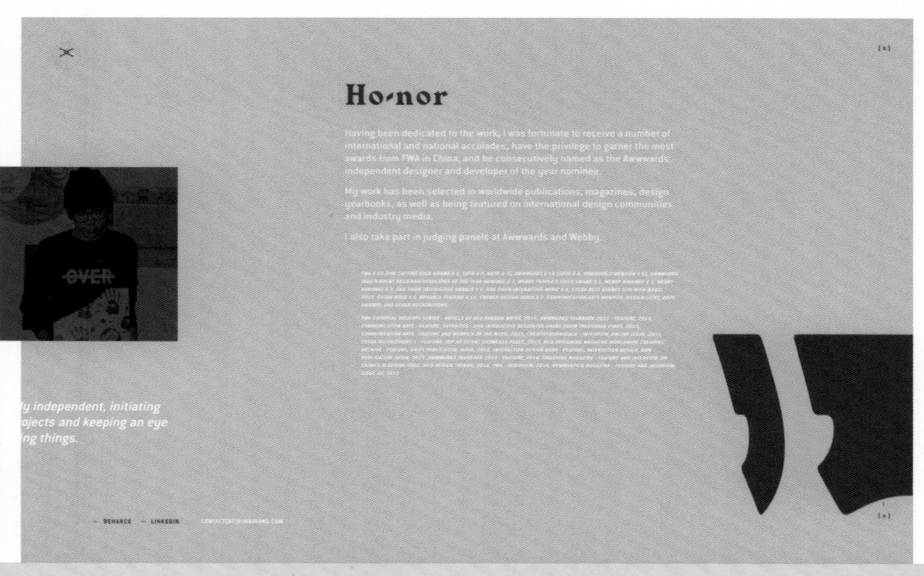

Du Haihang
Interactive
Designer & Developer
0-1
Logo And Noise Paint
Selected portfolio, 2016

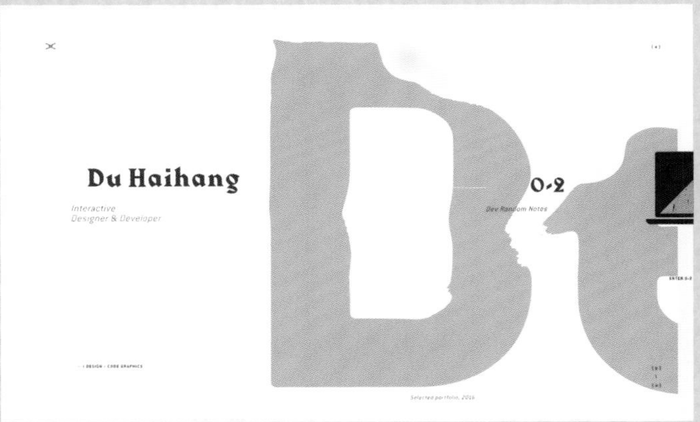

Du Haihang
Interactive
Designer & Developer
0-2
Dev Random Notes
Selected portfolio, 2016

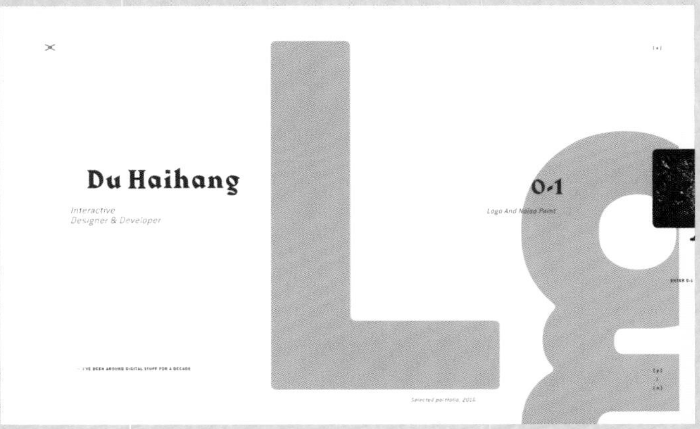

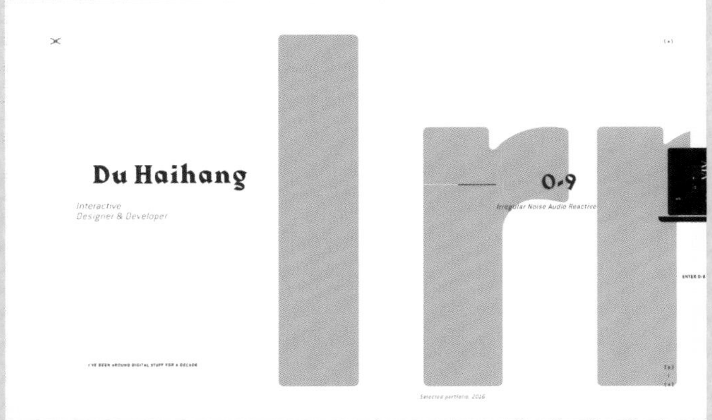

Du Haihang
Interactive
Designer & Developer
0-9
Irregular Noise Audio Reactive
Selected portfolio, 2016

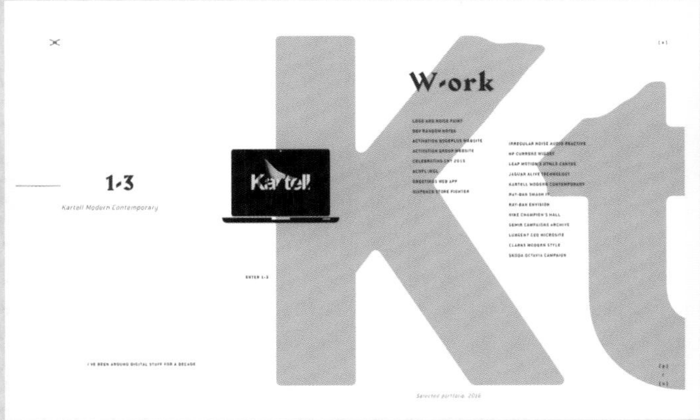

W-ork
1-3
Kartell Modern Contemporary
Selected portfolio, 2016

Music Story

Design Agency/
M—2—H

Web Design, UI/UX/
Alexander Laguta

Animation/
Alexey Smolkin

Music Story is a professional music education school based in Moscow. The school has more than 300 students and 15 professional teachers within several disciplines including vocal training, guitar, drums, and many others. M-2-H has created a full set of tools, guidelines, elements, and interactions. The fonts are used in variations to stress on different information when necessary. Such setting gives the site a bold, unconventional, and graceful look.

Title: Simsun; 16px \ ***Contents:*** Conduit; 12px \ ***Font-Kerning:*** Normal \ ***Line Height:*** 13px

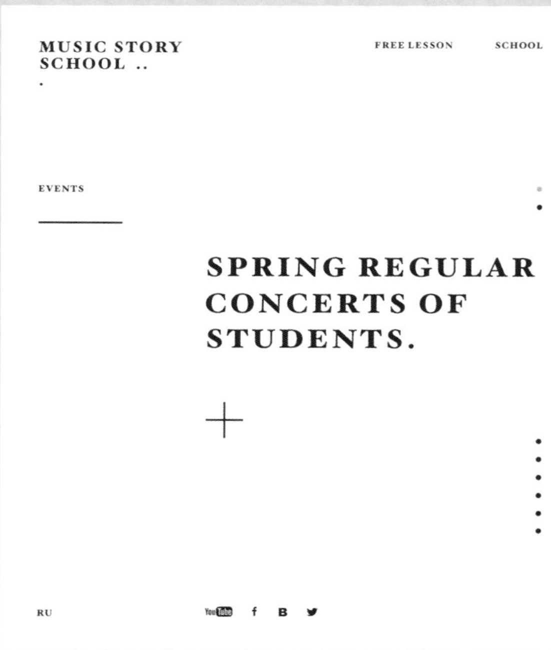

MUSIC STORY
SCHOOL ..
FREE LESSON
SCHOOL
ABOUT
GALLERY
CONCERTS
RECORDING
STUDIO.

MUSIC STORY SCHOOL ..

FREE LESSON SCHOOL TEACHERS STUDENTS

ABOUT GALLERY CONCERTS

I /6

TO REVEAL THE MYSTERY OF MUSIC.

In our school we have teachers of the highest class, everyone has a great experience and their interesting teaching methods.

RU

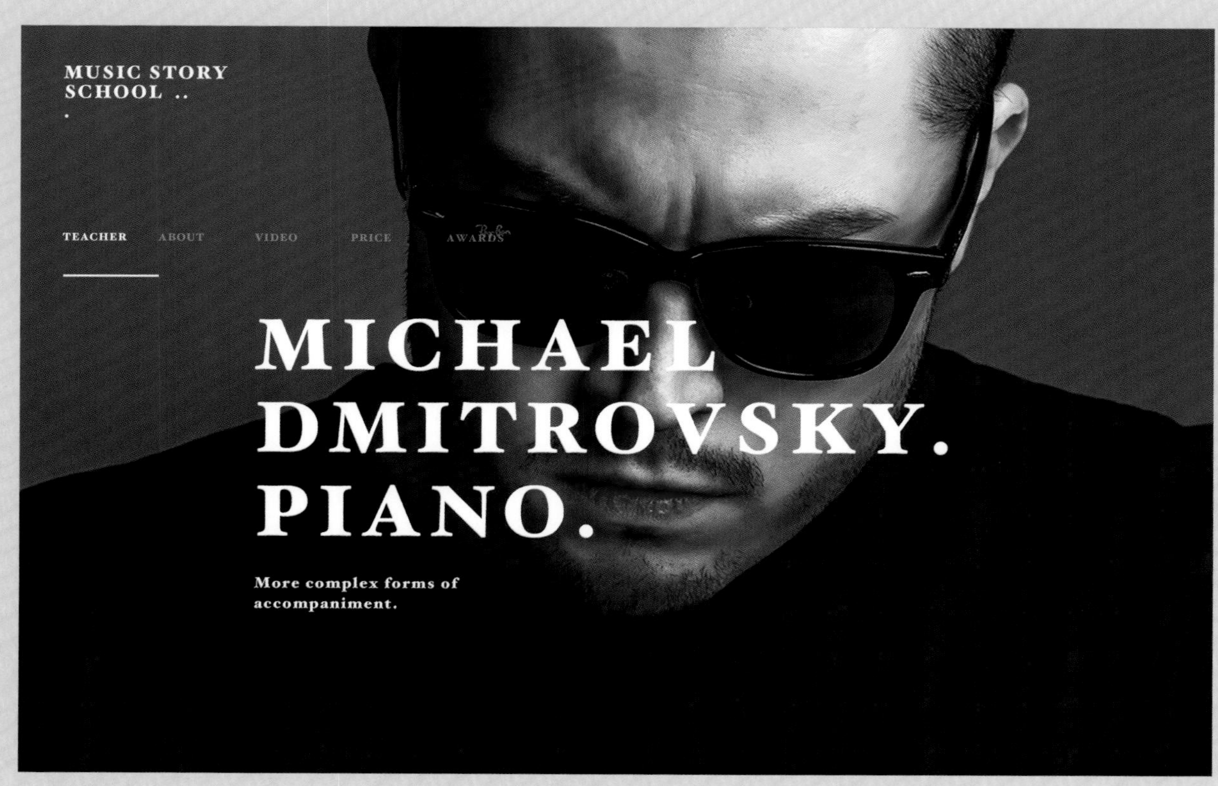

Te Oro

Design Agency/
Sons & Co.

Creative Directors/
Timothy Kelleher, Dean Poole

Designer/
Matthew Arnold, Greg Brown, Kris Lane, Tyrone Ohia, Jinki Cambronero

Client/
Auckland Council

URL/
http://www.teoro.org.nz

Te Oro is music and arts centre for young people. In this multi-purpose space young people and the local community gather together to perform, practice, and learn the arts; express their creativity and talents; and celebrate their cultures. The title and subtitles of the site are designed based on pixel, expressing an avant-garde spirits of the youths.

Title: Akkurat Regular \ ***Contents:*** Helvetica Neue; 13px \ ***Font-Kerning:*** Normal \ ***Line Height:*** 1.6px

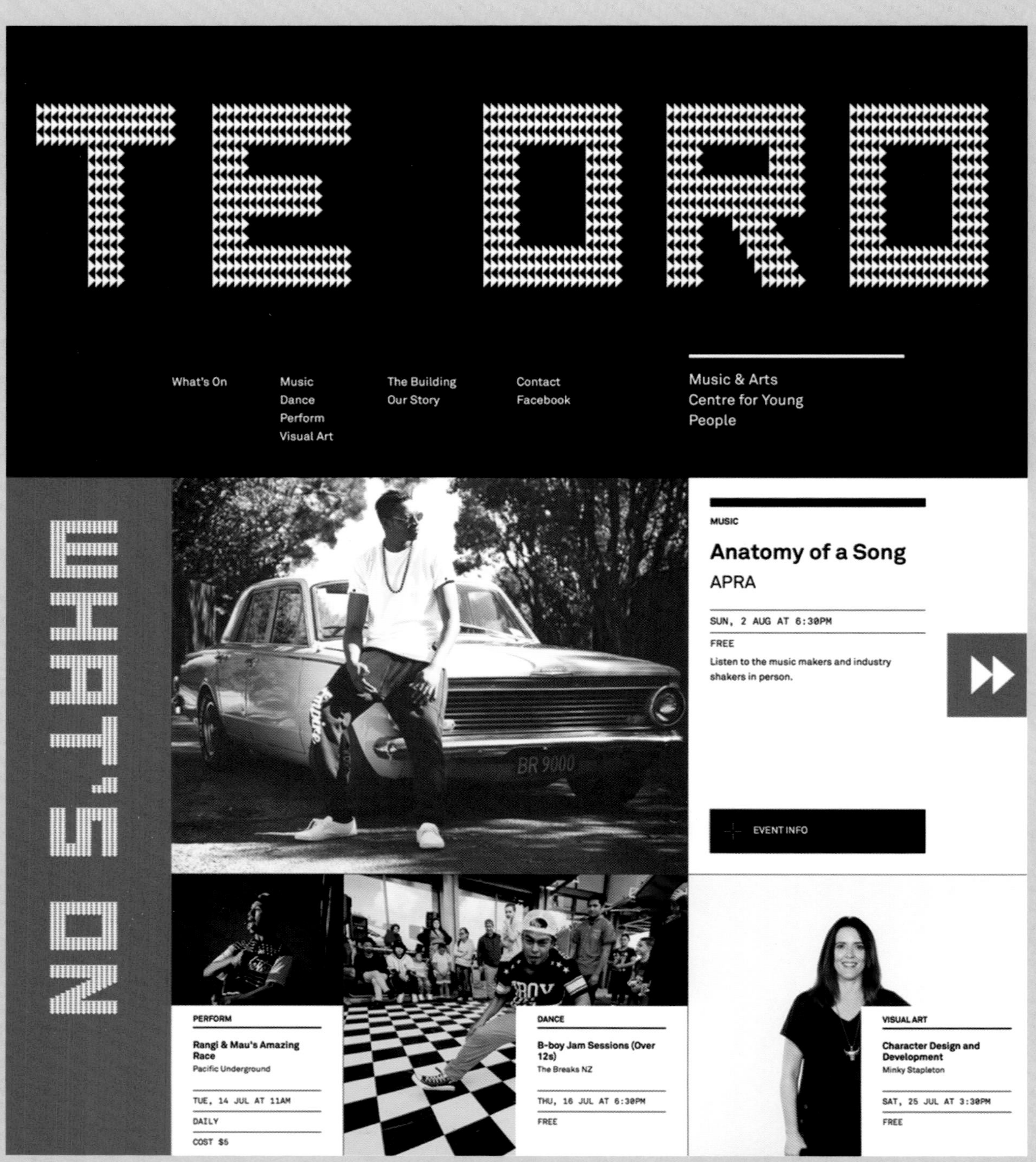

TE ORO
What's On
Music
Dance
Perform
Visual Art
The Building
Our Story
Contact
Facebook
TE ORO
OUR PLACE
INTRODUCTION
FLOOR PLAN
SOUND SITES
LEVEL 1
01. Te Wai O Taiki
LEVEL 2
01. Studio 2 / Hopu ōro 2

Mon - Fri
10:00 am - 7:00 pm
Saturday
9:00 am - 6:00 pm
98 Line Road
Glen Innes
Auckland
09 890 8560
info@teoro.org.nz
GET DIRECTIONS FROM:
Saint Johns Road
Point England Park
Waiatarua Reserve
Ellerslie Racecourse
Mount Wellington Domain
Jellicoe Road
Lagoon Drive
Great South Road
Pakuranga Road
Howick Golf Club
SIGN UP FOR EMAILS

INDIE EXPRESS

Art Direction/ Tseng Green
Designer/ Tseng Green, i-Mei Lee
Animation Design/ Phil Wu
Photography/ Tseng Green
Client/ THE WALL MUSIC

The project concept aims to present Indie Express as a media platform of music. For the visual design, the concept was set as "shuttling through space." Sound/Music is conveyed through sonic waves, which are invisible, only the experience of spirits can be perceived. And the listeners' spirits are the destinations of Sound/Music.

They then transferred the real space into an abstracted one, and Indie Express shuttles through this invisible space to deliver music into everyone's heart, to communicate over the culture of music.

Title: Helvetica Neue LT Std 95 Black (Bold) \ ***Contents:*** Helvetica Neue LT Std 65 Medium (Normal), Helvetica Neue LT Std 95 Black (Bold)
Font-Kerning: Normal \ ***Line Height:*** Normal

Index

◇◇◇

Carmen Nácher

Carmen Nácher is a Spanish graphic designer who has been living in Germany. Carmen studied graphic design in the EASD of Valencia. Currently, she works as a graphic designer in a design agency in Berlin, as well as freelance in different projects around the world.

http://www.carmennacher.com

146 – 147

Codefrisko

Codefrisko is a visual communication agency that provides a full-service for brands that want to position themselves on the stage of excellence by fine or unusual image. With its rich experience and network, Codefrisko and its creative director, Audrey Schayes, strengthen the image of its clients to achieve prominence in their fields. Their approach is strategic, using psychology and sociology, and taking account of the emotions guiding human spirits. Their added value must go far beyond appearances.

http://codefrisko.com

022 – 023; 102 – 103

CTDL Games

Love for games and graphic design is what brought CTDL Games to life. They are a studio founded by four independent designers focused on combining great ideas with passion for games, typography, and excellence in design.

http://ctdlgames.com

156 – 157

Current Haus

Current Haus focuses on creating digital experiences that connect brands with culture to inspire, entertain, and produce results. They are a team consisted of multi-skilled specialists hungry for new challenges and with a passion for great design. Working with clients all over the globe, their mission is to turn fresh ideas into bold brands and polished digital products.

http://currenthaus.com

134 – 137

Du Haihang

With 10-year multidisciplinary design experience, the award-winning digital designer Du Haihang wears different hats to bring digital experiences to life across a variety of design spectrums.

http://www.duhaihang.com

064 – 065; 104 – 105; 174 – 175; 226 – 227

Elisabeth Enthoven

Graduated from the Royal Academy of Arts in The Hague, Elisabeth Enthoven is an independent graphic designer from Amsterdam, the Netherlands. She works across magazines, visual identities, web design, packaging, books, illustrations, etc. in both commercial and cultural fields. After working for the design studio of Scotch & Soda for a few years she now returned to her own design studio in 2016 and regularly she teams up with other creative professionals.

http://www.elisabethenthoven.nl

084 – 087

Emanuele Cecini

Emanuele Cecini is an Italian multidisciplinary designer who works across a broad spectrum of media and fields. He has been living and working in Milan, London, Copenhagen, Frankfurt, San Francisco, and New York where he collaborated with a wide range of skilled partners. He creates strong and effective designs, with a simple and clean aesthetic and a meticulous attention to detail.

http://www.emanuelececini.com

110 – 113

FACE

FACE is a design studio of super modernists specialized in developing honest branding projects across the world. Their work is intended to stand the test of time. Their craft is the result of constant effort, talents, and commitments to quality of the highest international level. They are established in San Pedro Garza García, Mexico, and have delivered quality design products for both domestic and international clients since 2006.

http:// www.designbyface.com

114 – 115

Firman Suci Ananda

Firman Suci Ananda is a freelance UI designer since 2010. He has been working for global agencies and companies, such as Paper Tiger, Canva, Udemy, Freepik, and so forth. Apart from co-working with agencies, he works with his clients as a freelance designer on a diverse range of projects.

https://www.behance.net/firmansuciananda

054 – 057; 180 – 181

Florent Gomez

Inspired by European design philosophies especially Swiss design and Dutch design, Florent Gomez is ambitious to be a modernist designer. Embedded discipline and consistency beyond aesthetics, he tries to integrate this vision of design with sometimes a more contemporary approach. He also draws inspirations from experimental design and the way that it reverses the aesthetic codes to highlight strong concepts.

http://florentgomez.com

052 – 053; 116 – 119; 224 – 225

Héctor Sos

Héctor Sos is a graphic designer with a serious passion for the graphic world. With more than 10 years of experience in the field, He is always focused on the overall aim of the project. The areas in which he has most developed his skills and enthusiasm are identity, editorial design, art direction, packaging, web design, photography, and illustration.

http://hectorsos.net

042 – 043; 094 – 095; 198 – 199

Immersive Garden

Immersive Garden is a digital creative team based in Paris. Their expertise allows them to support projects from the brief to the launch. Their working scope is cross-disciplinary: design, development, film direction, photography, motion design, and so forth.

These artistic and technological skills, added to their knowledge of strategy and communicative culture, are the key to groundbreaking and successful productions.

http://immersive-g.com

176 – 177; 178 – 179; 206 – 207; 212 – 213

Inbal Lapidot Vidal

Inbal Lapidot Vidal is a multidisciplinary visual designer based in Tel Aviv, Israel. She graduated with excellence from the Visual Communication Department at Holon Institute of Technology. Her main domains are visual identities and branding, web design, product design, and print design. She creates bold and conceptual brands with a focus on image making and web design. She likes aesthetics and sensitive layouts and the dialogue between industry, design, business, and technology. She loves fresh and alternative culture, fashion, and travelling. She is enthusiastic to take new experiences and challenges.

https://www.behance.net/INBAL

128 – 129

Ira Banana

Ira Banana is a freelance UI/UX designer living between Minsk and Barcelona. She is specialized in creating modern, clean and user-friendly web and mobile design solutions.

http://irabanana.com

050 – 051

Irradié

Irradié is a multidisciplinary creative studio founded in 2016 by two brothers Alain and Laurent Vonck. L'atelier's skills express on branding, graphical systems, publications, and digital interfaces for a variety of clients, who are always with the same intellectual curiosity and passion, disregarding their scale and background. The studio promotes an open and respectful dialogue with each project executives in order to create the most appropriate and innovative visual solution.

http://irradie.com

022 – 023; 102 – 103

Javier Arizu

Javier Arizu is a Spanish graphic designer from Barcelona and currently based in New York. Graduated in 2012, he received a BA in Graphic Design in Eina, Centre Universitari de Disseny i Art de Barcelona and the London College of Communication. For almost 4 years he was part of Mucho's team in Barcelona, where he had the opportunity to design and art direct branding projects, publishing, packaging, web, and digital media for commercial, cultural, and institutional clients. In 2016, after leaving Mucho, he joined Pentagram New York.

https://www.behance.net/javierarizu

120 – 121

Kommigraphics Design Studio

Kommigraphics Design Studio is an award-winning communication agency, based in Athens, Greece. They specialize in effective branding and design paired with integrated marketing communication strategies and implementation, across a wide range of markets and media. They strongly believe in the power of creativity goes hand in hand with their strict conviction that a deep understanding of the market environment is vital to successful design and communication. They have a portfolio with varied projects that include branding, packaging, and website design and implementation as well as online and offline marketing services. They see all projects in a holistic way, so that they deliver effective, worthy, and memorable results that stand out of the market.

http://www.kommigraphics.com

088 – 089; 218 – 219

Lifeblood Agency

Lifeblood Agency is a digital design studio co-founded by Dominic Santalucia and Travis Weihermuller. Being a collective consciousness of creatives who are fearless, they craft meaningful human experiences that define brands in digital.

http://lifebloodagency.com

020 – 021

M—2—H

M—2—H creates unique digital experiences and branding solutions. They spend much of the time to make it very simple and straightforward to make the brands revive and blossom.

http://m-2-h.com

172 – 173; 194 – 195; 222 – 223; 228 – 229

Madelyn Bilsborough

Madelyn Bilsborough is a graphic designer based in Sydney, Australia. Her work encapsulates an eye for detail and simplicity. Although mainly focused on branding, editorial and digital layouts in graphic design, her passion stretches across numerous genres of creativity. Her work is inspired by surrounding environments and the ongoing supply of other talented designer's and creative projects across the world. She believes the details in design matter the most and are important in creating a strong foundation for a quality and polished piece of work.

https://madelyn.myportfolio.com

108 – 109

Mainstudio

Mainstudio is an Amsterdam based graphic design studio, founded by Edwin van Gelder in 2005. The studio creates projects deriving from the intersection of art, architecture, and fashion—including publications, digital media, and visual identities. Each is characterized by a content driven editorial approach, led by typography, to create a synthesis of form and content. The studio embeds inventive printing techniques in its traditional media, and explores innovative interaction design in its digital output, while an imaginative approach to art direction forms the studio's essential foundation. Mainstudio has been widely-honored with international awards, including the "Best Book Design from all over the World" (2013), the "Best Dutch Book Design" (2011 and 2012), and the "Art Directors Club New York" (2009).

http://mainstudio.com

100 – 101

Manon Moreau

Manon Moreau is a designer based in France.

https://www.behance.net/manonmoreau

122 – 123

Marija Erjavec

Marija Erjavec is a Helsinki based graphic designer from Ljubljana, Slovenia. She is interested in finding ways to make everyday processes smoother and more pleasant, to identify bottlenecks and little annoyances of everyday life and try to solve them with a holistic approach. She is currently studying her MA in Visual Communication Design at Aalto University's School of Arts, Design and Architecture in Finland.

https://www.behance.net/marijaerjavec

044 – 045; 142 – 143

Mashvp

Mashvp is a digital creative agency based in Toulouse, France. They provide art direction, innovative digital stuff for every screen. They empower brands through advice, digital strategy, project management, web design, user experience, custom and/or Open Source web development, community management, natural referencing (SEO), and finally payment reference. At Mashvp, they make customized websites and every other stuff that goes with it. They do their job with passion and they try to do it right. No formatted speech, no technical words or packaged solutions, they built customized websites and their best sales argument for their best marketing.

https://mashvp.com

182 – 183; 188 – 189

Milo Themes

Milo Themes is a small independent design studio located in Transilvania, working in graphic design, web development, and corporate branding. Milo is the artistic collaboration between two graphic designers: Loredana Papp-Dinea and Mihai Baldean.

Their partnership, in business and real life, brought together their strengths and creativity but also their different vision about design. Build with hard work, Milo is a successful project that is continuously growing.

http://milothemes.com

036 – 037

◇◇

moodley brand identity

moodley brand identity is an owner-operated and international award-winning strategic design agency. It has been developing corporate and product brands with its clients since Zggg. Brands live, breathe, and grow. Whether a startup, market launch or repositioning, moodley sees its creative responsibility in the strategic development of simple, intelligent, and emotionally appealing solutions to complex tasks. This is why moodley currently employs more than 6o specialists from the fields of strategy, design, consumer experience, architecture, journalism, and content publishing.

https://moodley.at

148 – 149

Morten Lybech

Morten Lybech is a Danish freelance multidisciplinary designer and creative director specialized in branding and interaction design. Through creative thinking, he creates immersive and strategic products helping global brands achieve their business goals.

http://mortenlybech.com

074 – 075; 130 – 131

Natalia Maltseva

Natalia Maltseva is a web designer based in Kharkiv, Ukraine.

https://behance.net/nataliyamaltseva

150 – 151

Nino Mamaladze

Nino Mamaladze is a graphic designer working for Leavingstone, which specializes in icon and logo design. She keeps her work fresh and up-to-date by actively engaging and publishing to her dribbble community.

https://dribbble.com/jelly-fishie

158 – 159

Oddds

Oddds was founded in 2013 by Reinold Lim (Penang) and Sarah Tan (Singapore). Their focuses are in branding, art direction, illustration, graphic design, packaging, to name a few. Oddds incorporates the study and evolution of cultures into their philosophy and attitude as their work reflects significantly on behaviors and futurism. They believe in aesthetics about how it draws attention and influences people.

https://oddds.com

138 – 141; 196 – 197

Phoenix the Creative Studio

By merging interaction and emotion, Phoenix the Creative Studio creates brand experiences that affect people. Creates brand experiences by reinventing them for the new interactive age, breaking with the industry's standards, and keeping them relevant and enjoyable to people to connect over. Though the studio is merely of human size, its creative audacity has already won more than 50 major awards and over 300 international mentions, which explains why Phoenix is considered amongst the best talent of his generation.

https://phoenix.cool

040 – 041; 066 – 067; 090 – 091; 154 – 155

Pierre Nguyen

Pierre Nguyen, aka Monsieur Caillou, is a French digital art director and UX designer based in Paris, working for agencies like AKQA, BETC, and Spintank. He is widely-recognized by FWA or Awwwards and known for his illustration work to the 1st Pick Me Up Fair in London. Inspired by magazines, his work is mainly composed of typographic and compositions of images.

http://www.monsieurcaillou.com

024 – 025; 166 – 169

Piotr Swierkowski

Graphics, being a huge passion for Piotr Swierkowski, enables him to stay spontaneous and gives him an opportunity for creative fulfillment. He puts a lot of commitment into his work, and take by the handful all the benefits offered by the Internet and contemporary advertising in order to satisfy his clients. He believes that the ability of creating new interesting solutions makes sense only when they are cooperating with other people. Together with teammates, it is much easier to achieve goals and set high standards of their service.

http://piotrswierkowski.com

038 – 039

Play&Type Studio

Founded by Raquel Orellana and Paco Díaz, Play&Type is a Barcelona-based studio that specializes in brand creation and visual communication for clients from fashion, art, design, luxury, and lifestyle industries. Believing that through the essence of simplification can be emphasized, and awareness of the importance of creating aspirational designs with business strategies, it approaches all projects from a strategic and creative view, taking care of every detail through a coherent, innovative, and specific language.

It works in multiple disciplines including brand identity, naming, print, editorial, packaging, web pages, digital platforms, as well as content creation and creative direction in audiovisual and photography productions.

http://www.playandtype.com

184 – 185

Project Projects LLC

Project Projects is an award-winning design studio specializing in work for art, architecture, education, and culture. Combining a conceptual and strategic approach with progressive modes of visual communication, the studio's practice encompasses the full range of contemporary graphic media—from books, exhibitions, magazines, and printed materials, to branding, signage, events, and interactive applications. The studio's work extends to editing and publishing books, curating exhibitions, and developing programs around a range of subjects. In recognition of its achievements, Project Projects was awarded the Cooper Hewitt's 2015 National Design Award in Communication Design, the United States' highest distinction in the field.

http://www.projectprojects.com

072 – 073; 096 – 097

Somewhere Else

Somewhere Else is about the constant shift away from the ordinary and the persistent journey to create work that goes beyond the basal need to communicate. The studio creates distinct and thoughtful work that communicates brand individually across diverse media, transforming brands from mere logos into experience worth sharing.

http://somewhere-else.co

098 – 099

Sons & Co.

Sons & Co. is an award-winning digital design agency in New Zealand. Instead of being big talkers, they believe in "talk less, work more," and they work quietly and studiously. They don't have a studio website, or blog, or Twitter due to the "less talk" policy. Their marketing is to show their works in which they instill the best quality and effects to achieve the best result for their clients.

http://sons.co.nz

048 – 049; 060 – 061; 070 – 071; 076 – 077; 078 – 079; 092 – 093; 162 – 165; 190 – 191; 192 – 193; 200 – 201; 230 – 231

Studio Gambetta

The Geneva based studio Gambetta was born from the close collaboration between two passionate and qualified designers in visual communication: Benoît Dumont and Franco Szymanski. Well-aligned with its time, this dynamic collective offers multiple services within the field of graphic design and visual communication such as: art direction, conception and creation of branding, book layout, magazine, poster design, packaging design, sign design, set design, illustration, multimedia, and web design.

http://studio-gambetta.ch

068 – 069; 214 – 215

Svetlana Tsybulevska

Svetlana Tsybulevska is a freelance designer from Kharkiv, Ukraine. She loves everything regarding web design, graphic design, and illustration. Working with passionate people gives her great satisfaction.

http://behance.com/anasveta

058 – 059

Taehee Kim & Hyemin Yoo

They are a cross-country design duo when Taehee is based in Berlin, Germany, and Heymin is living and working in Seoul. They share the same passion in web design, branding, print, digital design, and packaging design.

https://www.behance.net/taeheekim-design
https://www.behance.net/hyeminyooo

028 – 029

The Woork Co

The Woork Co is a Madrid-based studio founded by Debbie Martin and David Botella, two digital art directors with more than 25 years of experience together in digital advertising. The studio is specialized in branding, web design, illustration, branded content, and motion graphics.

http://www.thewoork.co

144 – 145

Thibaud Sabathier

Thibaud Sabathier is a young French designer graduated from École de Communication Visuelle (ECV) in Bordeaux in 2015. His work is related to art direction, editorial, visual, print, and interactive design. After his internships in different international studios, Thibaud has worked as a designer for Thonik, exploring the design issues in the cultural sector. In 2016 he opens a design studio with his fellow collaborator and friend Florent Gomez in Bordeaux France.

http://thibaud-sabathier.com

062 – 063

TIMA INSTITUTE

TIMA INSTITUTE is a design studio based in Beijing, China, founded by two Sanji Sun and qinxiaotong. They work through illustration, advertising, and web design to help their clients build up long-lasting impacts.

https://www.behance.net/timaworks

216 – 217

Tseng Green

Tseng Green graduated from the National Yunlin University of Science and Technology with a Bachelor Degree of Visual Communication Design. Currently he works as a freelancer to provide professional service in CIS, VI, branding, book cover, magazine layout, commercial photography, and filmmaking.

232

Vadim Kukin

Vadim Kukin is a designer from Riga, Latvia. With over 6 years experience in his field, the main focus is on the development of web sites. In the process, he pays special attention to the integration of new technological solutions that help to solve clients' problems as well as being a rethinking of user behavior in the pages or in an application. In his spare time he does a documentary video shooting.

This experience extends the worldview and allows his to offer original and non-standard solutions combining video files and html code.

http://www.vadimkukin.lv

032 – 033; 124 – 125

W&CO

W&CO is a digital design and development studio based in New York City, specializing in strategy, interface design, development, and technology for digital platforms. Since 2011, W&CO has designed and developed applications that couple intuitive and sophisticated user experiences with trend-setting technology. And with a strong background in wayfinding strategy applied to the digital domain, W&CO has become a thought leader in the fast-growing specialization of digital wayfinding.

http://winfieldco.com

012 – 015; 106 – 107

Waaark

Founded by designer Jimmy Raheriarisoa and developer Antoine Wodniack, Waaark is a two-person creative web studio that launched in 2016. The reason these two successful freelancers chose to join forces under the name of Waaark is simple: by combining their experience in the web design industry, the unique outcome is an attractive prospect to clients.

http://waaark.com

016 – 019